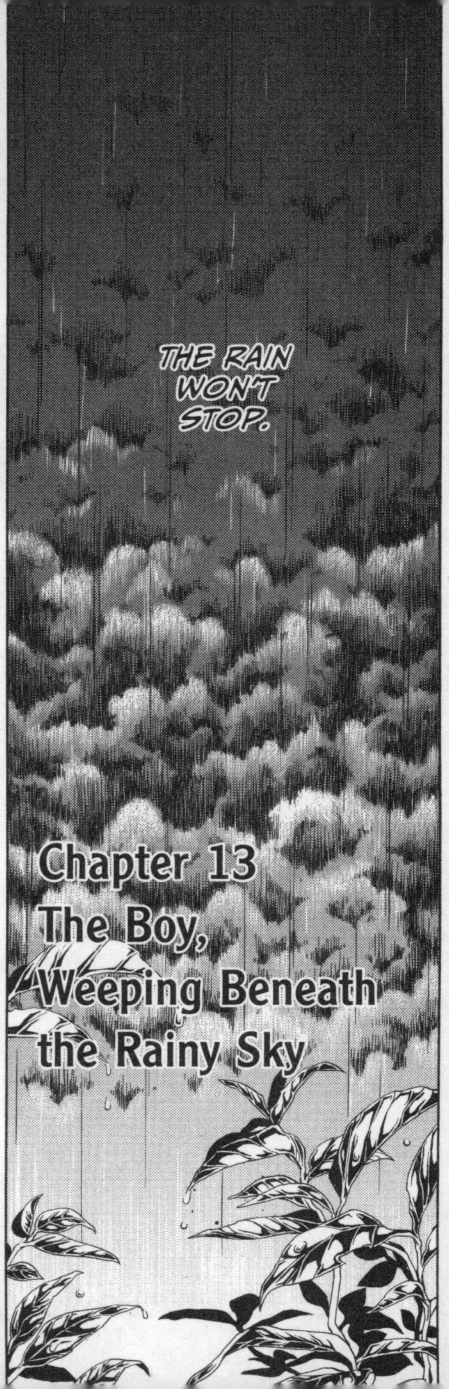
THE RAIN WON'T STOP.
Chapter 13
The Boy, Weeping Beneath the Rainy Sky

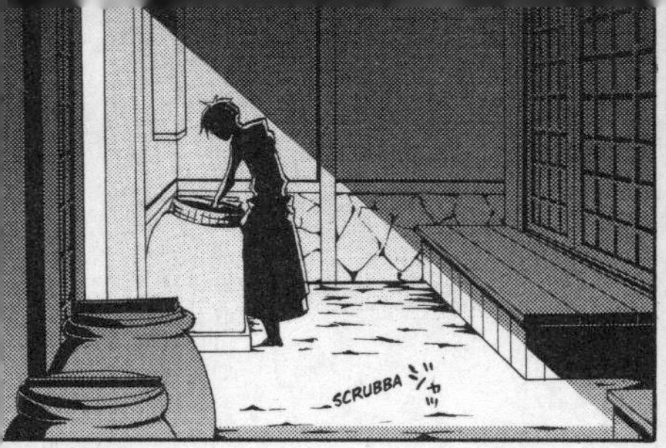
SCRUBBA

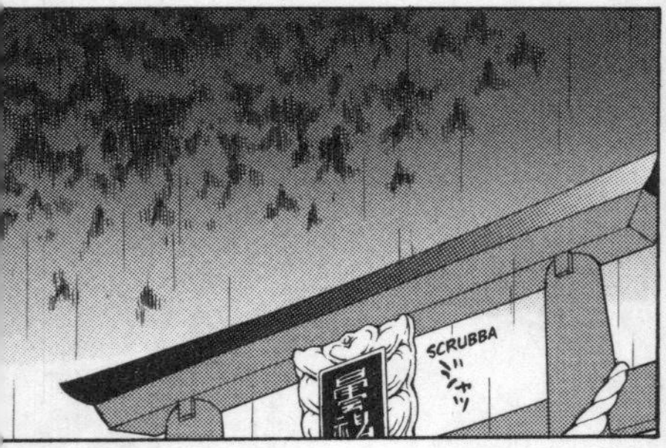
SCRUBBA

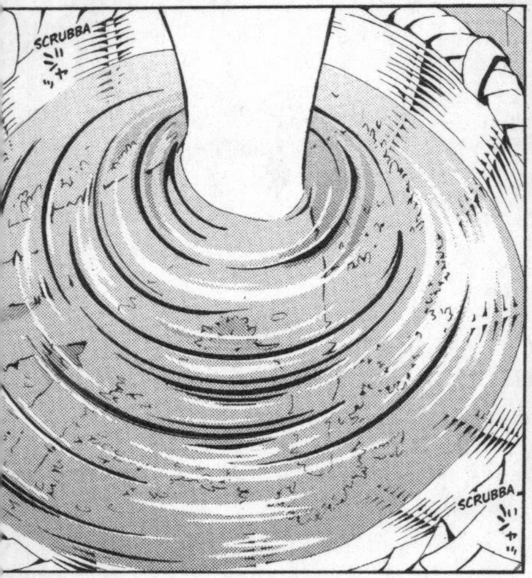
SCRUBBA
SCRUBBA

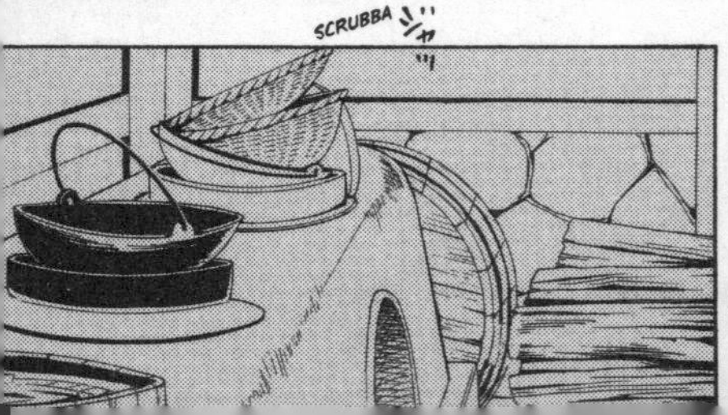
SCRUBBA

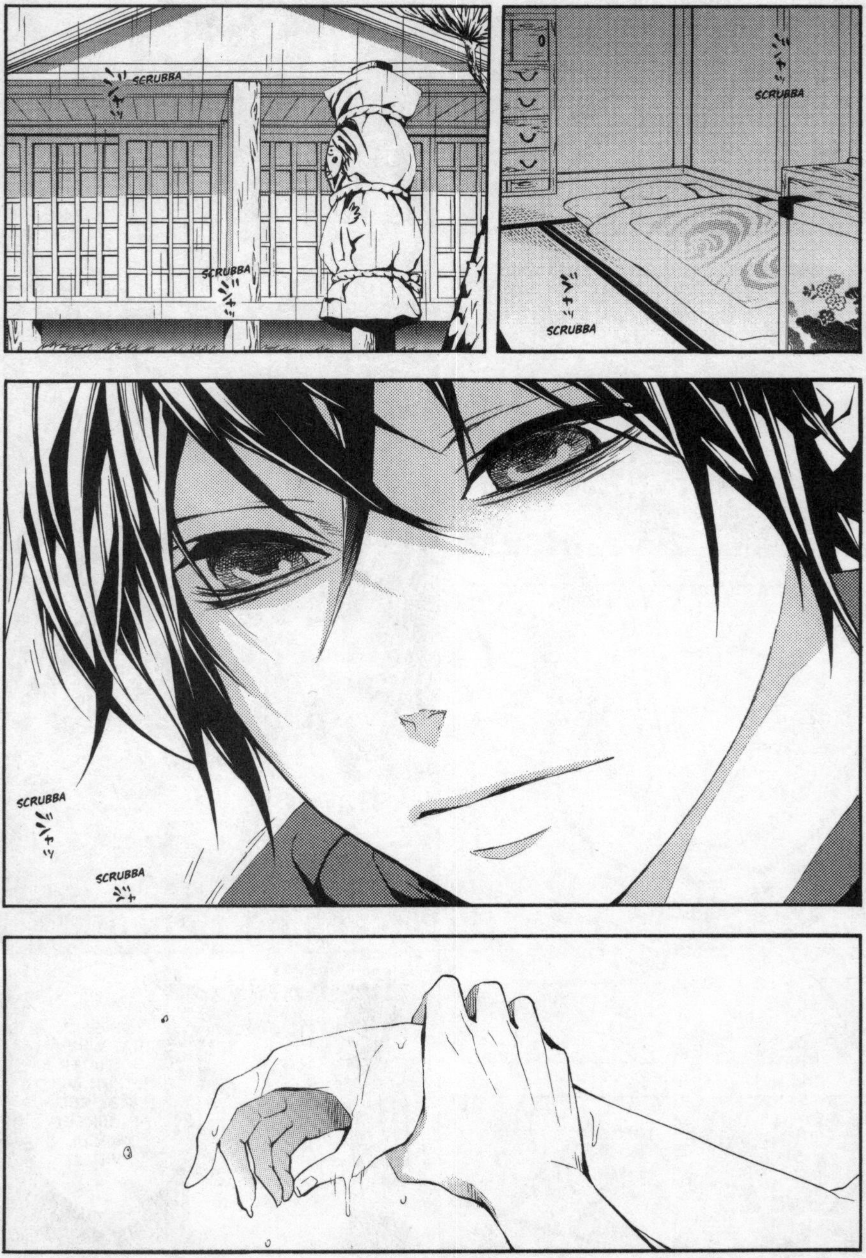
SCRUBBA
SCRUBBA
SCRUBBA
SCRUBBA
SCRUBBA
SCRUBBA

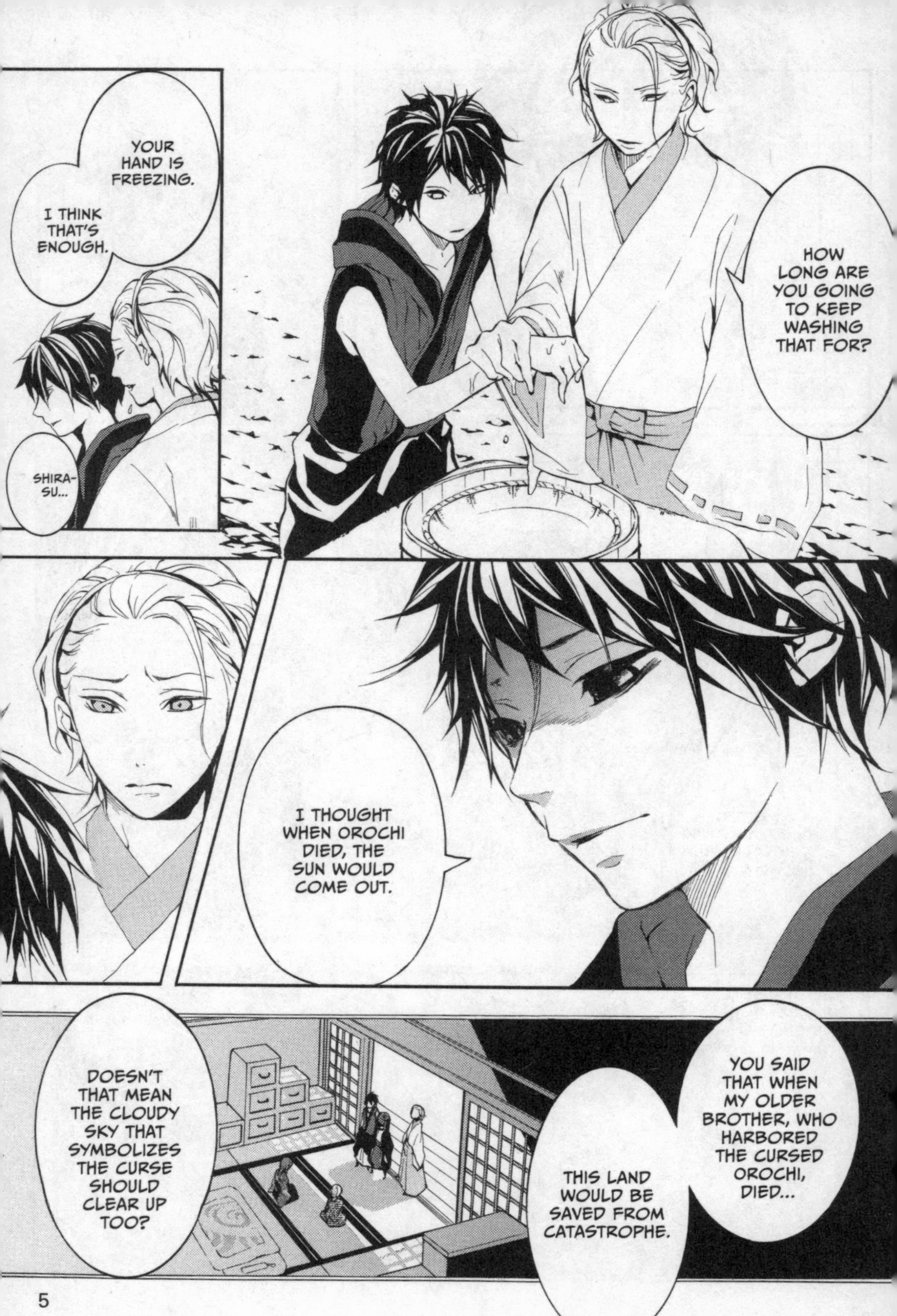
HOW LONG ARE YOU GOING TO KEEP WASHING THAT FOR?
YOUR HAND IS FREEZING.
I THINK THAT'S ENOUGH.
SHIRA-SU...
I THOUGHT WHEN OROCHI DIED, THE SUN WOULD COME OUT.
YOU SAID THAT WHEN MY OLDER BROTHER, WHO HARBORED THE CURSED OROCHI, DIED...
THIS LAND WOULD BE SAVED FROM CATASTROPHE.
DOESN'T THAT MEAN THE CLOUDY SKY THAT SYMBOLIZES THE CURSE SHOULD CLEAR UP TOO?

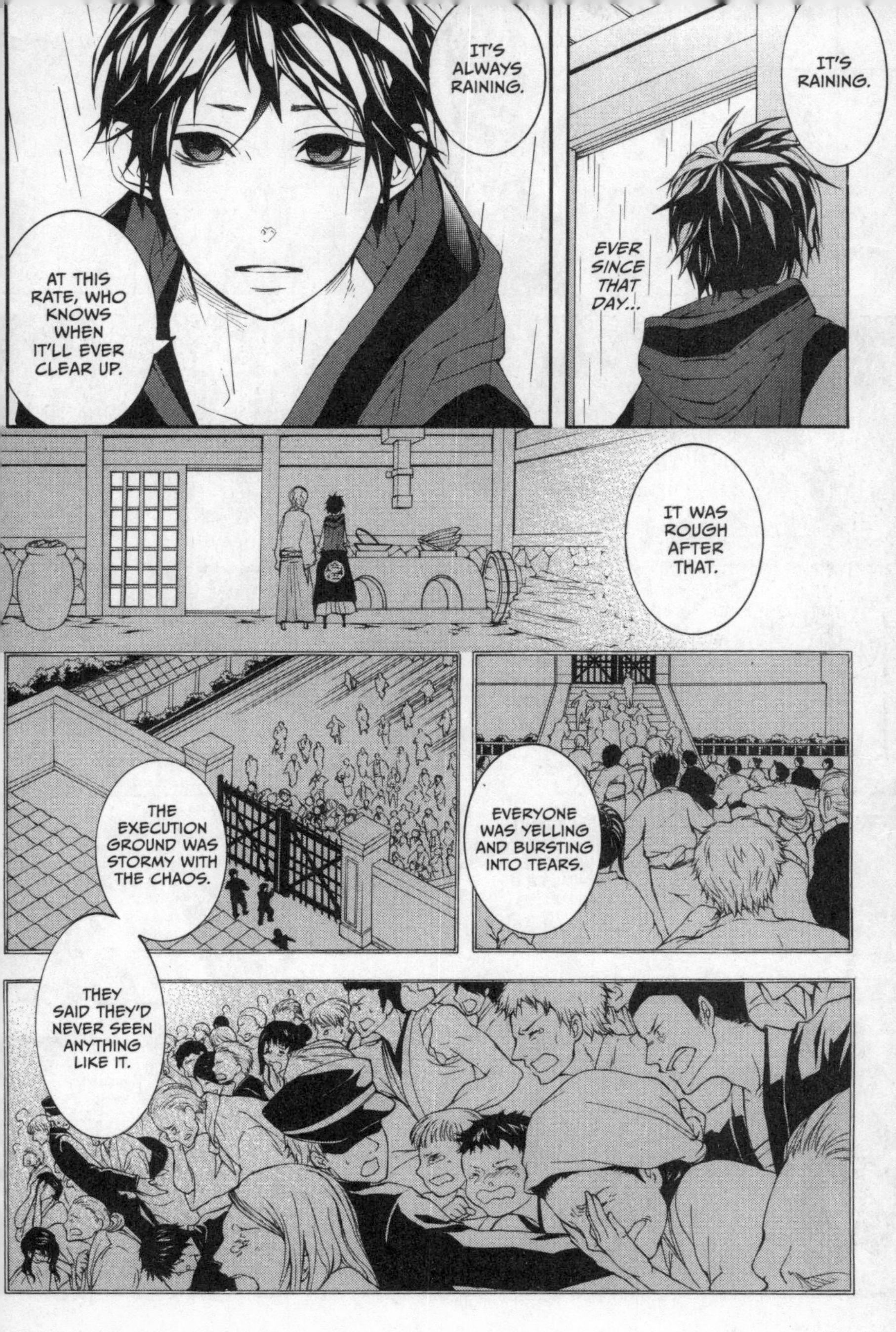
IT'S RAINING.
EVER SINCE THAT DAY...
IT'S ALWAYS RAINING.
AT THIS RATE, WHO KNOWS WHEN IT'LL EVER CLEAR UP.
IT WAS ROUGH AFTER THAT.
EVERYONE WAS YELLING AND BURSTING INTO TEARS.
THE EXECUTION GROUND WAS STORMY WITH THE CHAOS.
THEY SAID THEY'D NEVER SEEN ANYTHING LIKE IT.

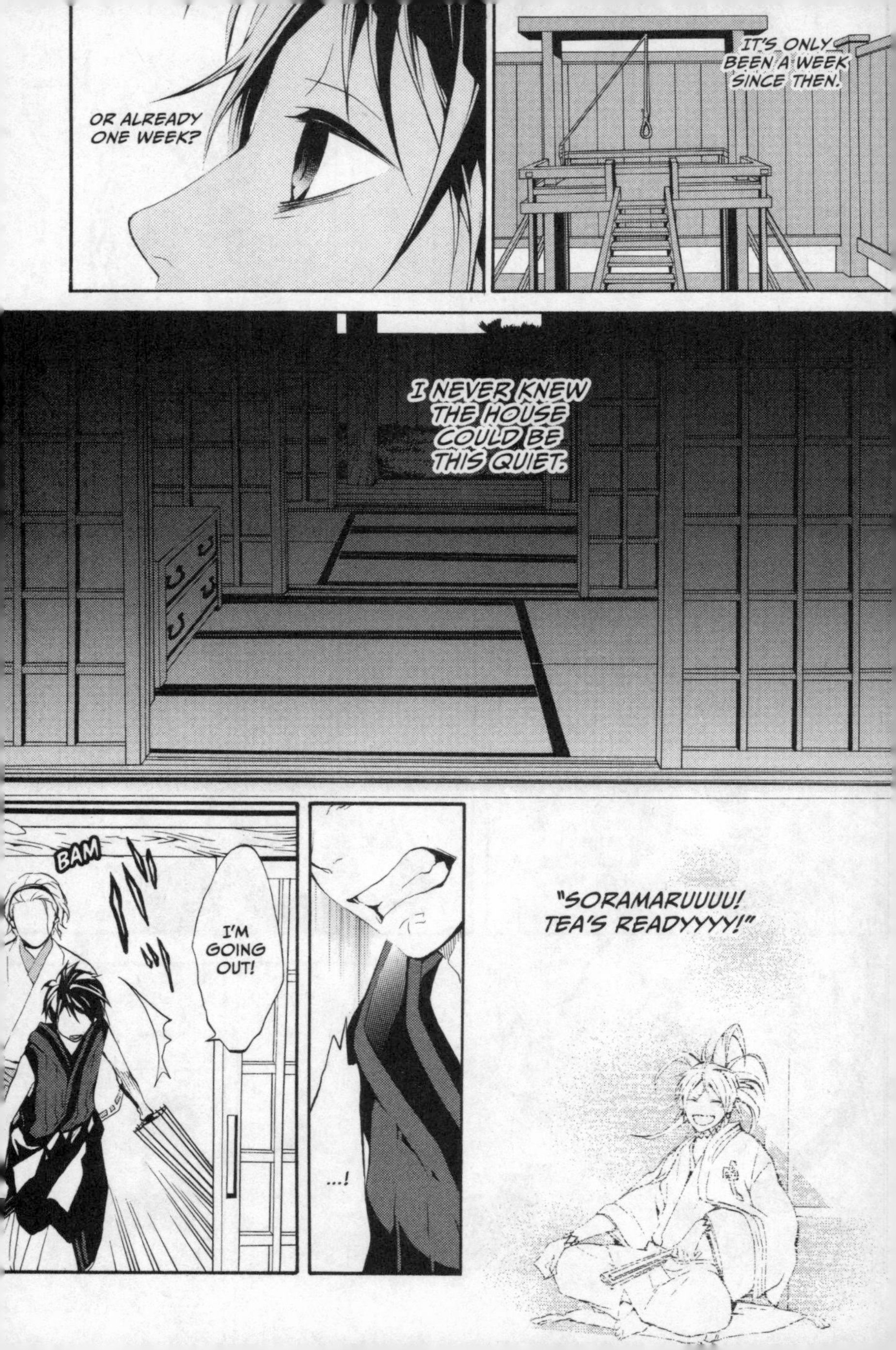
IT'S ONLY BEEN A WEEK SINCE THEN.
OR ALREADY ONE WEEK?
I NEVER KNEW THE HOUSE COULD BE THIS QUIET.
"SORAMARUUUU! TEA'S READYYYY!"
...!
BAM
I'M GOING OUT!

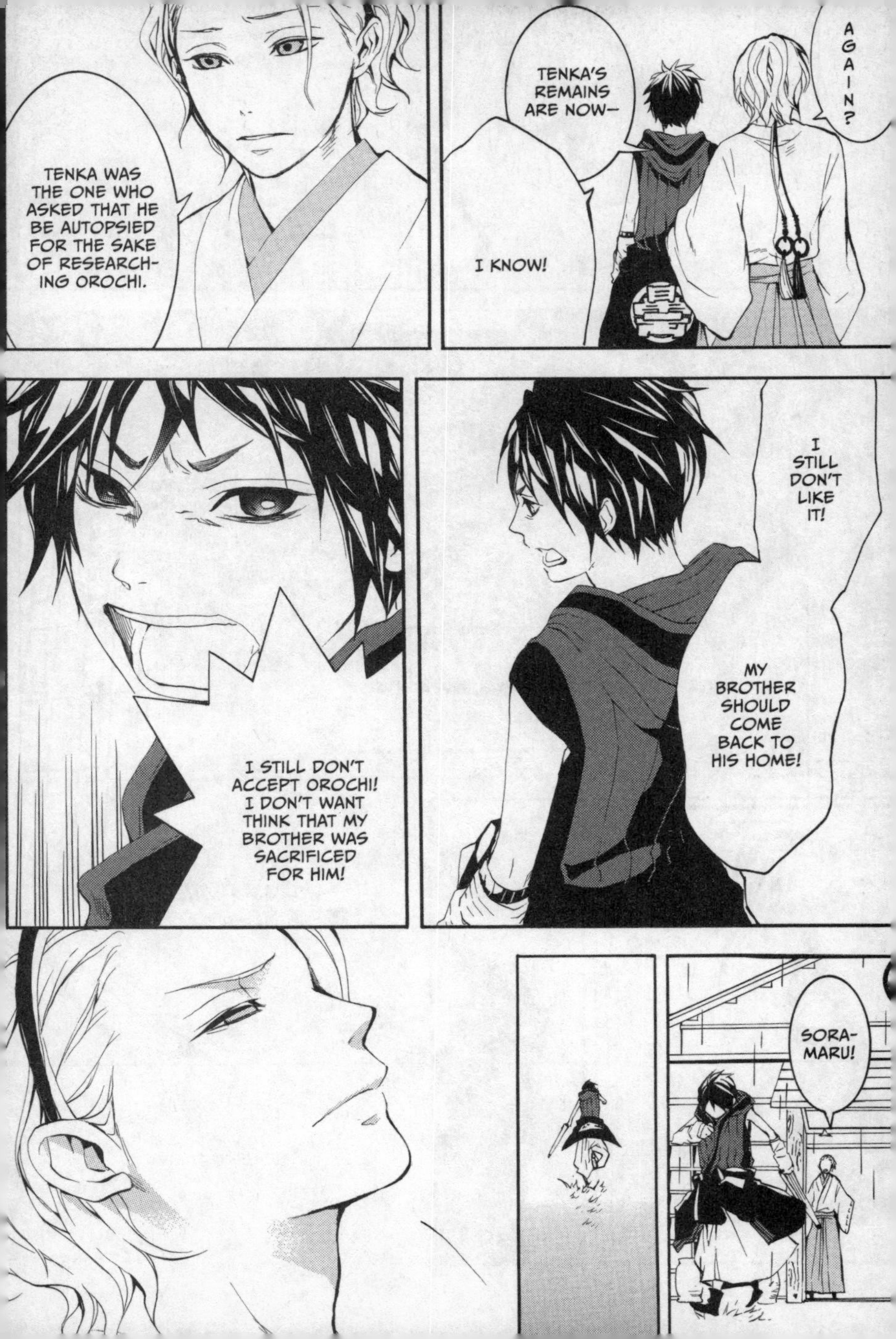
AGAIN?
TENKA'S REMAINS ARE NOW—
I KNOW!
TENKA WAS THE ONE WHO ASKED THAT HE BE AUTOPSIED FOR THE SAKE OF RESEARCH-ING OROCHI.
I STILL DON'T LIKE IT!
MY BROTHER SHOULD COME BACK TO HIS HOME!
I STILL DON'T ACCEPT OROCHI! I DON'T WANT THINK THAT MY BROTHER WAS SACRIFICED FOR HIM!
SORA-MARU!

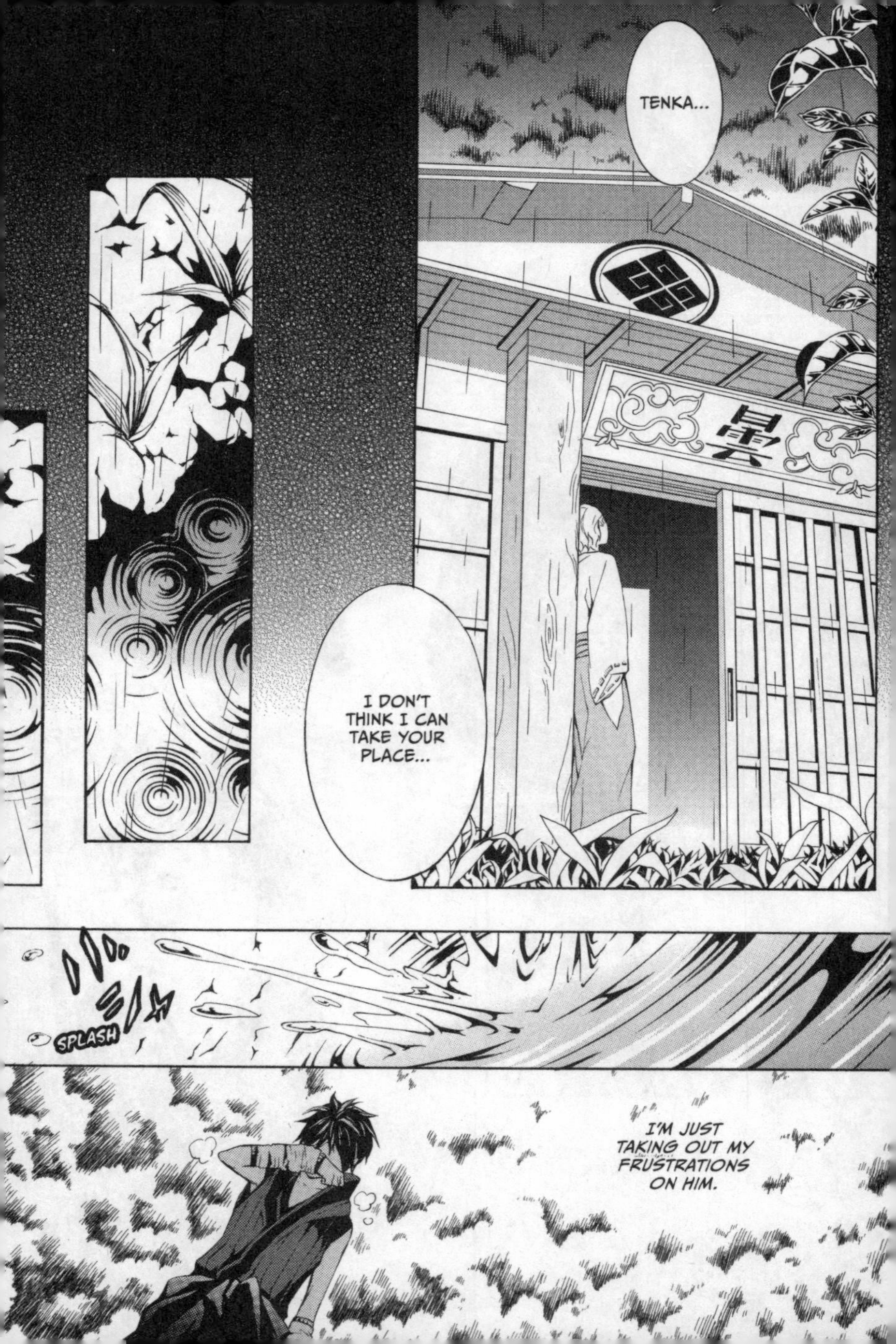
TENKA...
I DON'T THINK I CAN TAKE YOUR PLACE...
SPLASH
I'M JUST TAKING OUT MY FRUSTRATIONS ON HIM.

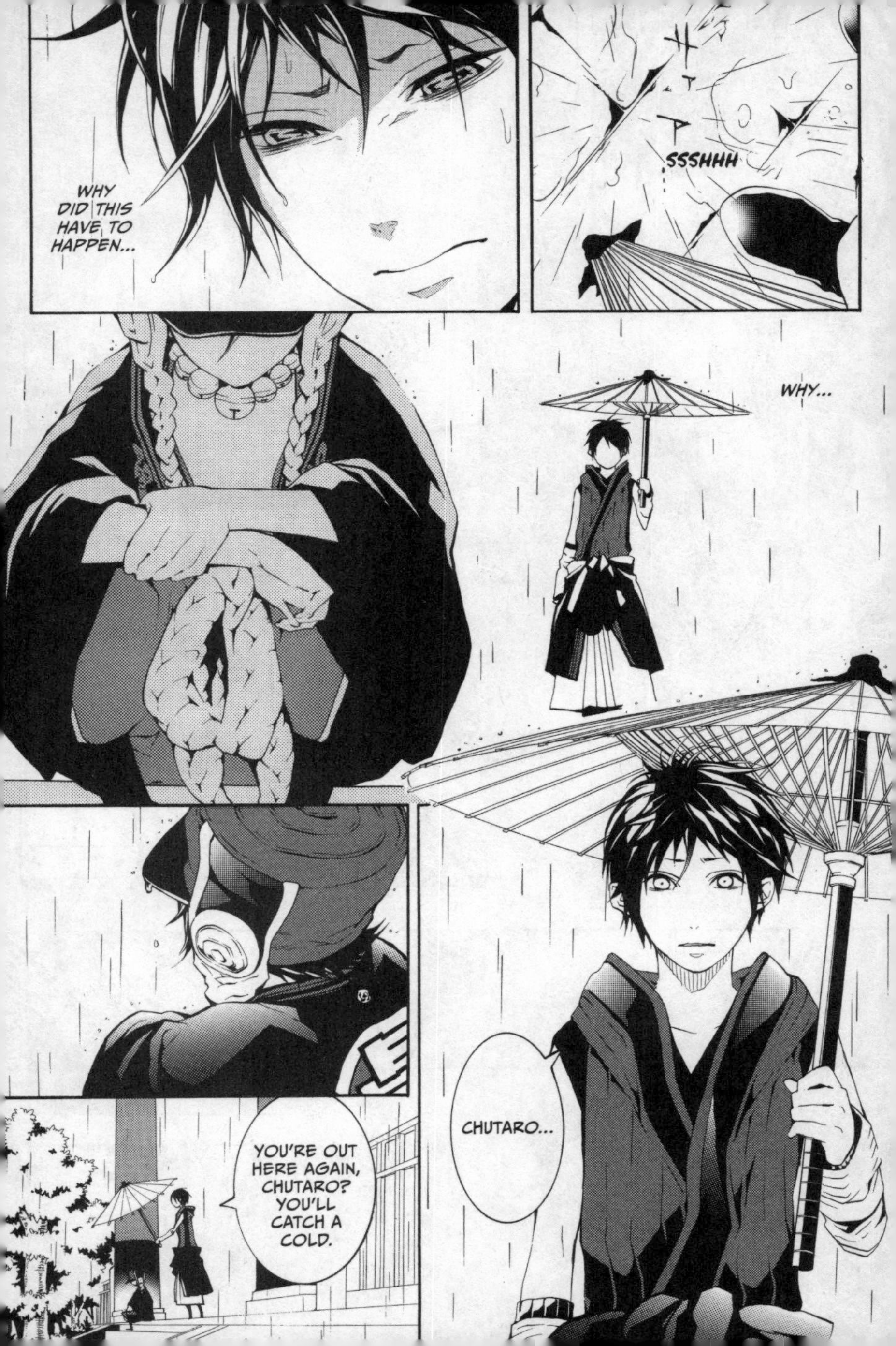
SSSHHH
WHY DID THIS HAVE TO HAPPEN...
WHY...
CHUTARO...
YOU'RE OUT HERE AGAIN, CHUTARO? YOU'LL CATCH A COLD.

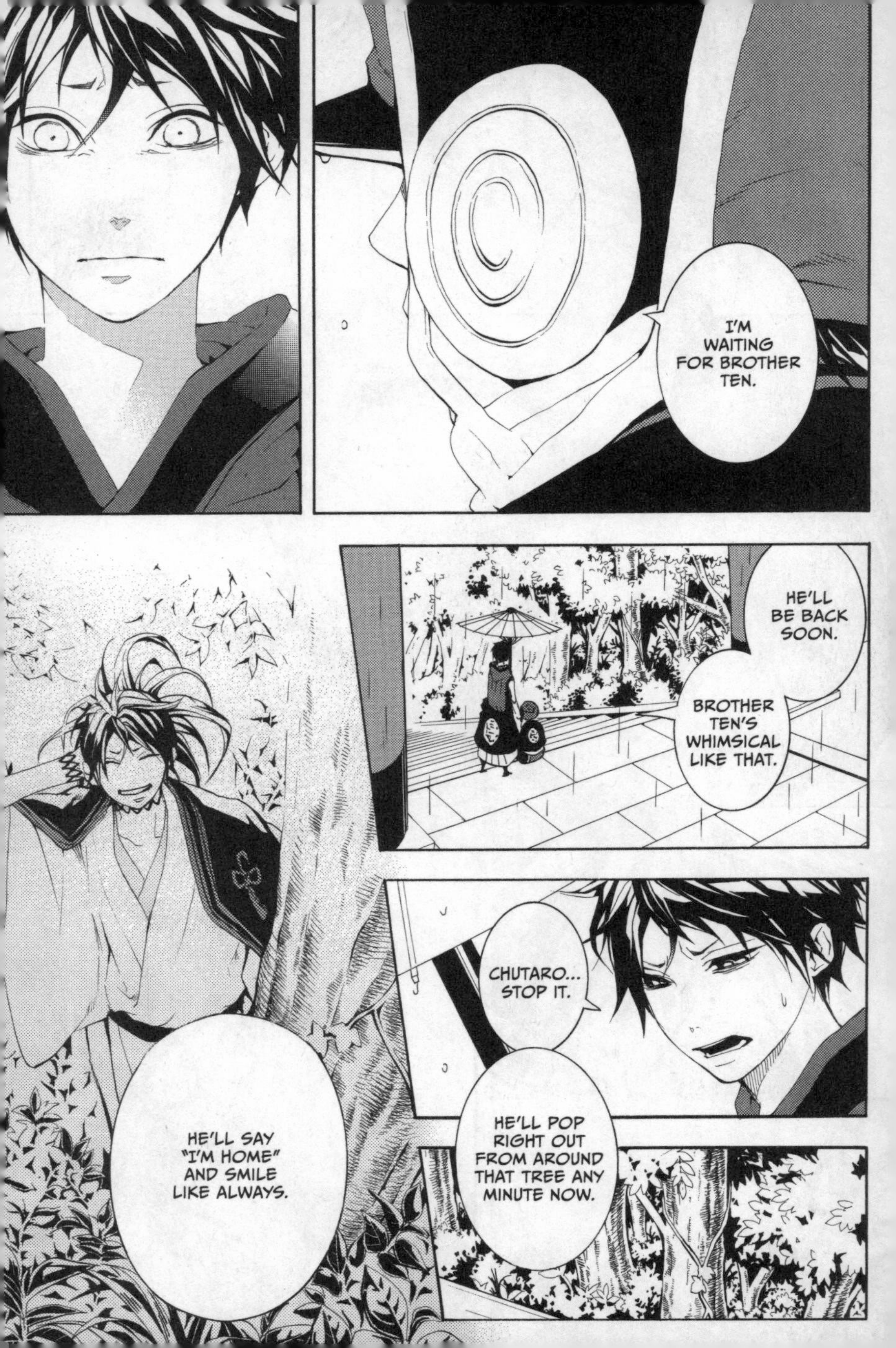
I'M WAITING FOR BROTHER TEN.
HE'LL BE BACK SOON.
BROTHER TEN'S WHIMSICAL LIKE THAT.
CHUTARO... STOP IT.
HE'LL POP RIGHT OUT FROM AROUND THAT TREE ANY MINUTE NOW.
HE'LL SAY "I'M HOME" AND SMILE LIKE ALWAYS.

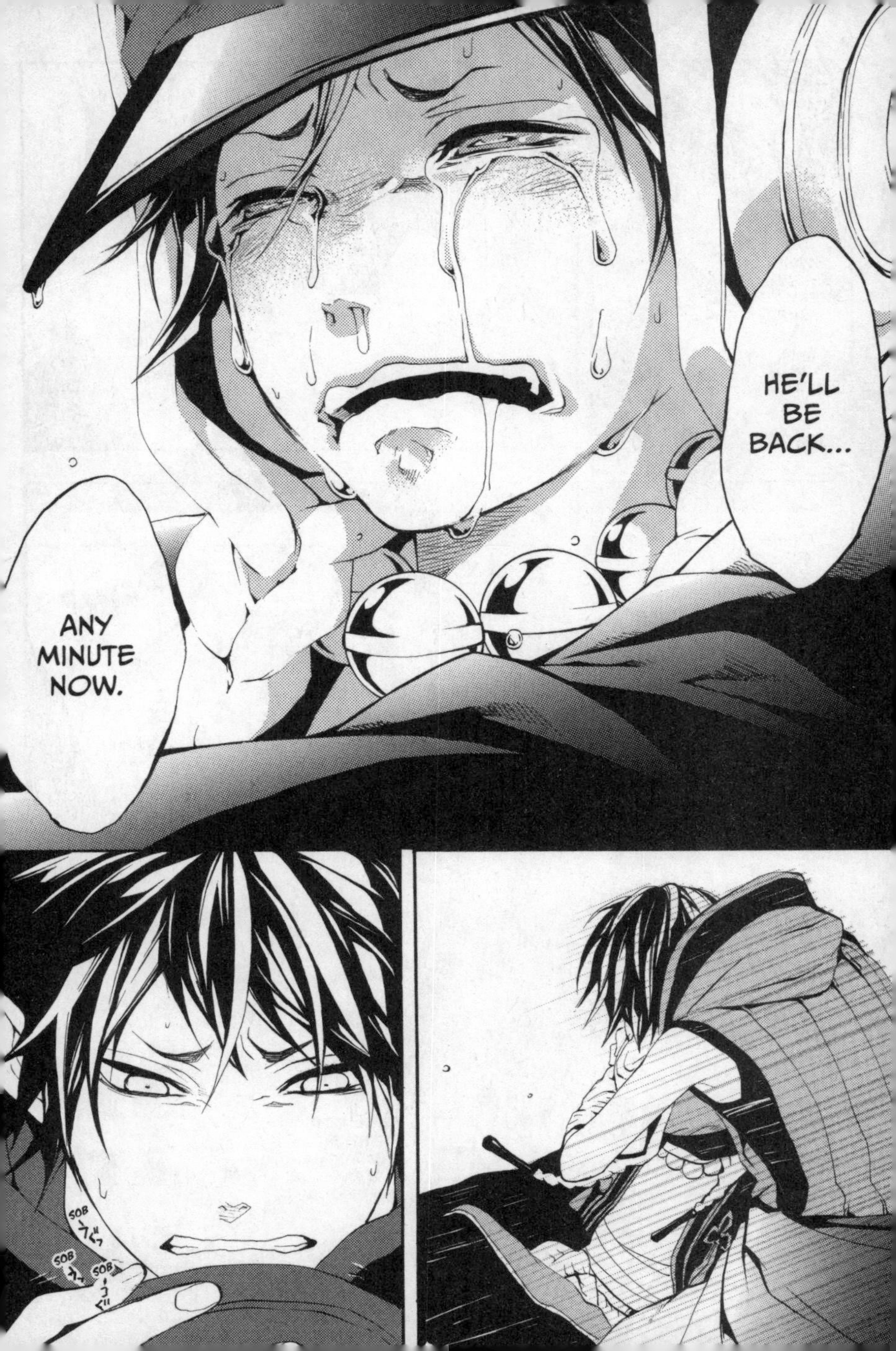
HE'LL BE BACK...
ANY MINUTE NOW.
SOB
SOB
SOB

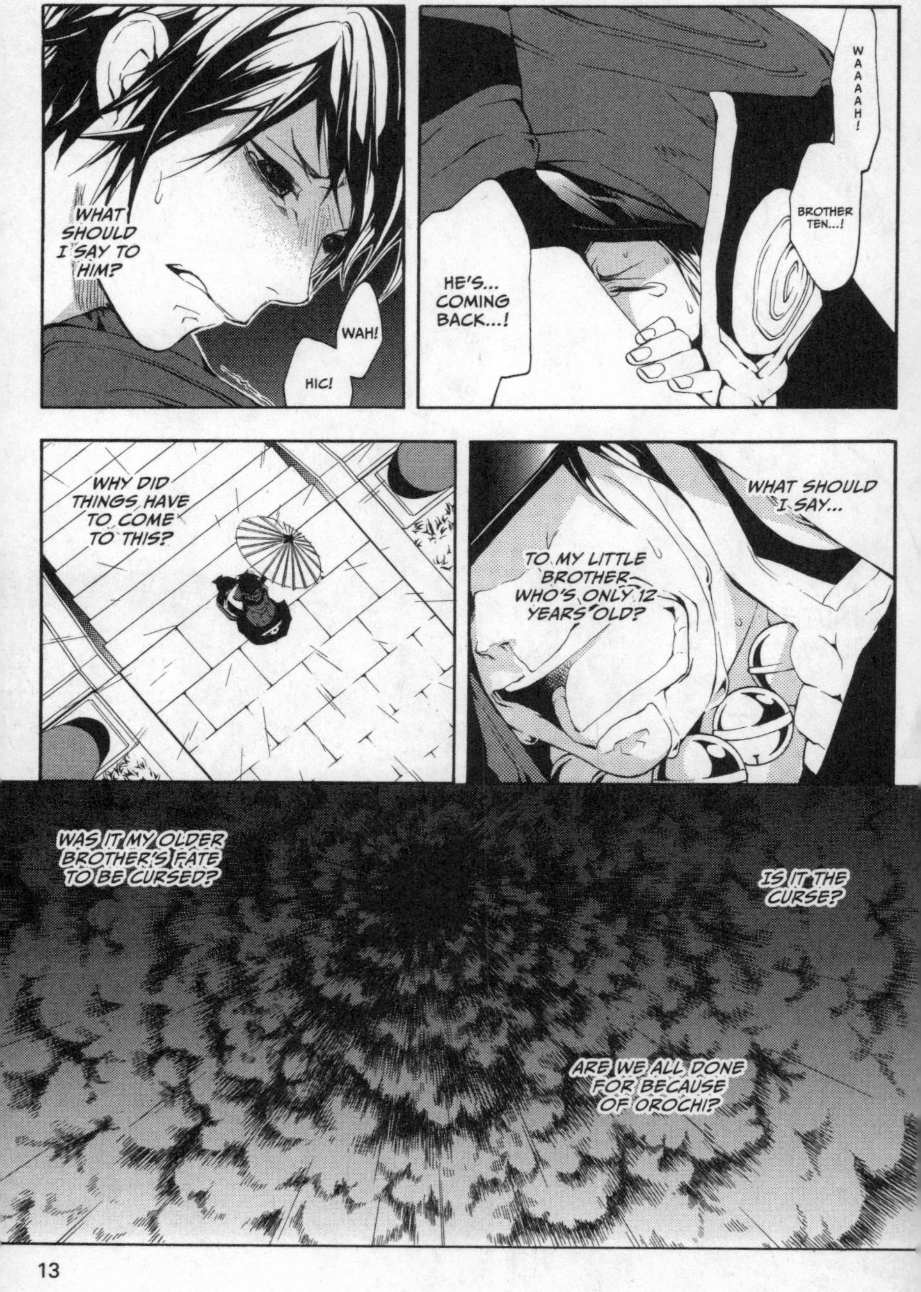
WAAAAH!
BROTHER TEN...!
HE'S... COMING BACK...!
WHAT SHOULD I SAY TO HIM?
WAH!
HIC!
WHAT SHOULD I SAY...
TO MY LITTLE BROTHER WHO'S ONLY 12 YEARS OLD?
WHY DID THINGS HAVE TO COME TO THIS?
IS IT THE CURSE?
WAS IT MY OLDER BROTHER'S FATE TO BE CURSED?
ARE WE ALL DONE FOR BECAUSE OF OROCHI?

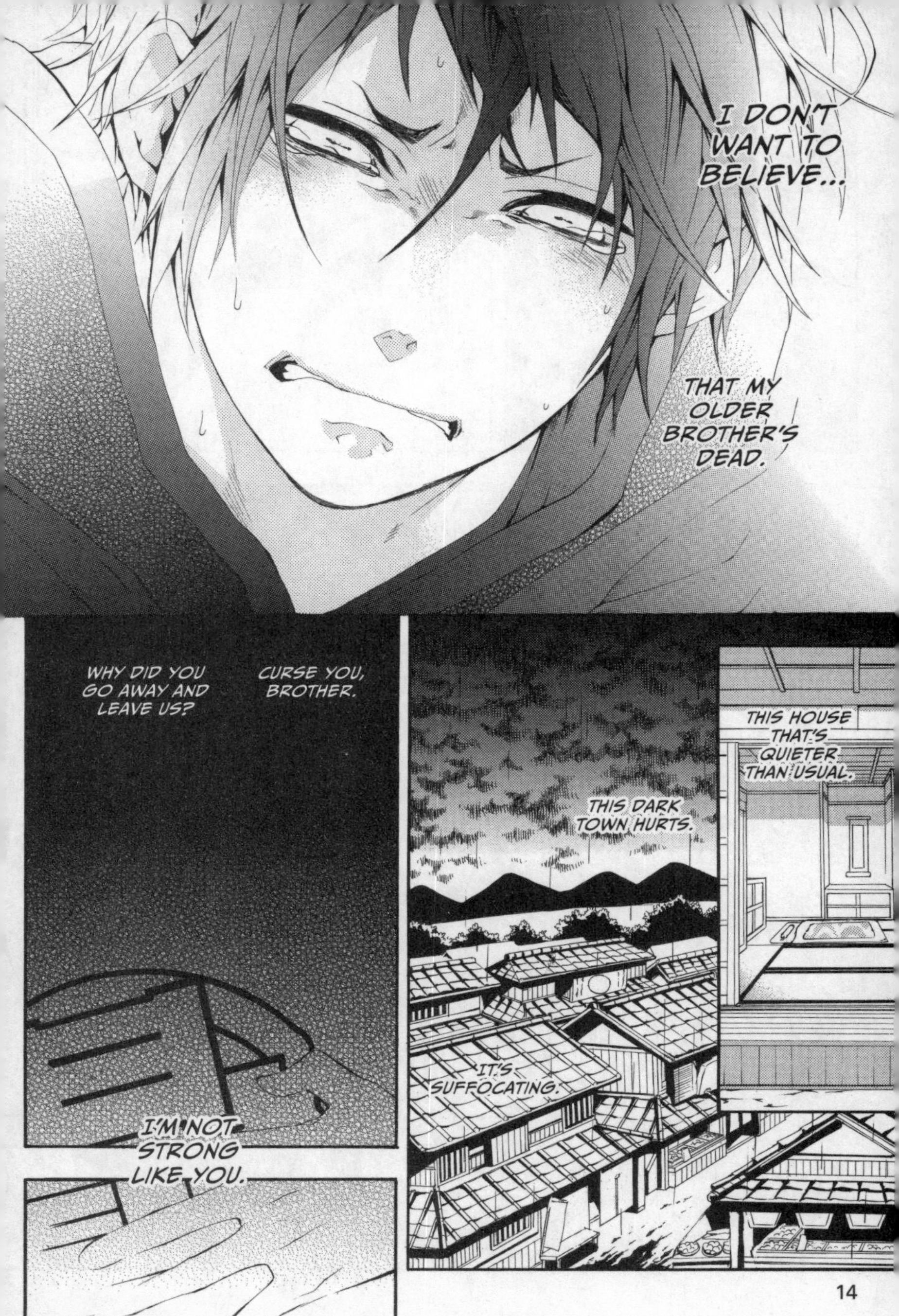
I DON'T WANT TO BELIEVE...
THAT MY OLDER BROTHER'S DEAD.
THIS HOUSE THAT'S QUIETER THAN USUAL.
THIS DARK TOWN HURTS.
IT'S SUFFOCATING.
CURSE YOU, BROTHER.
WHY DID YOU GO AWAY AND LEAVE US?
I'M NOT STRONG LIKE YOU.

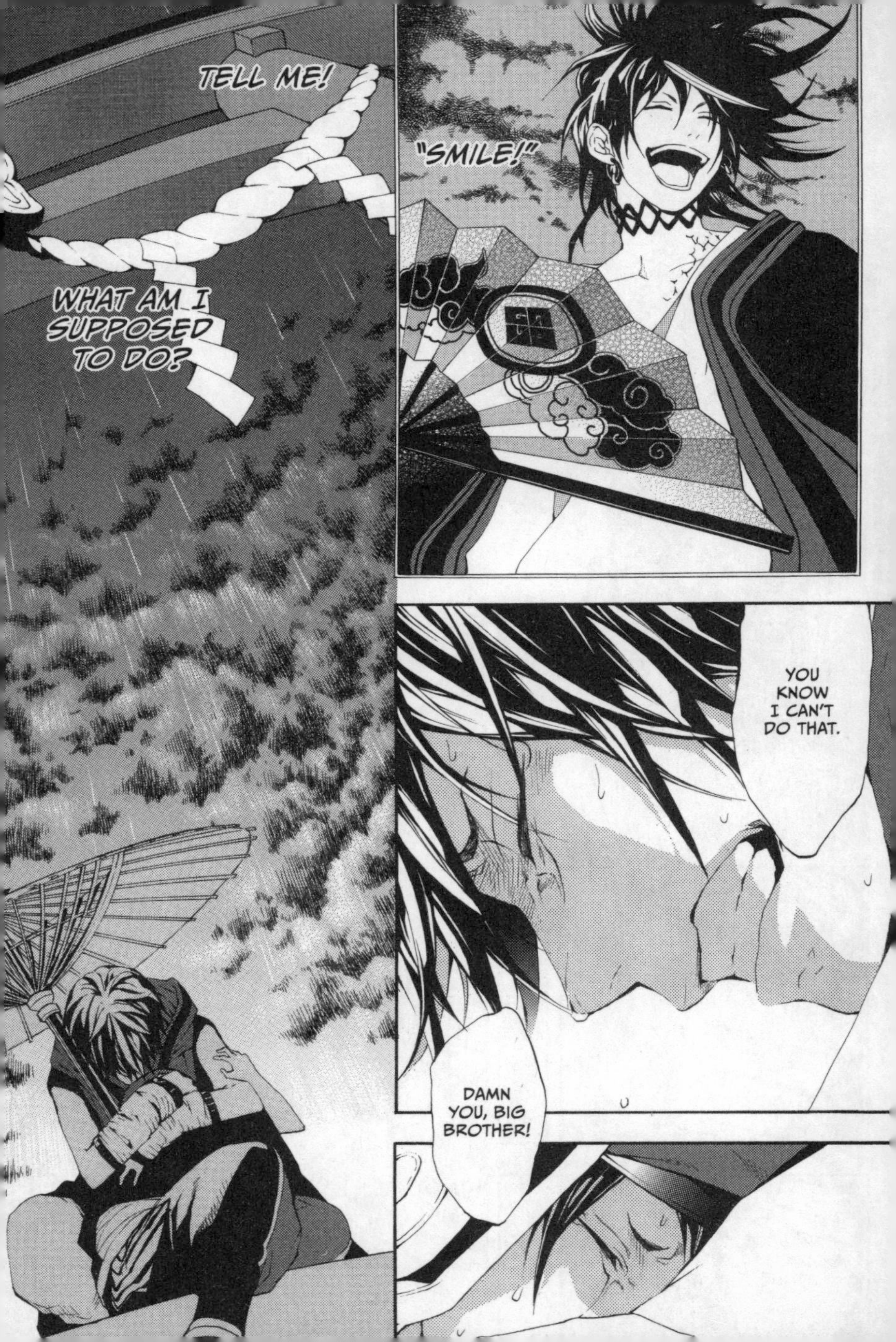
"SMILE!"
YOU KNOW I CAN'T DO THAT.
DAMN YOU, BIG BROTHER!
TELL ME!
WHAT AM I SUPPOSED TO DO?

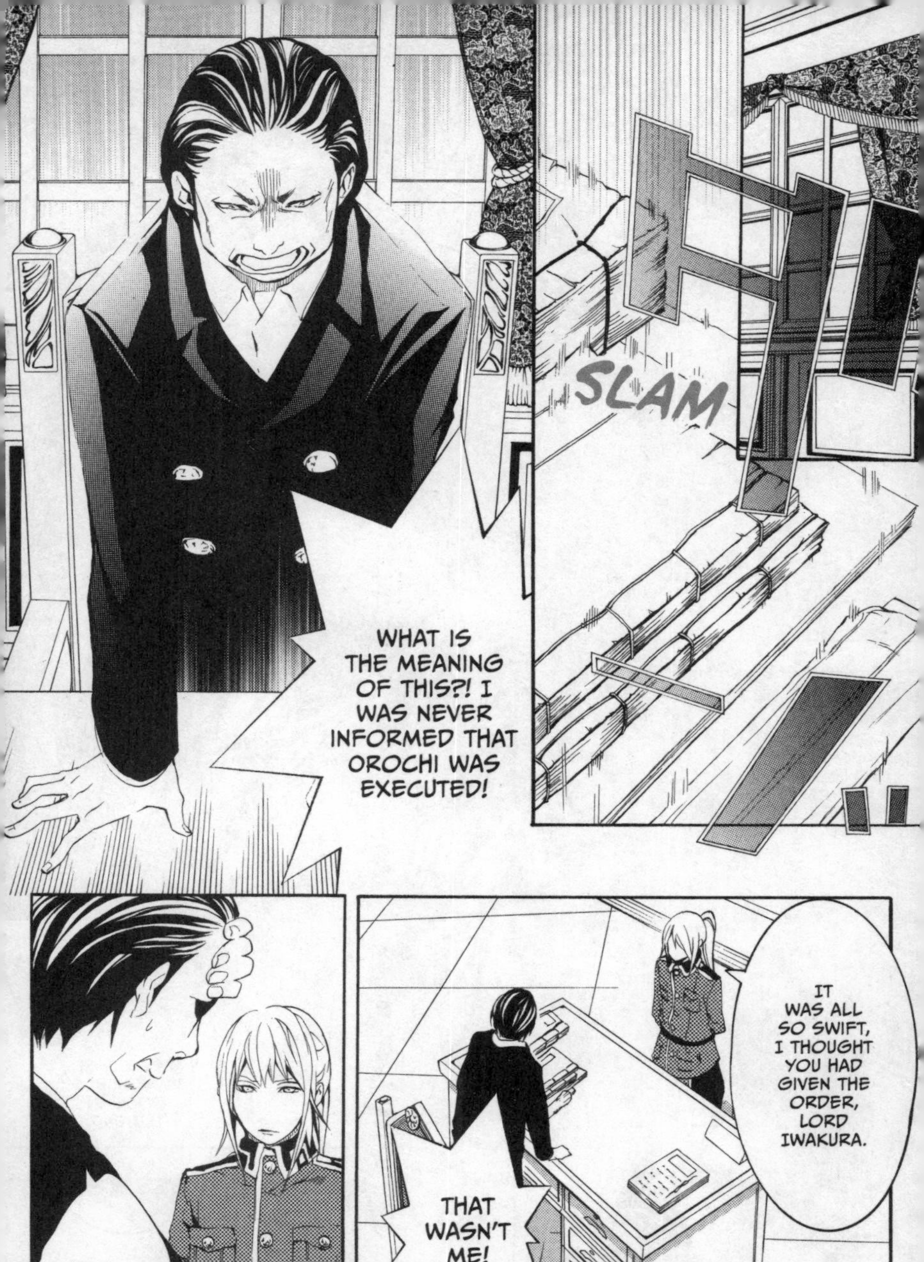
SLAM
WHAT IS THE MEANING OF THIS?! I WAS NEVER INFORMED THAT OROCHI WAS EXECUTED!
IT WAS ALL SO SWIFT, I THOUGHT YOU HAD GIVEN THE ORDER, LORD IWAKURA.
THAT WASN'T ME!
SOMEBODY GOT AHEAD OF ME!

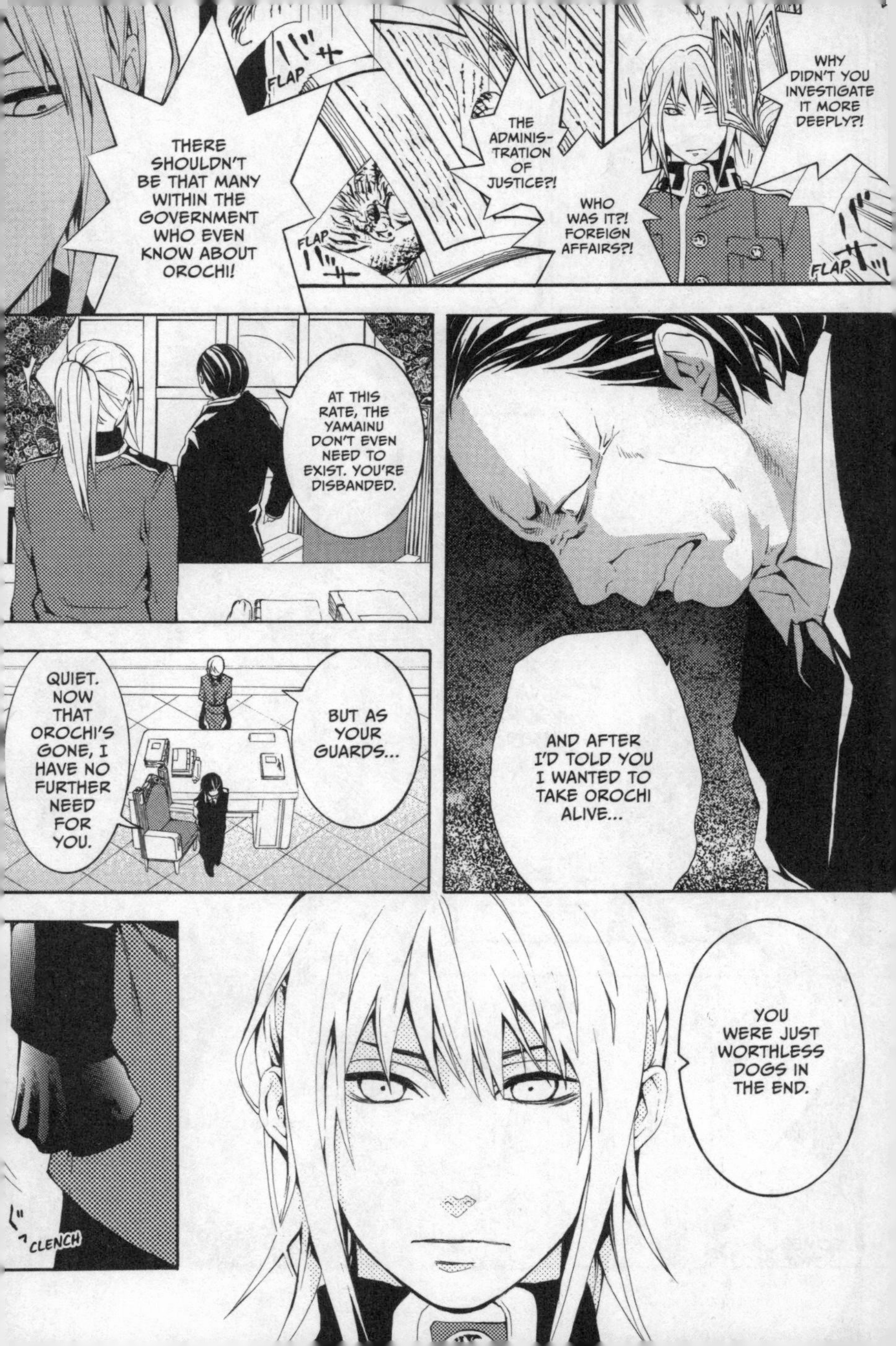
WHY DIDN'T YOU INVESTIGATE IT MORE DEEPLY?!
FLAP
WHO WAS IT?! FOREIGN AFFAIRS?!
THE ADMINIS-TRATION OF JUSTICE?!
FLAP
FLAP
THERE SHOULDN'T BE THAT MANY WITHIN THE GOVERNMENT WHO EVEN KNOW ABOUT OROCHI!
AND AFTER I'D TOLD YOU I WANTED TO TAKE OROCHI ALIVE...
AT THIS RATE, THE YAMAINU DON'T EVEN NEED TO EXIST. YOU'RE DISBANDED.
BUT AS YOUR GUARDS...
QUIET. NOW THAT OROCHI'S GONE, I HAVE NO FURTHER NEED FOR YOU.
YOU WERE JUST WORTHLESS DOGS IN THE END.
CLENCH

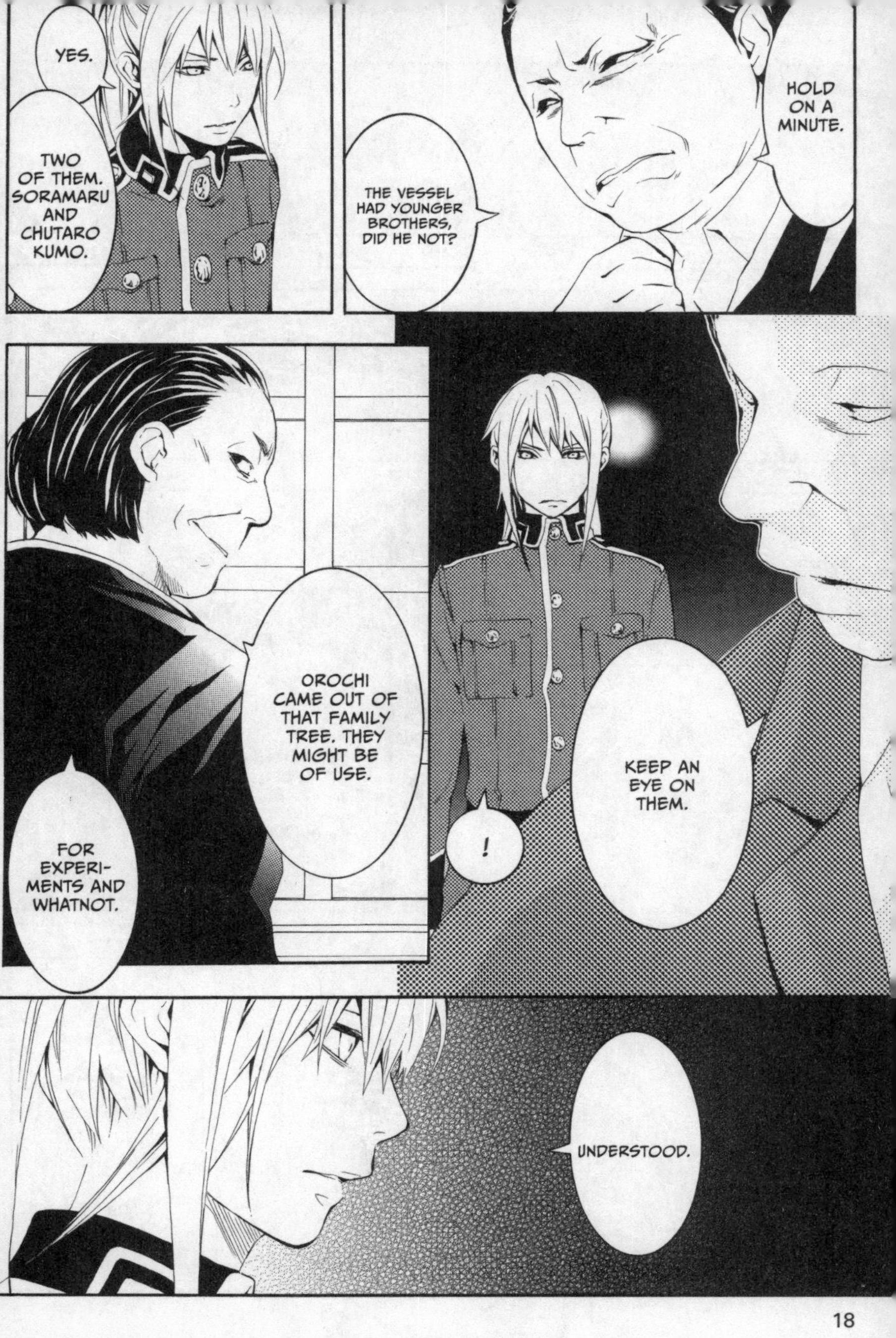
HOLD ON A MINUTE.
THE VESSEL HAD YOUNGER BROTHERS, DID HE NOT?
YES.
TWO OF THEM. SORAMARU AND CHUTARO KUMO.
KEEP AN EYE ON THEM.
!
OROCHI CAME OUT OF THAT FAMILY TREE. THEY MIGHT BE OF USE.
FOR EXPERI-MENTS AND WHATNOT.
UNDERSTOOD.

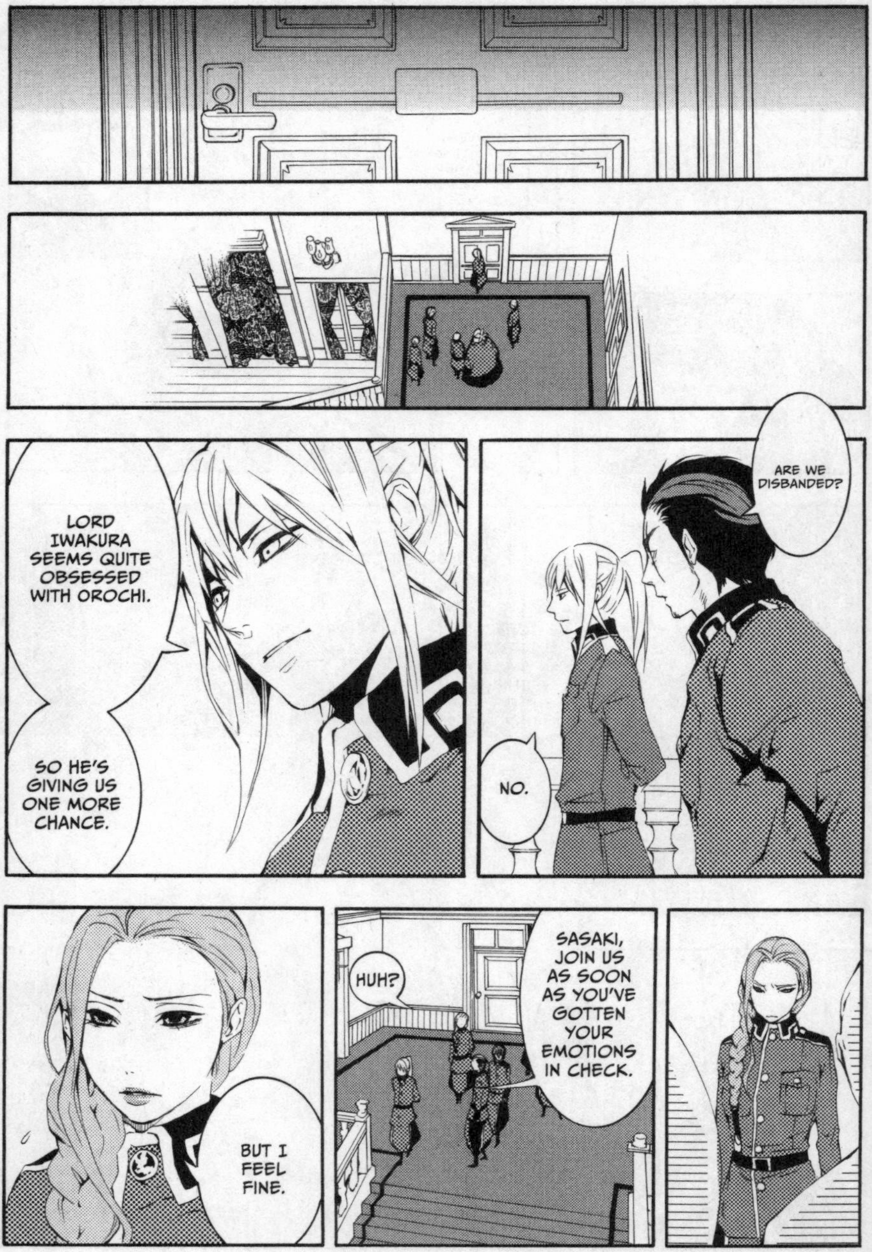
ARE WE DISBANDED?
NO.
LORD IWAKURA SEEMS QUITE OBSESSED WITH OROCHI.
SO HE'S GIVING US ONE MORE CHANCE.
SASAKI, JOIN US AS SOON AS YOU'VE GOTTEN YOUR EMOTIONS IN CHECK.
HUH?
BUT I FEEL FINE.

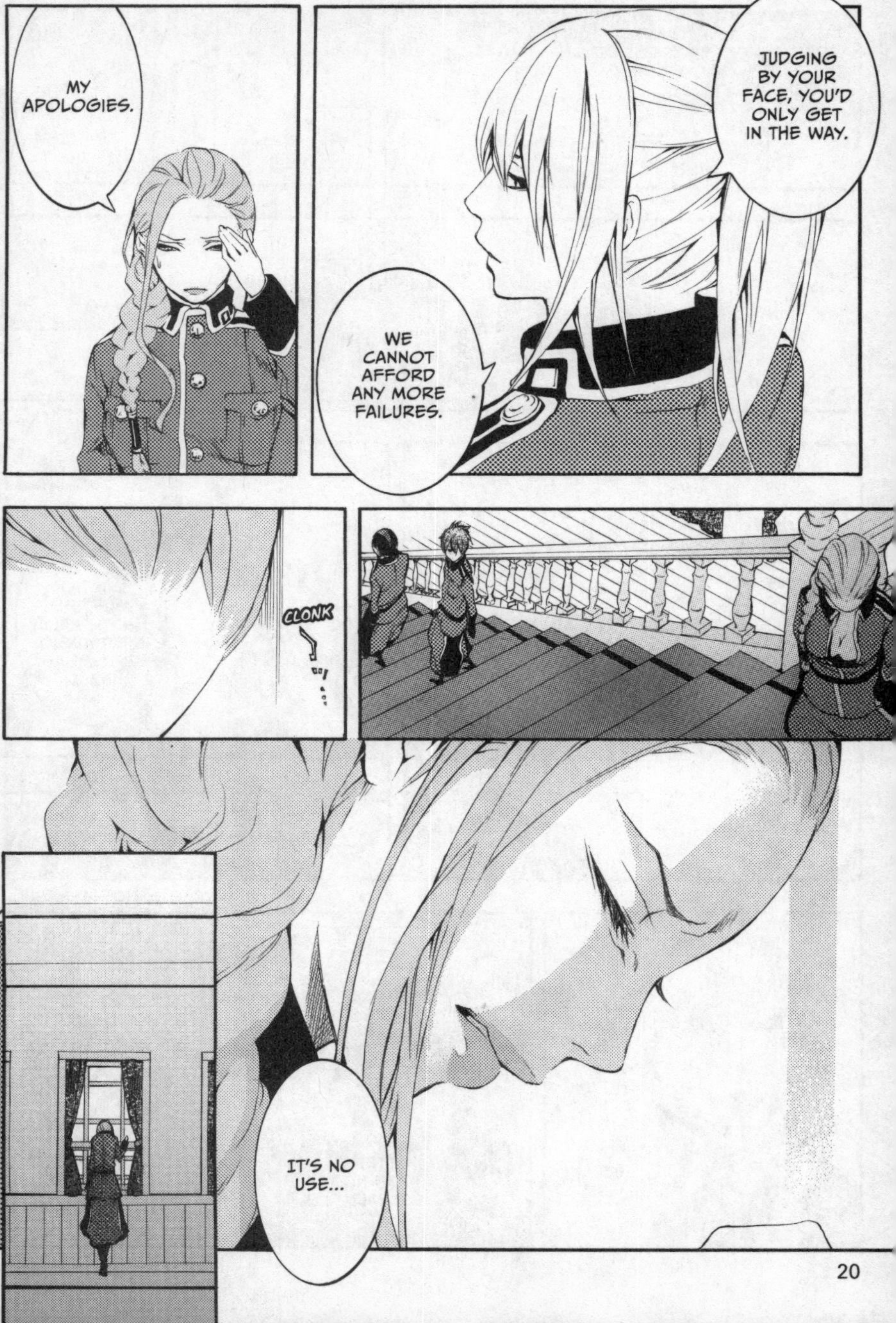
JUDGING BY YOUR FACE, YOU'D ONLY GET IN THE WAY.
WE CANNOT AFFORD ANY MORE FAILURES.
MY APOLOGIES.
CLONK
IT'S NO USE...

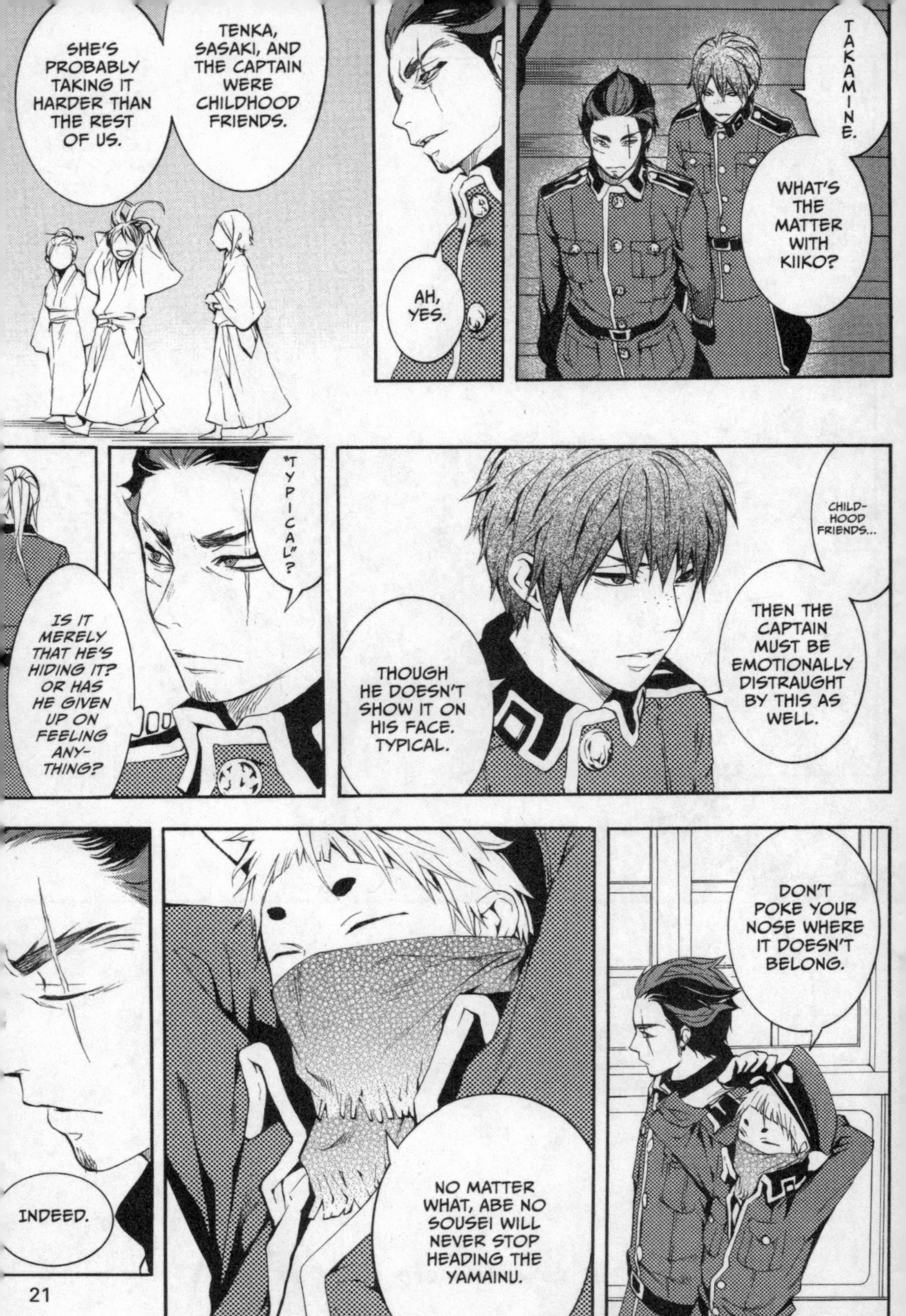
TAKAMINE.
WHAT'S THE MATTER WITH KIIKO?
AH, YES.
TENKA, SASAKI, AND THE CAPTAIN WERE CHILDHOOD FRIENDS.
SHE'S PROBABLY TAKING IT HARDER THAN THE REST OF US.
CHILDHOOD FRIENDS...
THEN THE CAPTAIN MUST BE EMOTIONALLY DISTRAUGHT BY THIS AS WELL.
THOUGH HE DOESN'T SHOW IT ON HIS FACE. TYPICAL.
"TYPICAL"?
IS IT MERELY THAT HE'S HIDING IT? OR HAS HE GIVEN UP ON FEELING ANYTHING?
DON'T POKE YOUR NOSE WHERE IT DOESN'T BELONG.
NO MATTER WHAT, ABE NO SOUSEI WILL NEVER STOP HEADING THE YAMAINU.
INDEED.

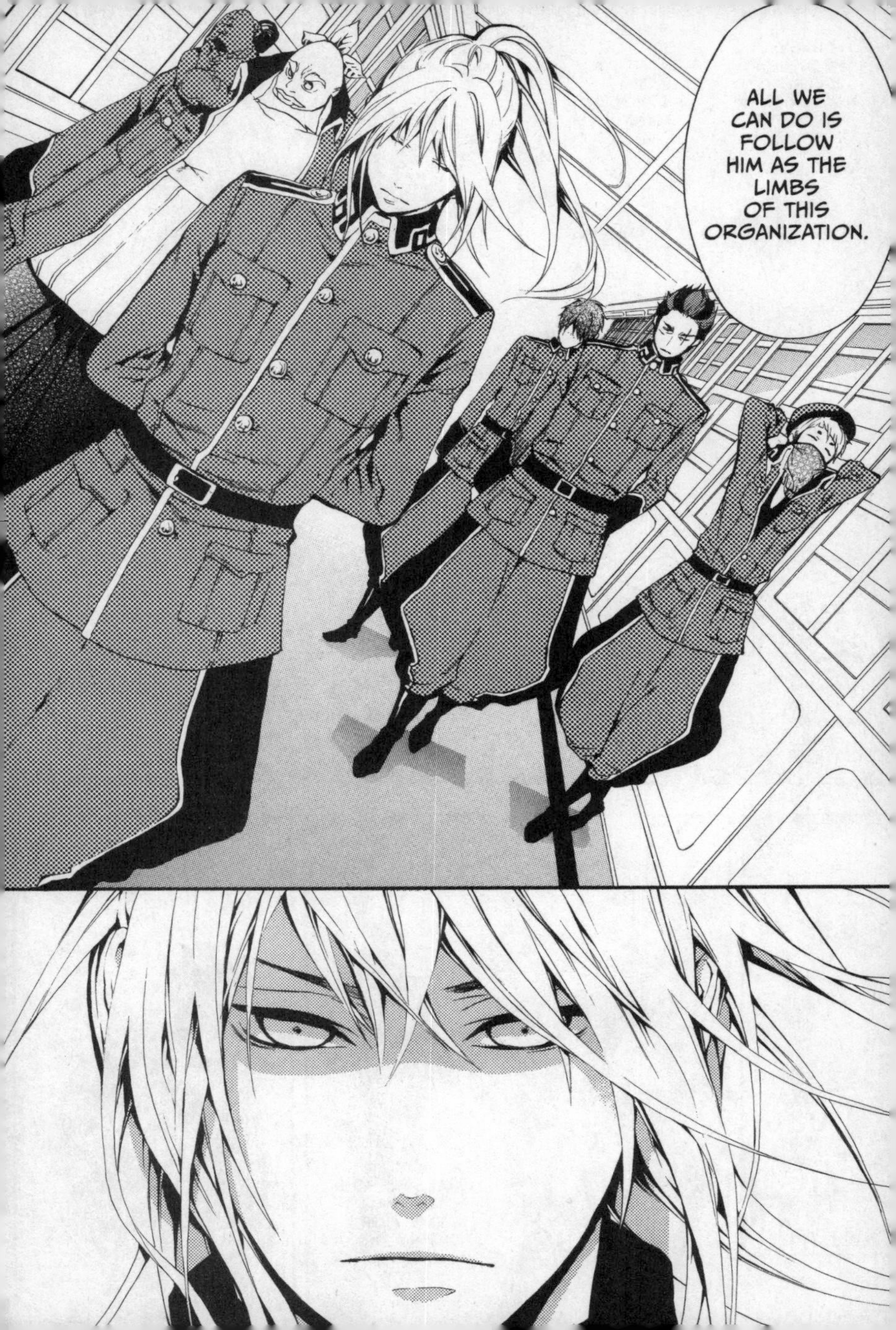
ALL WE CAN DO IS FOLLOW HIM AS THE LIMBS OF THIS ORGANIZATION.

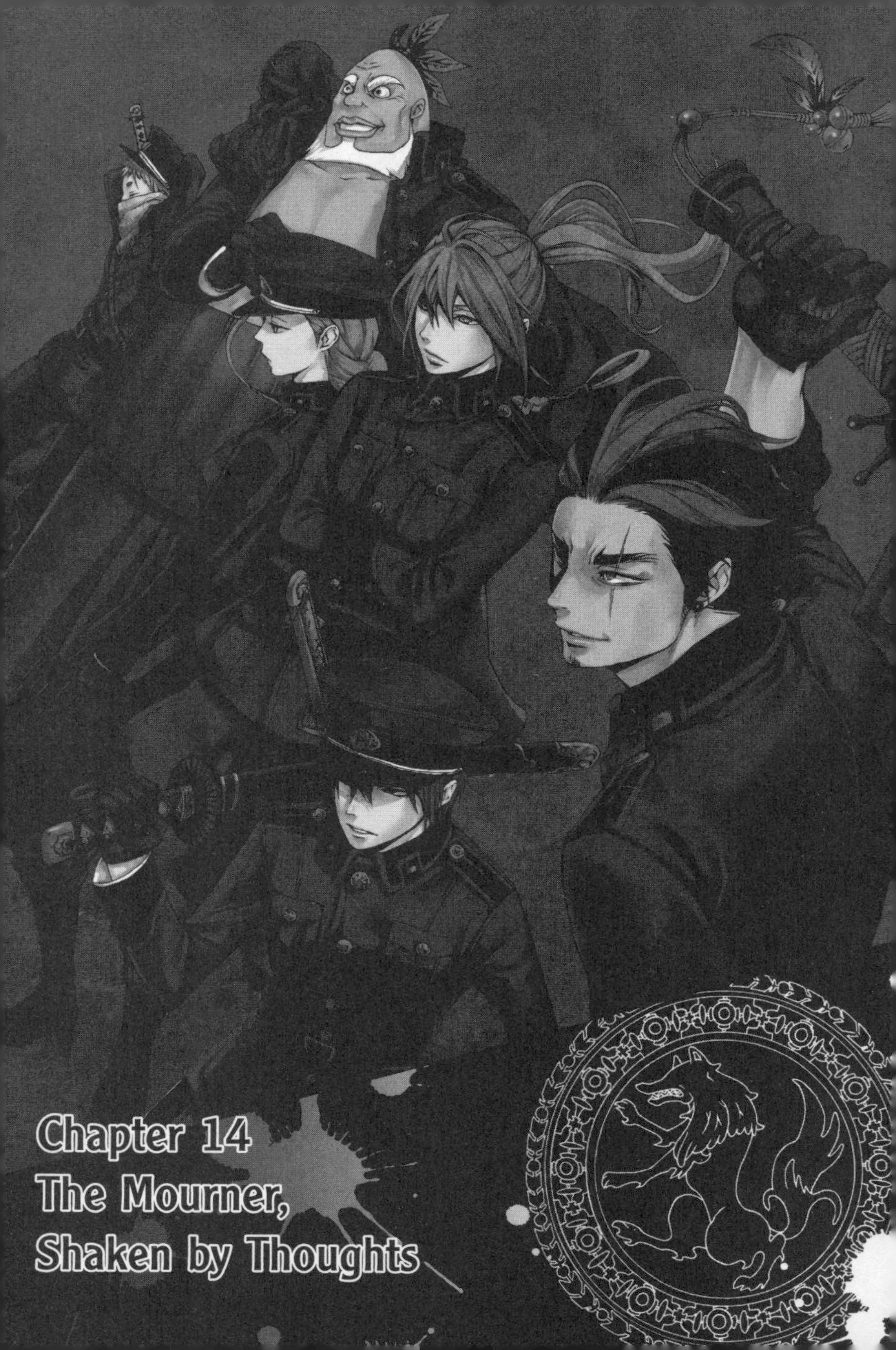
Chapter 14
The Mourner, Shaken by Thoughts

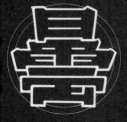

LAUGHING UNDER THE CLOUDS

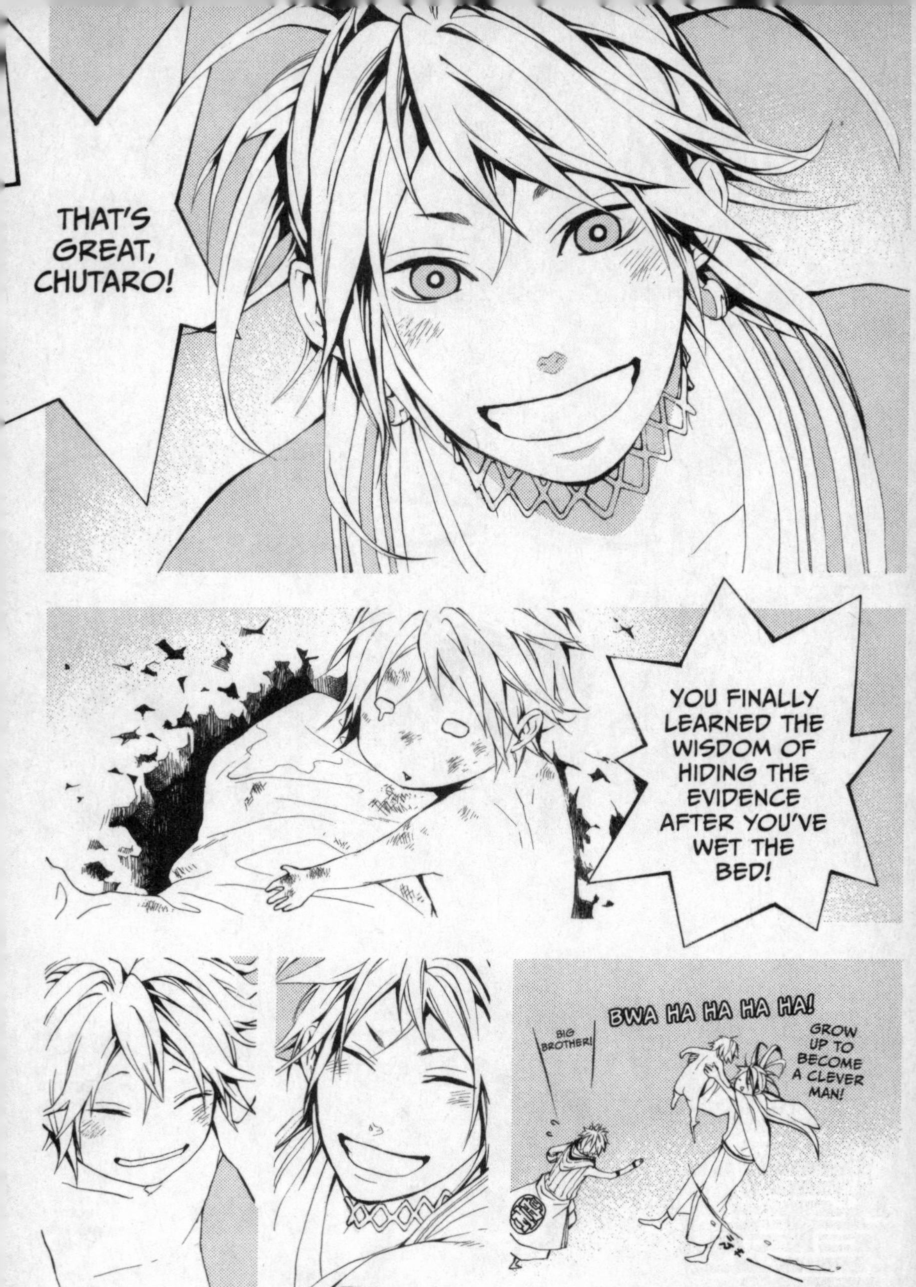
THAT'S GREAT, CHUTARO!
YOU FINALLY LEARNED THE WISDOM OF HIDING THE EVIDENCE AFTER YOU'VE WET THE BED!
GROW UP TO BECOME A CLEVER MAN!
BWA HA HA HA HA!
BIG BROTHER!

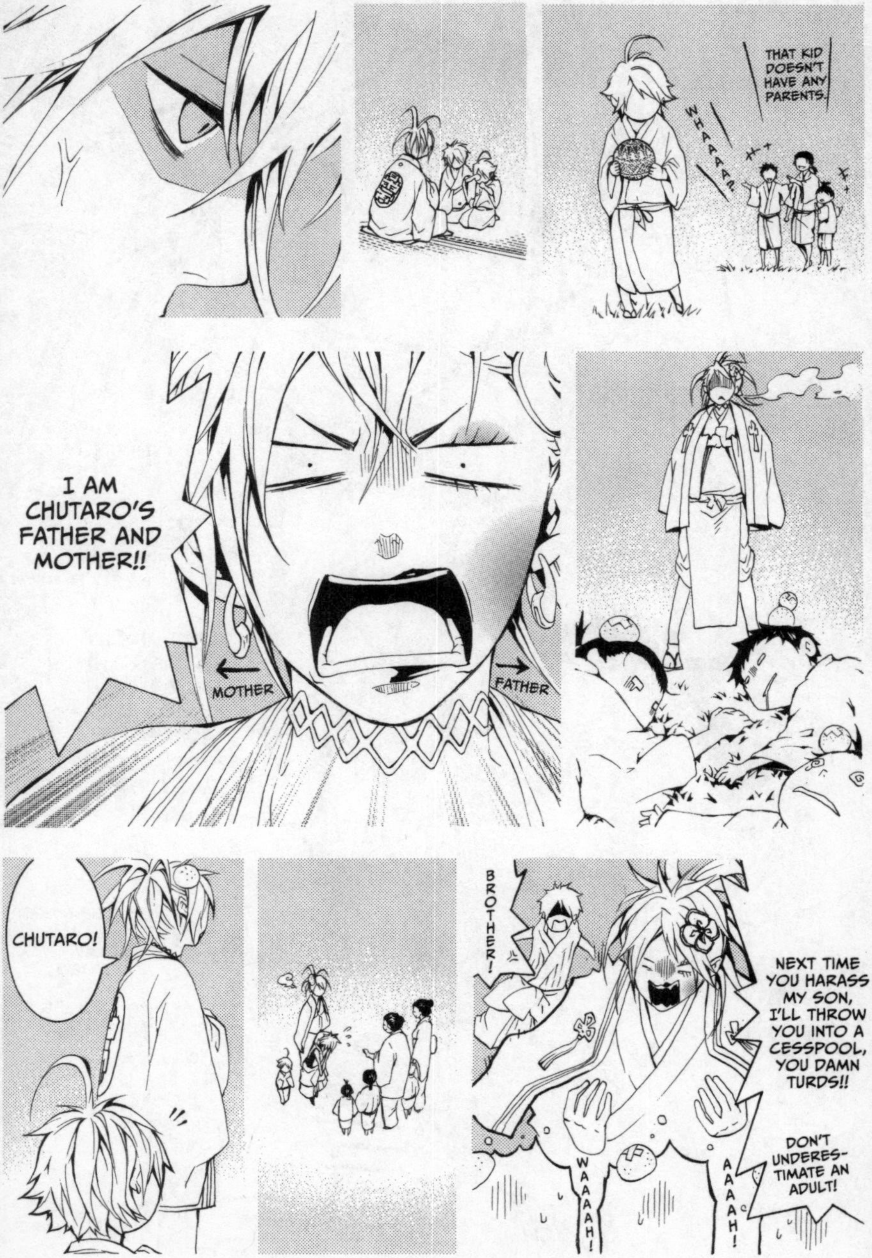
THAT KID DOESN'T HAVE ANY PARENTS.
WHAAAA?
I AM CHUTARO'S FATHER AND MOTHER!!
MOTHER
FATHER
NEXT TIME YOU HARASS MY SON, I'LL THROW YOU INTO A CESSPOOL, YOU DAMN TURDS!!
BROTHER!
DON'T UNDERES-TIMATE AN ADULT!
AAAAAH!
WAAAAH!
CHUTARO!

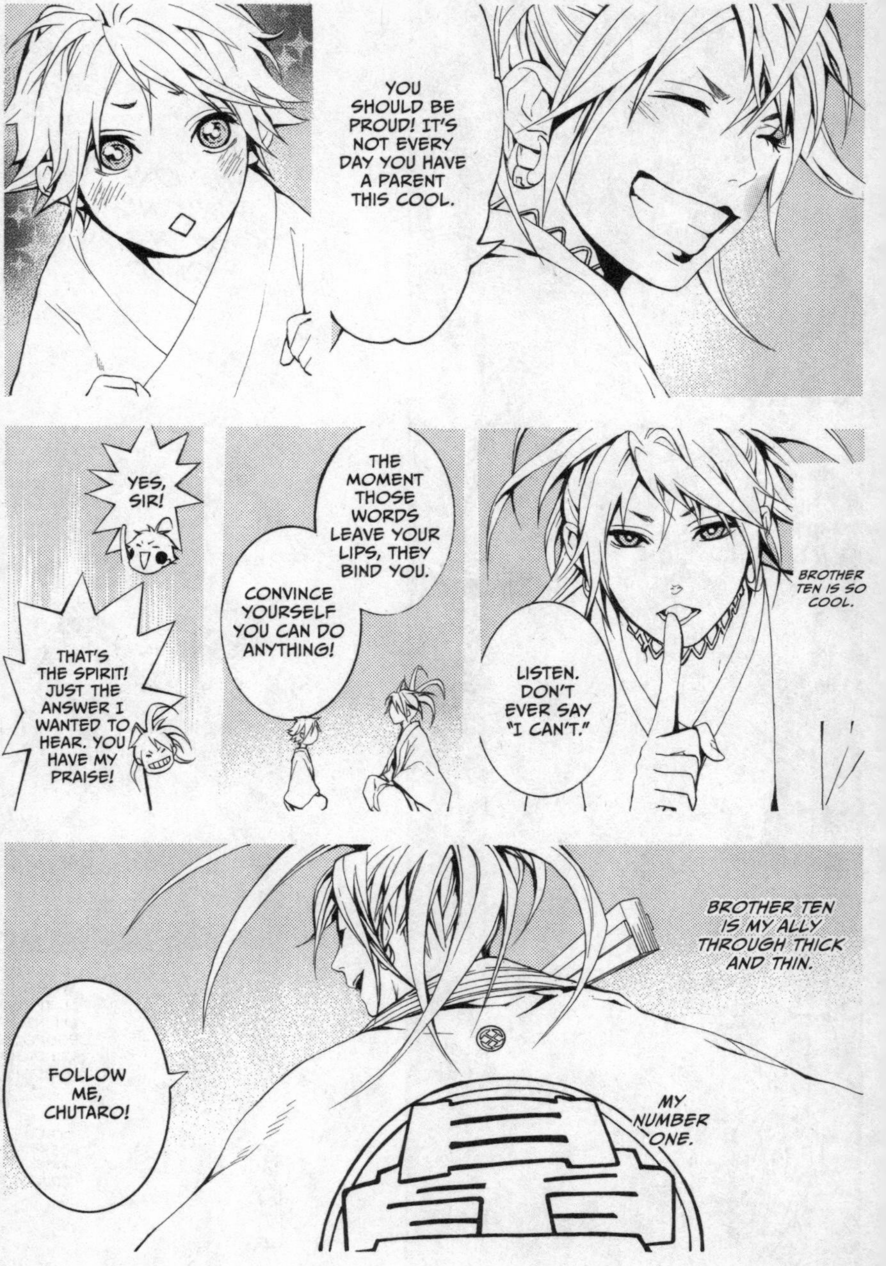
YOU SHOULD BE PROUD! IT'S NOT EVERY DAY YOU HAVE A PARENT THIS COOL.
LISTEN. DON'T EVER SAY "I CAN'T."
BROTHER TEN IS SO COOL.
THE MOMENT THOSE WORDS LEAVE YOUR LIPS, THEY BIND YOU.
CONVINCE YOURSELF YOU CAN DO ANYTHING!
YES, SIR!
THAT'S THE SPIRIT! JUST THE ANSWER I WANTED TO HEAR. YOU HAVE MY PRAISE!
BROTHER TEN IS MY ALLY THROUGH THICK AND THIN.
FOLLOW ME, CHUTARO!
MY NUMBER ONE.

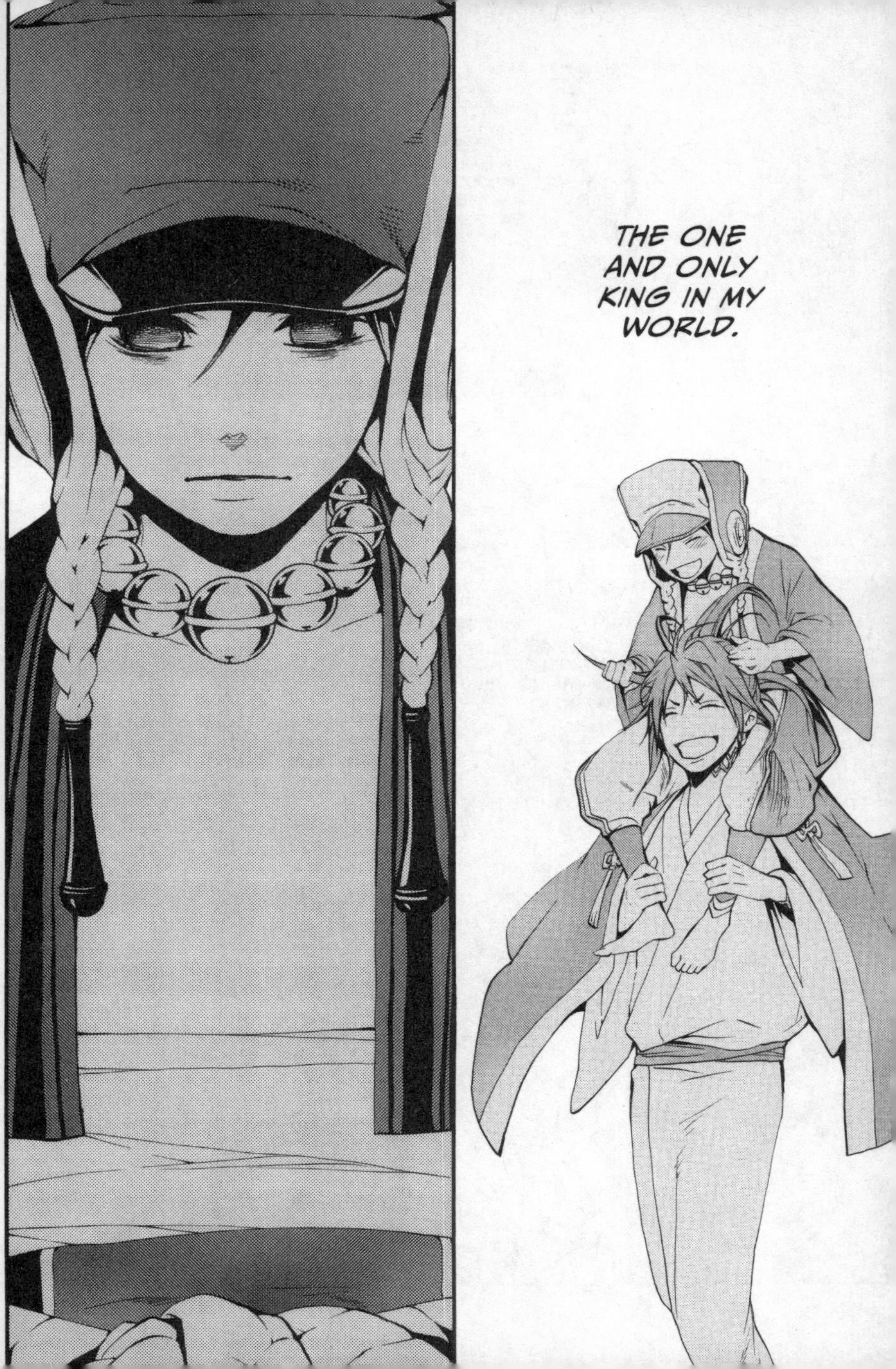
THE ONE AND ONLY KING IN MY WORLD.

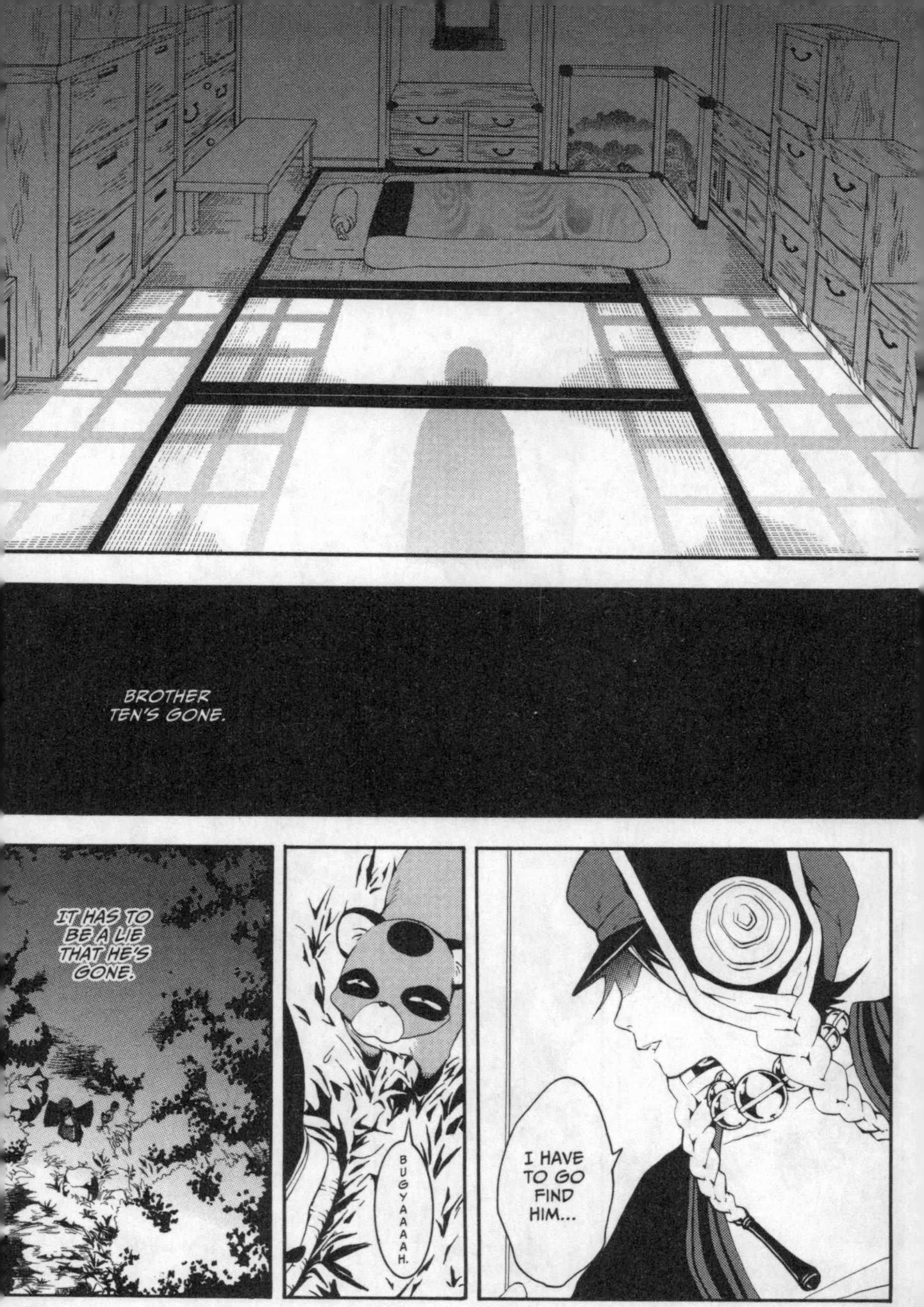
BROTHER TEN'S GONE.
I HAVE TO GO FIND HIM...
BUGYAAAAAH.
IT HAS TO BE A LIE THAT HE'S GONE.

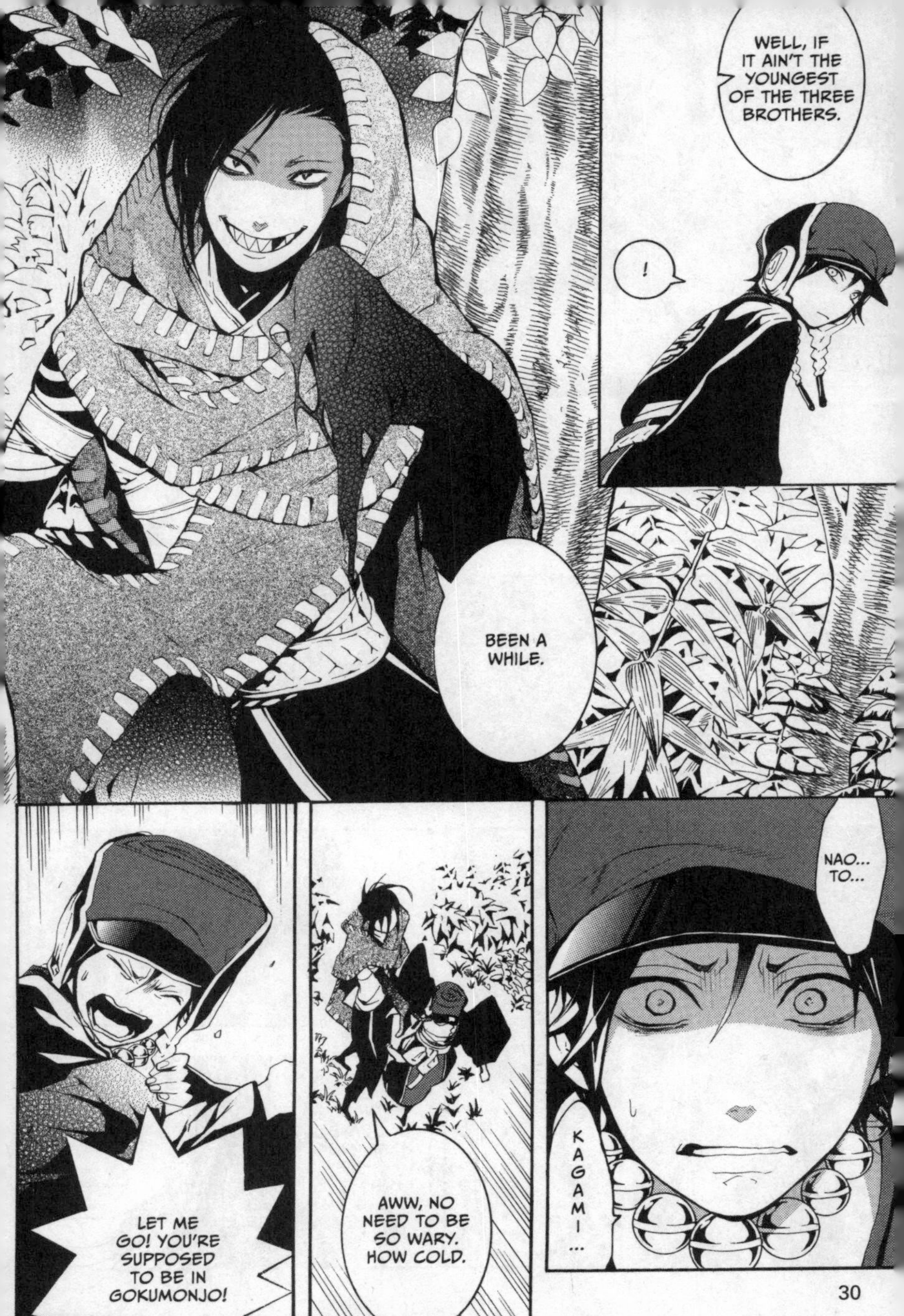
WELL, IF IT AIN'T THE YOUNGEST OF THE THREE BROTHERS.
!
BEEN A WHILE.
NAO... TO...
KAGAMI...
AWW, NO NEED TO BE SO WARY. HOW COLD.
LET ME GO! YOU'RE SUPPOSED TO BE IN GOKUMONJO!

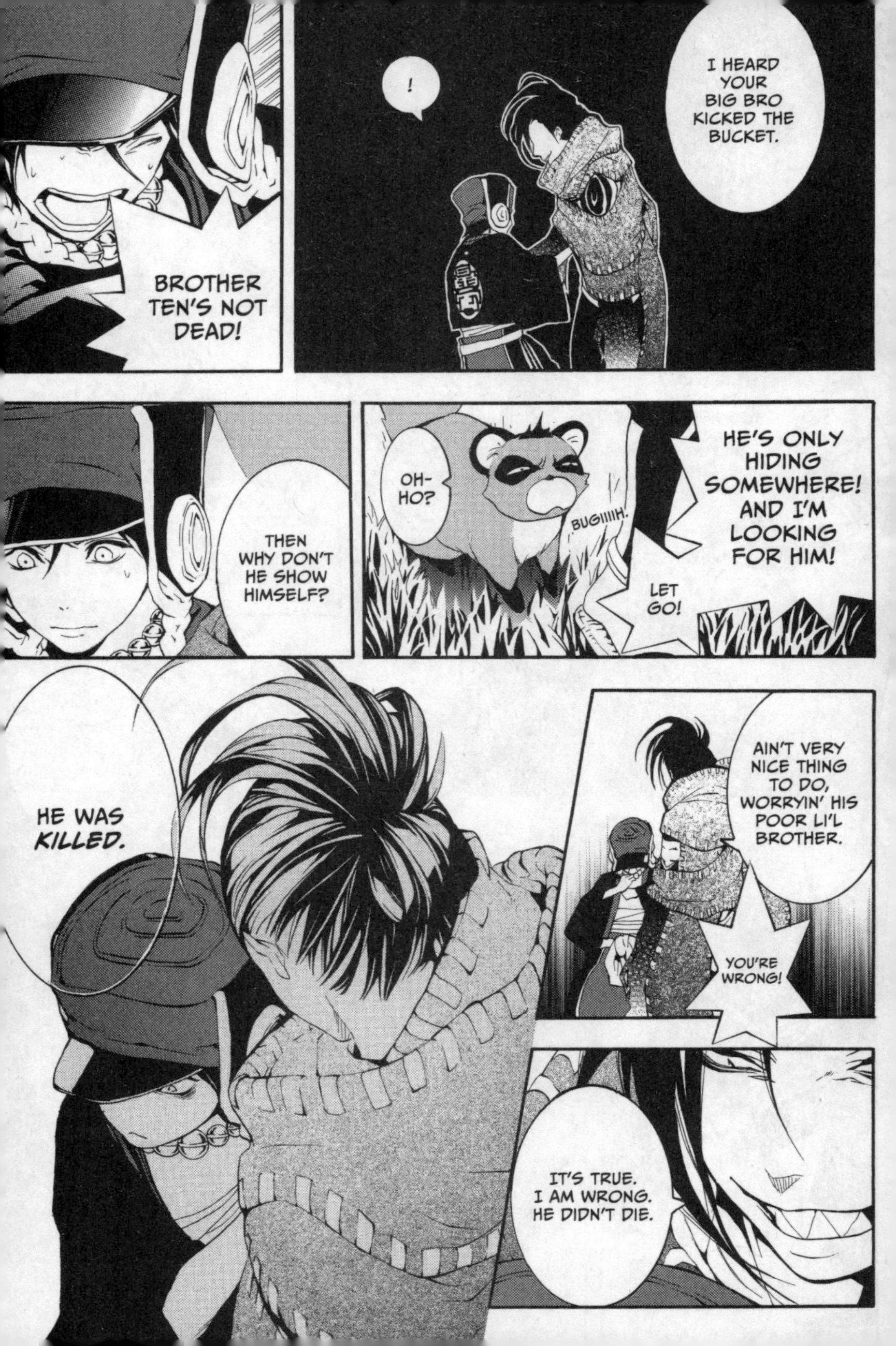
I HEARD YOUR BIG BRO KICKED THE BUCKET.
!
BROTHER TEN'S NOT DEAD!
HE'S ONLY HIDING SOMEWHERE! AND I'M LOOKING FOR HIM!
LET GO!
BUGIIIIH.
OH-HO?
THEN WHY DON'T HE SHOW HIMSELF?
AIN'T VERY NICE THING TO DO, WORRYIN' HIS POOR LI'L BROTHER.
YOU'RE WRONG!
IT'S TRUE. I AM WRONG. HE DIDN'T DIE.
HE WAS *KILLED*.

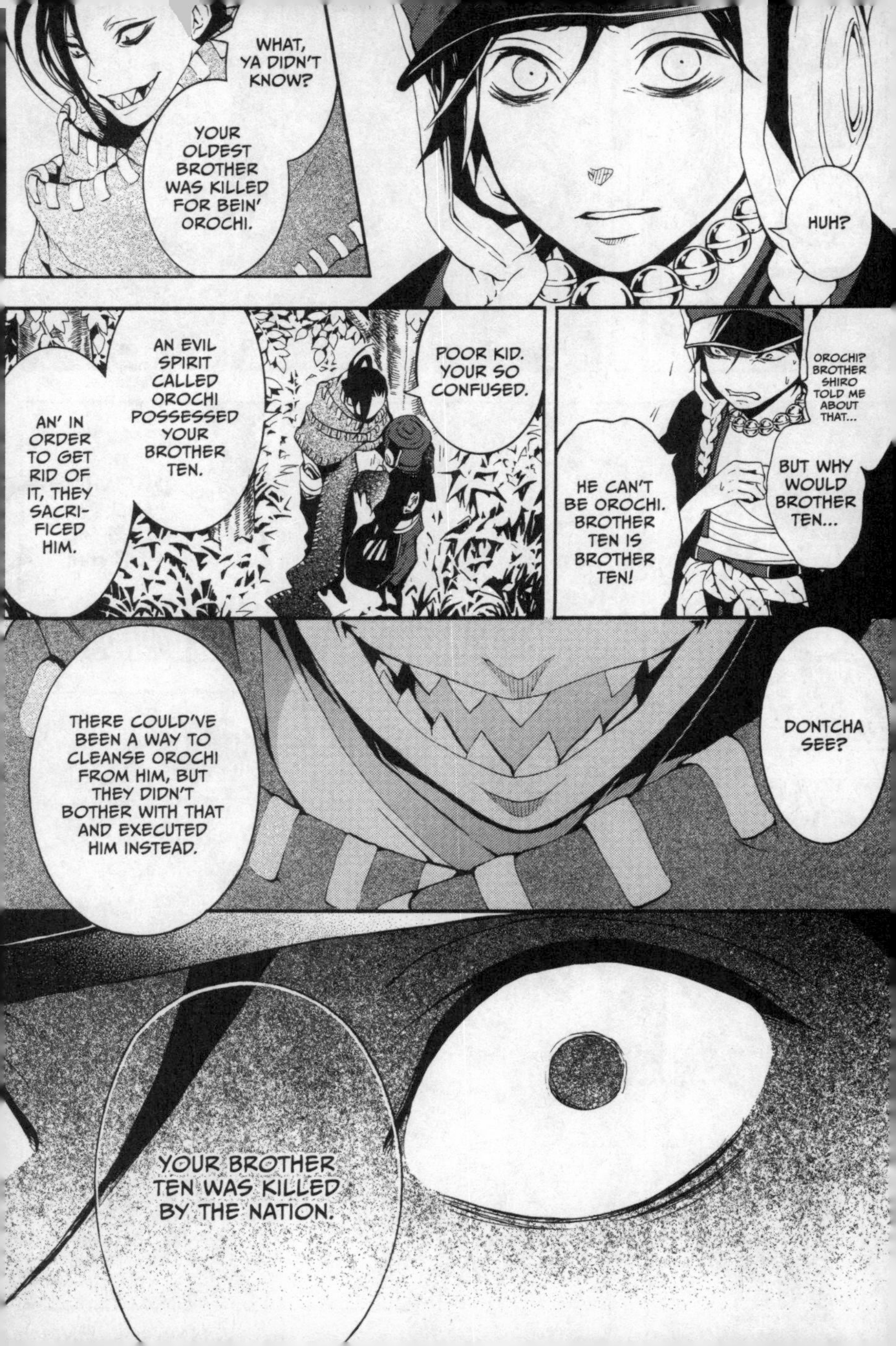
HUH?
WHAT, YA DIDN'T KNOW?
YOUR OLDEST BROTHER WAS KILLED FOR BEIN' OROCHI.
OROCHI? BROTHER SHIRO TOLD ME ABOUT THAT...
BUT WHY WOULD BROTHER TEN...
HE CAN'T BE OROCHI. BROTHER TEN IS BROTHER TEN!
POOR KID. YOUR SO CONFUSED.
AN EVIL SPIRIT CALLED OROCHI POSSESSED YOUR BROTHER TEN.
AN' IN ORDER TO GET RID OF IT, THEY SACRIFICED HIM.
DONTCHA SEE?
THERE COULD'VE BEEN A WAY TO CLEANSE OROCHI FROM HIM, BUT THEY DIDN'T BOTHER WITH THAT AND EXECUTED HIM INSTEAD.
YOUR BROTHER TEN WAS KILLED BY THE NATION.

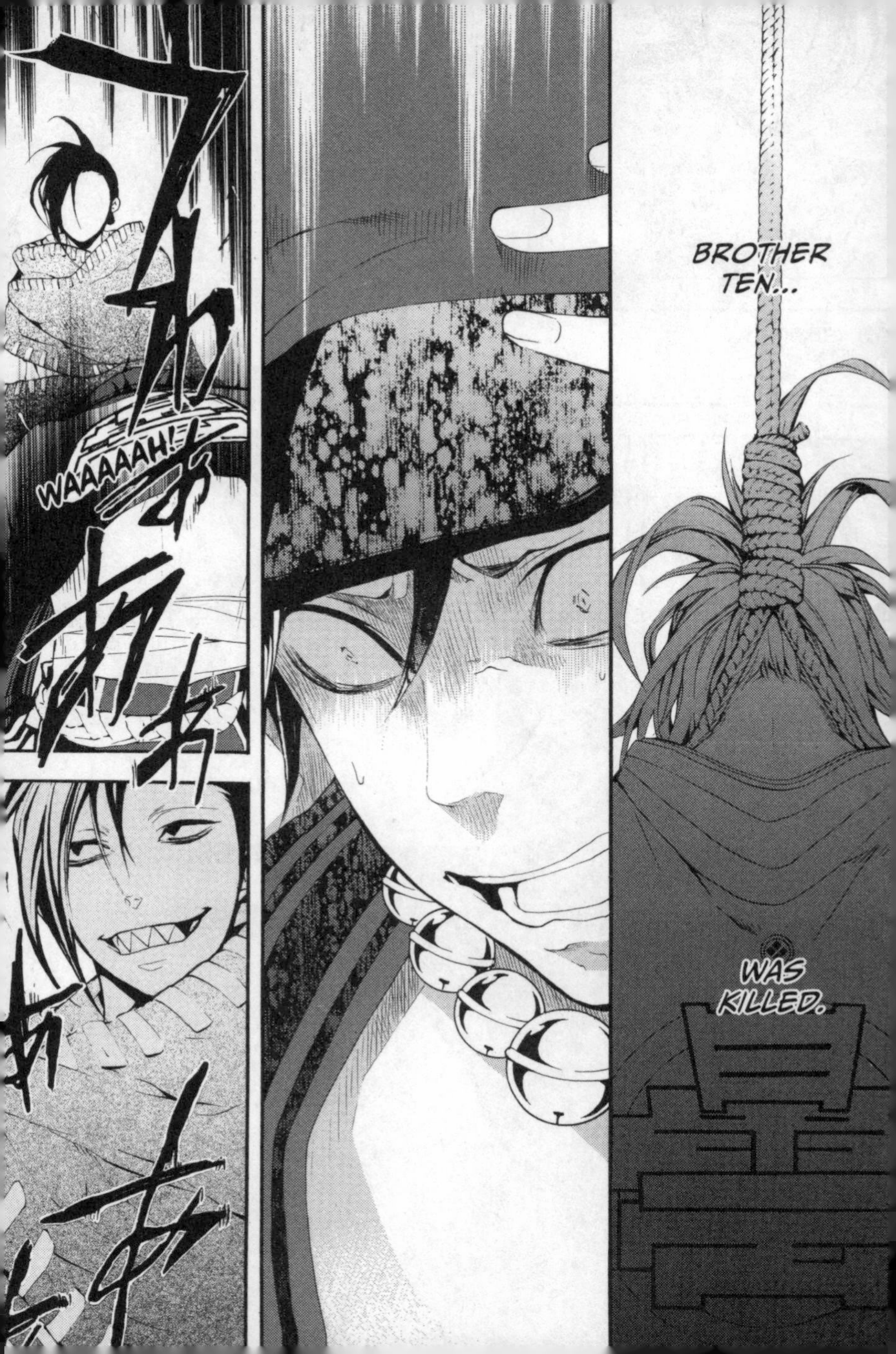
BROTHER TEN...
WAS KILLED.
WAAAAAH!

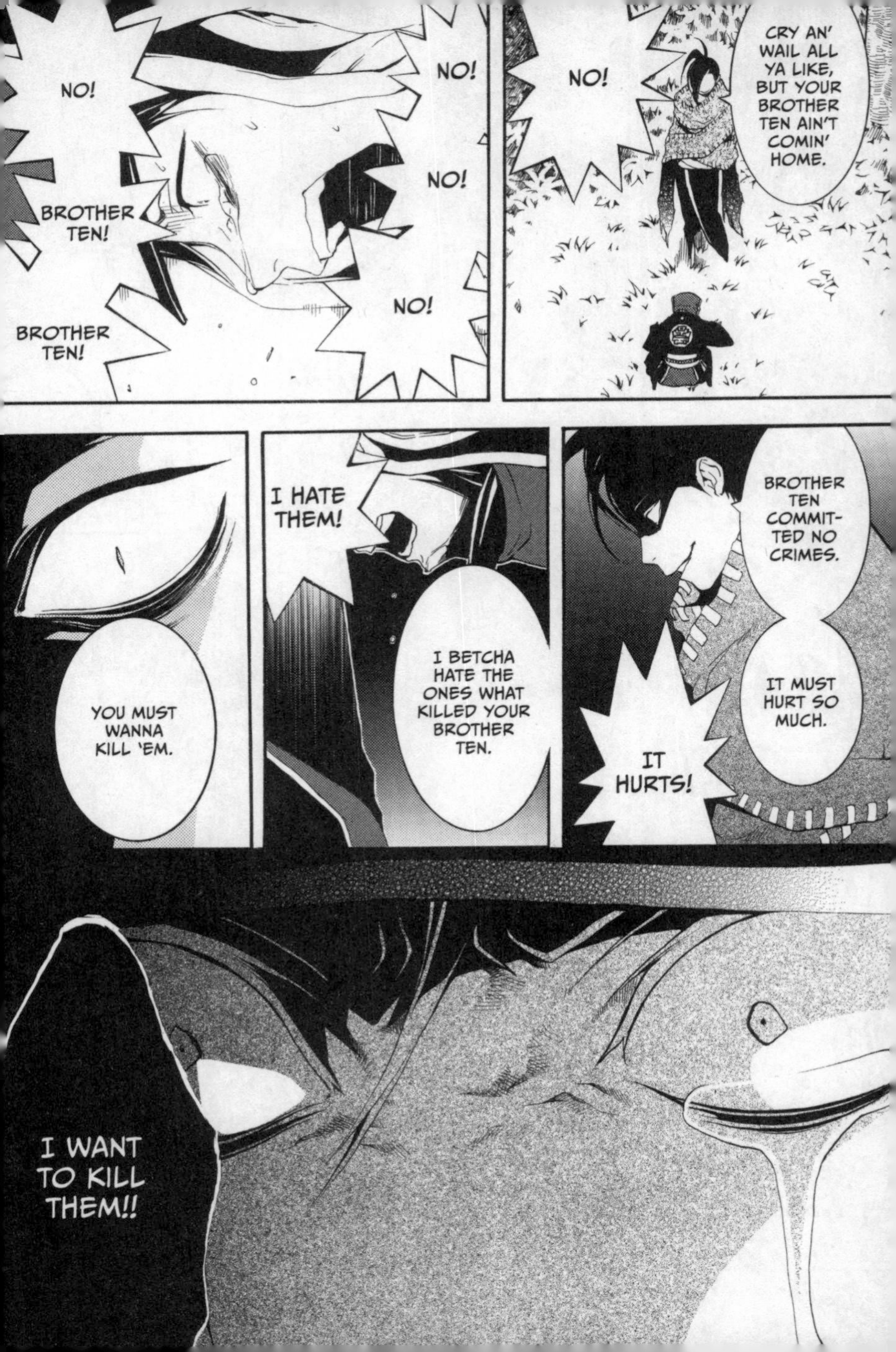
CRY AN' WAIL ALL YA LIKE, BUT YOUR BROTHER TEN AIN'T COMIN' HOME.
NO!
NO!
NO!
NO!
NO!
BROTHER TEN!
BROTHER TEN!
BROTHER TEN COMMIT-TED NO CRIMES.
IT MUST HURT SO MUCH.
IT HURTS!
I BETCHA HATE THE ONES WHAT KILLED YOUR BROTHER TEN.
I HATE THEM!
YOU MUST WANNA KILL 'EM.
I WANT TO KILL THEM!!

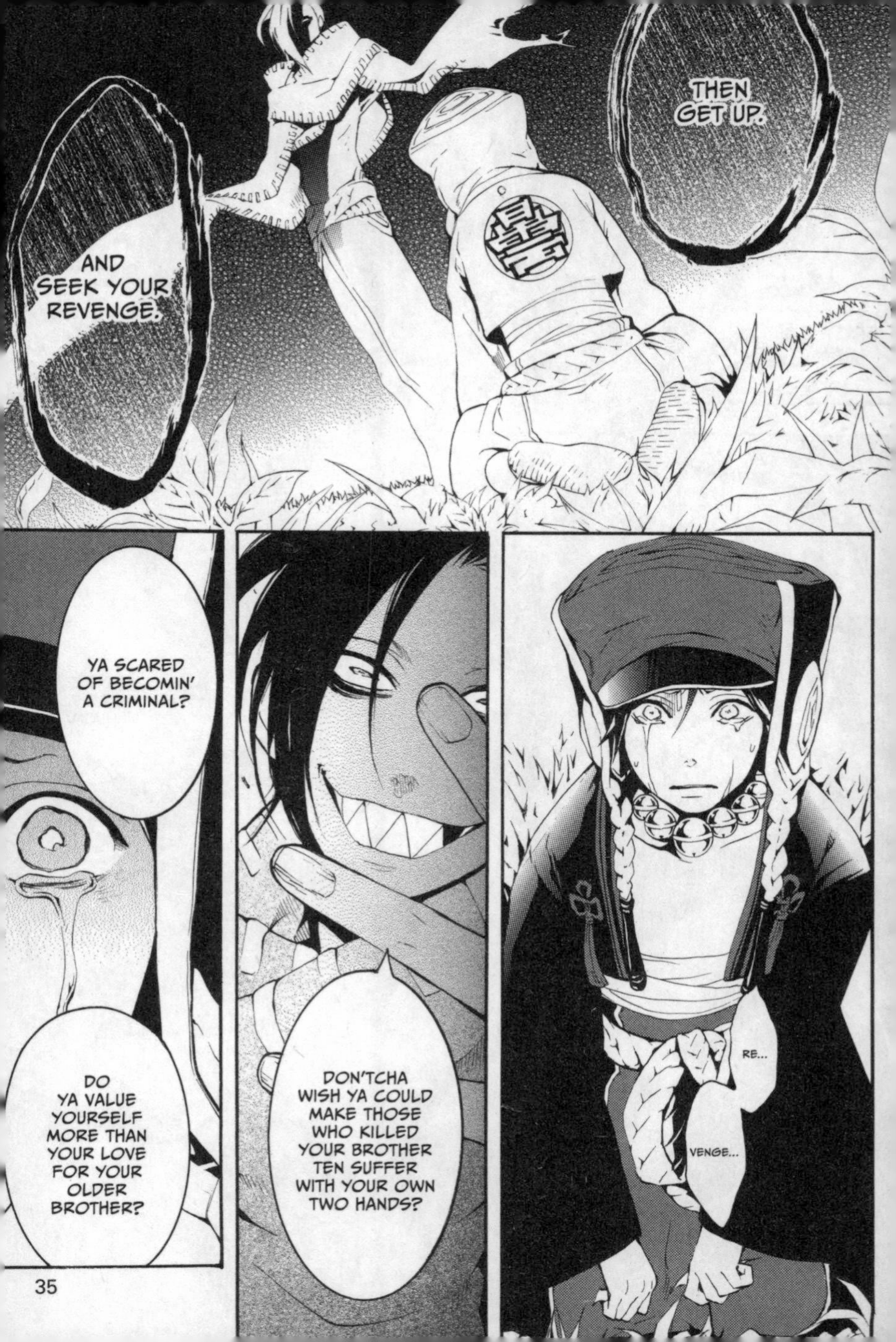
THEN GET UP.
AND SEEK YOUR REVENGE.
RE...
VENGE...
DON'TCHA WISH YA COULD MAKE THOSE WHO KILLED YOUR BROTHER TEN SUFFER WITH YOUR OWN TWO HANDS?
YA SCARED OF BECOMIN' A CRIMINAL?
DO YA VALUE YOURSELF MORE THAN YOUR LOVE FOR YOUR OLDER BROTHER?

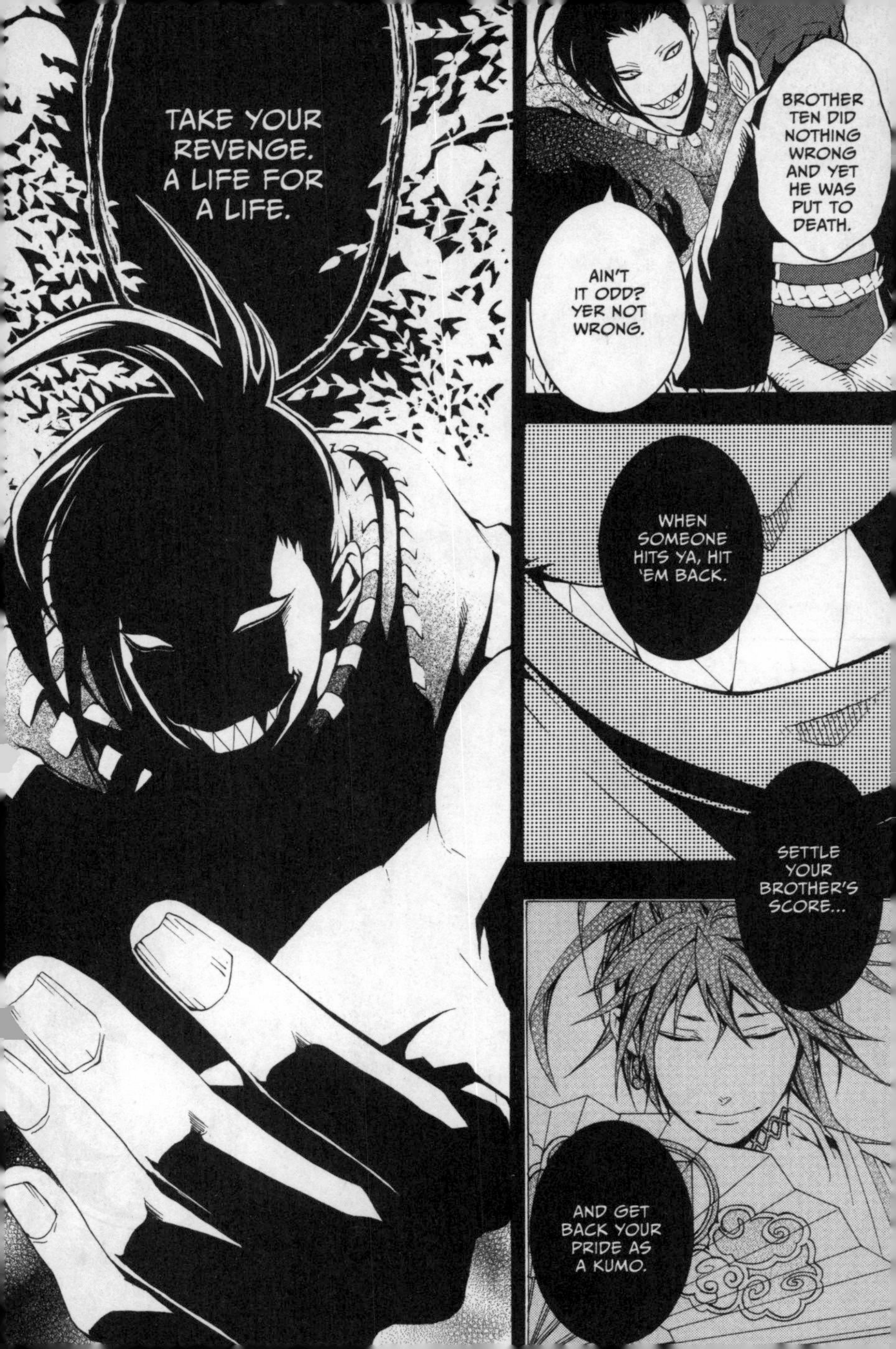
BROTHER TEN DID NOTHING WRONG AND YET HE WAS PUT TO DEATH.
AIN'T IT ODD? YER NOT WRONG.
WHEN SOMEONE HITS YA, HIT 'EM BACK.
SETTLE YOUR BROTHER'S SCORE...
AND GET BACK YOUR PRIDE AS A KUMO.
TAKE YOUR REVENGE. A LIFE FOR A LIFE.

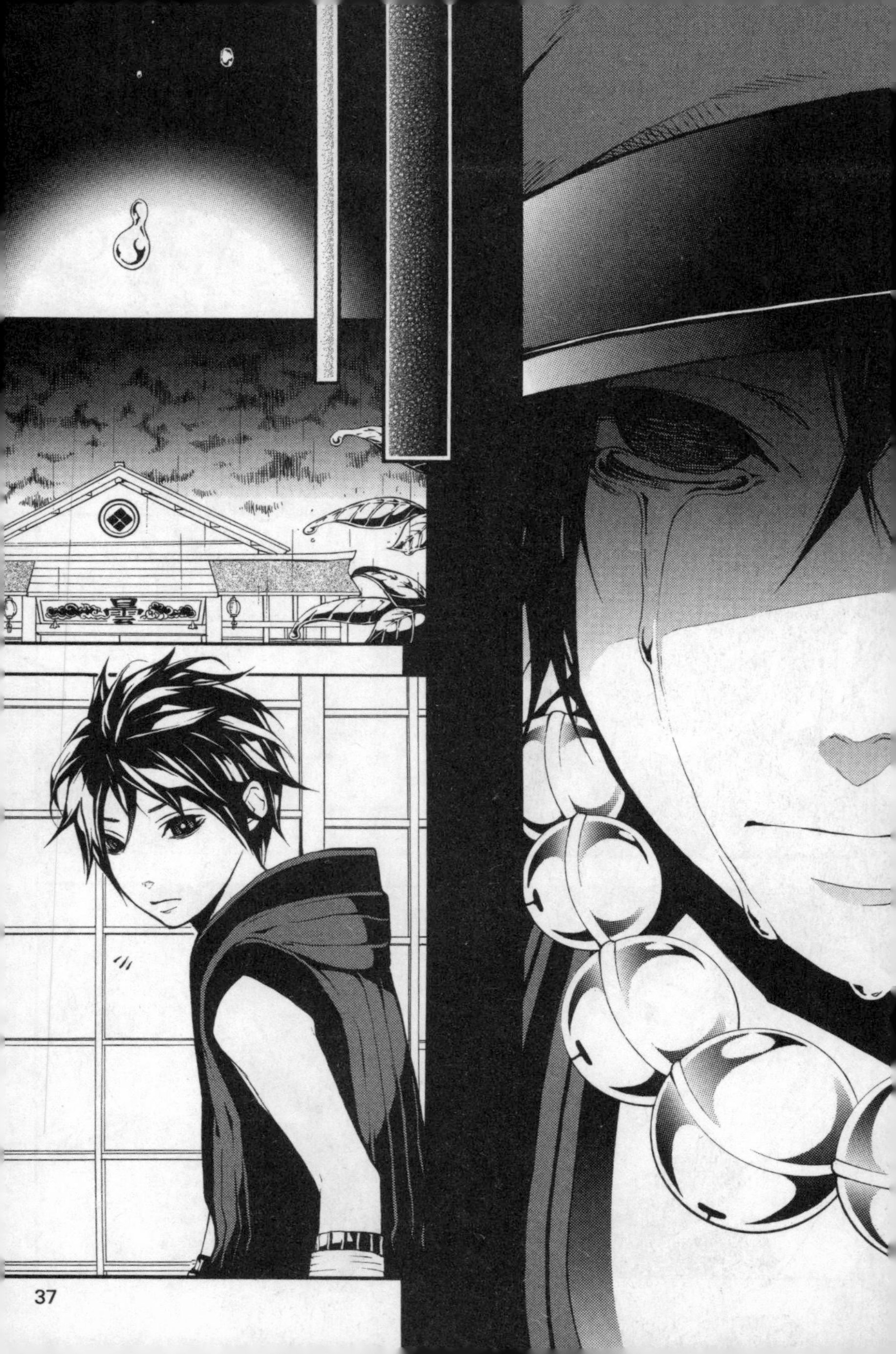

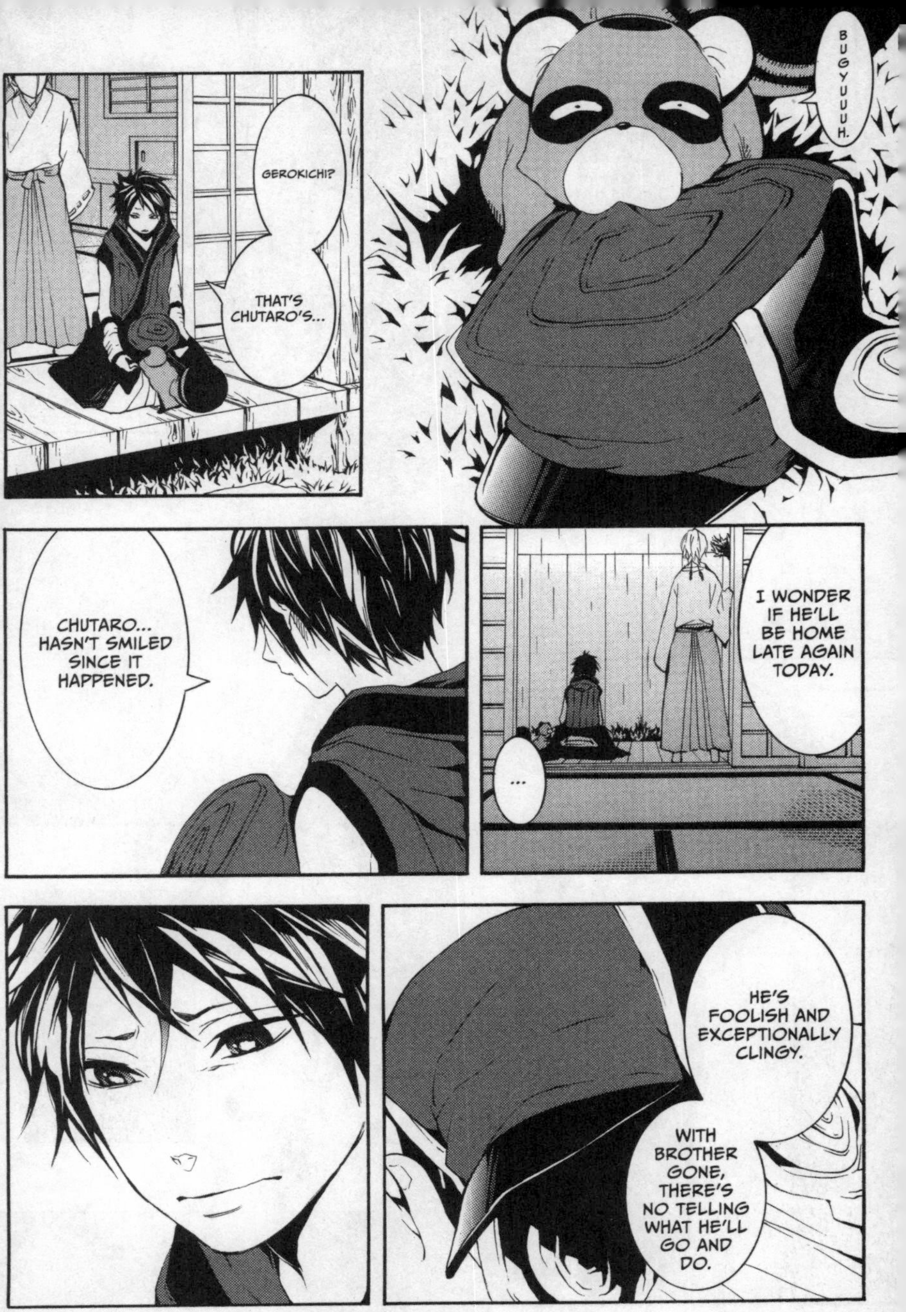
BUGYUUUH.
GEROKICHI?
THAT'S CHUTARO'S...
I WONDER IF HE'LL BE HOME LATE AGAIN TODAY.
...
CHUTARO... HASN'T SMILED SINCE IT HAPPENED.
HE'S FOOLISH AND EXCEPTIONALLY CLINGY.
WITH BROTHER GONE, THERE'S NO TELLING WHAT HE'LL GO AND DO.

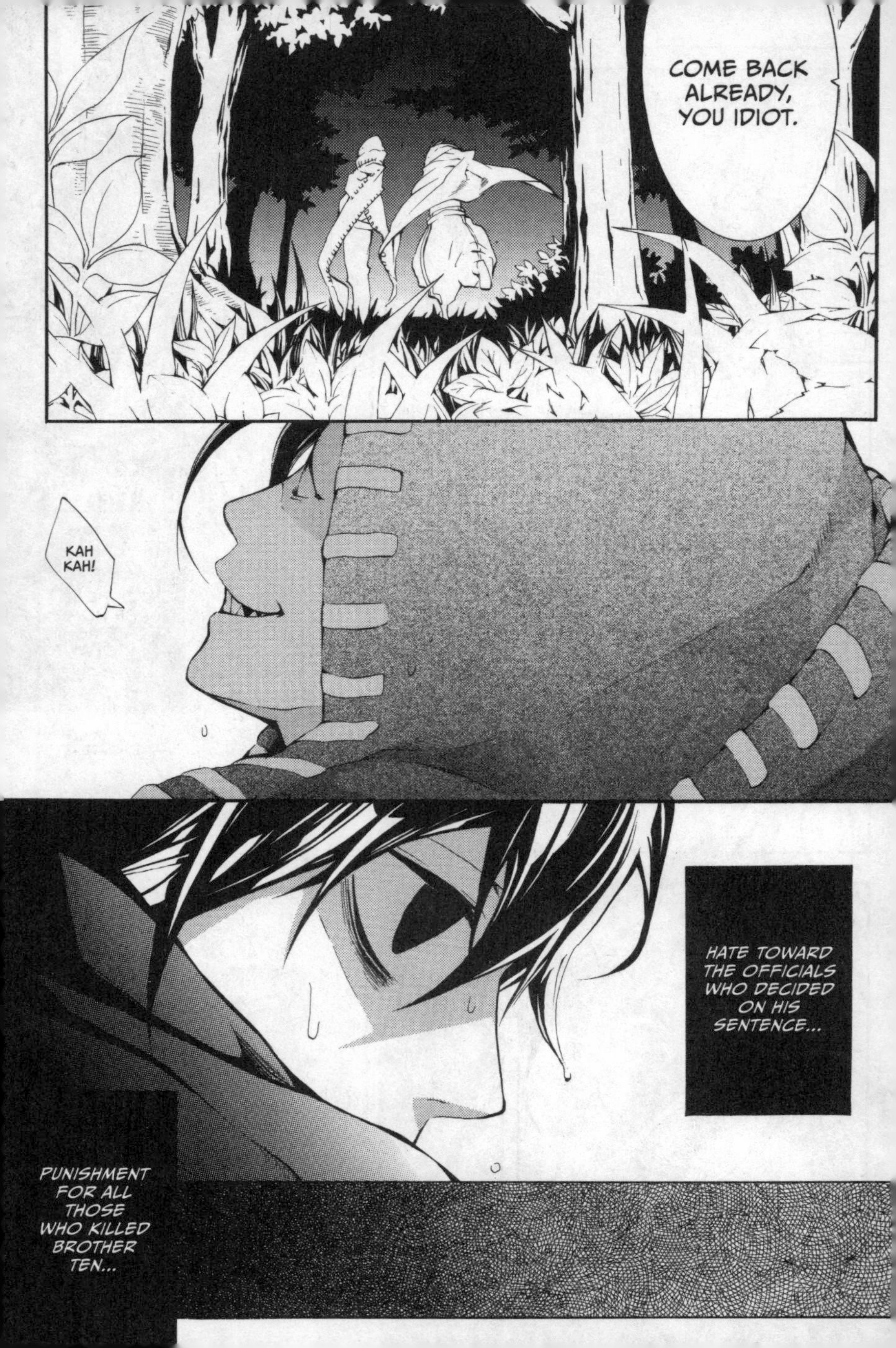
COME BACK ALREADY, YOU IDIOT.
KAH KAH!
HATE TOWARD THE OFFICIALS WHO DECIDED ON HIS SENTENCE...
PUNISHMENT FOR ALL THOSE WHO KILLED BROTHER TEN...

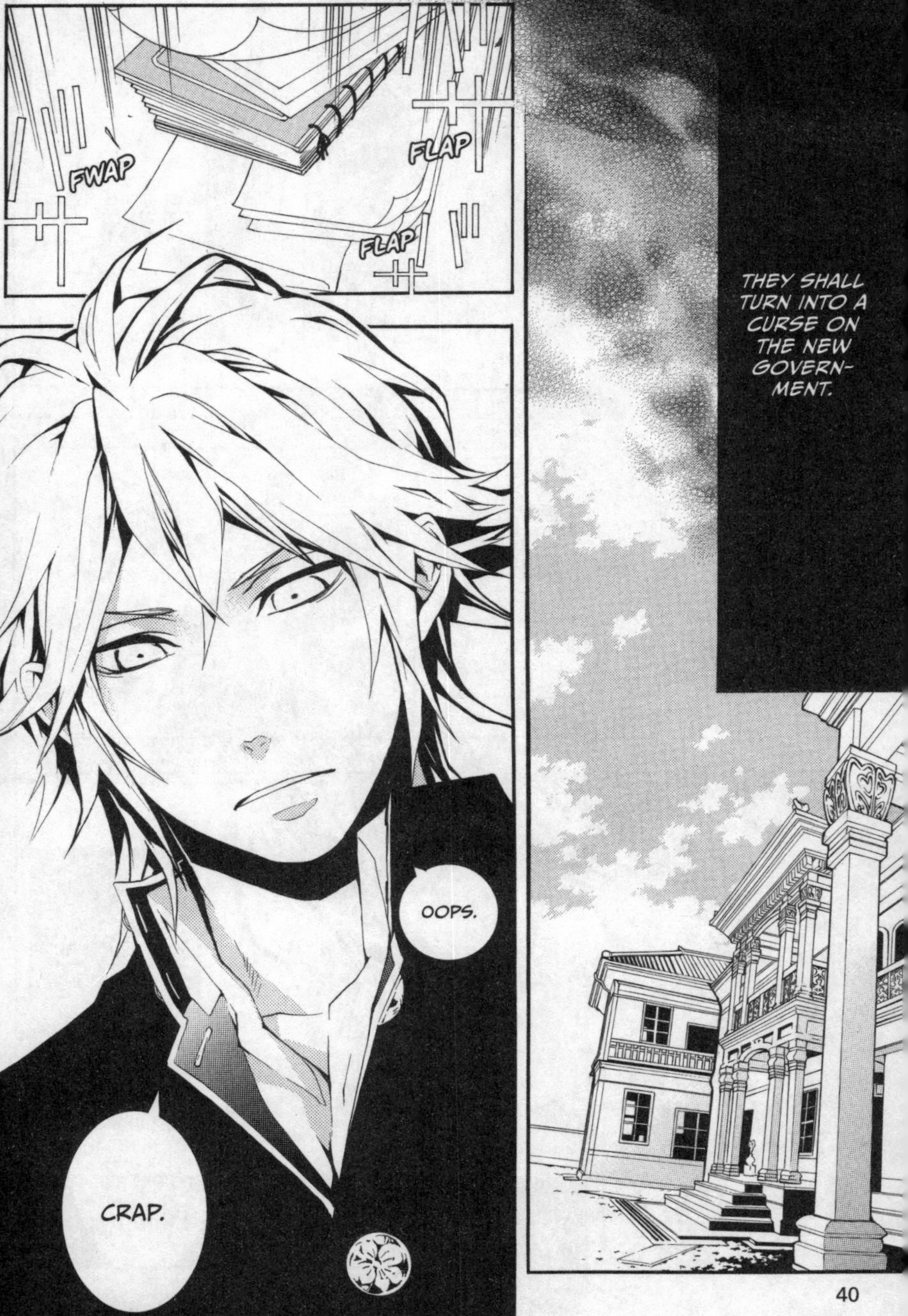
THEY SHALL TURN INTO A CURSE ON THE NEW GOVERNMENT.
FLAP
FWAP
FLAP
OOPS.
CRAP.

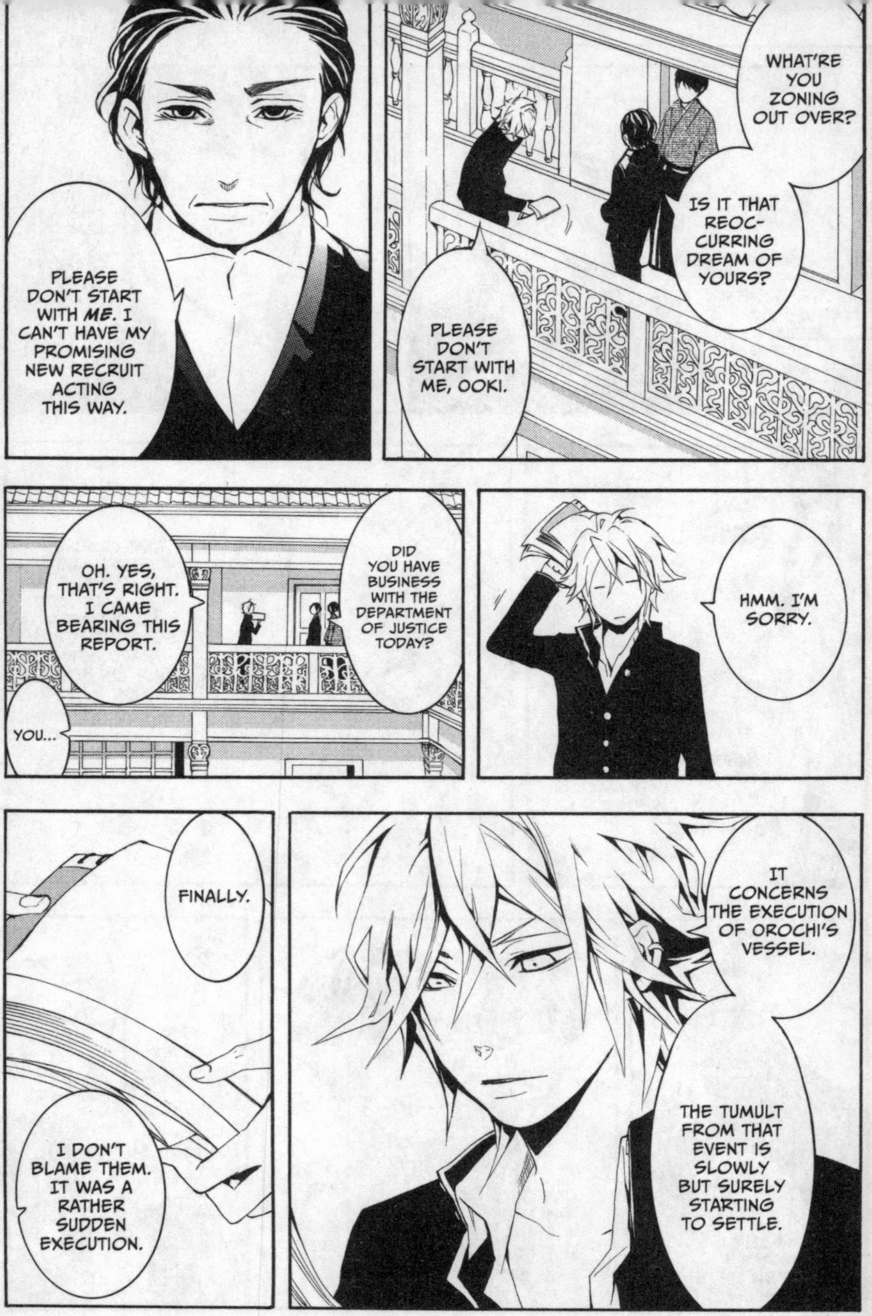
WHAT'RE YOU ZONING OUT OVER?
IS IT THAT REOC-CURRING DREAM OF YOURS?
PLEASE DON'T START WITH ME, OOKI.
PLEASE DON'T START WITH *ME*. I CAN'T HAVE MY PROMISING NEW RECRUIT ACTING THIS WAY.
HMM. I'M SORRY.
DID YOU HAVE BUSINESS WITH THE DEPARTMENT OF JUSTICE TODAY?
OH. YES, THAT'S RIGHT. I CAME BEARING THIS REPORT.
YOU...
IT CONCERNS THE EXECUTION OF OROCHI'S VESSEL.
THE TUMULT FROM THAT EVENT IS SLOWLY BUT SURELY STARTING TO SETTLE.
FINALLY.
I DON'T BLAME THEM. IT WAS A RATHER SUDDEN EXECUTION.

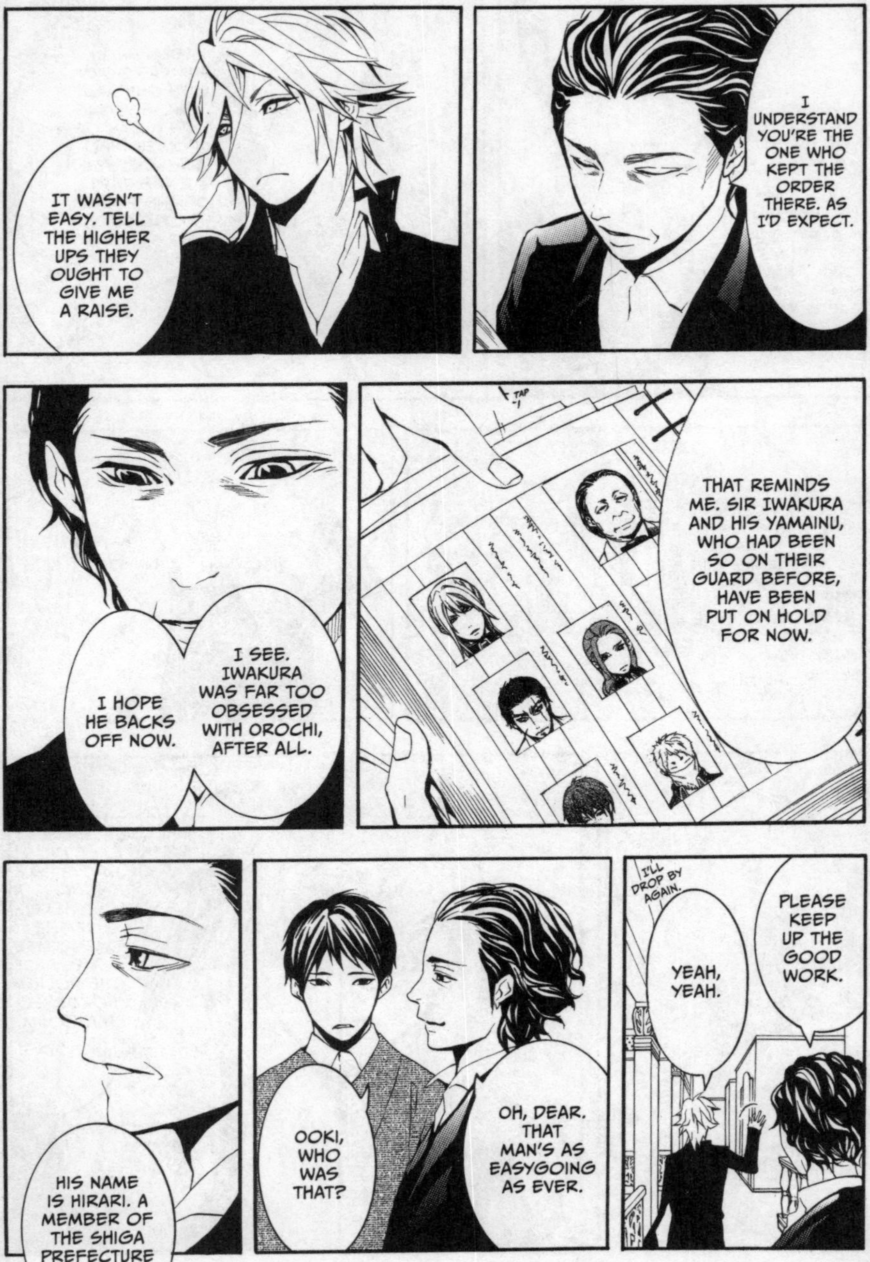
I UNDERSTAND YOU'RE THE ONE WHO KEPT THE ORDER THERE. AS I'D EXPECT.
IT WASN'T EASY. TELL THE HIGHER UPS THEY OUGHT TO GIVE ME A RAISE.
TAP
THAT REMINDS ME. SIR IWAKURA AND HIS YAMAINU, WHO HAD BEEN SO ON THEIR GUARD BEFORE, HAVE BEEN PUT ON HOLD FOR NOW.
I SEE. IWAKURA WAS FAR TOO OBSESSED WITH OROCHI, AFTER ALL.
I HOPE HE BACKS OFF NOW.
PLEASE KEEP UP THE GOOD WORK.
I'LL DROP BY AGAIN.
YEAH, YEAH.
OH, DEAR. THAT MAN'S AS EASYGOING AS EVER.
OOKI, WHO WAS THAT?
HIS NAME IS HIRARI. A MEMBER OF THE SHIGA PREFECTURE GUARD.

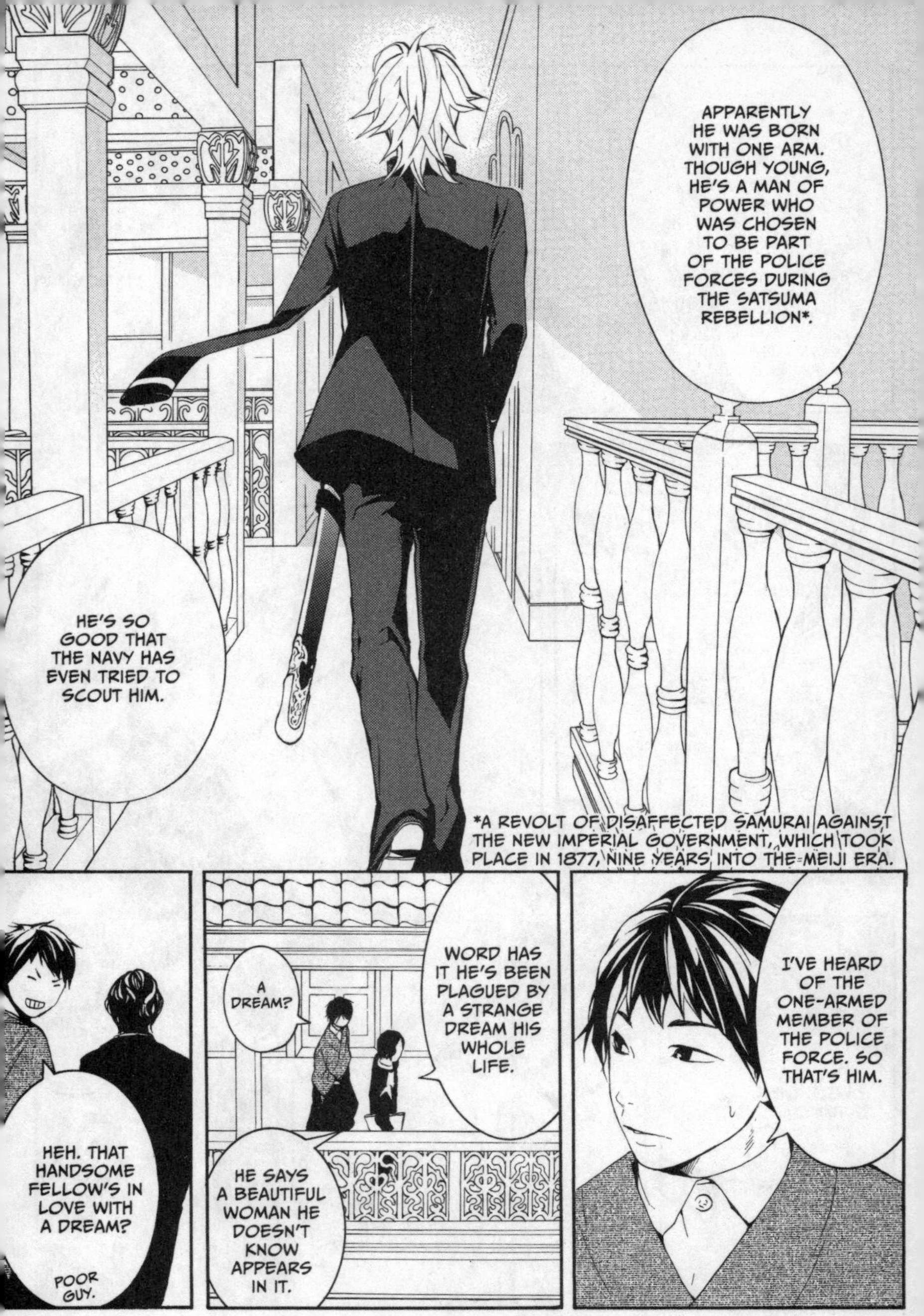
APPARENTLY HE WAS BORN WITH ONE ARM. THOUGH YOUNG, HE'S A MAN OF POWER WHO WAS CHOSEN TO BE PART OF THE POLICE FORCES DURING THE SATSUMA REBELLION*.
HE'S SO GOOD THAT THE NAVY HAS EVEN TRIED TO SCOUT HIM.
*A REVOLT OF DISAFFECTED SAMURAI AGAINST THE NEW IMPERIAL GOVERNMENT, WHICH TOOK PLACE IN 1877, NINE YEARS INTO THE MEIJI ERA.
I'VE HEARD OF THE ONE-ARMED MEMBER OF THE POLICE FORCE. SO THAT'S HIM.
WORD HAS IT HE'S BEEN PLAGUED BY A STRANGE DREAM HIS WHOLE LIFE.
A DREAM?
HE SAYS A BEAUTIFUL WOMAN HE DOESN'T KNOW APPEARS IN IT.
HEH. THAT HANDSOME FELLOW'S IN LOVE WITH A DREAM?
POOR GUY.

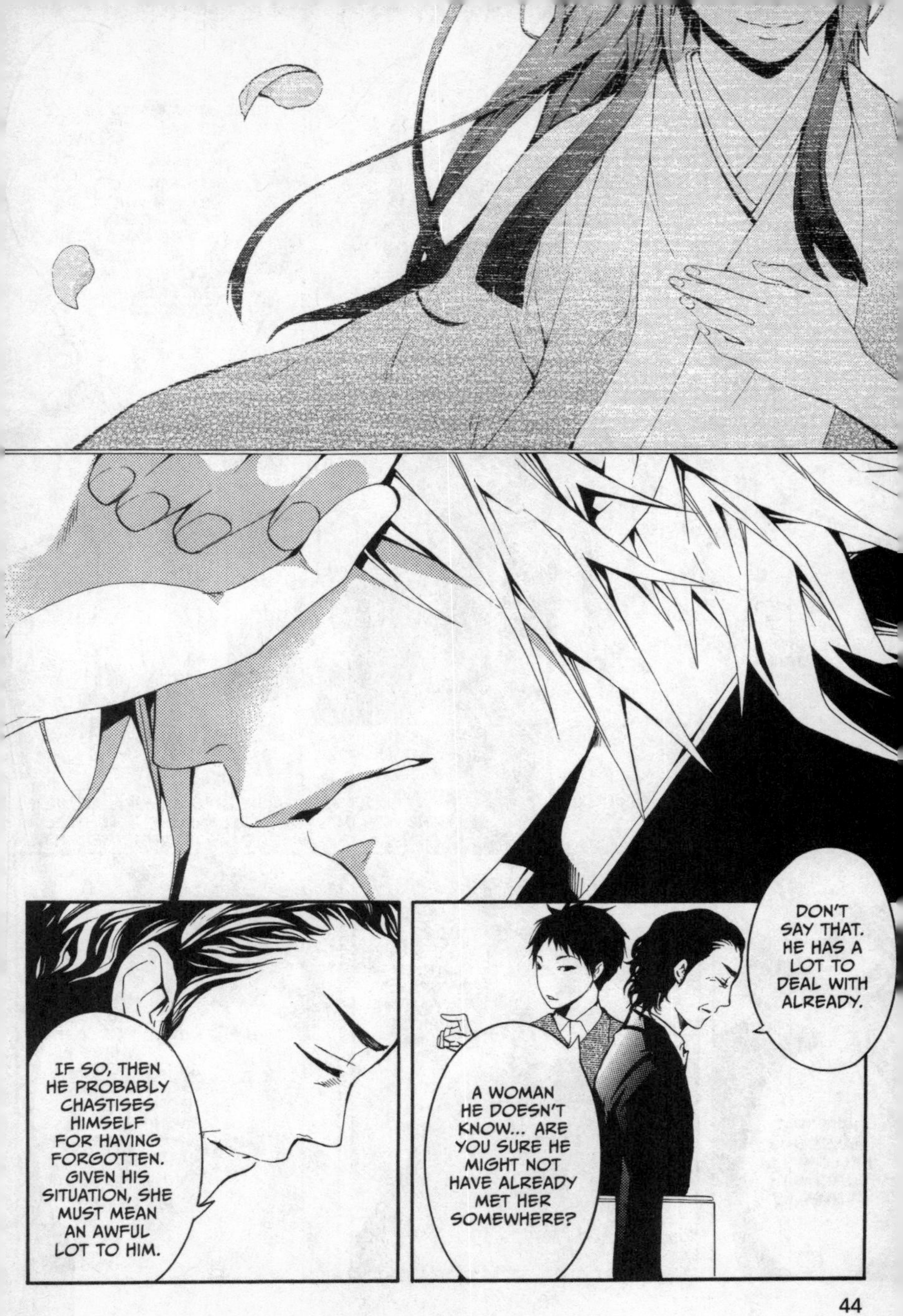
DON'T SAY THAT. HE HAS A LOT TO DEAL WITH ALREADY.
A WOMAN HE DOESN'T KNOW... ARE YOU SURE HE MIGHT NOT HAVE ALREADY MET HER SOMEWHERE?
IF SO, THEN HE PROBABLY CHASTISES HIMSELF FOR HAVING FORGOTTEN. GIVEN HIS SITUATION, SHE MUST MEAN AN AWFUL LOT TO HIM.

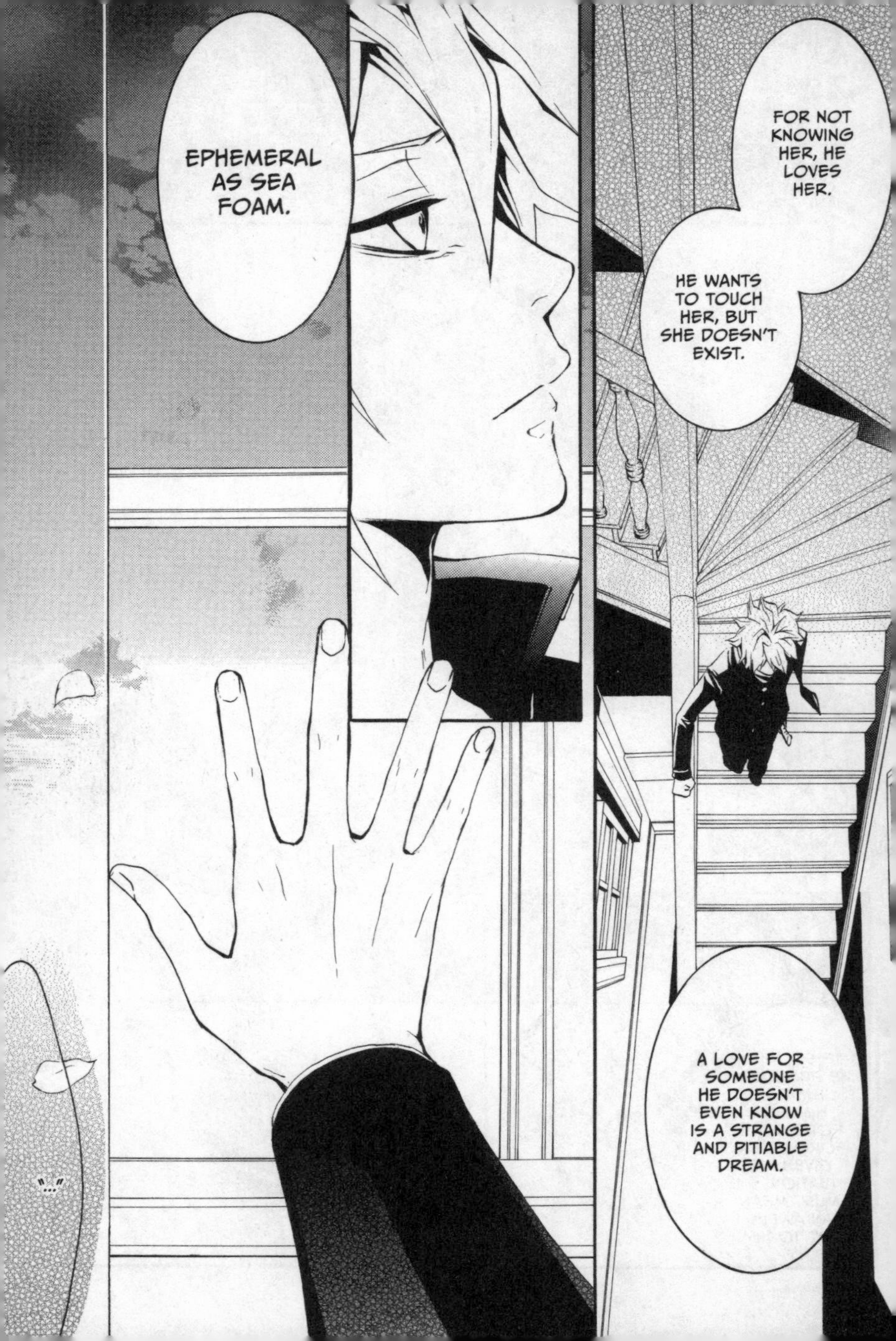
FOR NOT KNOWING HER, HE LOVES HER.
HE WANTS TO TOUCH HER, BUT SHE DOESN'T EXIST.
A LOVE FOR SOMEONE HE DOESN'T EVEN KNOW IS A STRANGE AND PITIABLE DREAM.
EPHEMERAL AS SEA FOAM.
"..."

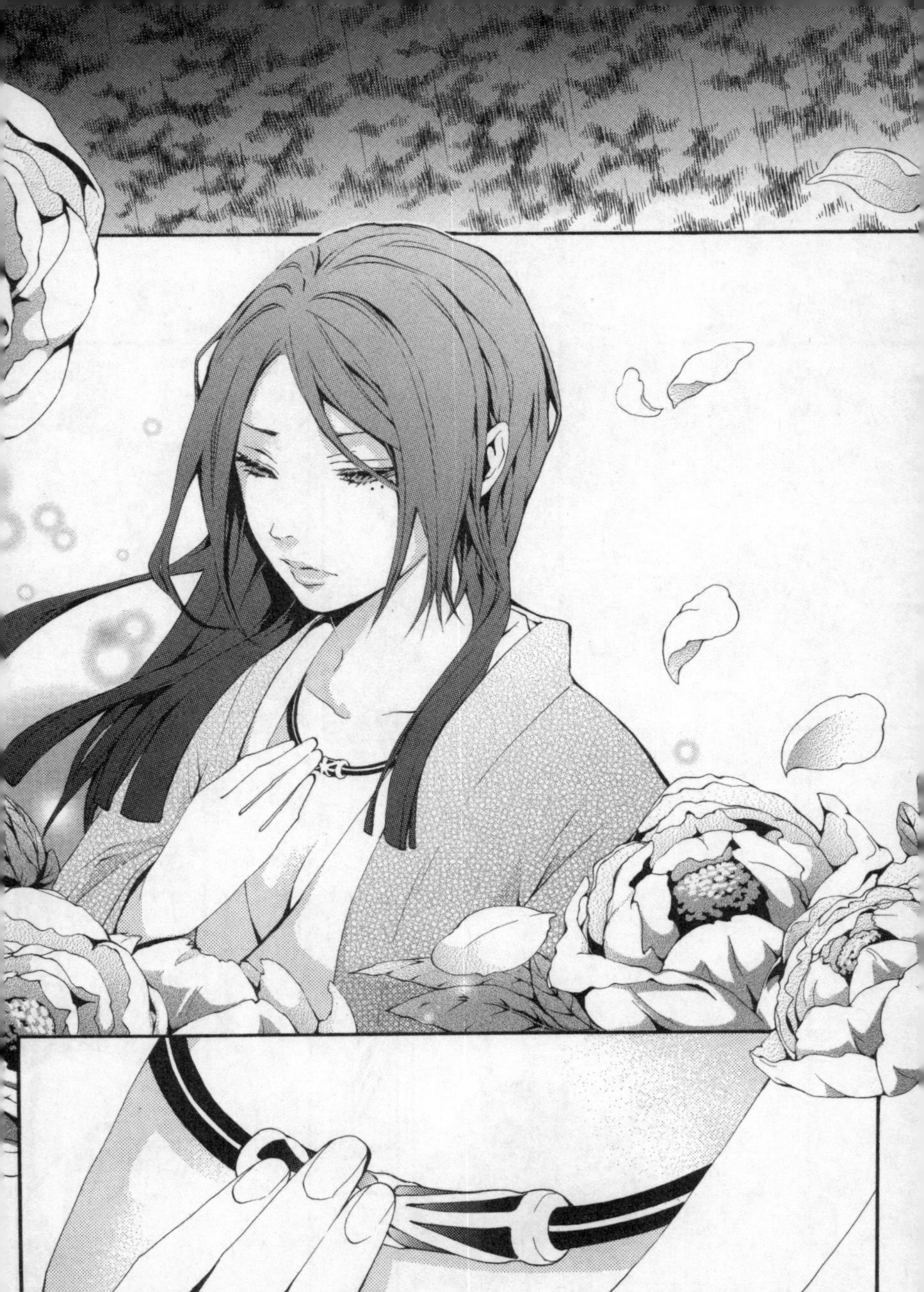

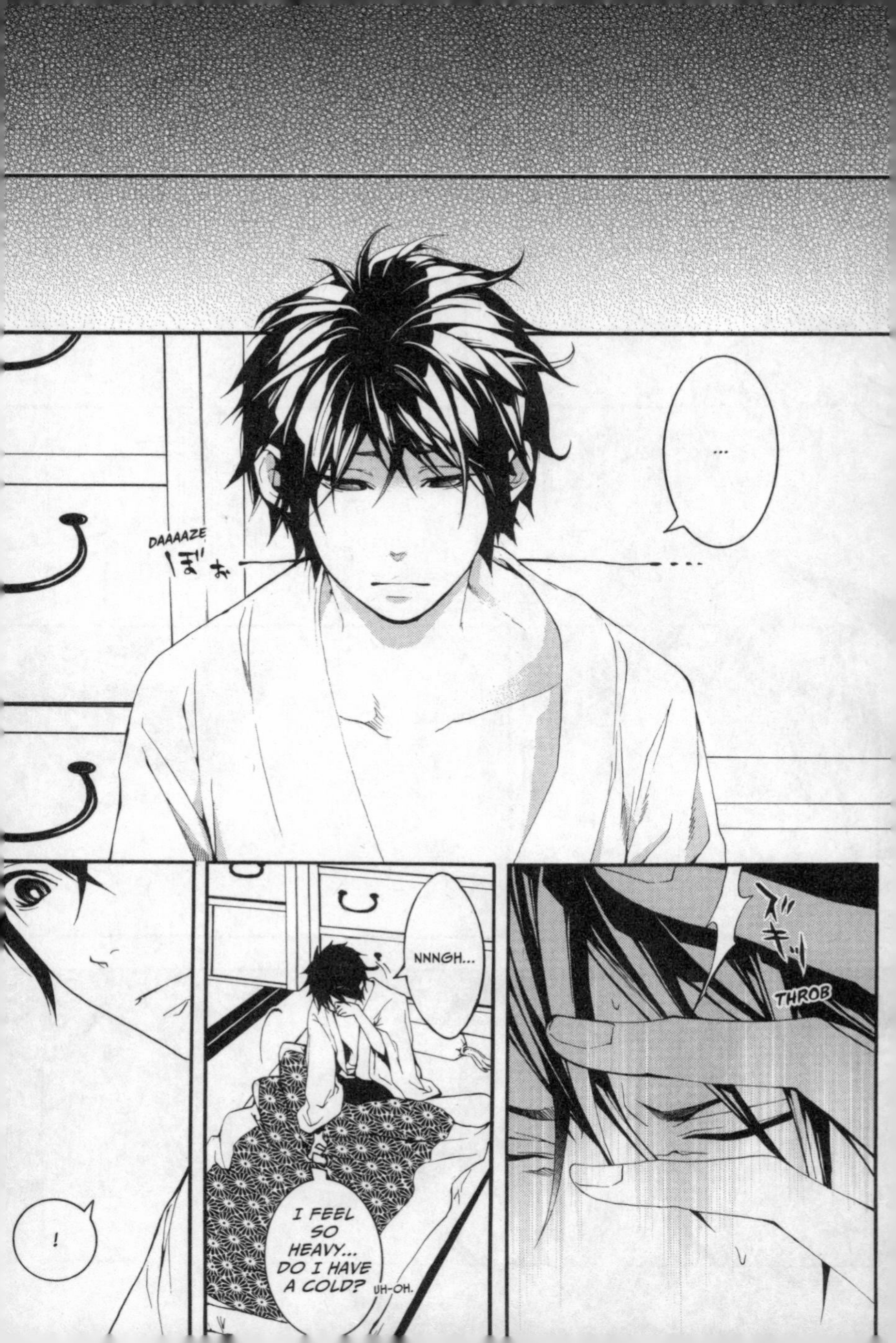
...
DAAAAZE
ぼぉーーー…
ズキッ
THROB
NNNGH...
I FEEL SO HEAVY... DO I HAVE A COLD?
UH-OH.
!

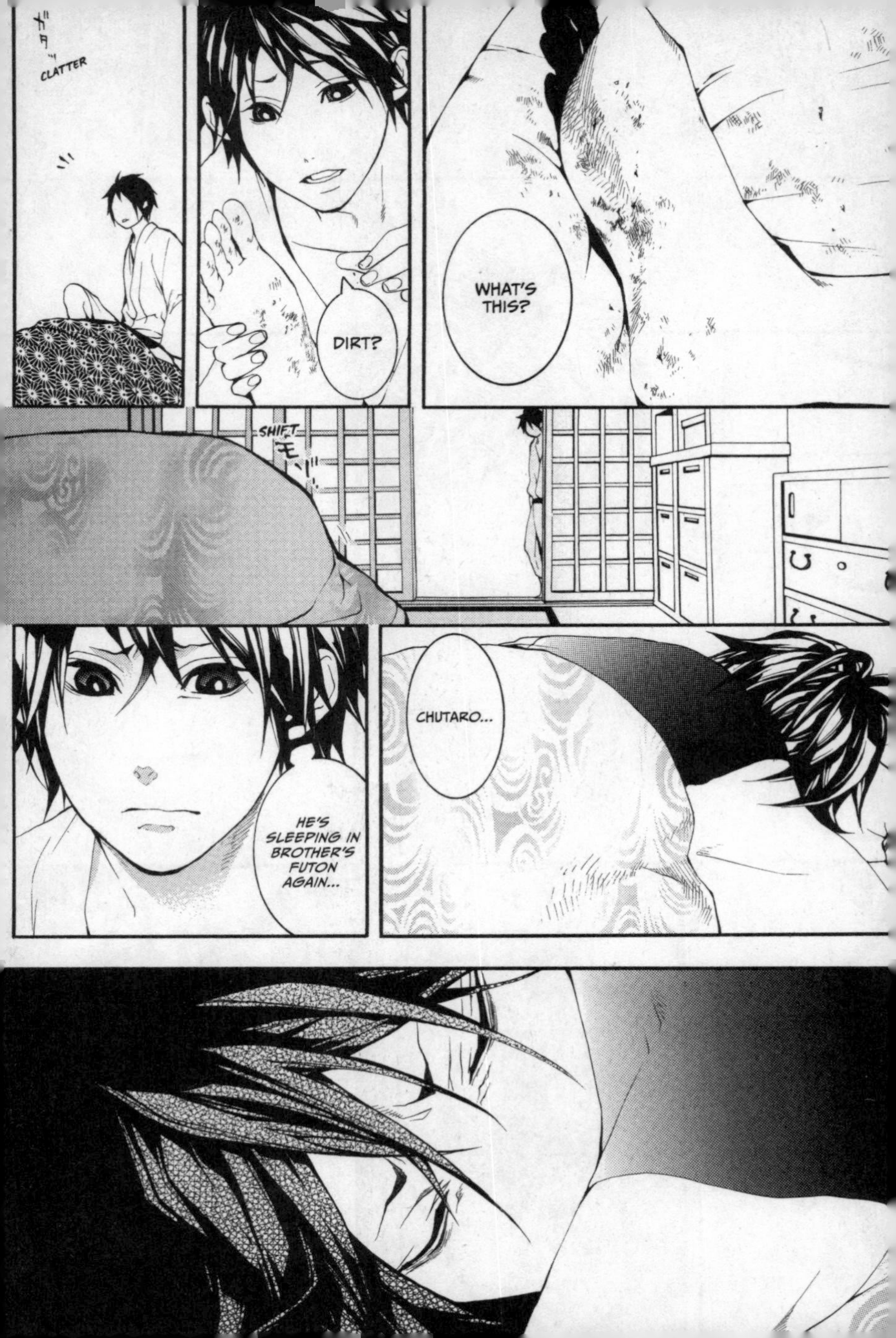
WHAT'S THIS?
DIRT?
CLATTER
SHIFT
CHUTARO...
HE'S SLEEPING IN BROTHER'S FUTON AGAIN...

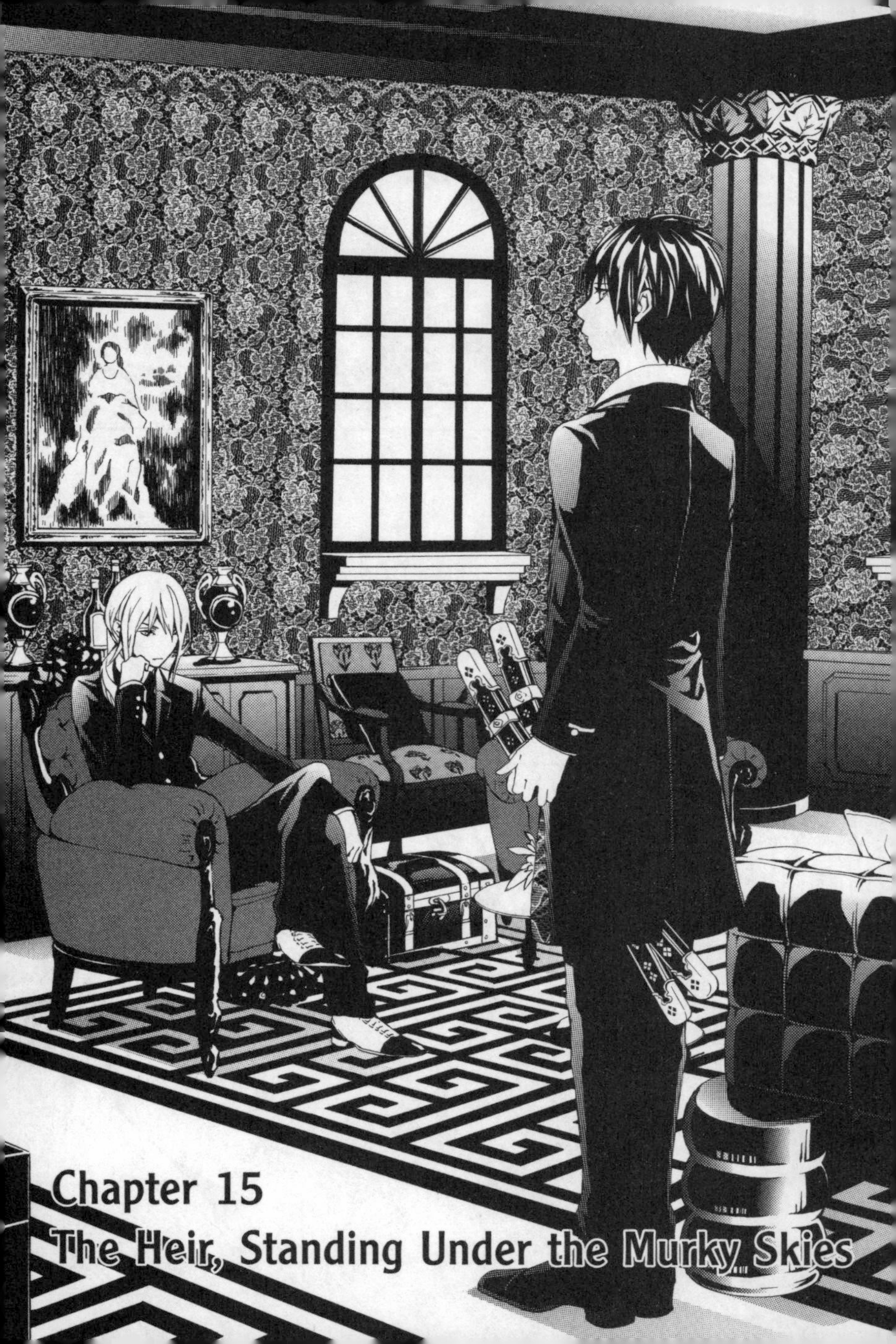
Chapter 15
The Heir, Standing Under the Murky Skies

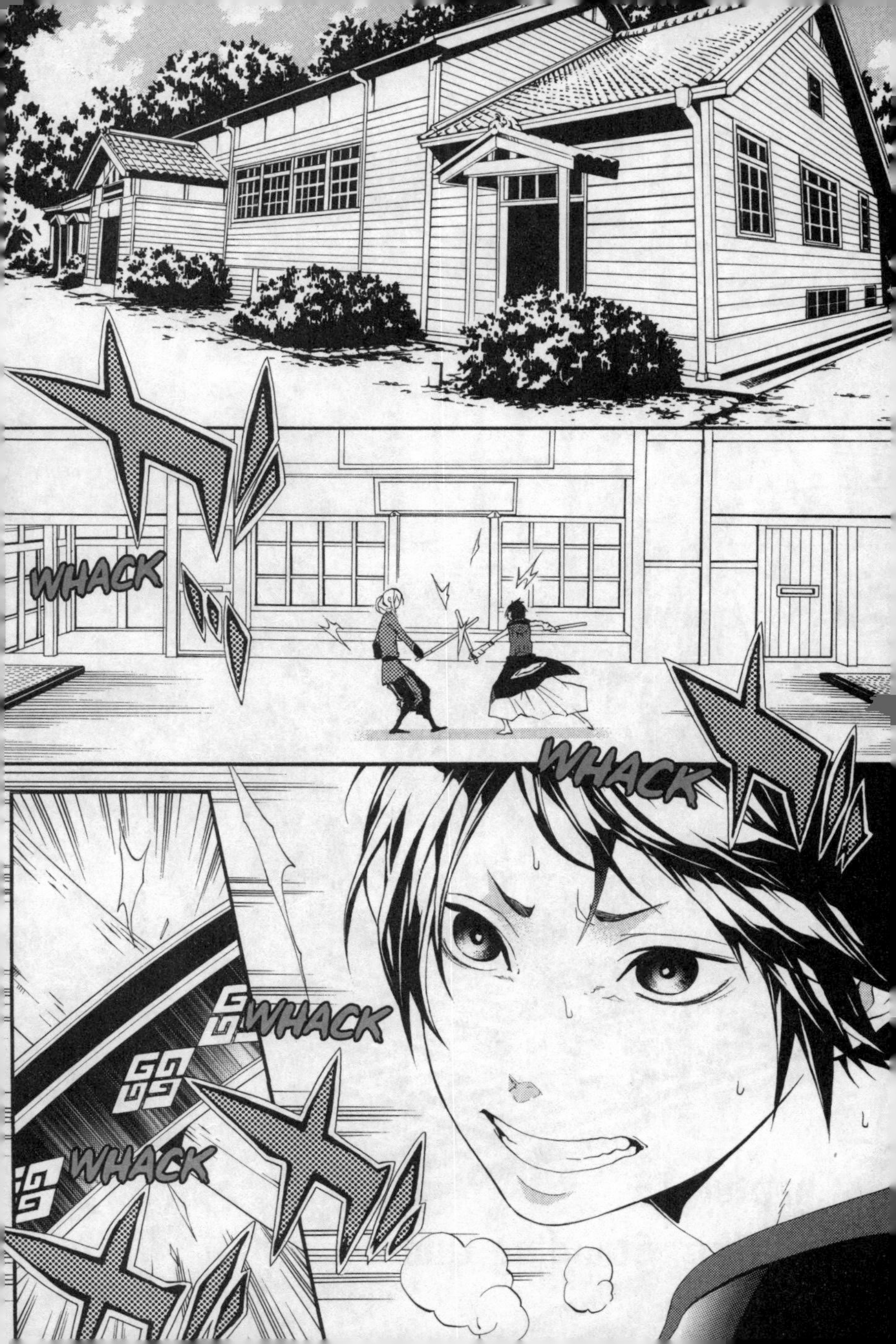
WHACK
WHACK
WHACK
WHACK

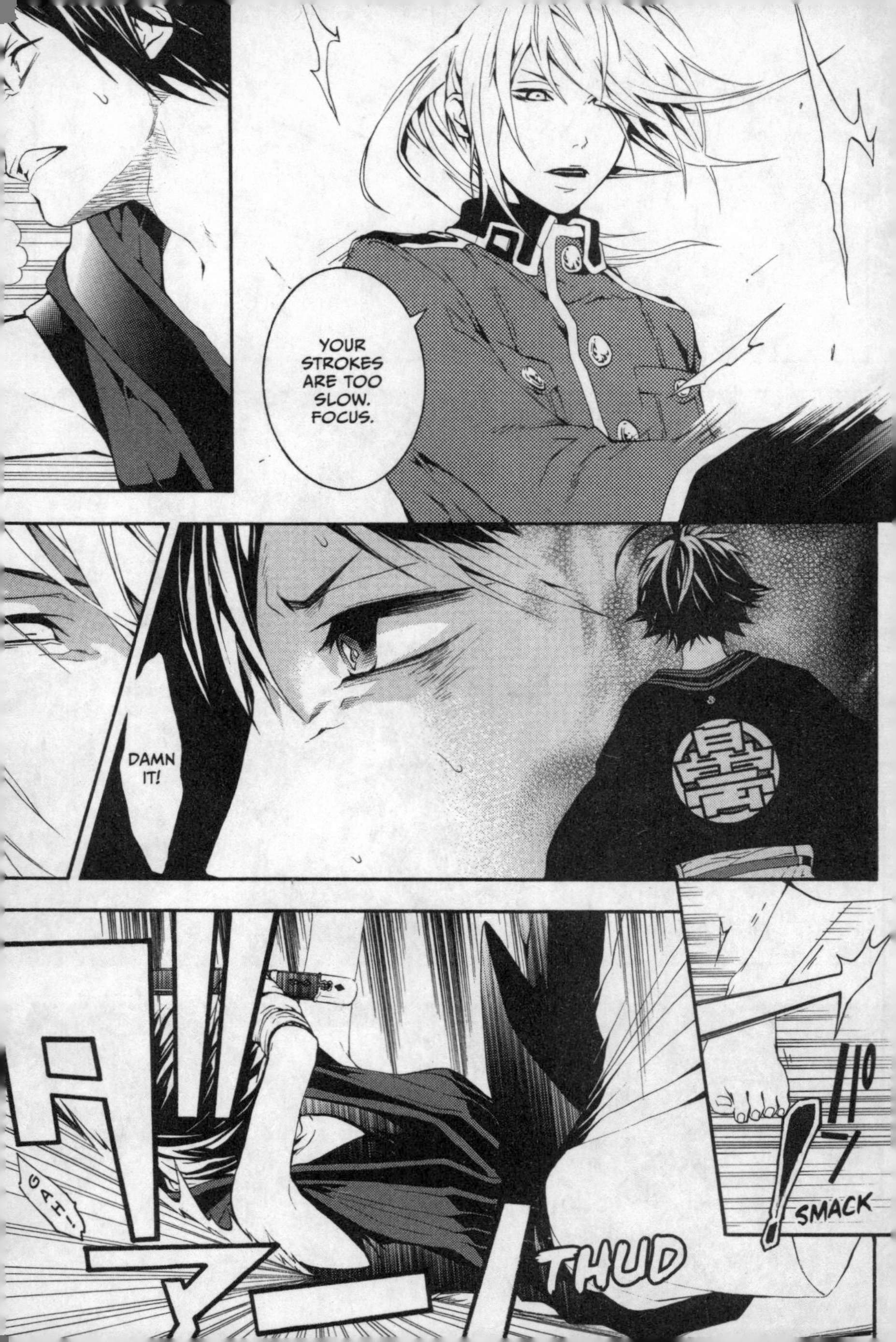
YOUR STROKES ARE TOO SLOW. FOCUS.
DAMN IT!
SMACK
THUD
GAI-!

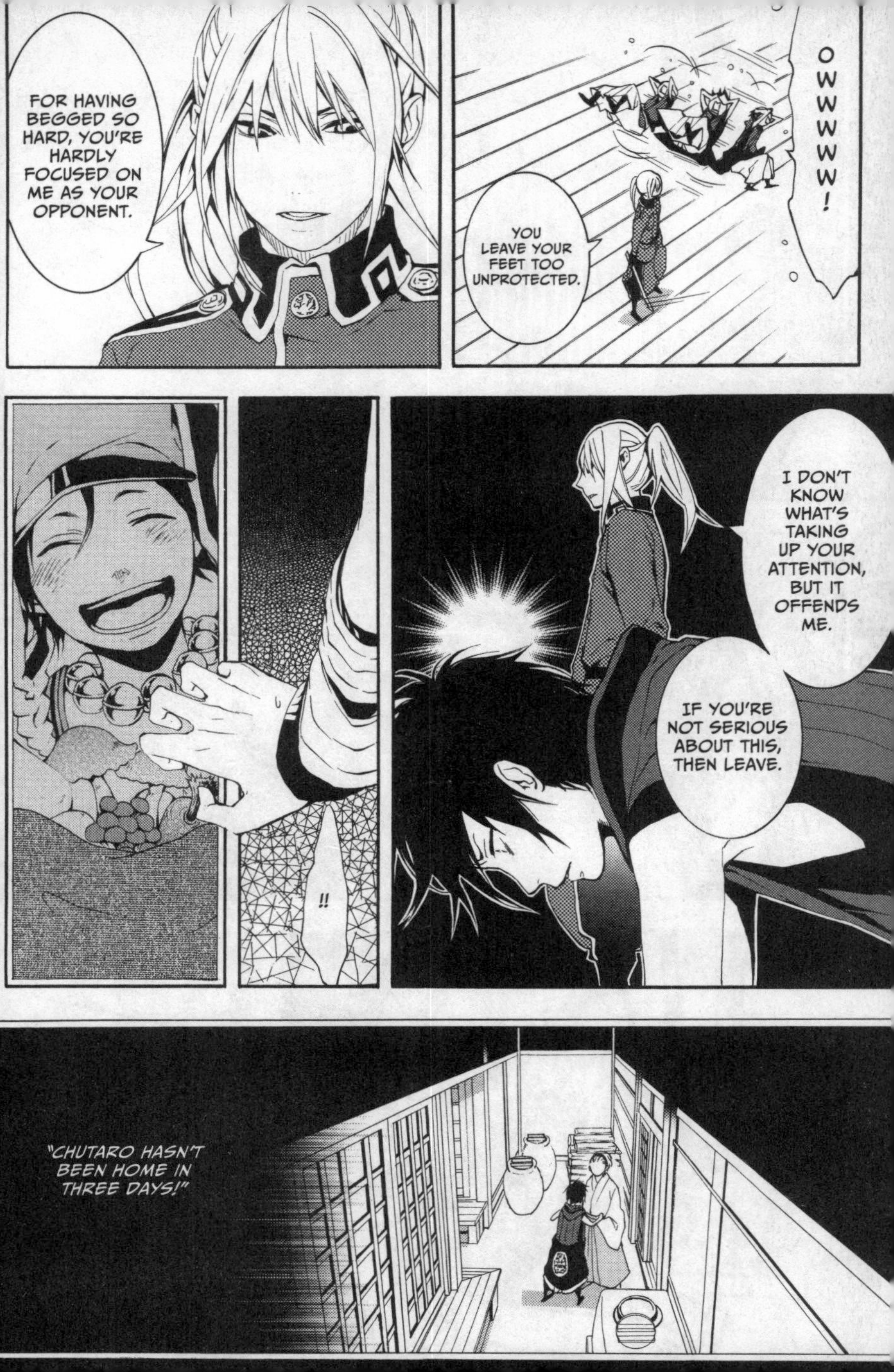
OWWWWWW!
YOU LEAVE YOUR FEET TOO UNPROTECTED.
FOR HAVING BEGGED SO HARD, YOU'RE HARDLY FOCUSED ON ME AS YOUR OPPONENT.
I DON'T KNOW WHAT'S TAKING UP YOUR ATTENTION, BUT IT OFFENDS ME.
IF YOU'RE NOT SERIOUS ABOUT THIS, THEN LEAVE.
!!
"CHUTARO HASN'T BEEN HOME IN THREE DAYS!"

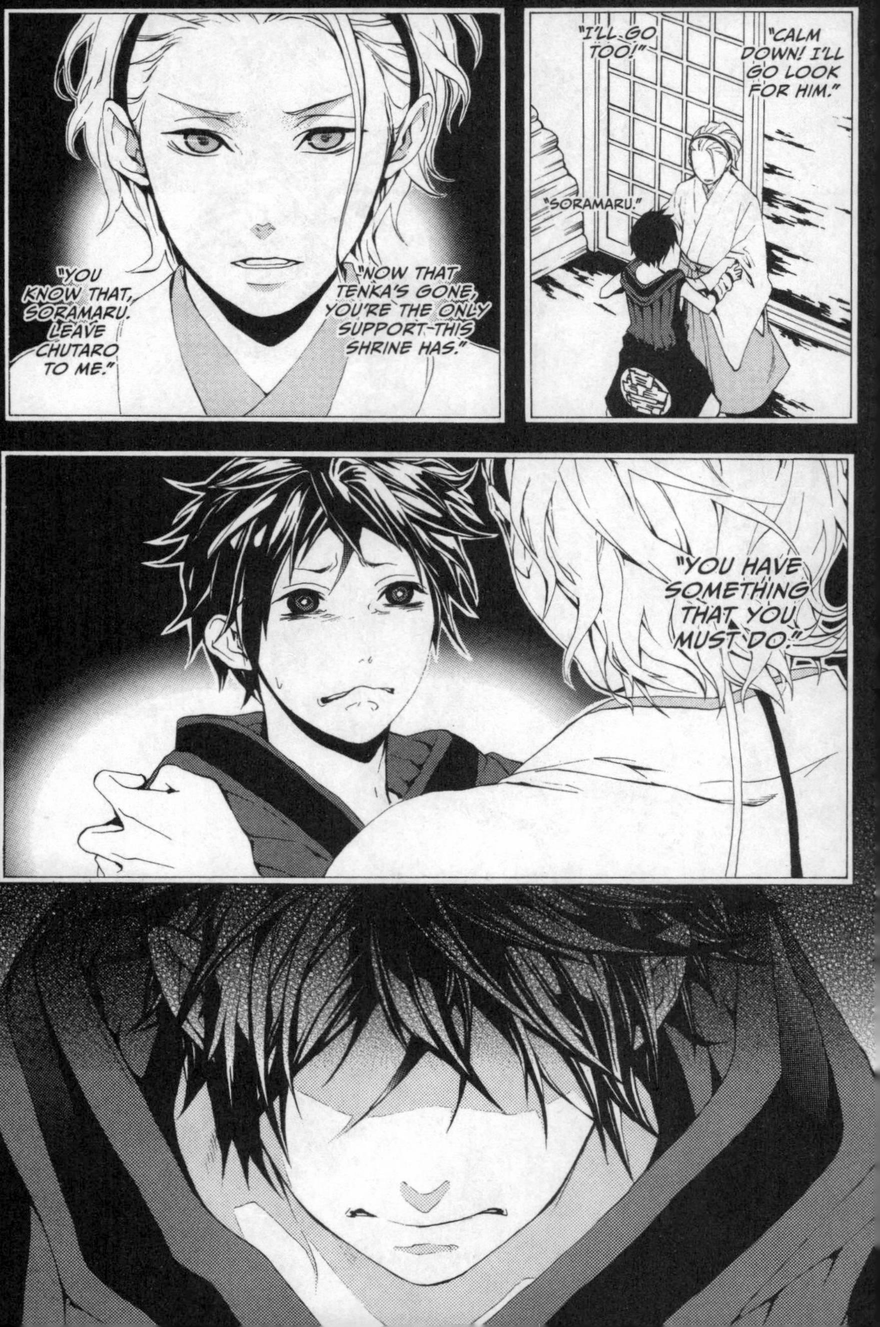
"CALM DOWN! I'LL GO LOOK FOR HIM."
"I'LL GO TOO!"
"SORAMARU."
"NOW THAT TENKA'S GONE, YOU'RE THE ONLY SUPPORT THIS SHRINE HAS."
"YOU KNOW THAT, SORAMARU. LEAVE CHUTARO TO ME."
"YOU HAVE SOMETHING THAT YOU MUST DO."

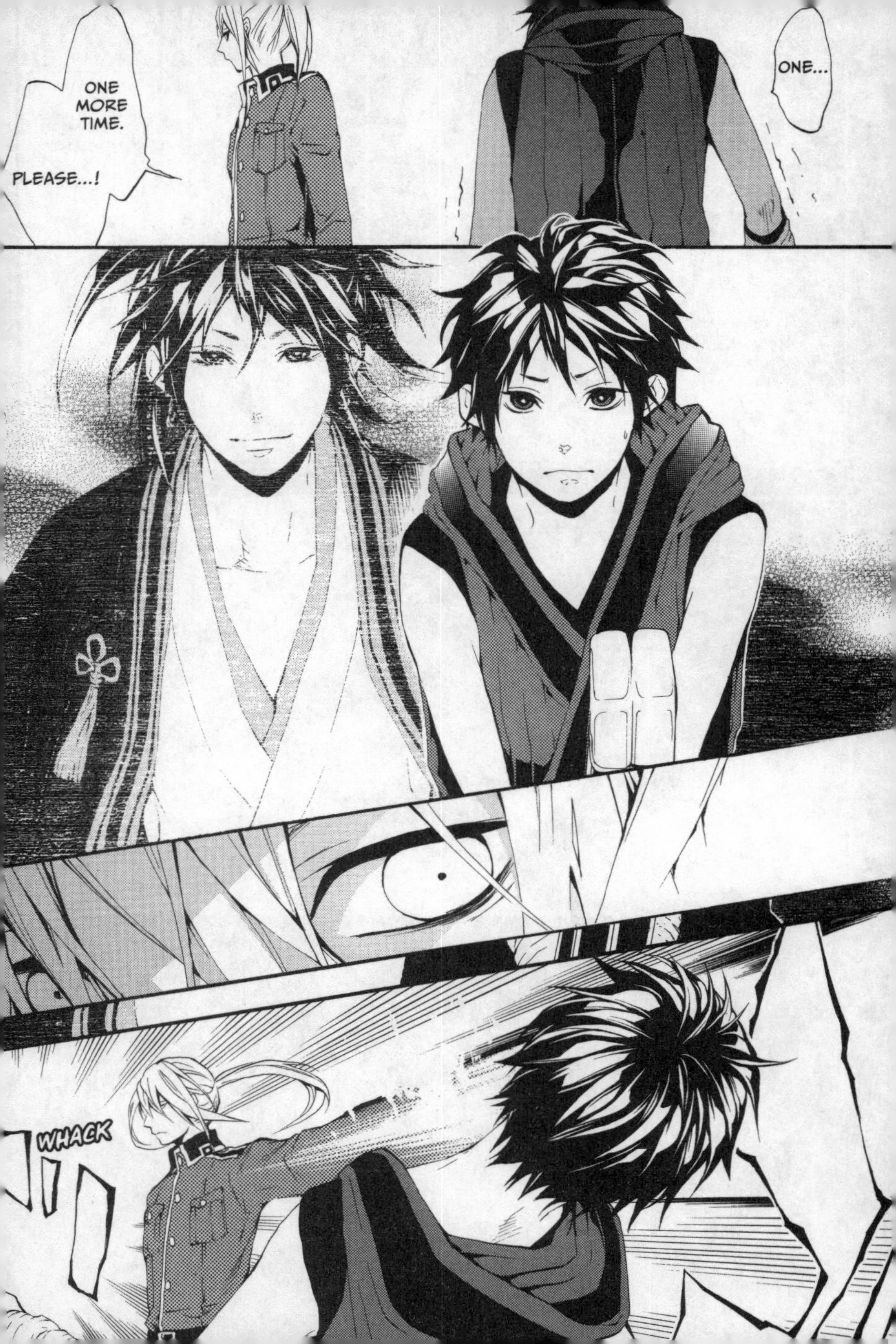
ONE...
ONE MORE TIME.
PLEASE...!
WHACK

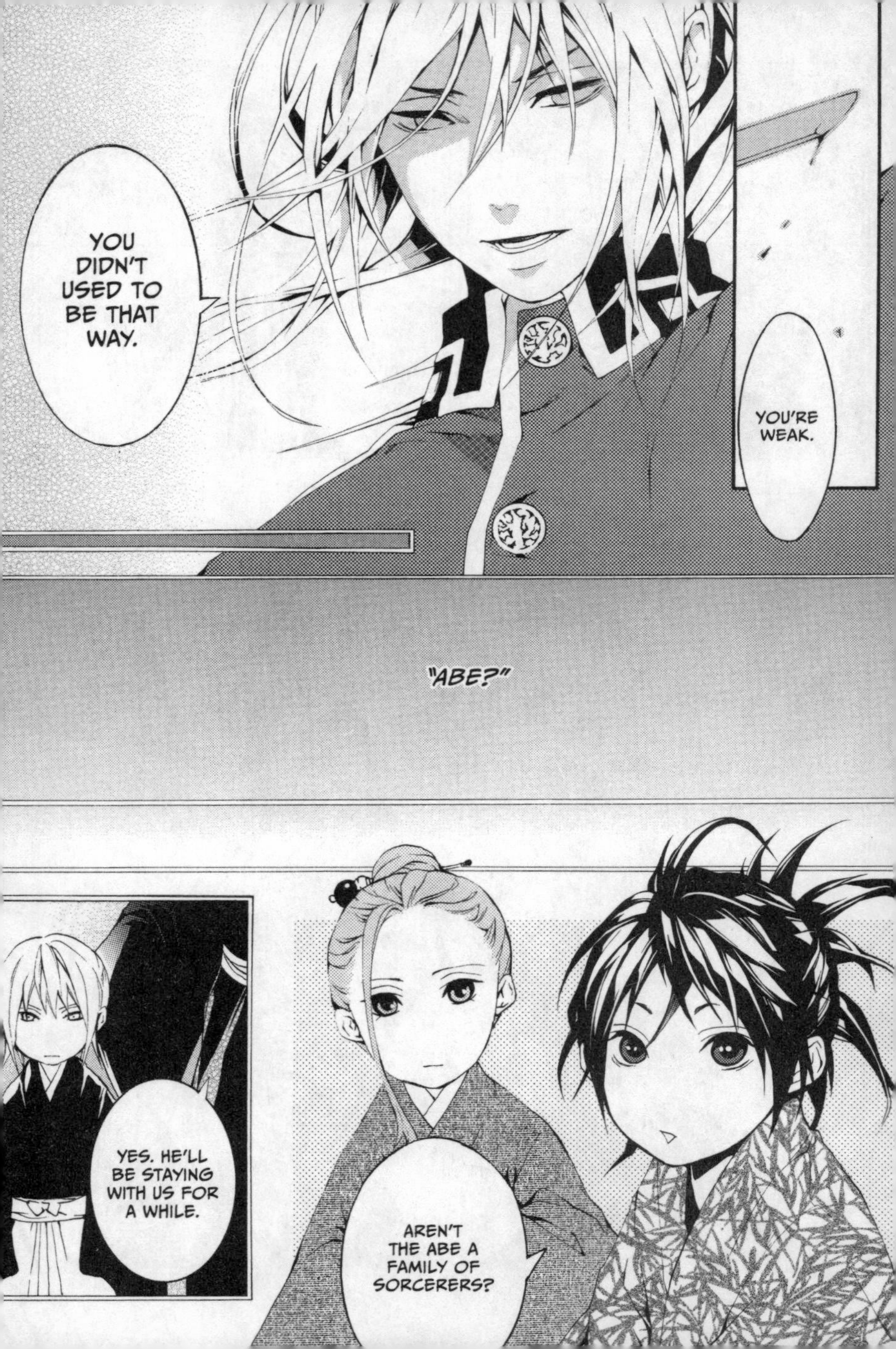
YOU'RE WEAK.
YOU DIDN'T USED TO BE THAT WAY.
"ABE?"
AREN'T THE ABE A FAMILY OF SORCERERS?
YES. HE'LL BE STAYING WITH US FOR A WHILE.

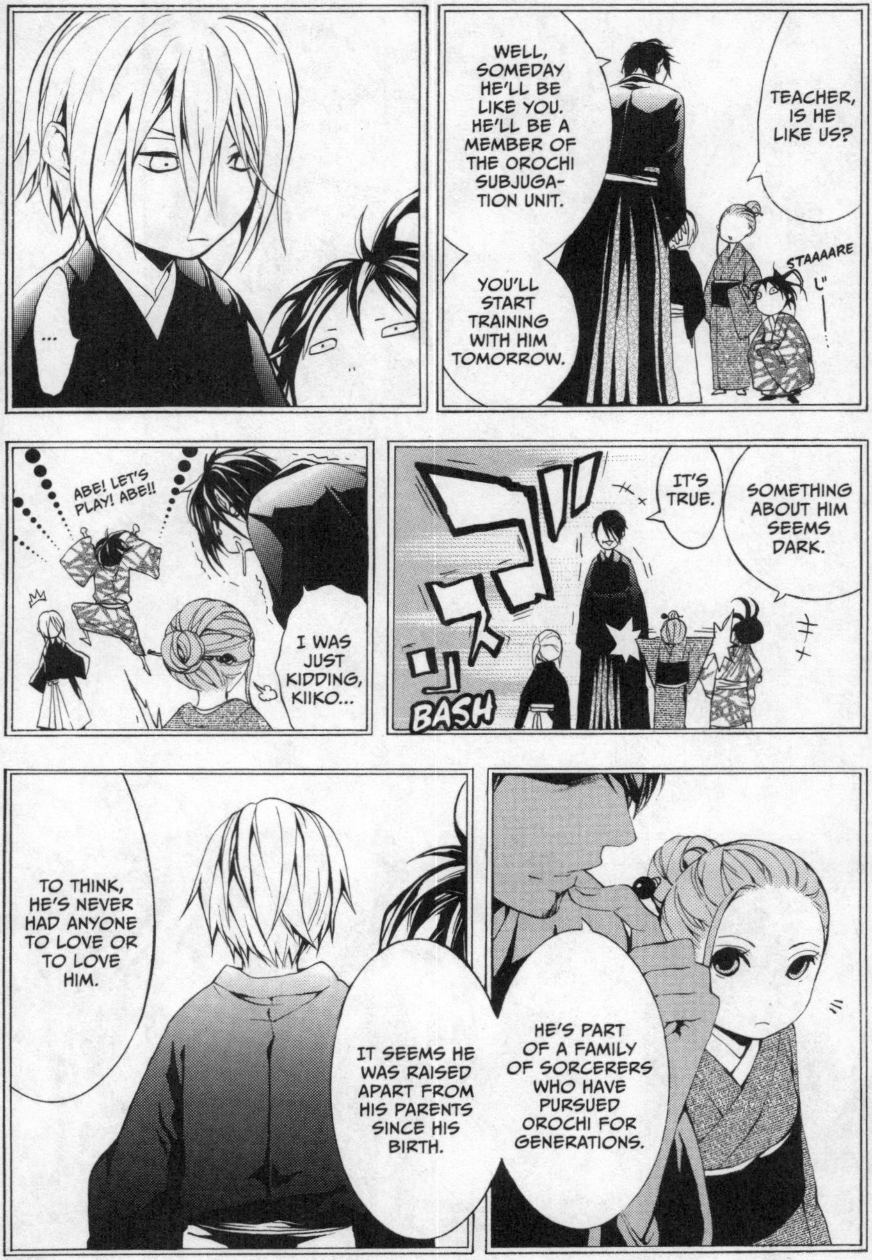
TEACHER, IS HE LIKE US?
WELL, SOMEDAY HE'LL BE LIKE YOU. HE'LL BE A MEMBER OF THE OROCHI SUBJUGA-TION UNIT.
YOU'LL START TRAINING WITH HIM TOMORROW.
STAAAARE
じー
...
SOMETHING ABOUT HIM SEEMS DARK.
IT'S TRUE.
BASH
ABE! LET'S PLAY! ABE!!
I WAS JUST KIDDING, KIIKO...
HE'S PART OF A FAMILY OF SORCERERS WHO HAVE PURSUED OROCHI FOR GENERATIONS.
IT SEEMS HE WAS RAISED APART FROM HIS PARENTS SINCE HIS BIRTH.
TO THINK, HE'S NEVER HAD ANYONE TO LOVE OR TO LOVE HIM.

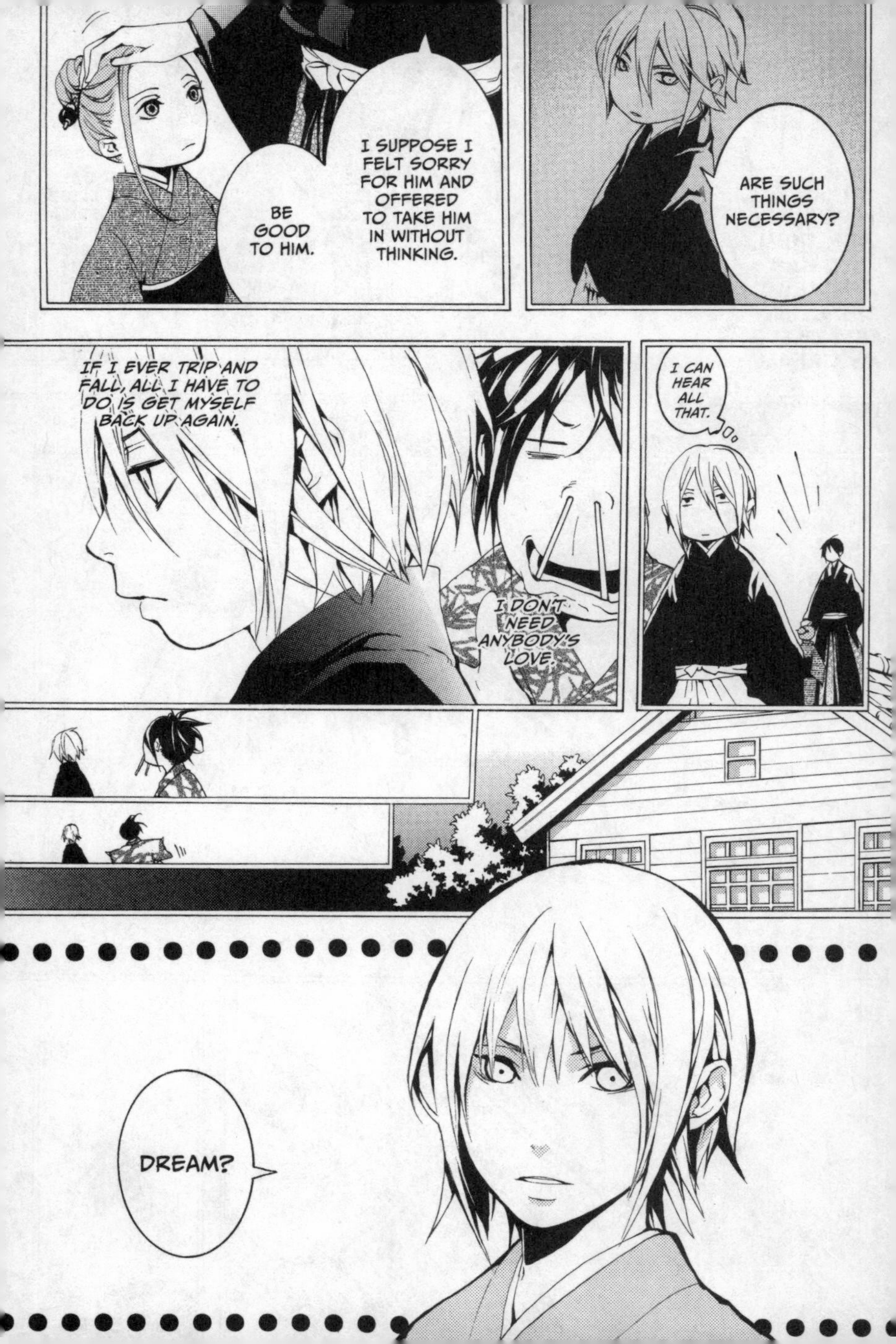
ARE SUCH THINGS NECESSARY?
I SUPPOSE I FELT SORRY FOR HIM AND OFFERED TO TAKE HIM IN WITHOUT THINKING.
BE GOOD TO HIM.
I CAN HEAR ALL THAT.
IF I EVER TRIP AND FALL, ALL I HAVE TO DO IS GET MYSELF BACK UP AGAIN.
I DON'T NEED ANYBODY'S LOVE.
DREAM?

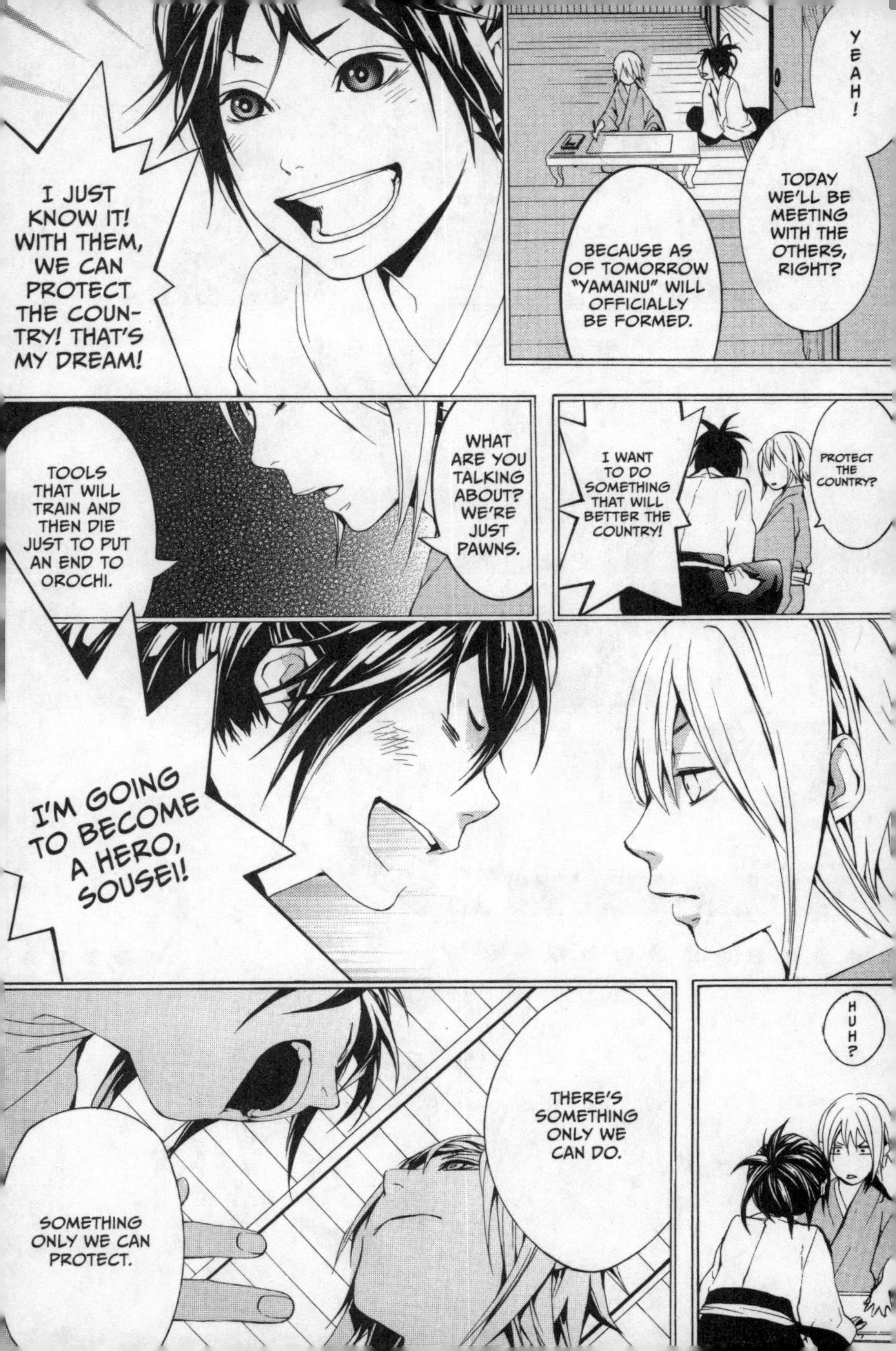
YEAH!
TODAY WE'LL BE MEETING WITH THE OTHERS, RIGHT?
BECAUSE AS OF TOMORROW "YAMAINU" WILL OFFICIALLY BE FORMED.
I JUST KNOW IT! WITH THEM, WE CAN PROTECT THE COUN-TRY! THAT'S MY DREAM!
PROTECT THE COUNTRY?
I WANT TO DO SOMETHING THAT WILL BETTER THE COUNTRY!
WHAT ARE YOU TALKING ABOUT? WE'RE JUST PAWNS.
TOOLS THAT WILL TRAIN AND THEN DIE JUST TO PUT AN END TO OROCHI.
I'M GOING TO BECOME A HERO, SOUSEI!
HUH?
THERE'S SOMETHING ONLY WE CAN DO.
SOMETHING ONLY WE CAN PROTECT.

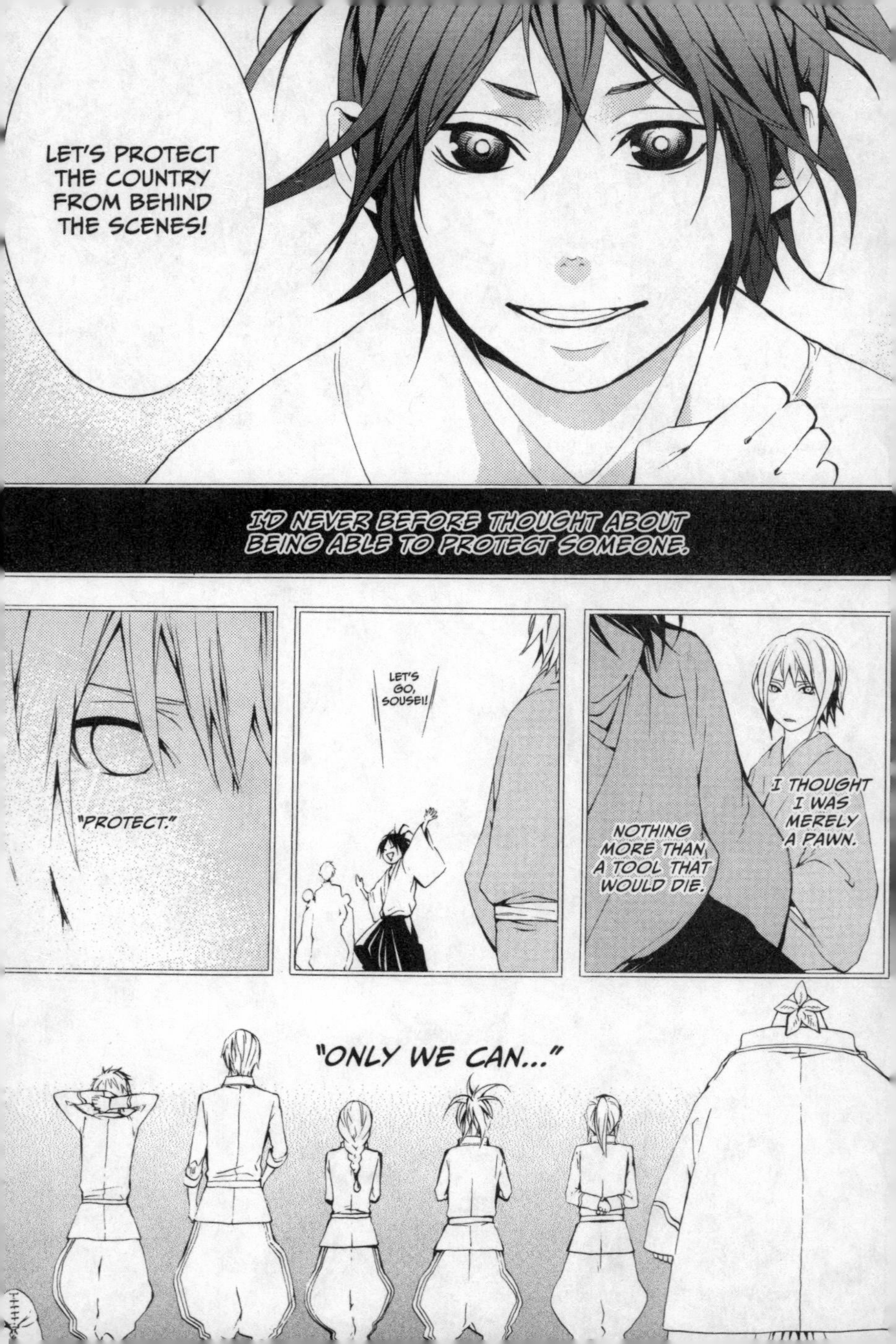
LET'S PROTECT THE COUNTRY FROM BEHIND THE SCENES!
I'D NEVER BEFORE THOUGHT ABOUT BEING ABLE TO PROTECT SOMEONE.
I THOUGHT I WAS MERELY A PAWN.
NOTHING MORE THAN A TOOL THAT WOULD DIE.
LET'S GO, SOUSEI!
"PROTECT."
"ONLY WE CAN..."

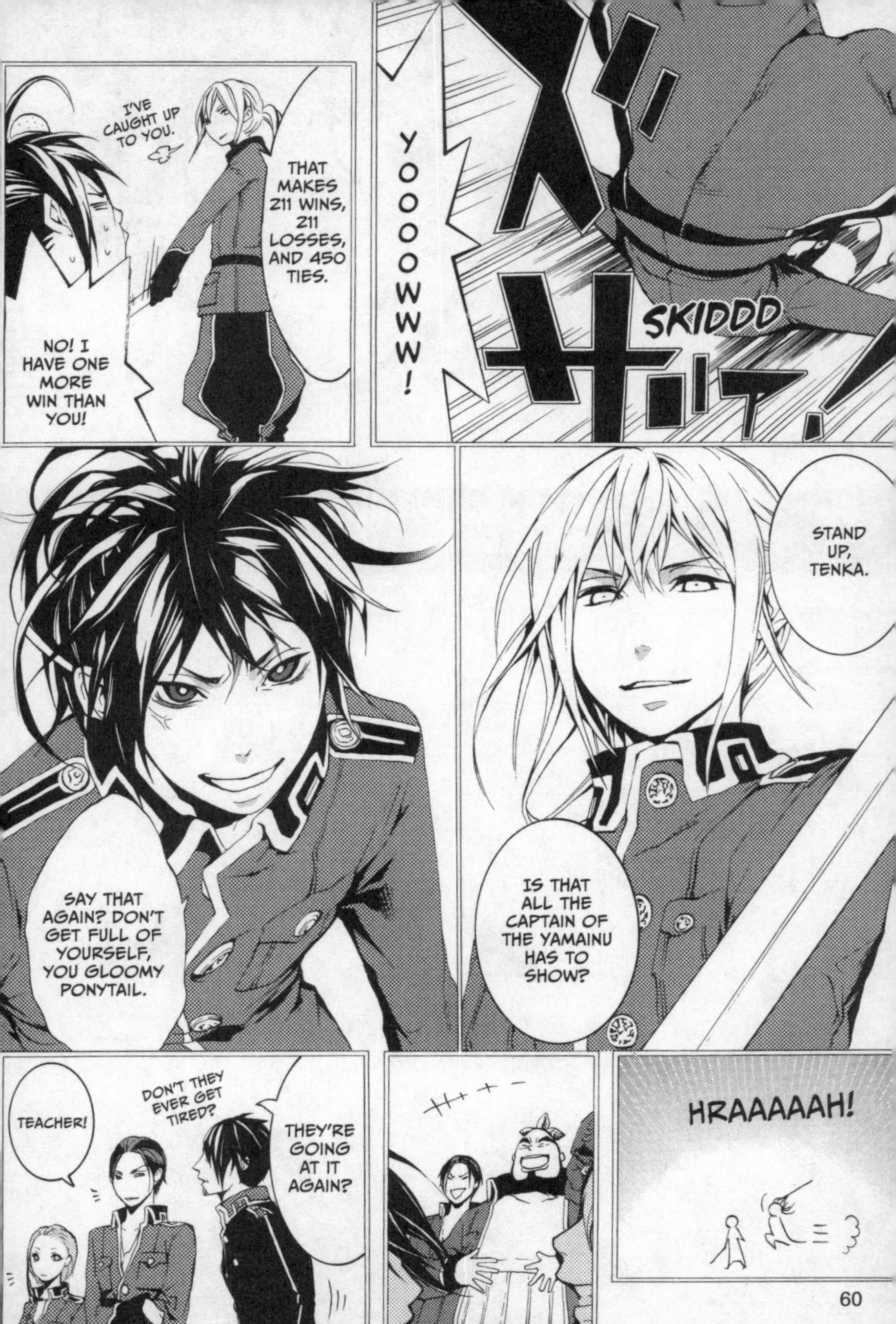
SKIDDD
YOOOOOWWW!
I'VE CAUGHT UP TO YOU.
THAT MAKES 211 WINS, 211 LOSSES, AND 450 TIES.
NO! I HAVE ONE MORE WIN THAN YOU!
STAND UP, TENKA.
IS THAT ALL THE CAPTAIN OF THE YAMAINU HAS TO SHOW?
SAY THAT AGAIN? DON'T GET FULL OF YOURSELF, YOU GLOOMY PONYTAIL.
HRAAAAAH!
THEY'RE GOING AT IT AGAIN?
DON'T THEY EVER GET TIRED?
TEACHER!

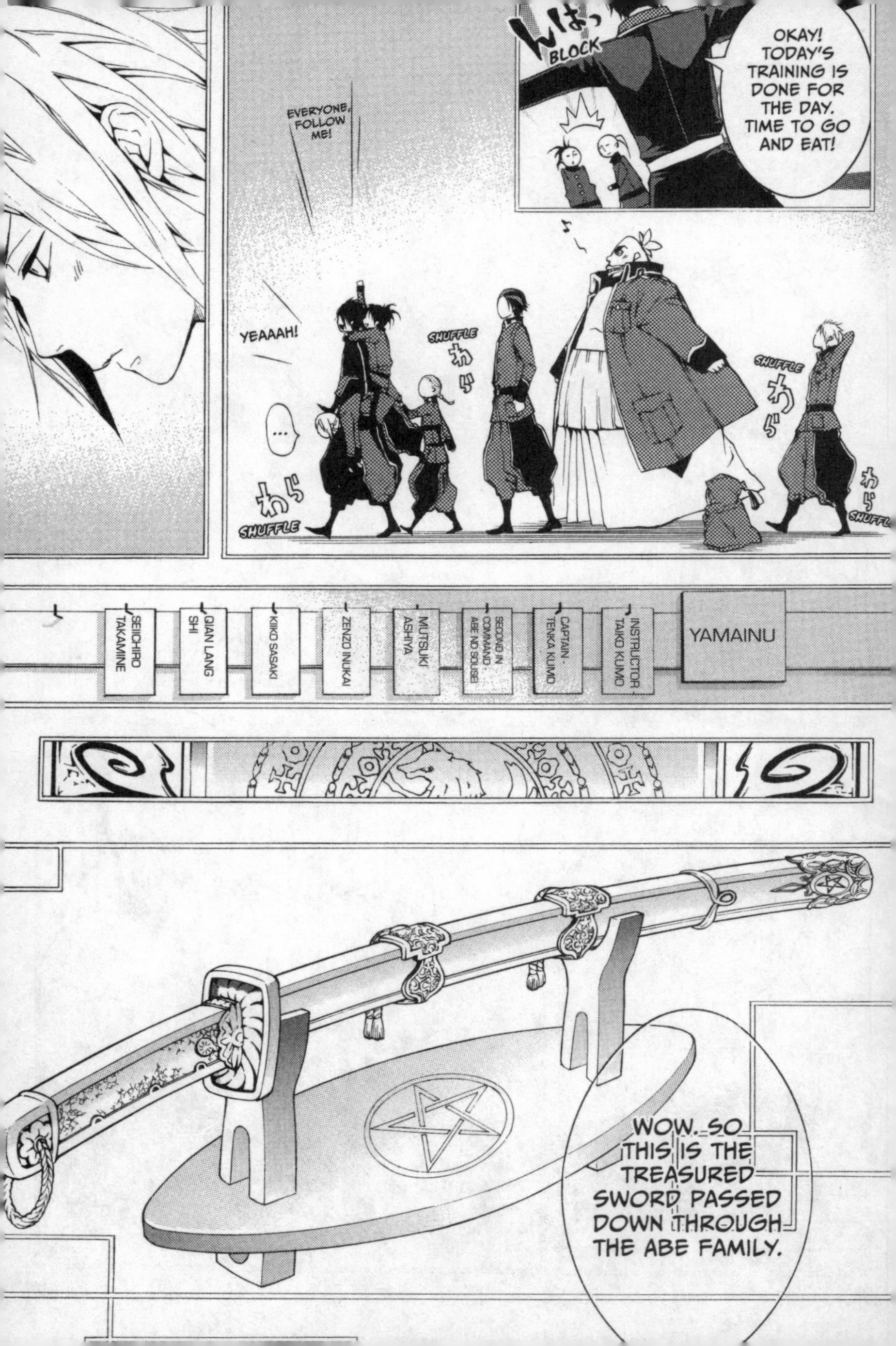
BLOCK
OKAY! TODAY'S TRAINING IS DONE FOR THE DAY. TIME TO GO AND EAT!
EVERYONE, FOLLOW ME!
YEAAAH!
SHUFFLE
SHUFFLE
SHUFFLE
SHUFFLE
...
YAMAINU
INSTRUCTOR TAIKO KUMO
CAPTAIN TENKA KUMO
SECOND IN COMMAND ABE NO SOUSEI
MUTSUKI ASHIYA
ZENZO INUKAI
KIIKO SASAKI
QIAN LANG SHI
SEICHIRO TAKAMINE
WOW... SO THIS IS THE TREASURED SWORD PASSED DOWN THROUGH THE ABE FAMILY.

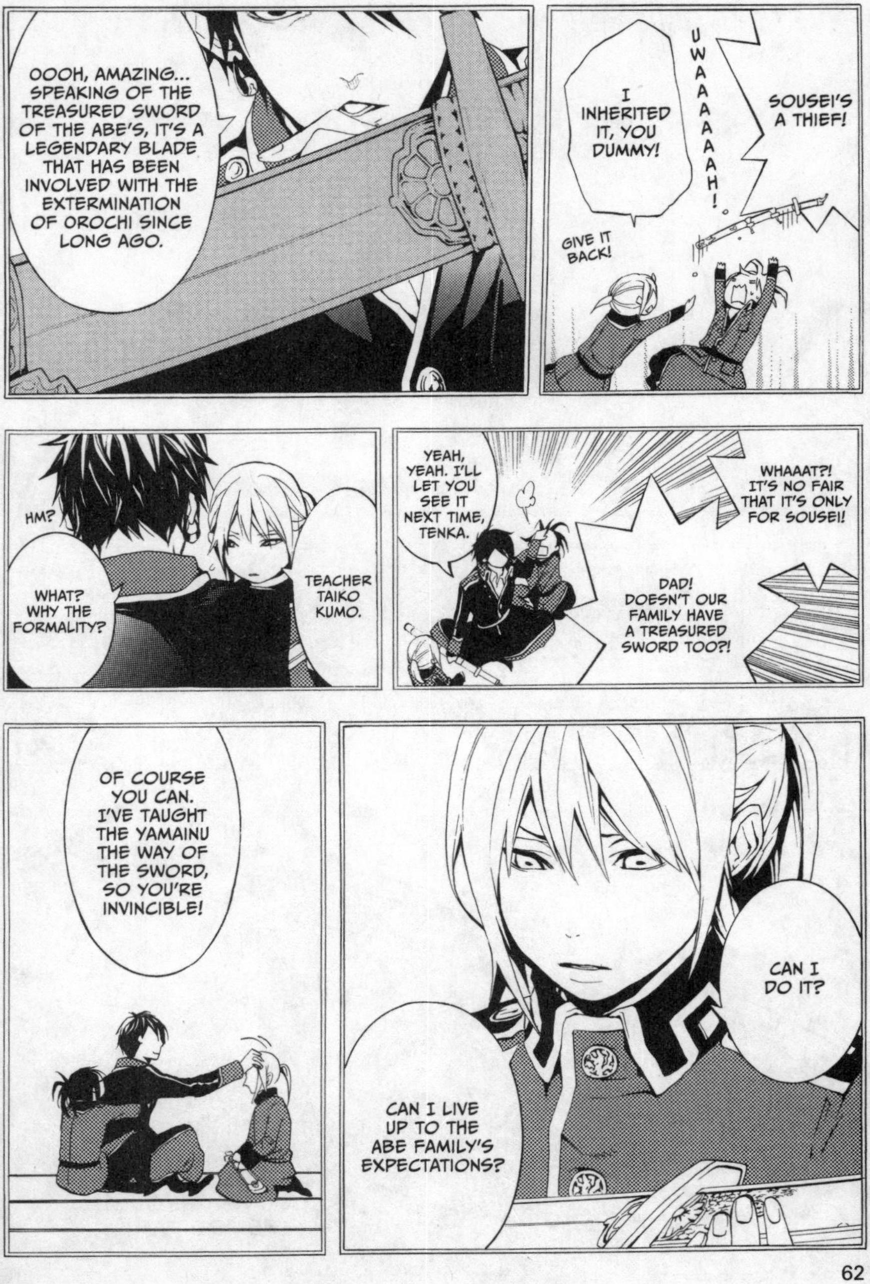
SOUSEI'S A THIEF!
UWAAAAAAAH!
I INHERITED IT, YOU DUMMY!
GIVE IT BACK!
OOOH, AMAZING... SPEAKING OF THE TREASURED SWORD OF THE ABE'S, IT'S A LEGENDARY BLADE THAT HAS BEEN INVOLVED WITH THE EXTERMINATION OF OROCHI SINCE LONG AGO.
WHAAAT?! IT'S NO FAIR THAT IT'S ONLY FOR SOUSEI!
DAD! DOESN'T OUR FAMILY HAVE A TREASURED SWORD TOO?!
YEAH, YEAH. I'LL LET YOU SEE IT NEXT TIME, TENKA.
TEACHER TAIKO KUMO.
HM?
WHAT? WHY THE FORMALITY?
CAN I DO IT?
CAN I LIVE UP TO THE ABE FAMILY'S EXPECTATIONS?
OF COURSE YOU CAN. I'VE TAUGHT THE YAMAINU THE WAY OF THE SWORD, SO YOU'RE INVINCIBLE!

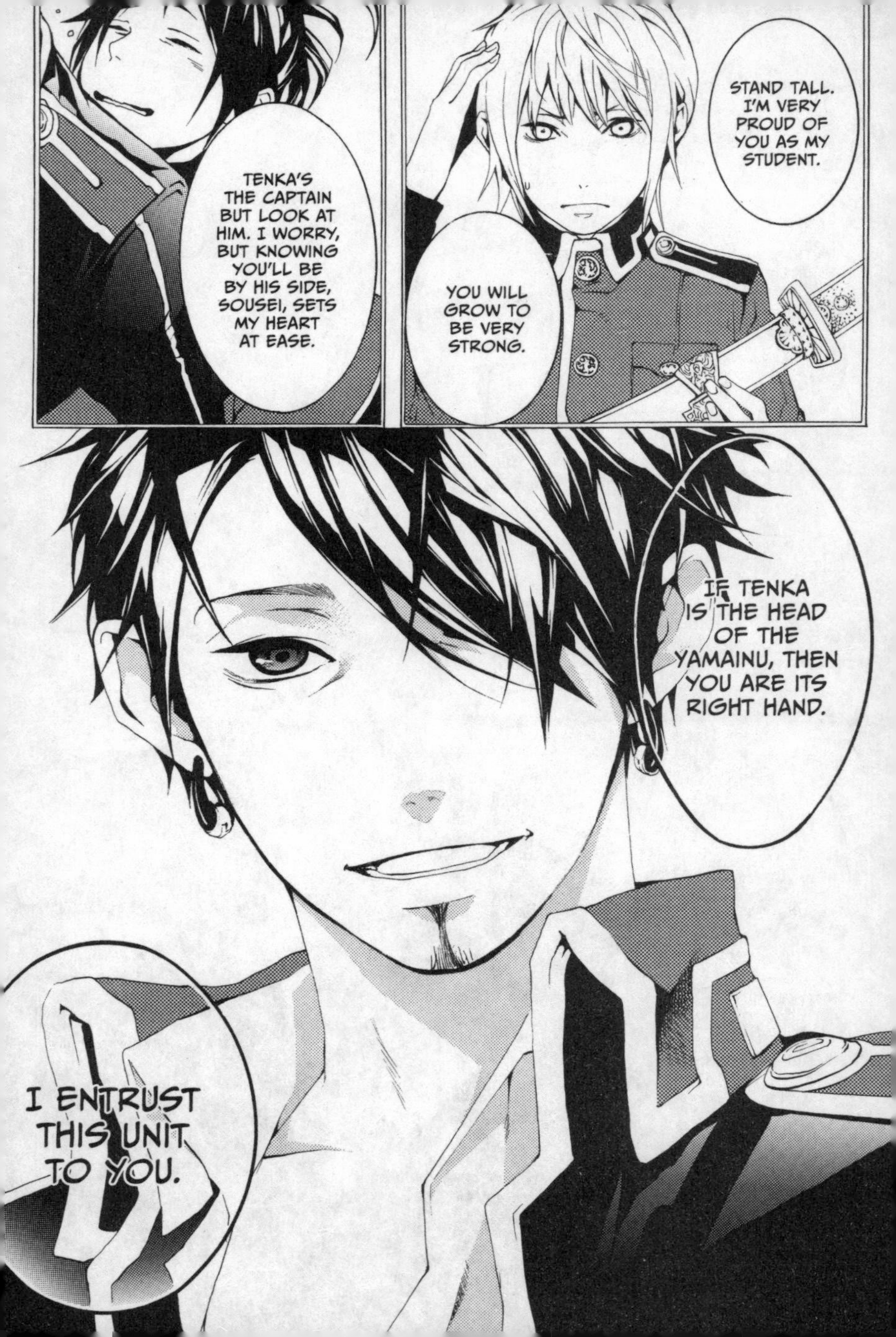
STAND TALL. I'M VERY PROUD OF YOU AS MY STUDENT.
YOU WILL GROW TO BE VERY STRONG.
TENKA'S THE CAPTAIN BUT LOOK AT HIM. I WORRY, BUT KNOWING YOU'LL BE BY HIS SIDE, SOUSEI, SETS MY HEART AT EASE.
IF TENKA IS THE HEAD OF THE YAMAINU, THEN YOU ARE ITS RIGHT HAND.
I ENTRUST THIS UNIT TO YOU.

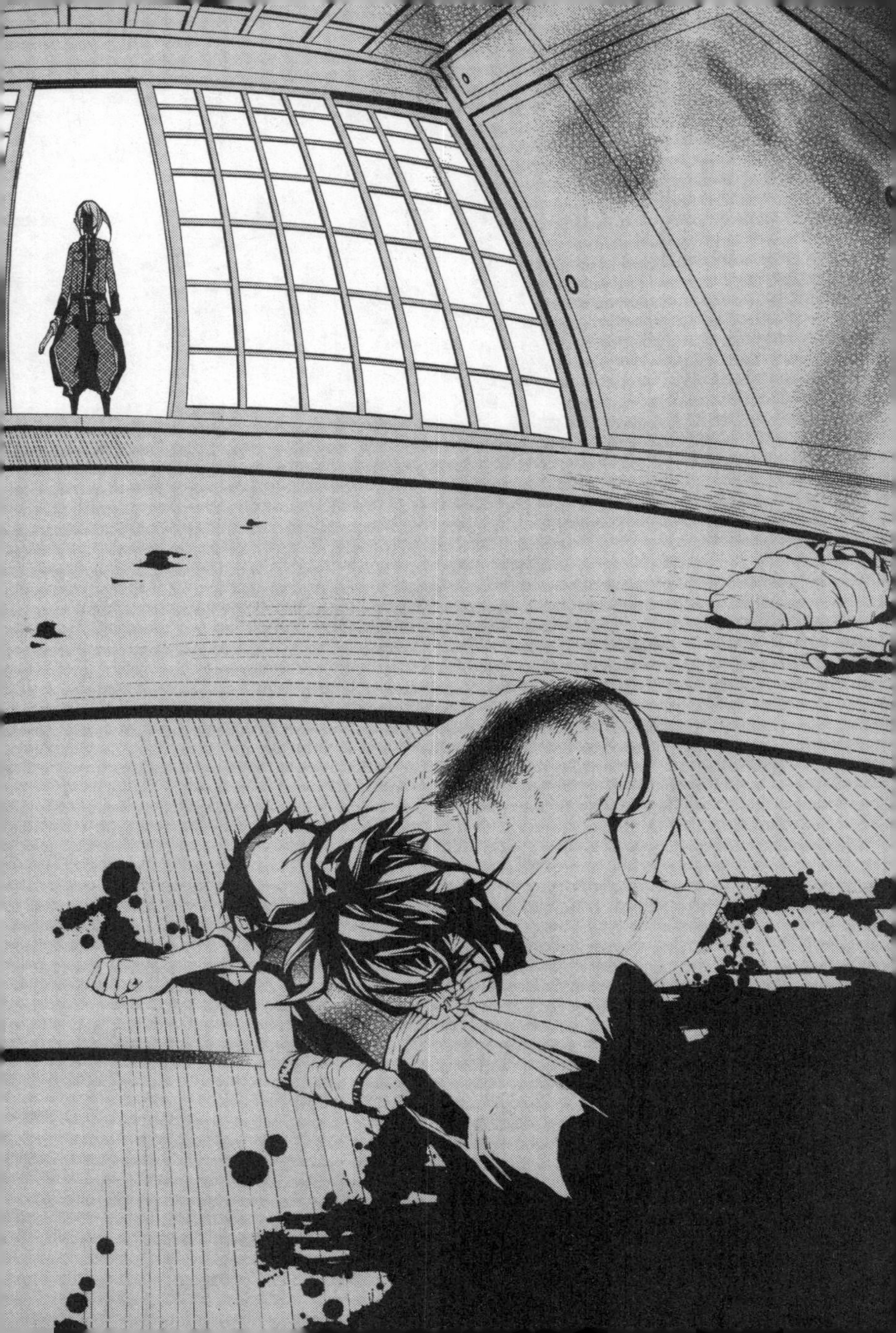

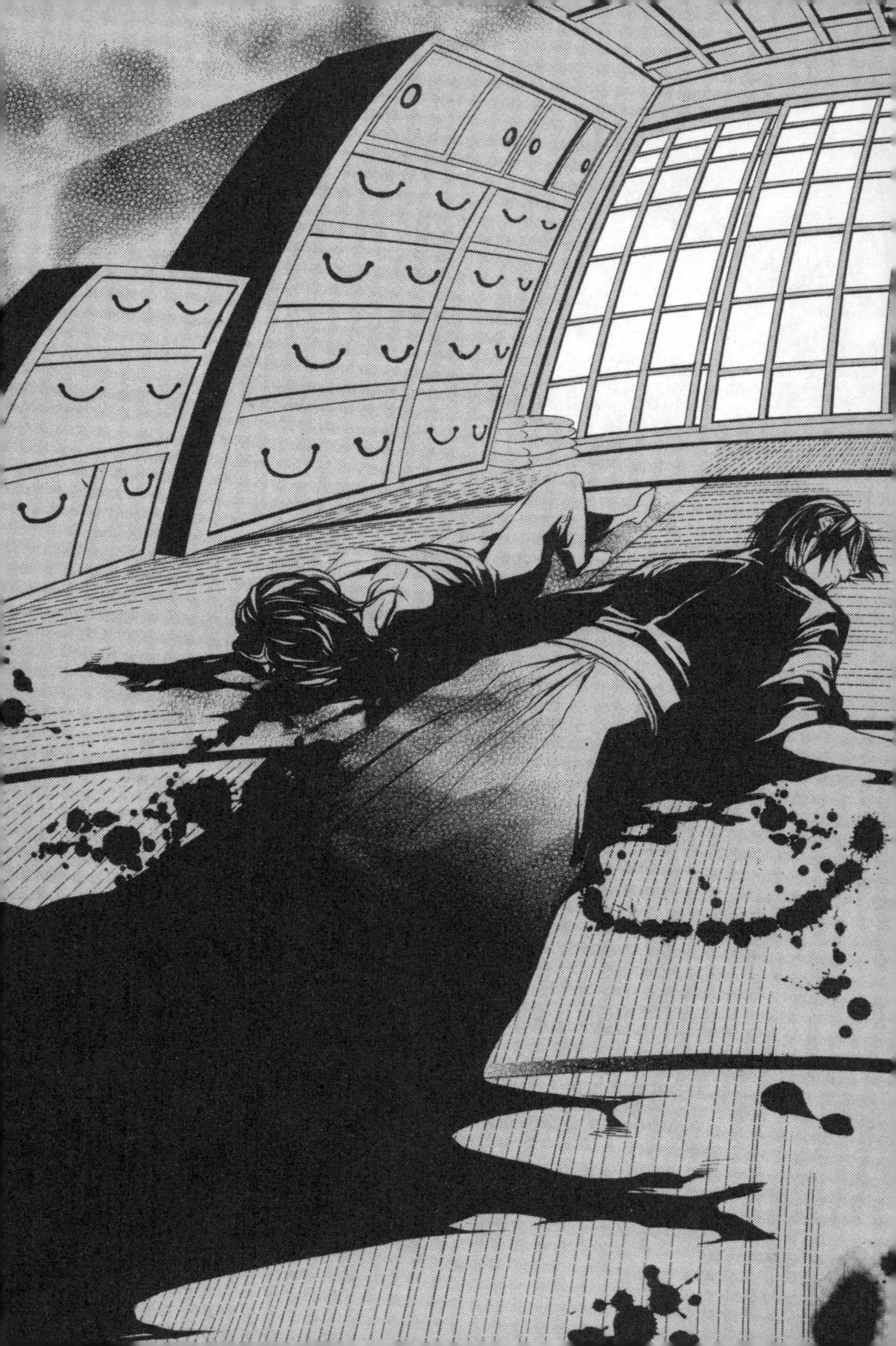

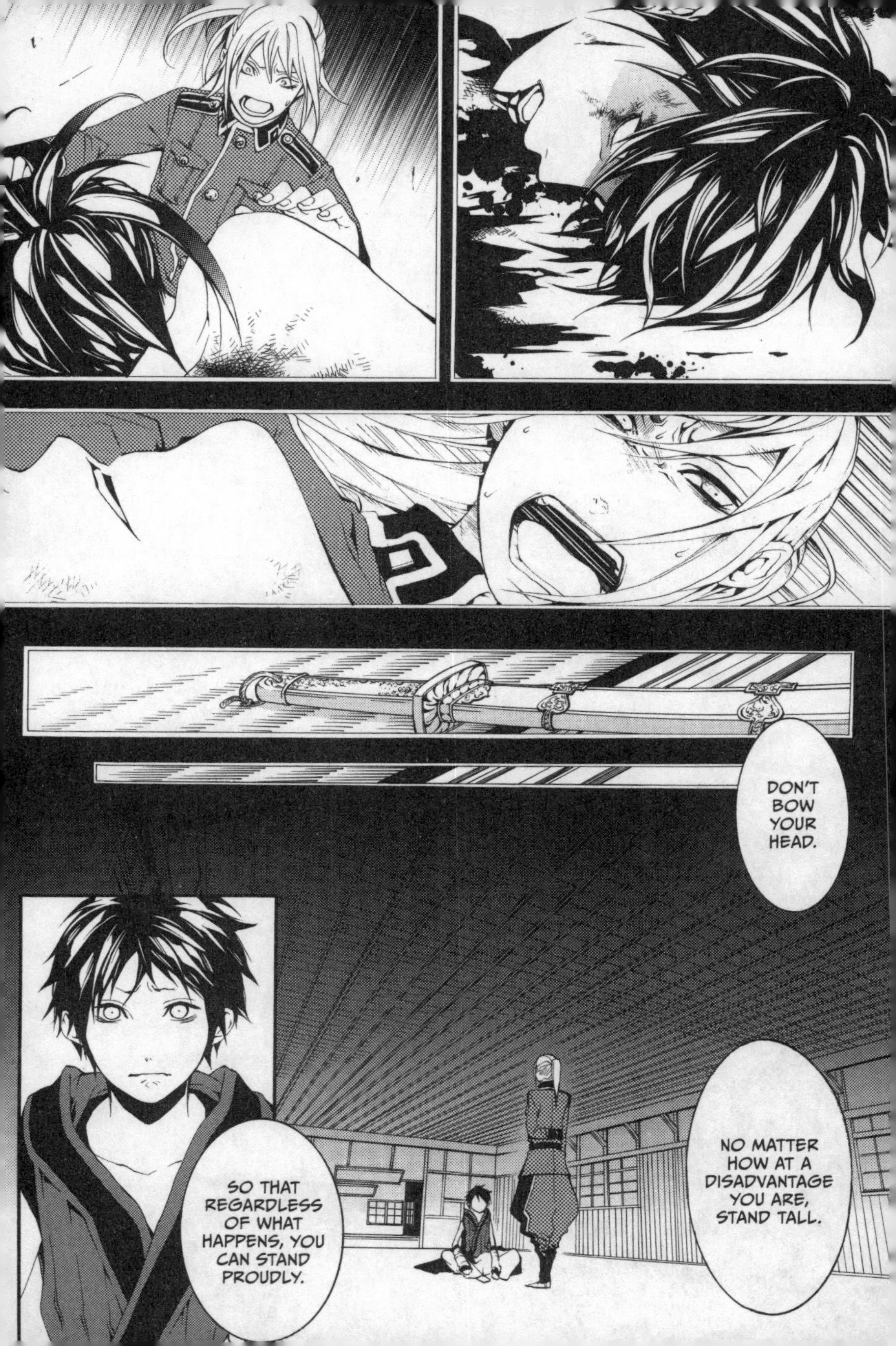
DON'T BOW YOUR HEAD.
NO MATTER HOW AT A DISADVANTAGE YOU ARE, STAND TALL.
SO THAT REGARDLESS OF WHAT HAPPENS, YOU CAN STAND PROUDLY.

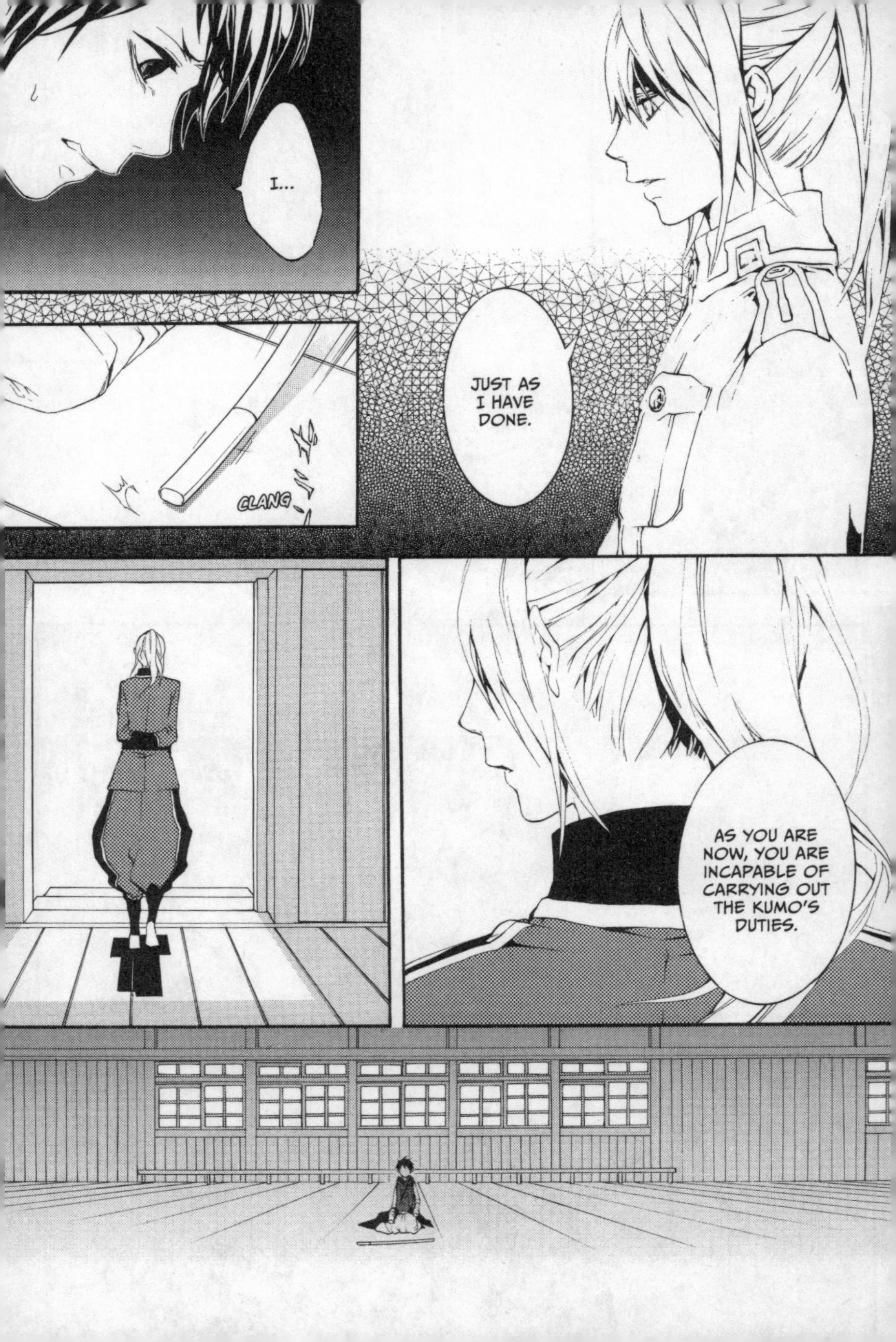
JUST AS I HAVE DONE.
I...
CLANG
AS YOU ARE NOW, YOU ARE INCAPABLE OF CARRYING OUT THE KUMO'S DUTIES.

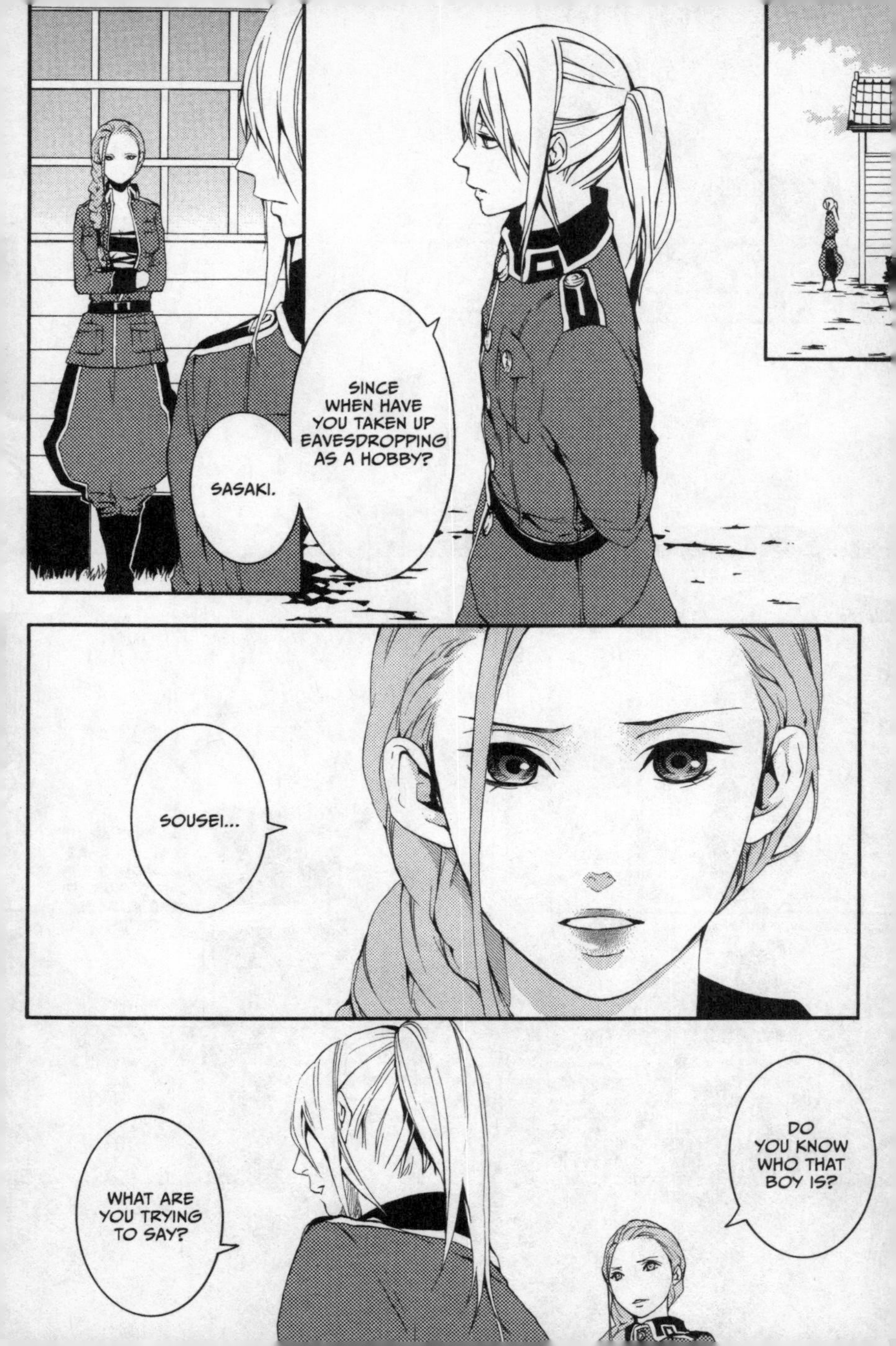
SINCE WHEN HAVE YOU TAKEN UP EAVESDROPPING AS A HOBBY?
SASAKI.
SOUSEI...
DO YOU KNOW WHO THAT BOY IS?
WHAT ARE YOU TRYING TO SAY?

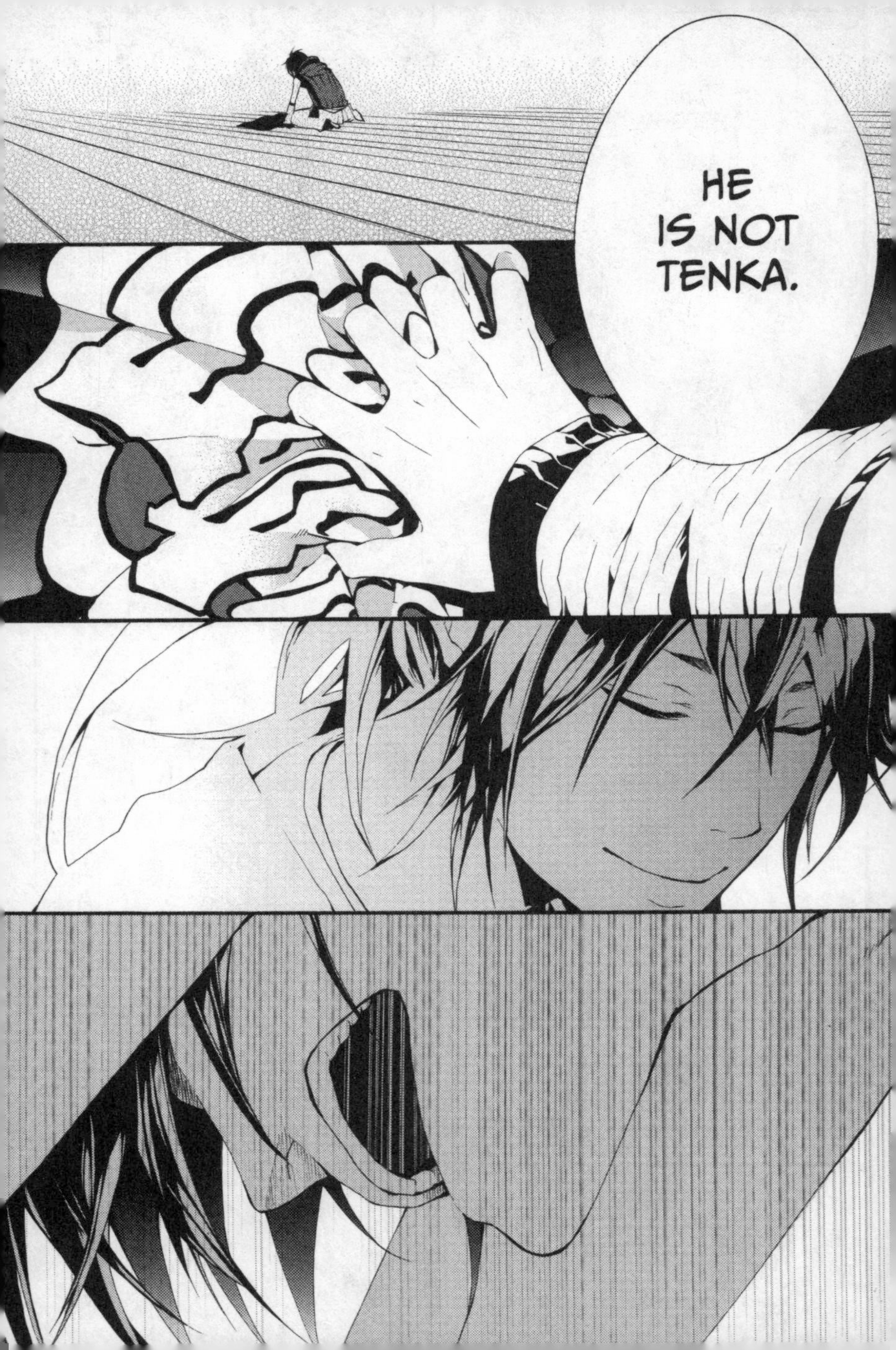
HE IS NOT TENKA.

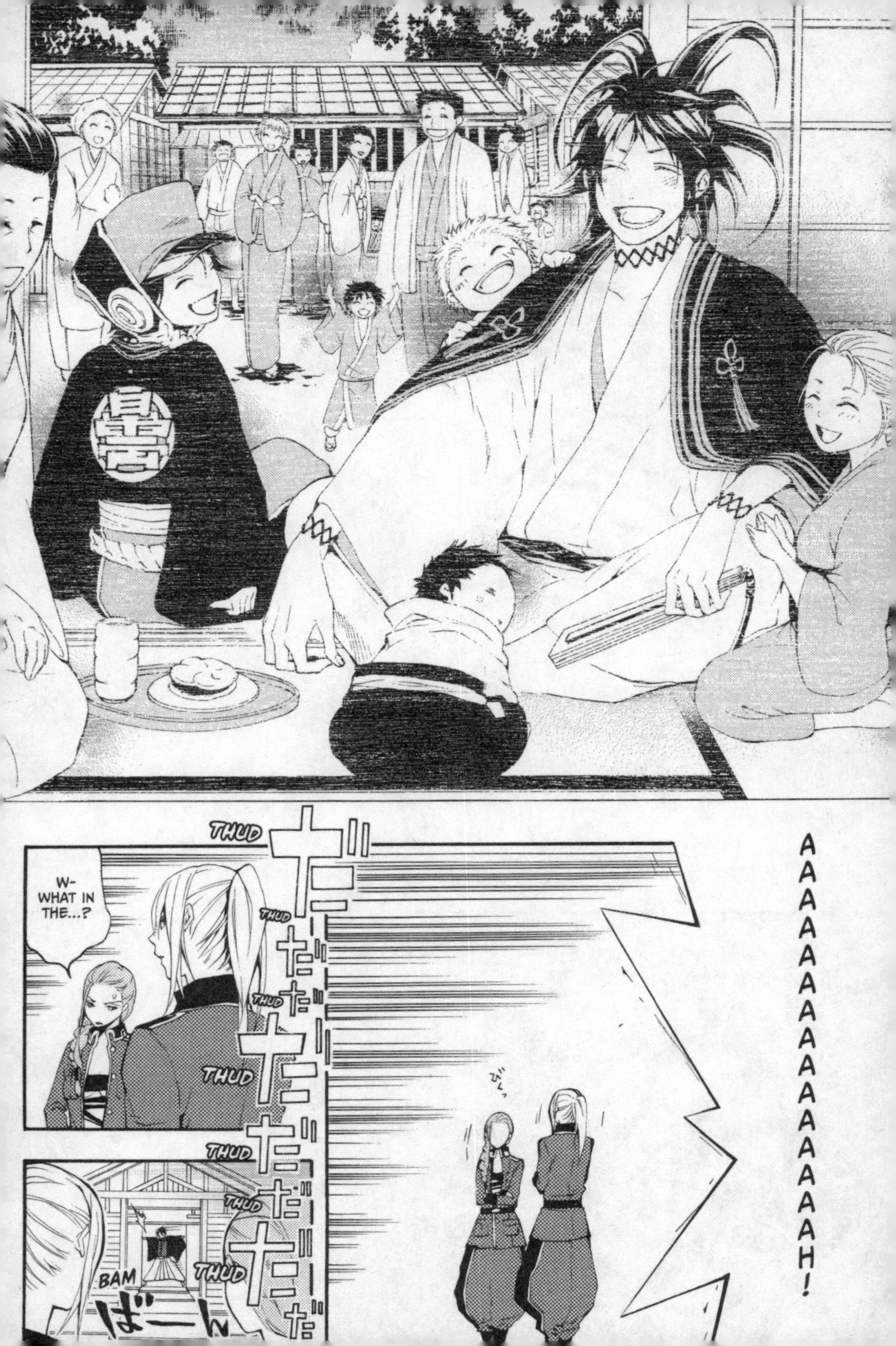
AAAAAAAAAAAAAAAH!
THUD
W-WHAT IN THE...?
THUD
THUD
THUD
THUD
THUD
THUD
BAM

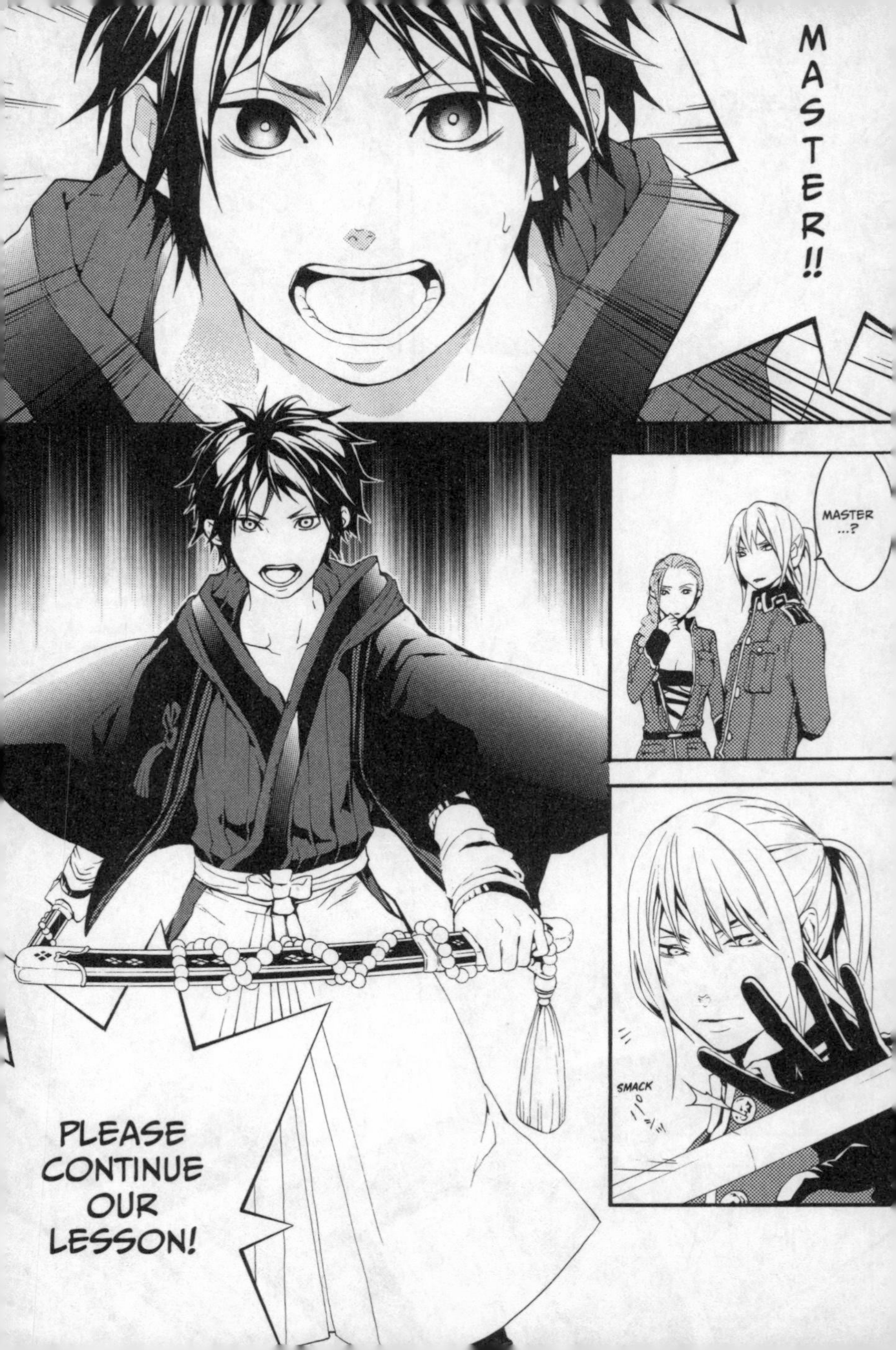
MASTER!!
MASTER ...?
SMACK
PLEASE CONTINUE OUR LESSON!

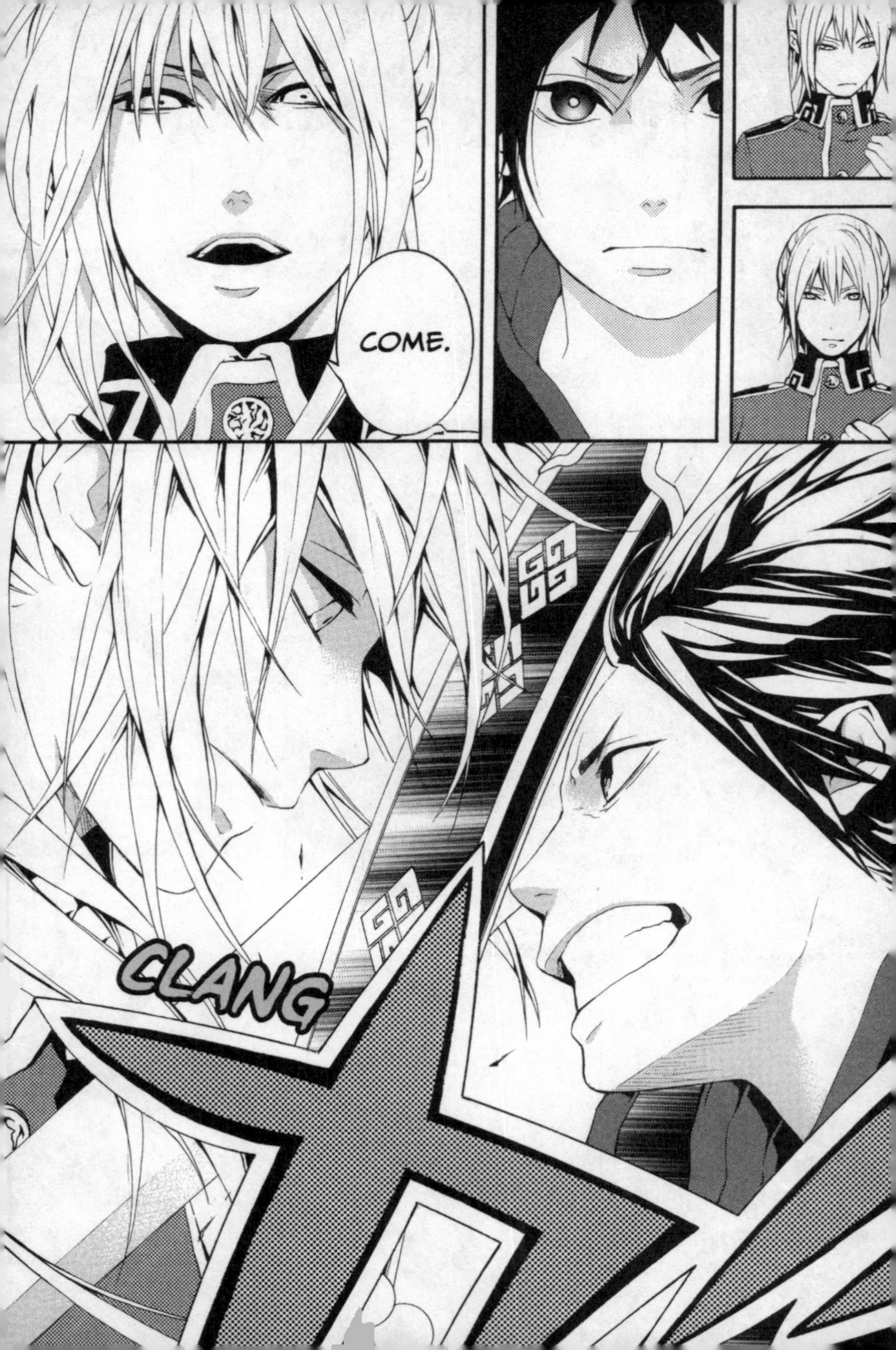
COME.
CLANG

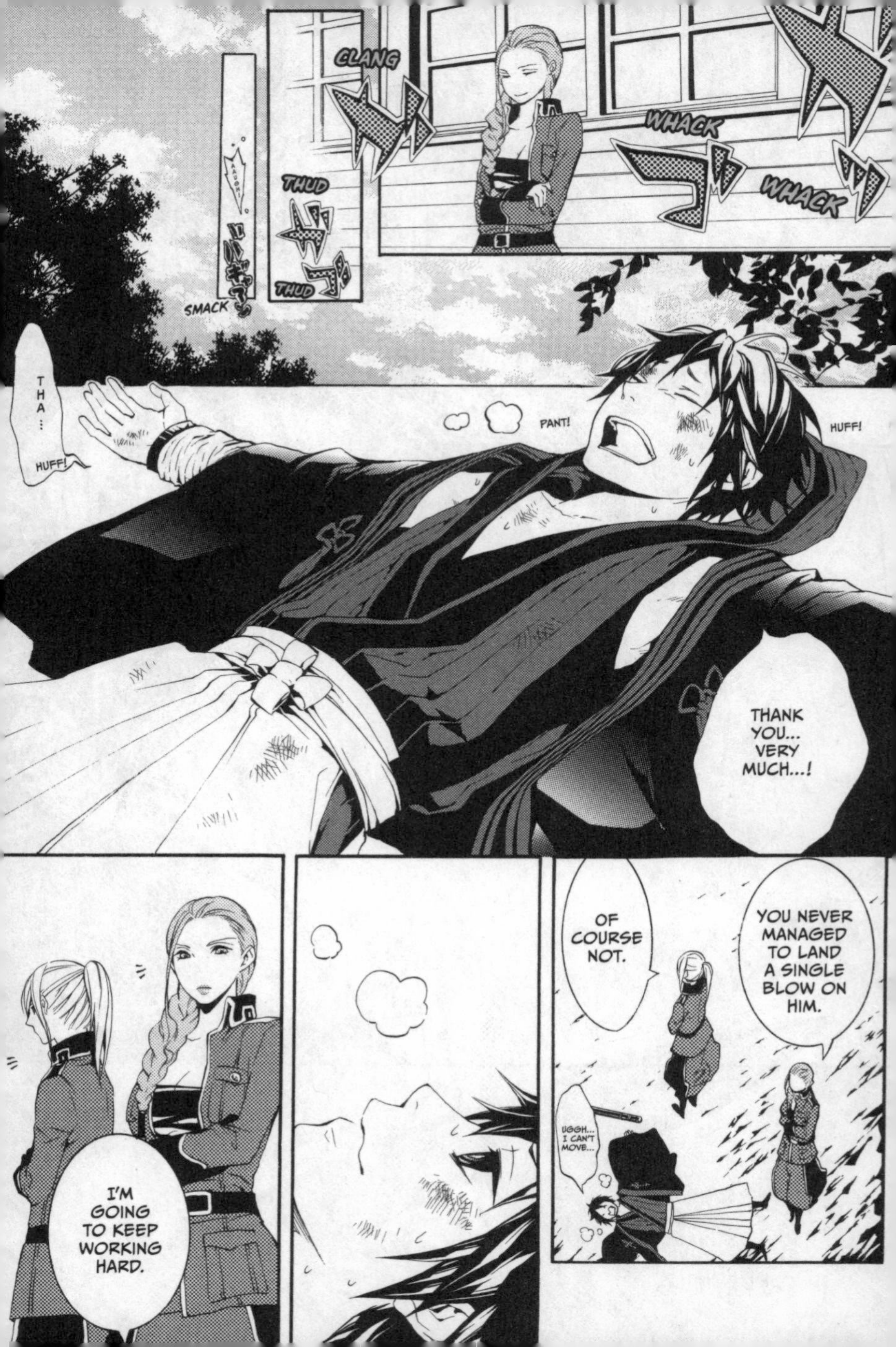

WHACK
WHACK
CLANG
THUD
THUD
AAUGH!
SMACK
HUFF!
PANT!
THA... HUFF!
THANK YOU... VERY MUCH...!
YOU NEVER MANAGED TO LAND A SINGLE BLOW ON HIM.
OF COURSE NOT.
UGGH... I CAN'T MOVE...
I'M GOING TO KEEP WORKING HARD.

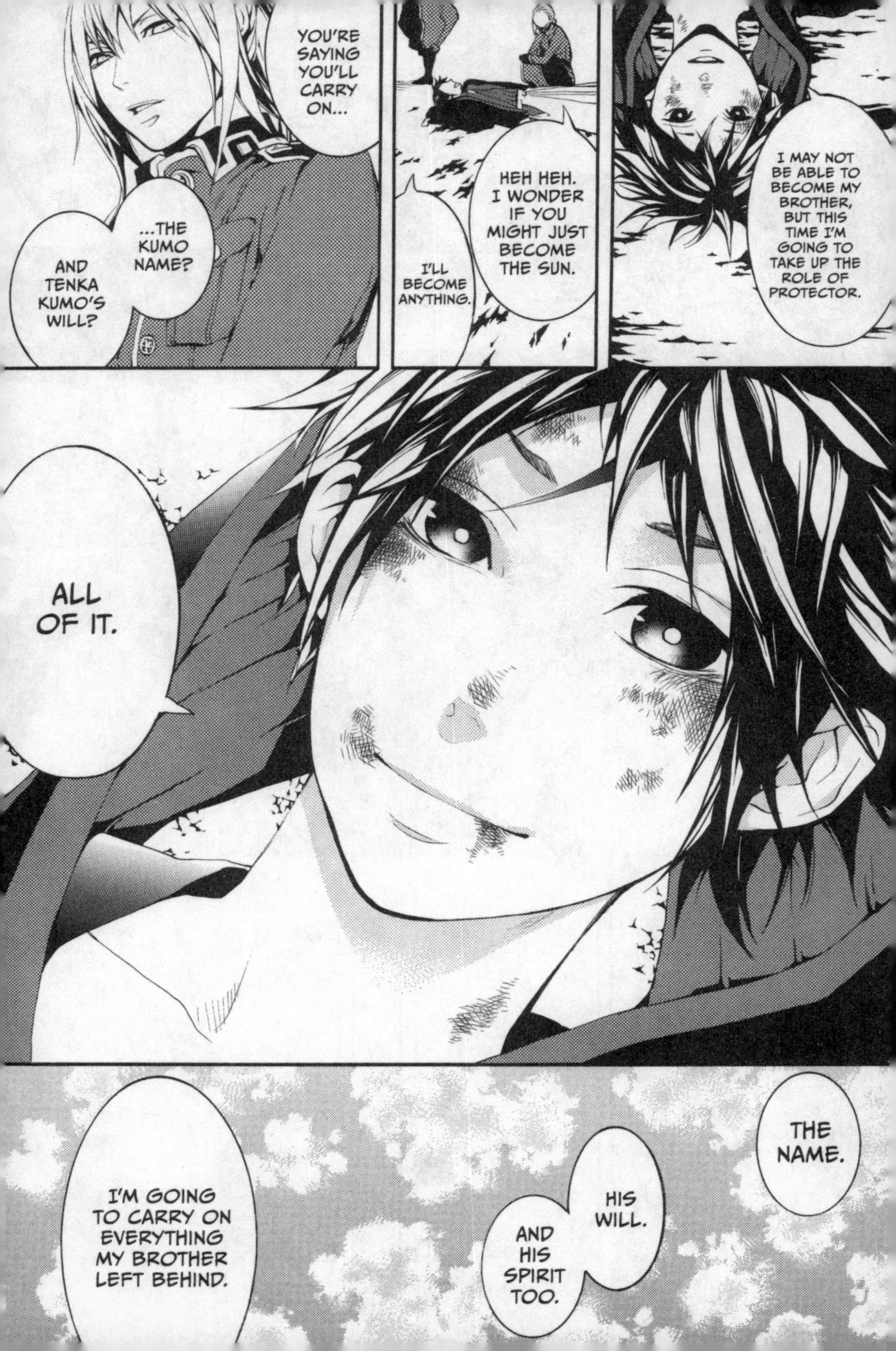
I MAY NOT BE ABLE TO BECOME MY BROTHER, BUT THIS TIME I'M GOING TO TAKE UP THE ROLE OF PROTECTOR.
HEH HEH. I WONDER IF YOU MIGHT JUST BECOME THE SUN.
I'LL BECOME ANYTHING.
YOU'RE SAYING YOU'LL CARRY ON...
...THE KUMO NAME?
AND TENKA KUMO'S WILL?
ALL OF IT.
THE NAME.
HIS WILL.
AND HIS SPIRIT TOO.
I'M GOING TO CARRY ON EVERYTHING MY BROTHER LEFT BEHIND.

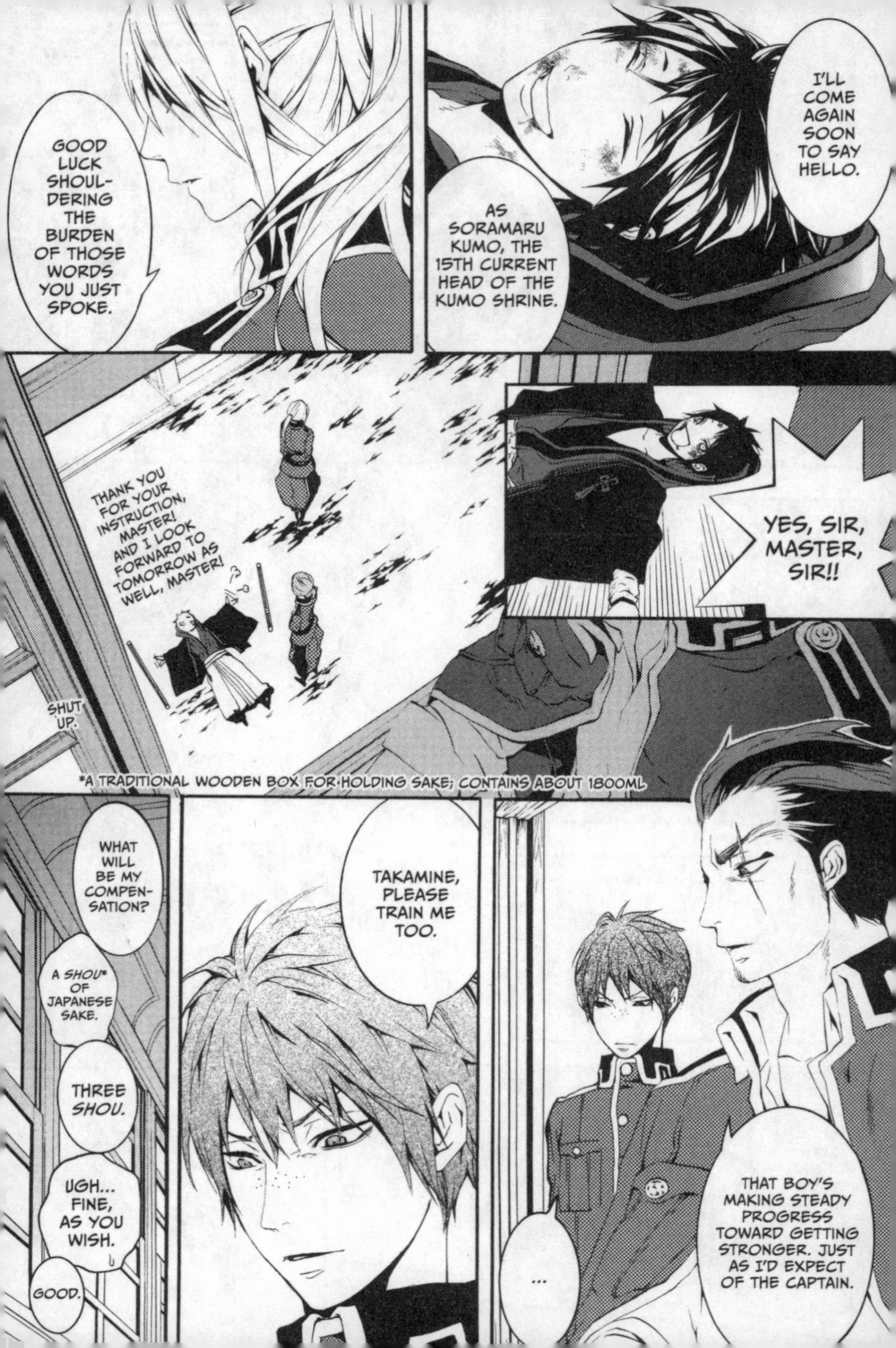
I'LL COME AGAIN SOON TO SAY HELLO.
AS SORAMARU KUMO, THE 15TH CURRENT HEAD OF THE KUMO SHRINE.
GOOD LUCK SHOULDERING THE BURDEN OF THOSE WORDS YOU JUST SPOKE.
YES, SIR, MASTER, SIR!!
THANK YOU FOR YOUR INSTRUCTION, MASTER! AND I LOOK FORWARD TO TOMORROW AS WELL, MASTER!
SHUT UP.
THAT BOY'S MAKING STEADY PROGRESS TOWARD GETTING STRONGER. JUST AS I'D EXPECT OF THE CAPTAIN.
...
TAKAMINE, PLEASE TRAIN ME TOO.
WHAT WILL BE MY COMPENSATION?
A *SHOU** OF JAPANESE SAKE.
THREE *SHOU*.
UGH... FINE, AS YOU WISH.
GOOD.
*A TRADITIONAL WOODEN BOX FOR HOLDING SAKE; CONTAINS ABOUT 1800ML

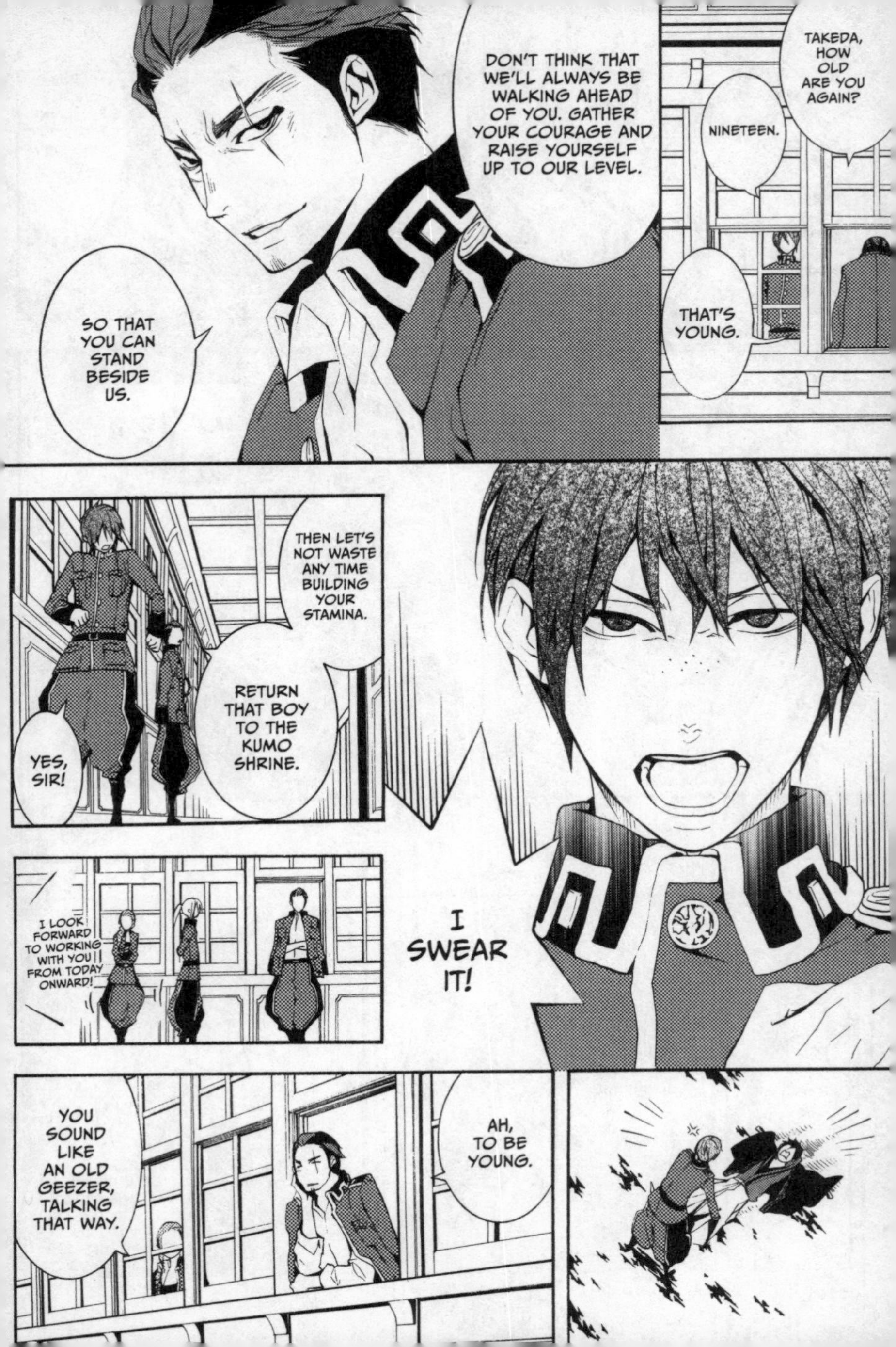
TAKEDA, HOW OLD ARE YOU AGAIN?
NINETEEN.
THAT'S YOUNG.
DON'T THINK THAT WE'LL ALWAYS BE WALKING AHEAD OF YOU. GATHER YOUR COURAGE AND RAISE YOURSELF UP TO OUR LEVEL.
SO THAT YOU CAN STAND BESIDE US.
I SWEAR IT!
THEN LET'S NOT WASTE ANY TIME BUILDING YOUR STAMINA.
RETURN THAT BOY TO THE KUMO SHRINE.
YES, SIR!
I LOOK FORWARD TO WORKING WITH YOU FROM TODAY ONWARD!
AH, TO BE YOUNG.
YOU SOUND LIKE AN OLD GEEZER, TALKING THAT WAY.

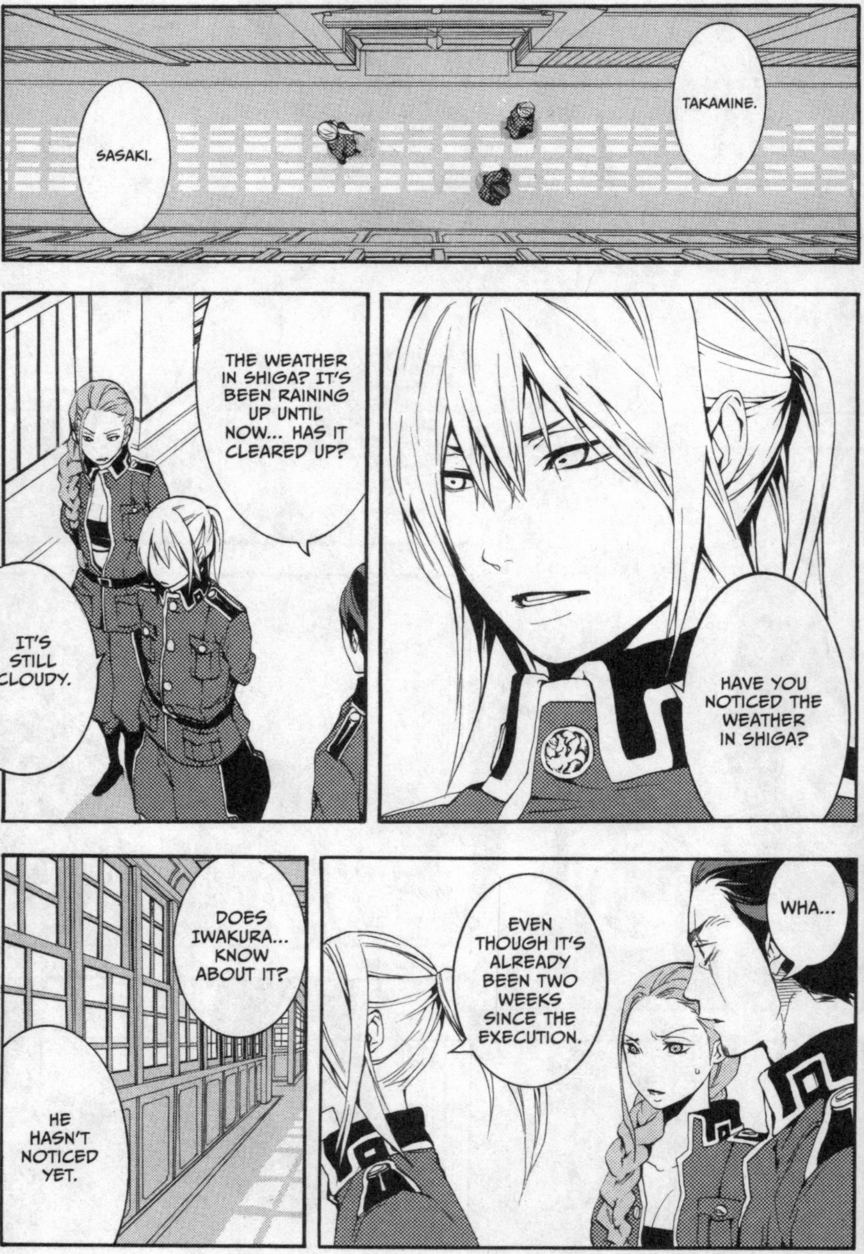
TAKAMINE.
SASAKI.
HAVE YOU NOTICED THE WEATHER IN SHIGA?
THE WEATHER IN SHIGA? IT'S BEEN RAINING UP UNTIL NOW... HAS IT CLEARED UP?
IT'S STILL CLOUDY.
WHA...
EVEN THOUGH IT'S ALREADY BEEN TWO WEEKS SINCE THE EXECUTION.
DOES IWAKURA... KNOW ABOUT IT?
HE HASN'T NOTICED YET.

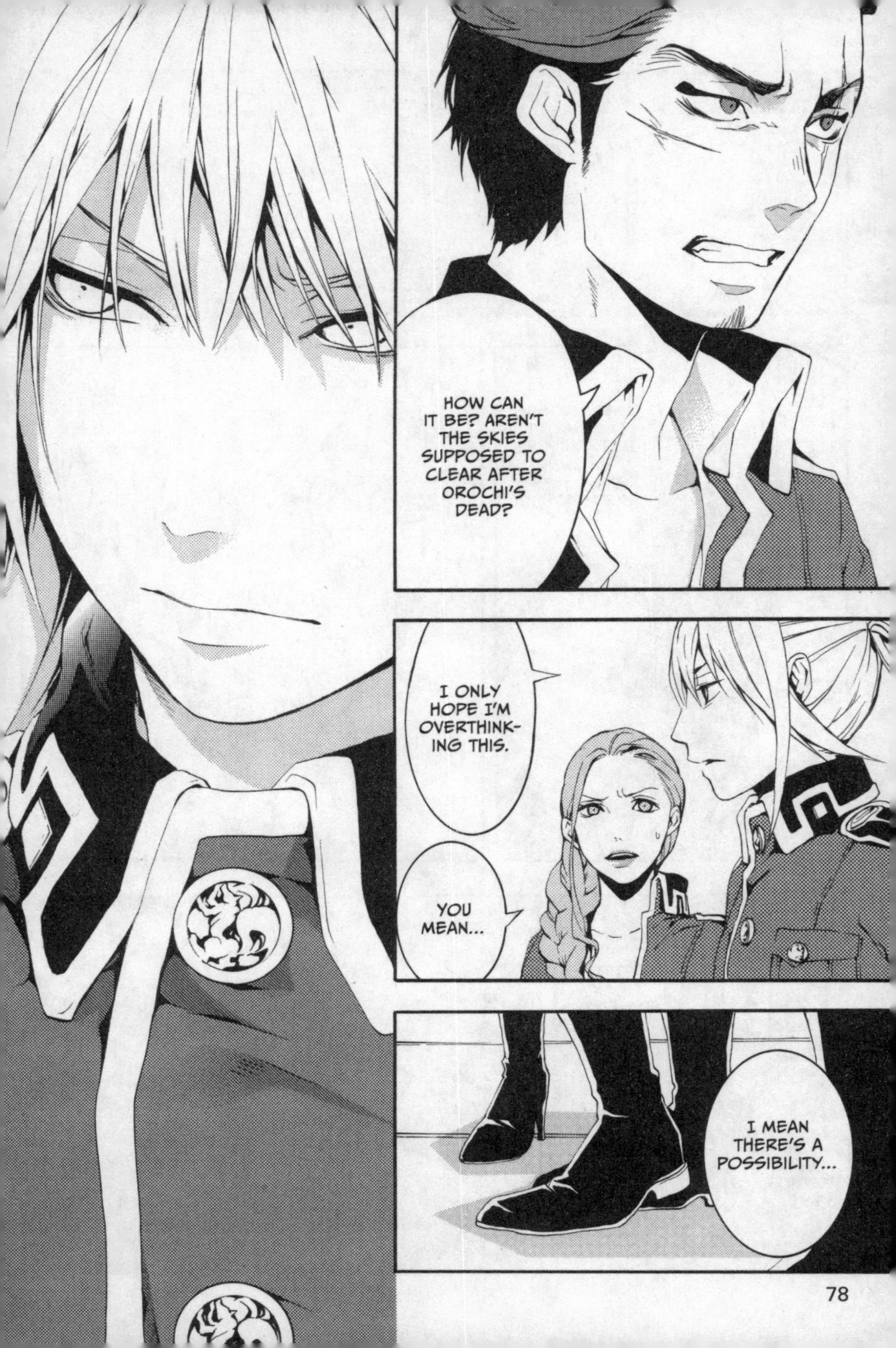
HOW CAN IT BE? AREN'T THE SKIES SUPPOSED TO CLEAR AFTER OROCHI'S DEAD?
I ONLY HOPE I'M OVERTHINKING THIS.
YOU MEAN...
I MEAN THERE'S A POSSIBILITY...

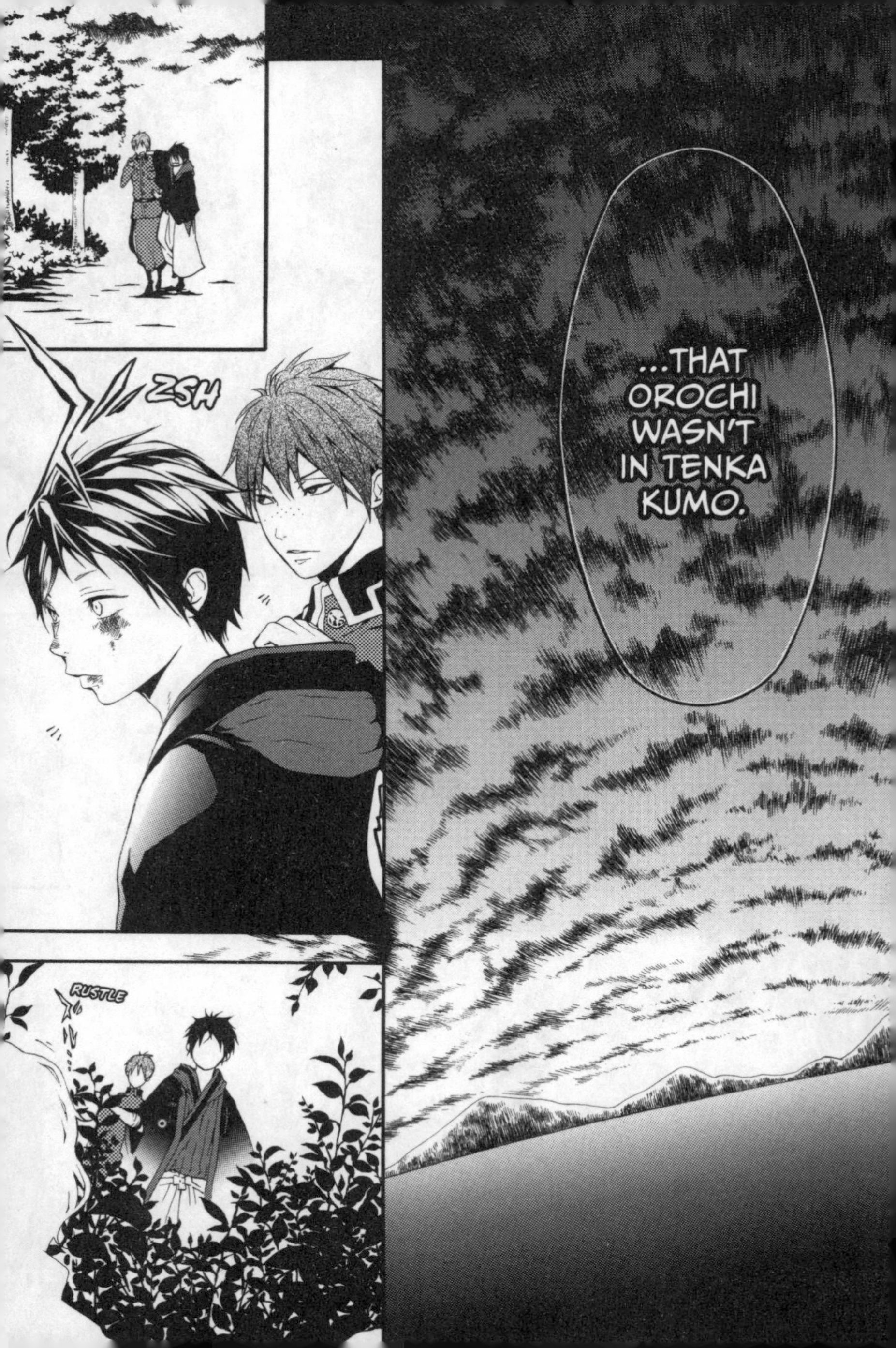
...THAT OROCHI WASN'T IN TENKA KUMO.
ZSH
RUSTLE

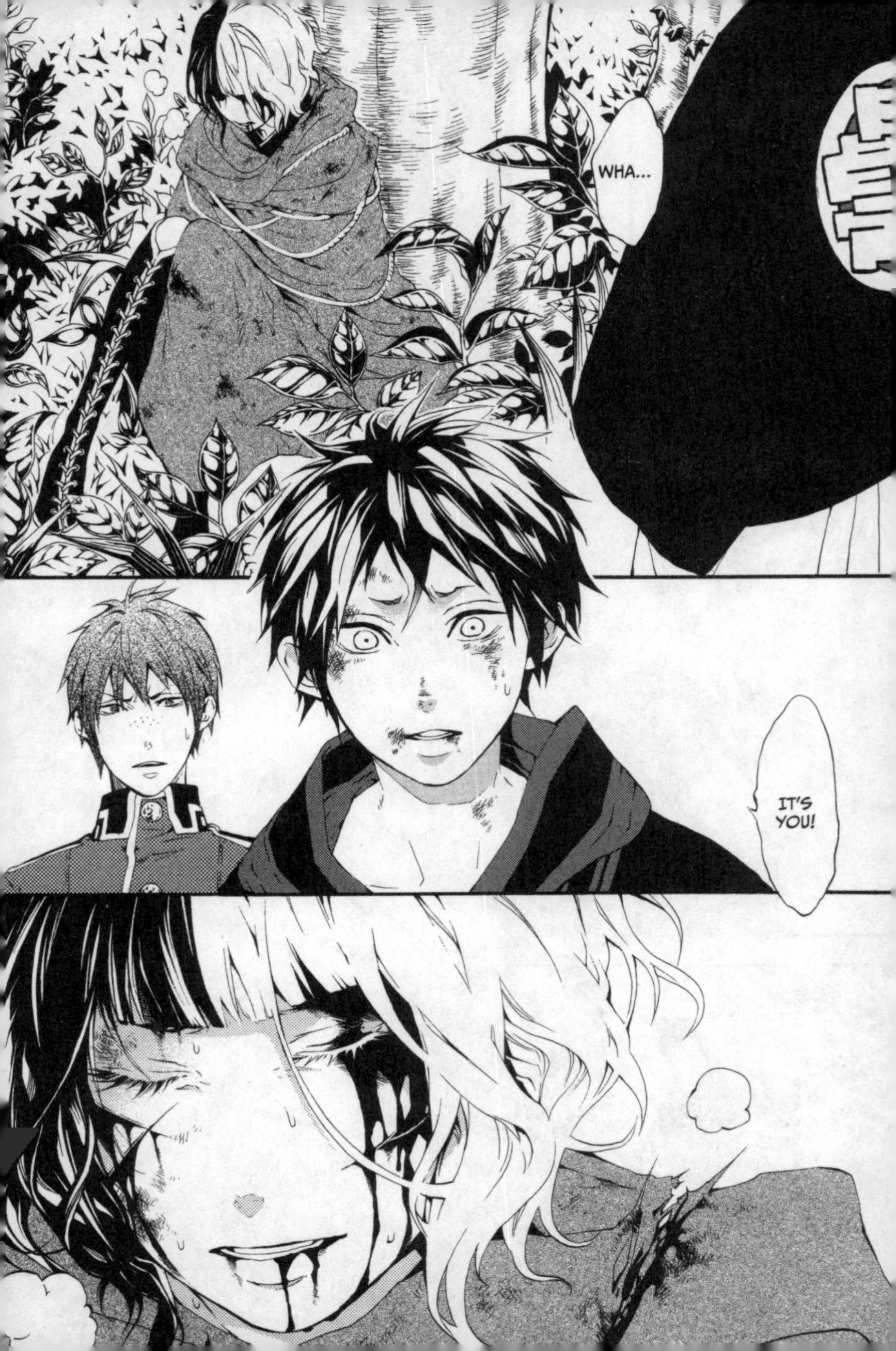
WHA...
IT'S YOU!

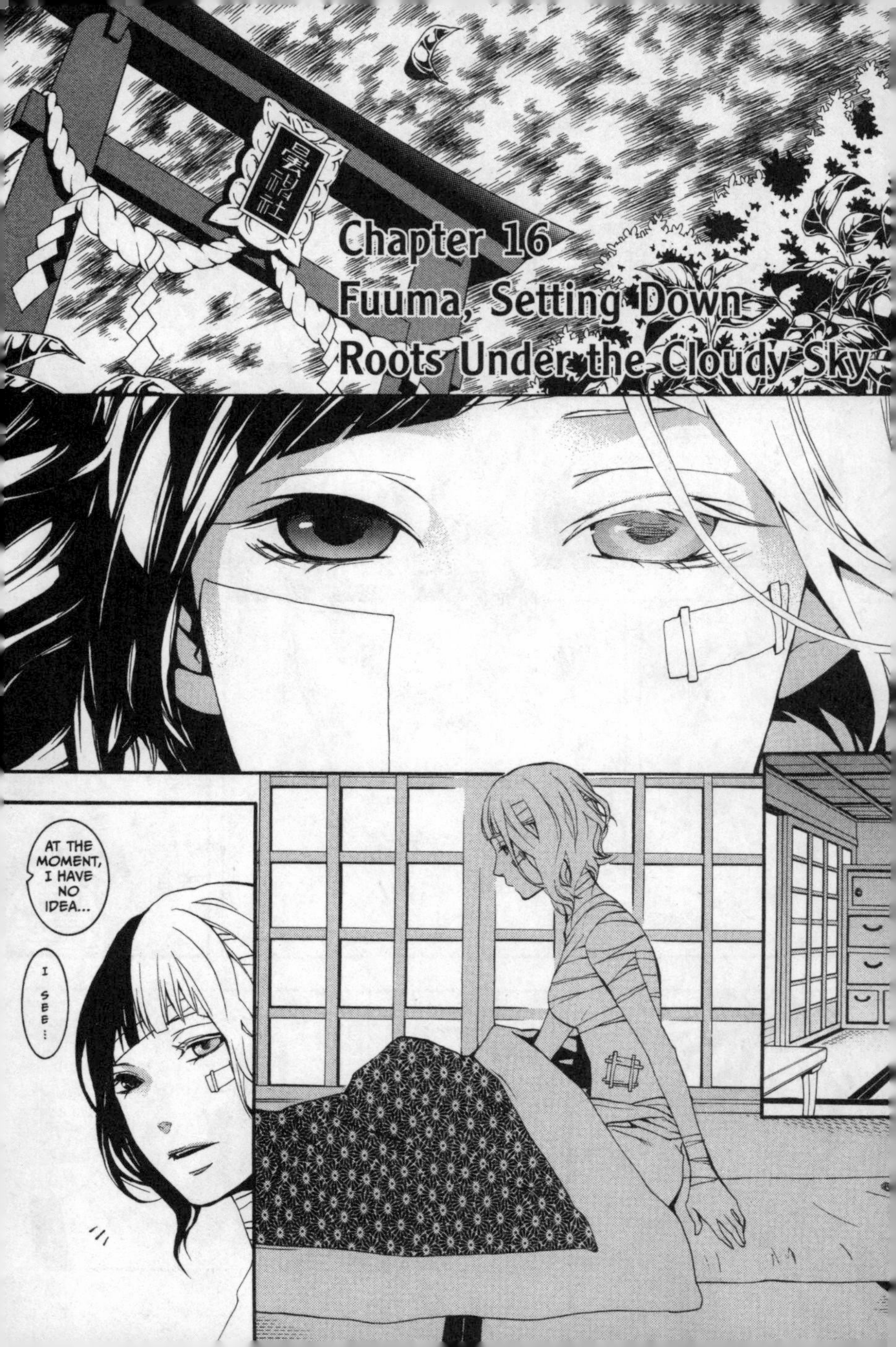
Chapter 16
Fuuma, Setting Down Roots Under the Cloudy Sky
AT THE MOMENT, I HAVE NO IDEA...
I SEE...

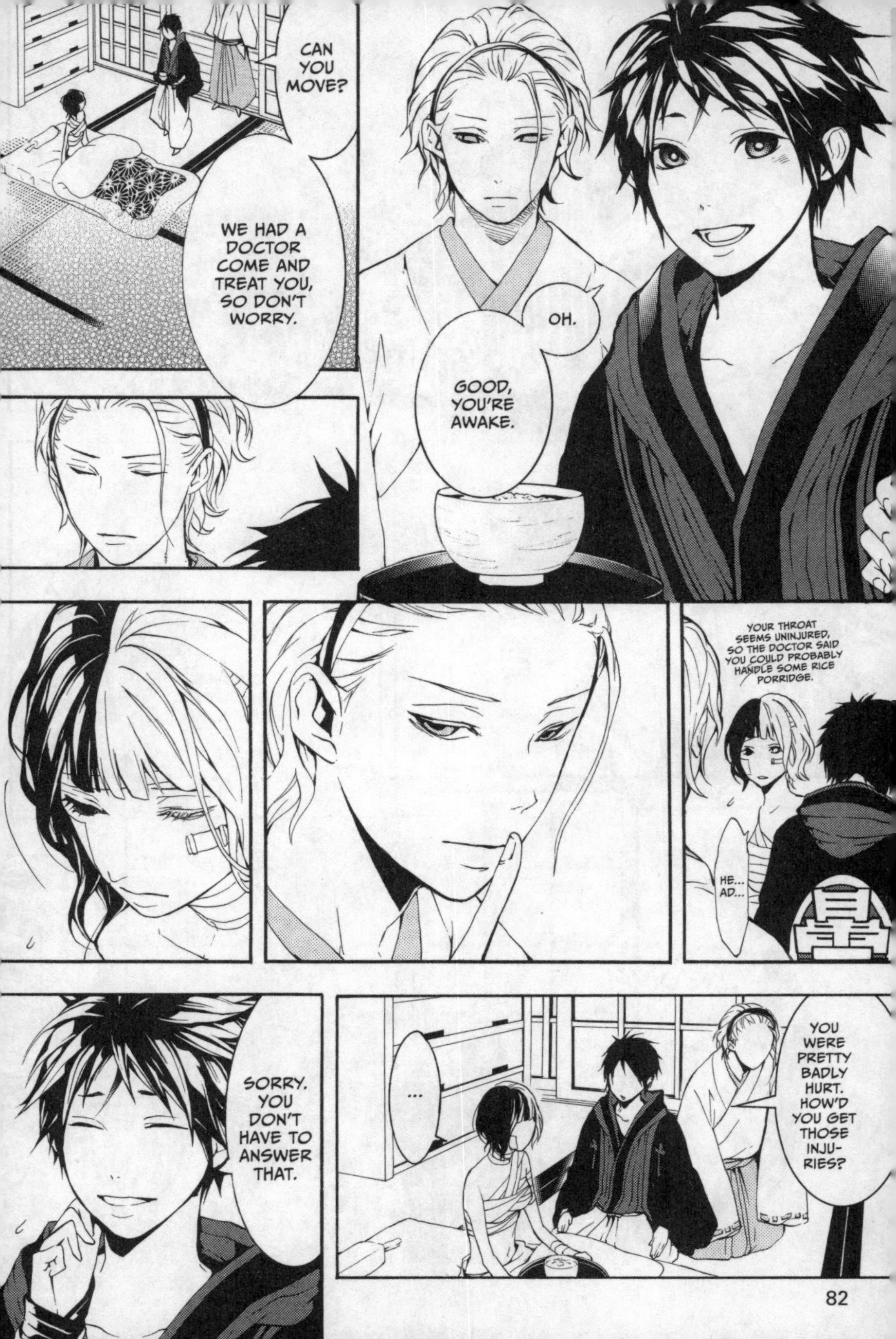
OH.
GOOD, YOU'RE AWAKE.
CAN YOU MOVE?
WE HAD A DOCTOR COME AND TREAT YOU, SO DON'T WORRY.
YOUR THROAT SEEMS UNINJURED, SO THE DOCTOR SAID YOU COULD PROBABLY HANDLE SOME RICE PORRIDGE.
HE... AD...
YOU WERE PRETTY BADLY HURT. HOW'D YOU GET THOSE INJU-RIES?
...
SORRY. YOU DON'T HAVE TO ANSWER THAT.

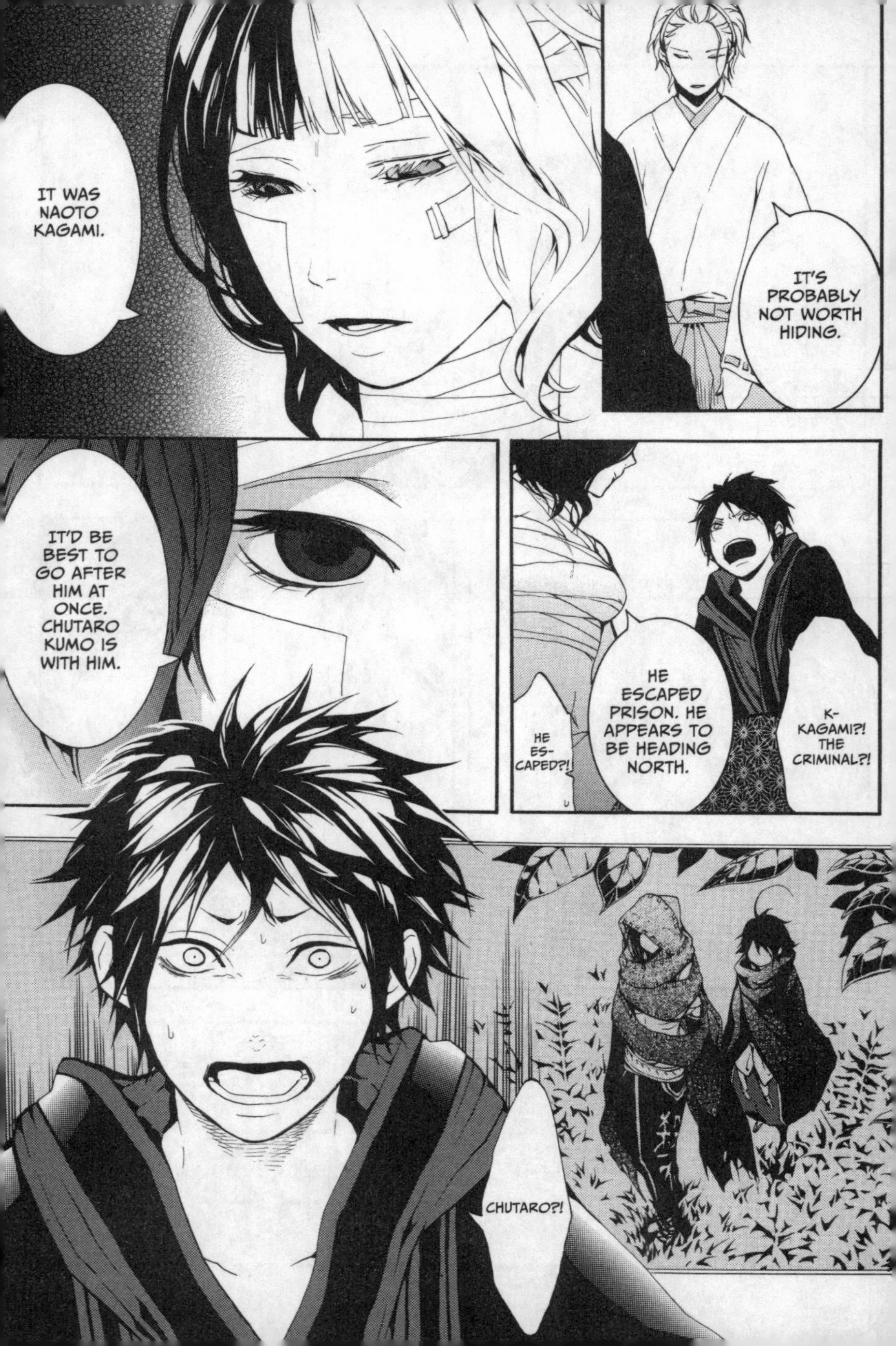
IT'S PROBABLY NOT WORTH HIDING.
IT WAS NAOTO KAGAMI.
K-KAGAMI?! THE CRIMINAL?!
HE ESCAPED PRISON. HE APPEARS TO BE HEADING NORTH.
HE ES-CAPED?!
IT'D BE BEST TO GO AFTER HIM AT ONCE. CHUTARO KUMO IS WITH HIM.
CHUTARO?!

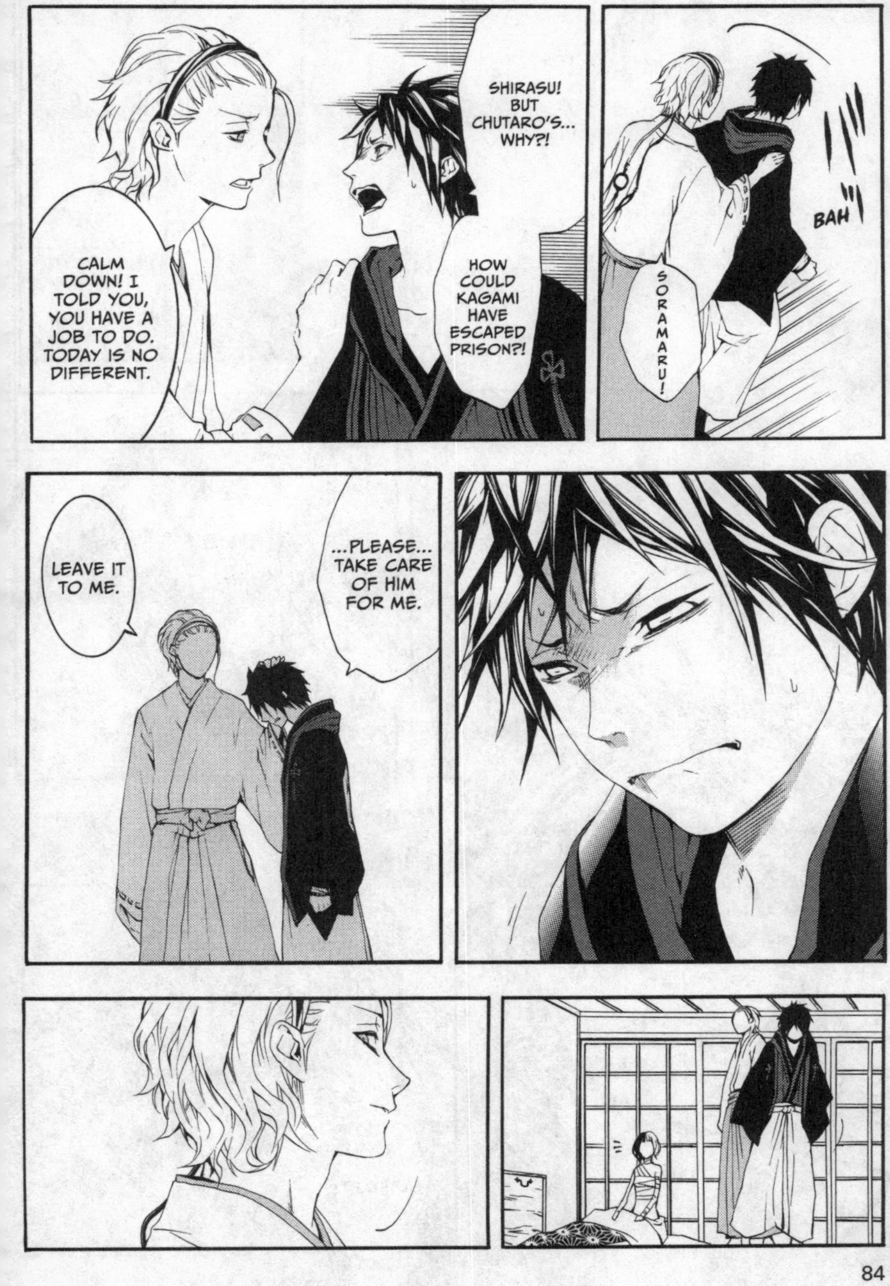
SORAMARU!
BAH
SHIRASU! BUT CHUTARO'S... WHY?!
HOW COULD KAGAMI HAVE ESCAPED PRISON?!
CALM DOWN! I TOLD YOU, YOU HAVE A JOB TO DO. TODAY IS NO DIFFERENT.
...PLEASE... TAKE CARE OF HIM FOR ME.
LEAVE IT TO ME.

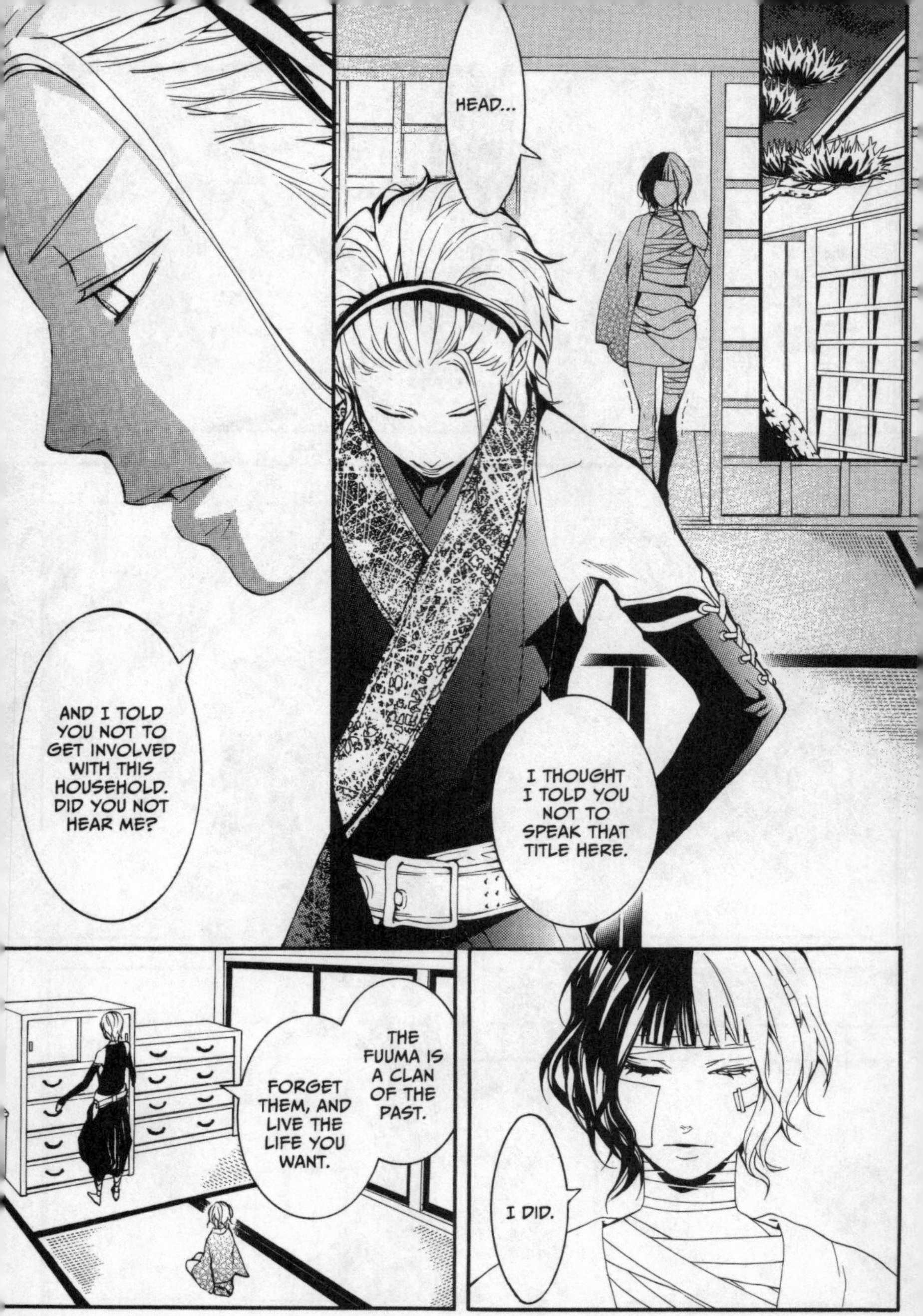
HEAD...
I THOUGHT I TOLD YOU NOT TO SPEAK THAT TITLE HERE.
AND I TOLD YOU NOT TO GET INVOLVED WITH THIS HOUSEHOLD. DID YOU NOT HEAR ME?
I DID.
THE FUUMA IS A CLAN OF THE PAST.
FORGET THEM, AND LIVE THE LIFE YOU WANT.

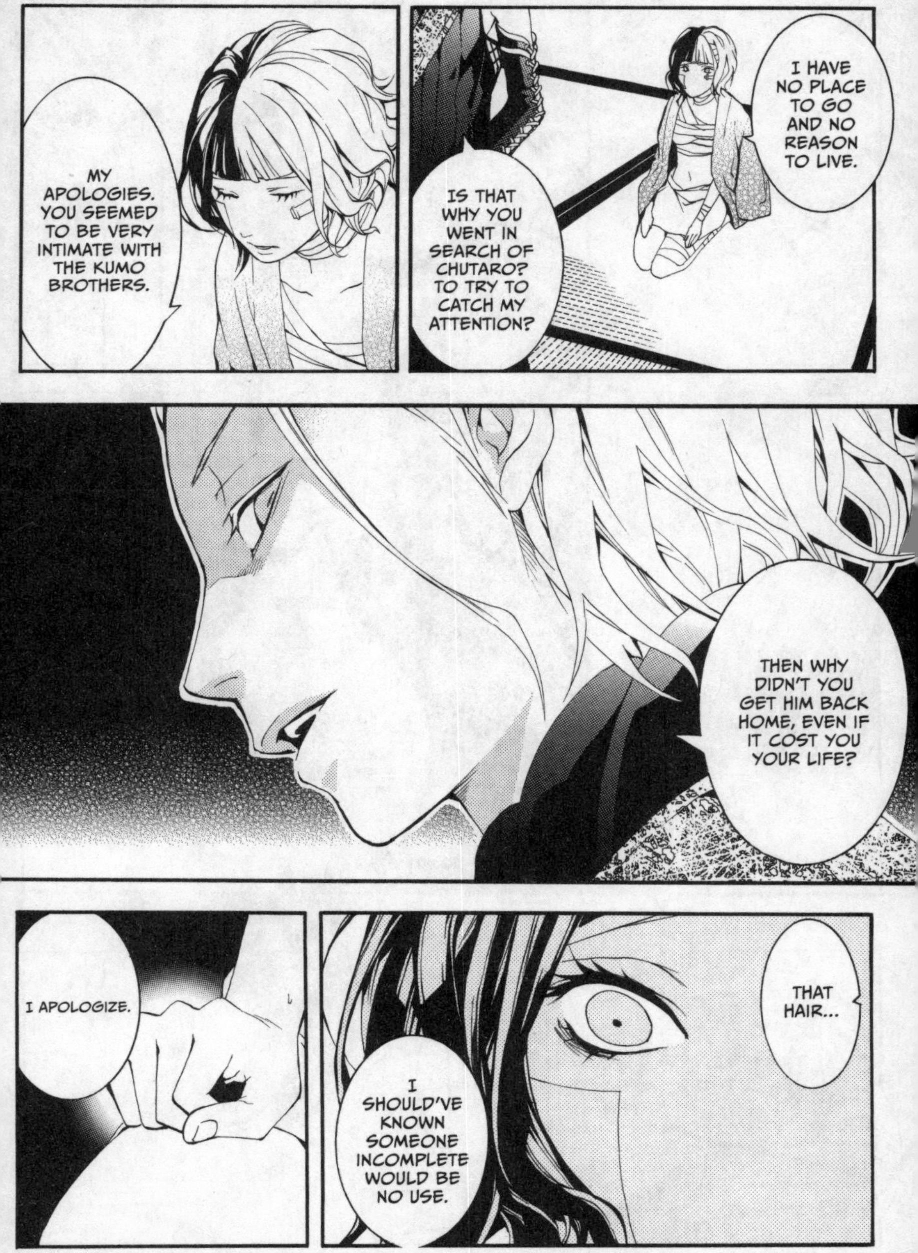
I HAVE NO PLACE TO GO AND NO REASON TO LIVE.
IS THAT WHY YOU WENT IN SEARCH OF CHUTARO? TO TRY TO CATCH MY ATTENTION?
MY APOLOGIES. YOU SEEMED TO BE VERY INTIMATE WITH THE KUMO BROTHERS.
THEN WHY DIDN'T YOU GET HIM BACK HOME, EVEN IF IT COST YOU YOUR LIFE?
THAT HAIR...
I SHOULD'VE KNOWN SOMEONE INCOMPLETE WOULD BE NO USE.
I APOLOGIZE.

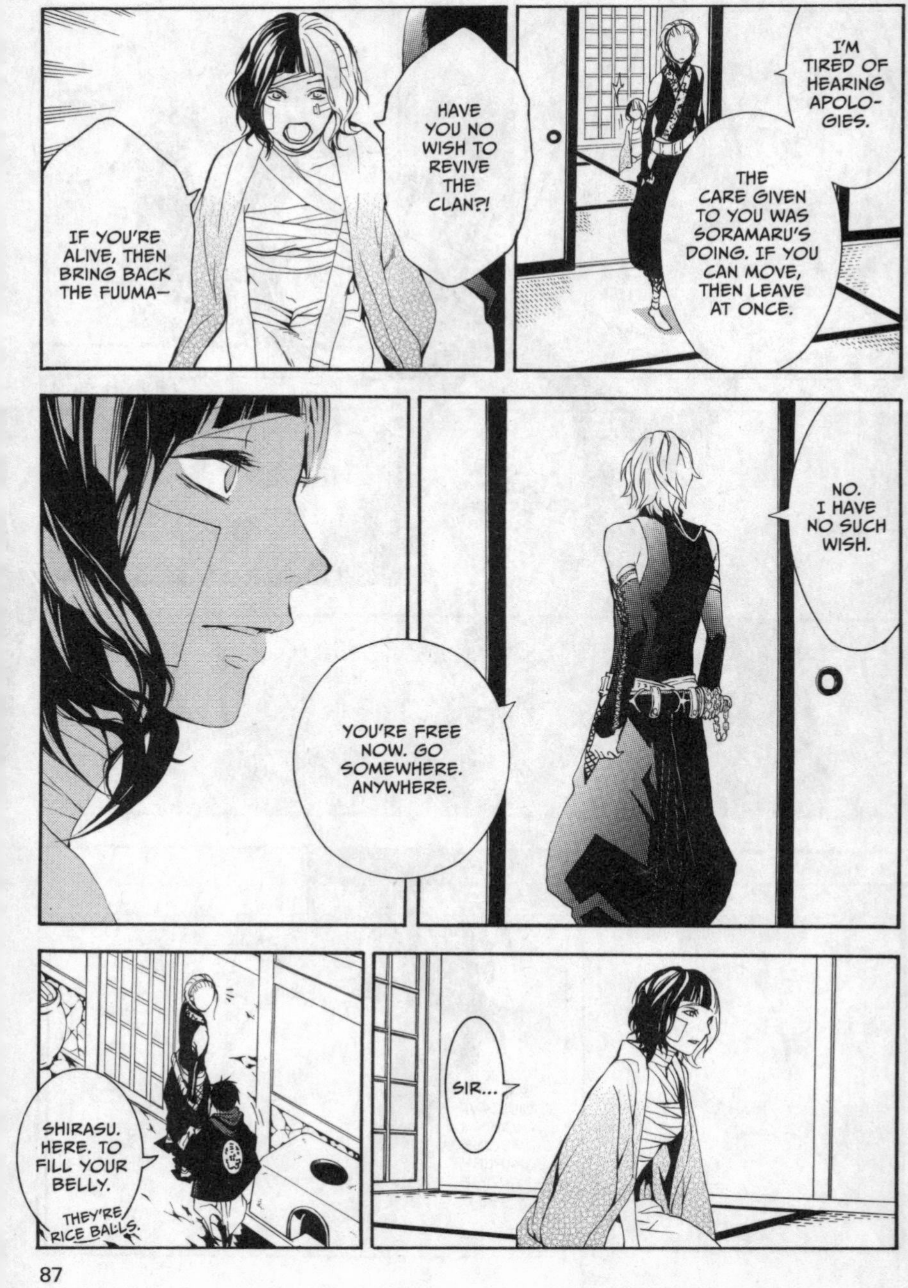
I'M TIRED OF HEARING APOLO-GIES.
THE CARE GIVEN TO YOU WAS SORAMARU'S DOING. IF YOU CAN MOVE, THEN LEAVE AT ONCE.
HAVE YOU NO WISH TO REVIVE THE CLAN?!
IF YOU'RE ALIVE, THEN BRING BACK THE FUUMA—
NO. I HAVE NO SUCH WISH.
YOU'RE FREE NOW. GO SOMEWHERE. ANYWHERE.
SIR...
SHIRASU. HERE. TO FILL YOUR BELLY.
THEY'RE RICE BALLS.

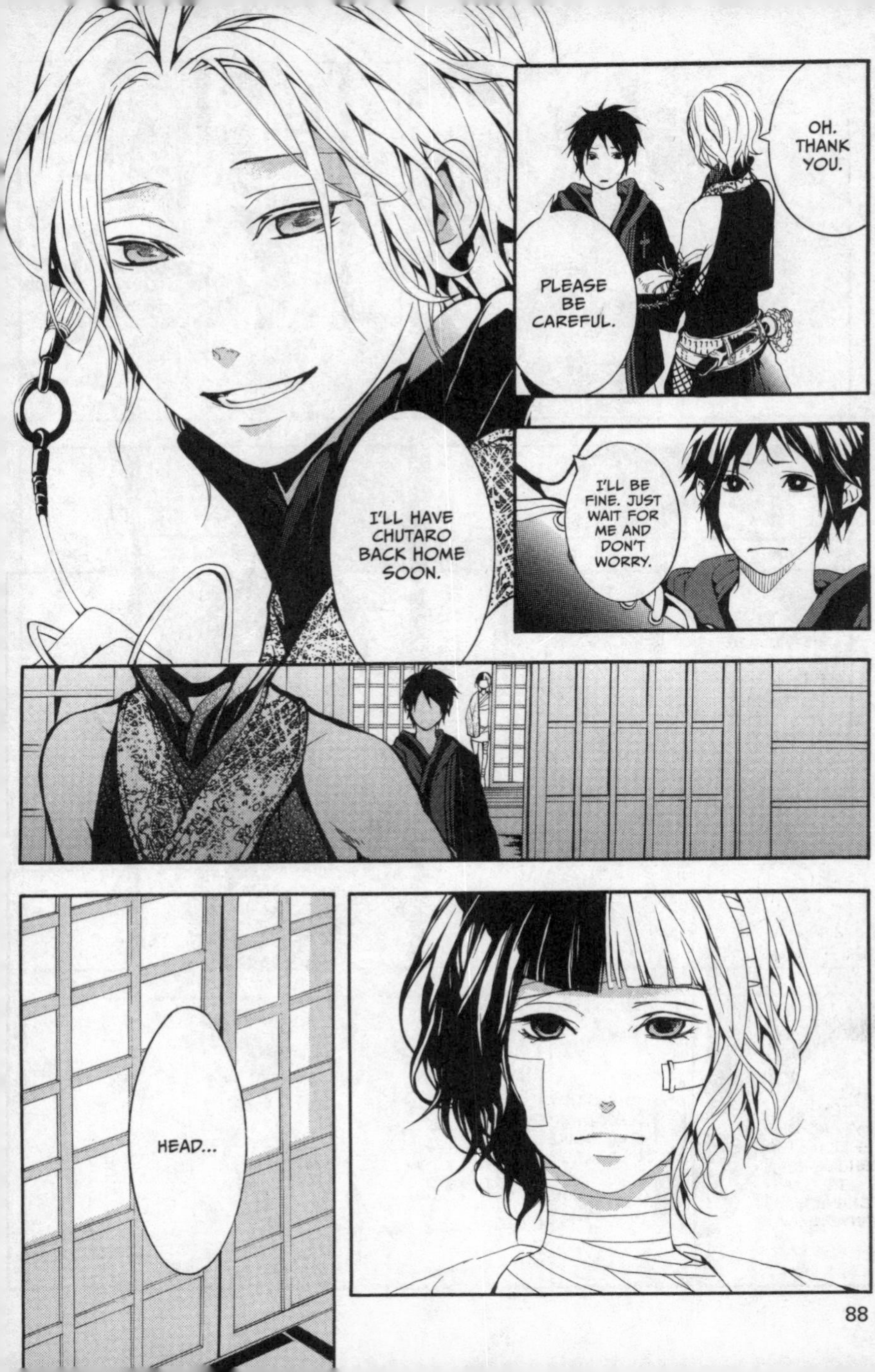
OH. THANK YOU.
PLEASE BE CAREFUL.
I'LL BE FINE. JUST WAIT FOR ME AND DON'T WORRY.
I'LL HAVE CHUTARO BACK HOME SOON.
HEAD...

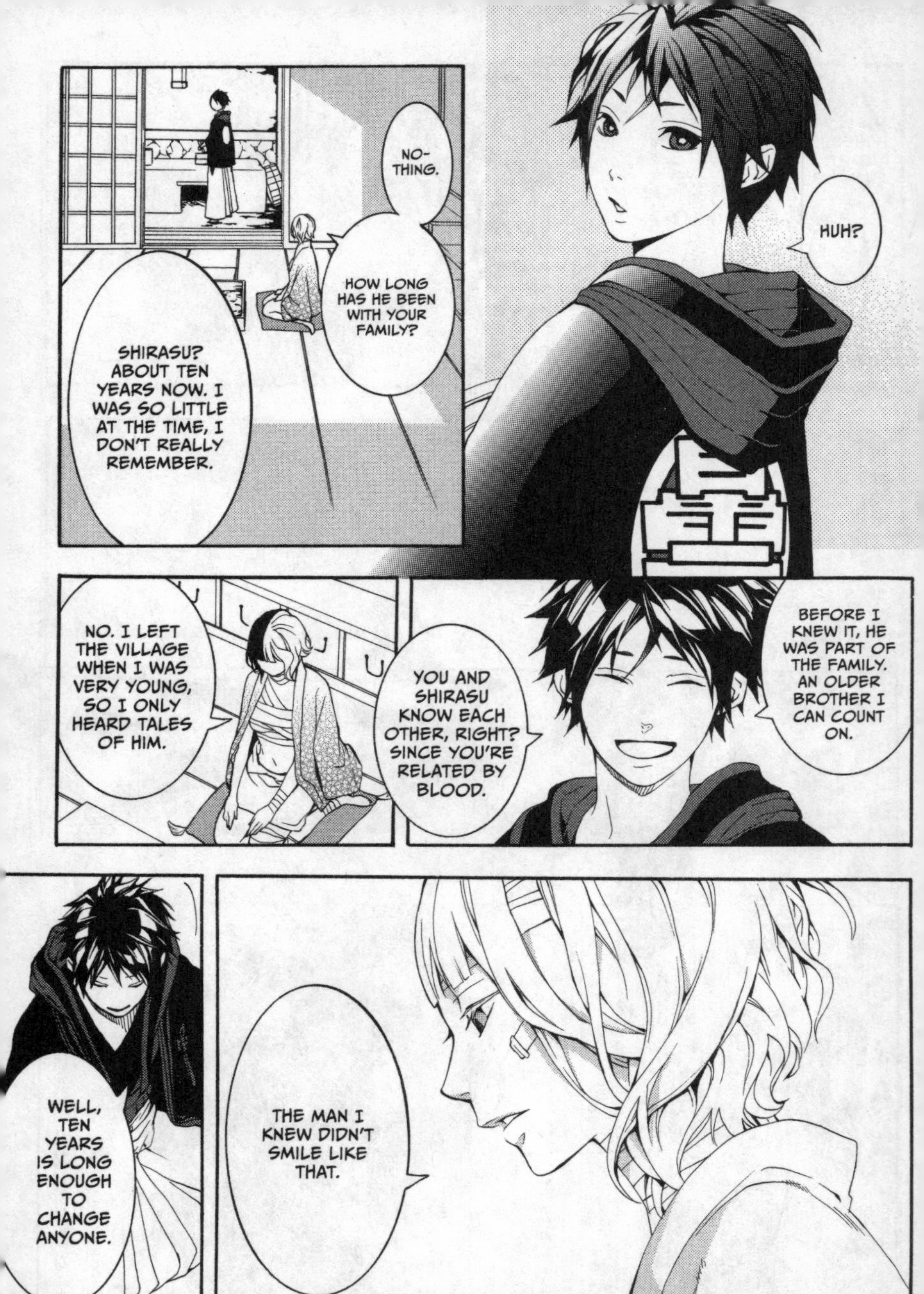

HUH?
NO-THING.
HOW LONG HAS HE BEEN WITH YOUR FAMILY?
SHIRASU? ABOUT TEN YEARS NOW. I WAS SO LITTLE AT THE TIME, I DON'T REALLY REMEMBER.
BEFORE I KNEW IT, HE WAS PART OF THE FAMILY. AN OLDER BROTHER I CAN COUNT ON.
YOU AND SHIRASU KNOW EACH OTHER, RIGHT? SINCE YOU'RE RELATED BY BLOOD.
NO. I LEFT THE VILLAGE WHEN I WAS VERY YOUNG, SO I ONLY HEARD TALES OF HIM.
THE MAN I KNEW DIDN'T SMILE LIKE THAT.
WELL, TEN YEARS IS LONG ENOUGH TO CHANGE ANYONE.

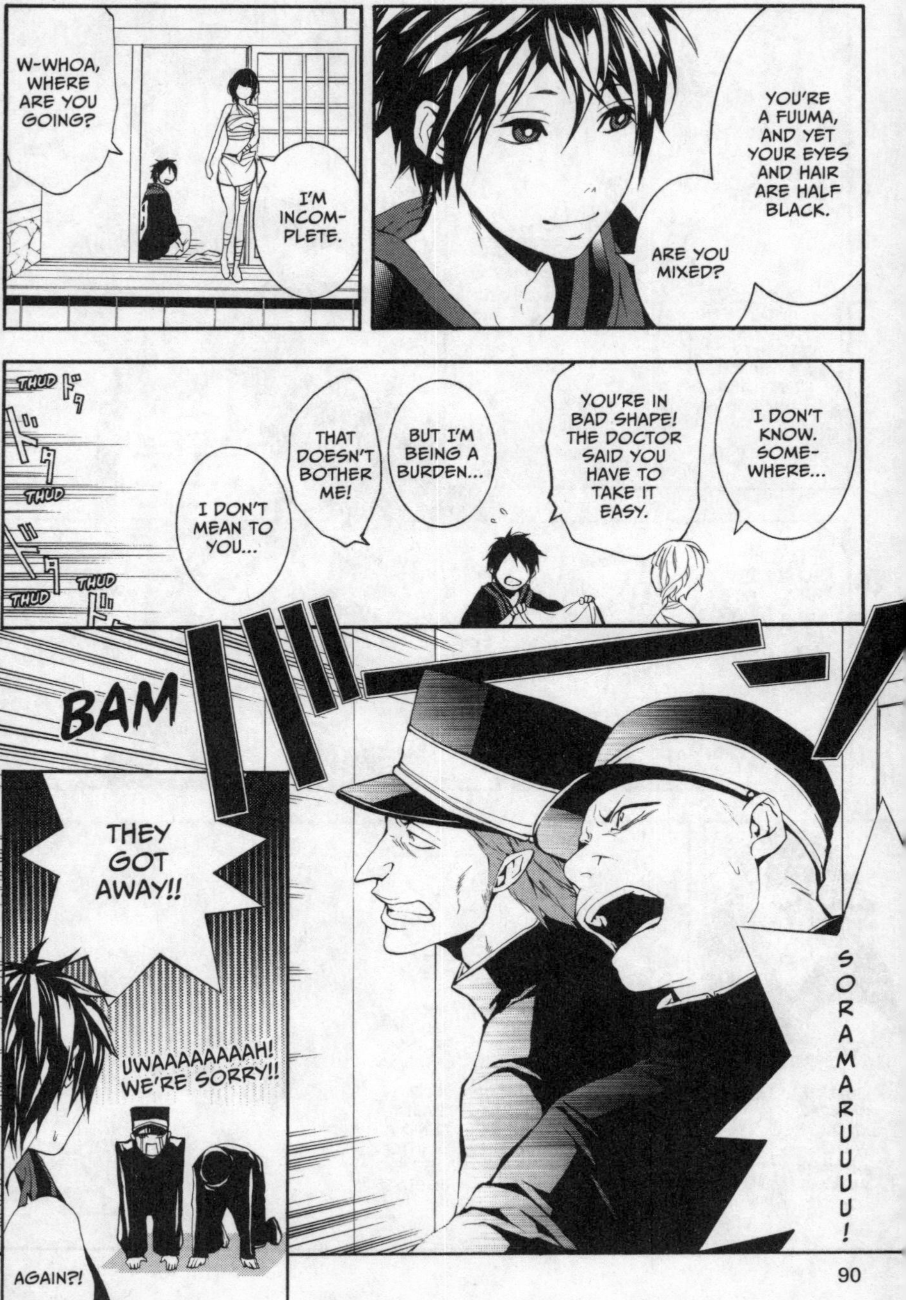
YOU'RE A FUUMA, AND YET YOUR EYES AND HAIR ARE HALF BLACK.
ARE YOU MIXED?
I'M INCOMPLETE.
W-WHOA, WHERE ARE YOU GOING?
I DON'T KNOW. SOMEWHERE...
YOU'RE IN BAD SHAPE! THE DOCTOR SAID YOU HAVE TO TAKE IT EASY.
BUT I'M BEING A BURDEN...
THAT DOESN'T BOTHER ME!
I DON'T MEAN TO YOU...
THUD
THUD
THUD
THUD
BAM
SORAMARUUUU!
THEY GOT AWAY!!
UWAAAAAAAAH! WE'RE SORRY!!
AGAIN?!

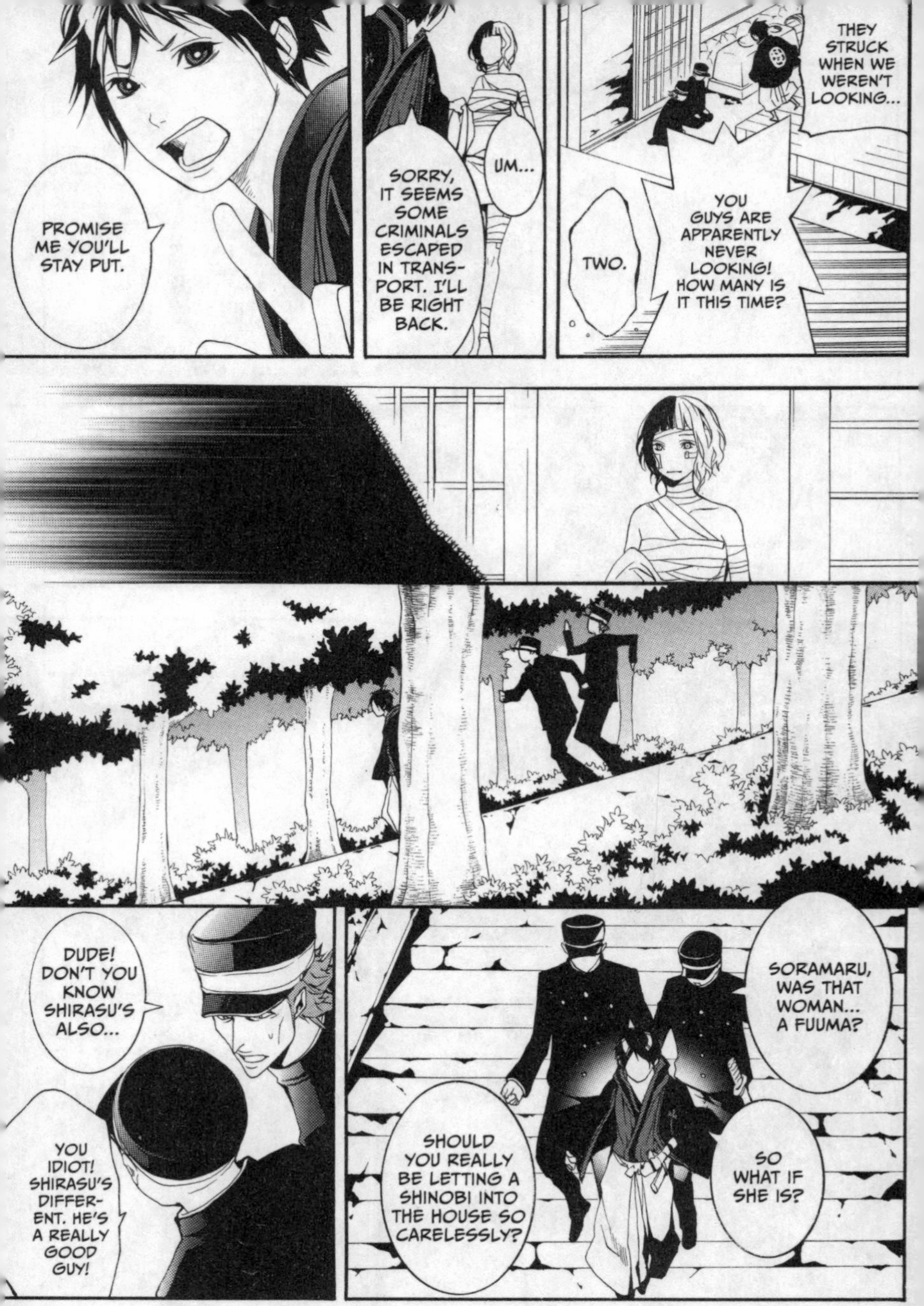
THEY STRUCK WHEN WE WEREN'T LOOKING...
YOU GUYS ARE APPARENTLY NEVER LOOKING! HOW MANY IS IT THIS TIME?
TWO.
UM...
SORRY, IT SEEMS SOME CRIMINALS ESCAPED IN TRANS-PORT. I'LL BE RIGHT BACK.
PROMISE ME YOU'LL STAY PUT.
SORAMARU, WAS THAT WOMAN... A FUUMA?
SO WHAT IF SHE IS?
SHOULD YOU REALLY BE LETTING A SHINOBI INTO THE HOUSE SO CARELESSLY?
DUDE! DON'T YOU KNOW SHIRASU'S ALSO...
YOU IDIOT! SHIRASU'S DIFFER-ENT. HE'S A REALLY GOOD GUY!

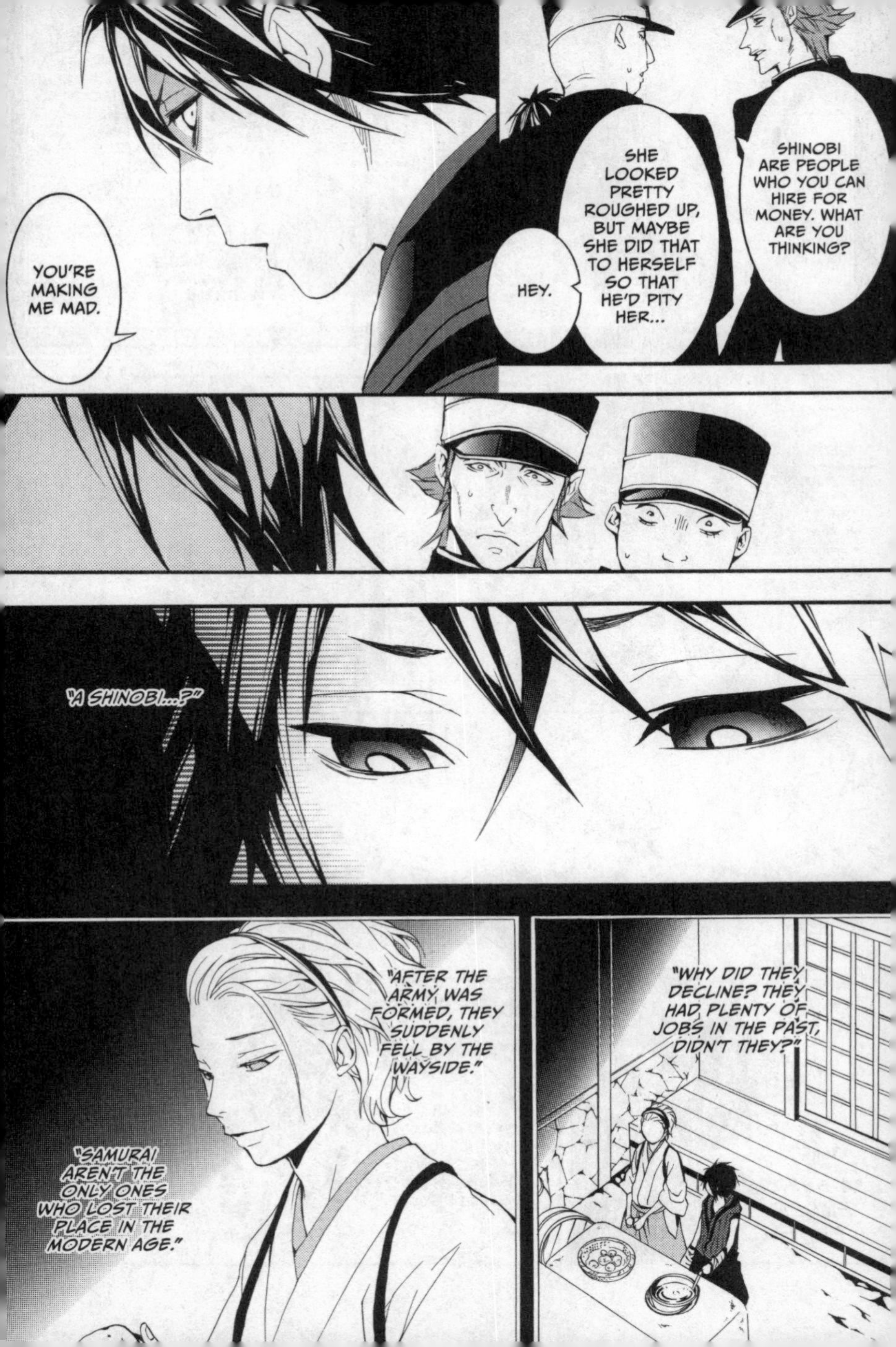
SHINOBI ARE PEOPLE WHO YOU CAN HIRE FOR MONEY. WHAT ARE YOU THINKING?
SHE LOOKED PRETTY ROUGHED UP, BUT MAYBE SHE DID THAT TO HERSELF SO THAT HE'D PITY HER...
HEY.
YOU'RE MAKING ME MAD.
"A SHINOBI...?"
"WHY DID THEY DECLINE? THEY HAD PLENTY OF JOBS IN THE PAST, DIDN'T THEY?"
"AFTER THE ARMY WAS FORMED, THEY SUDDENLY FELL BY THE WAYSIDE."
"SAMURAI AREN'T THE ONLY ONES WHO LOST THEIR PLACE IN THE MODERN AGE."

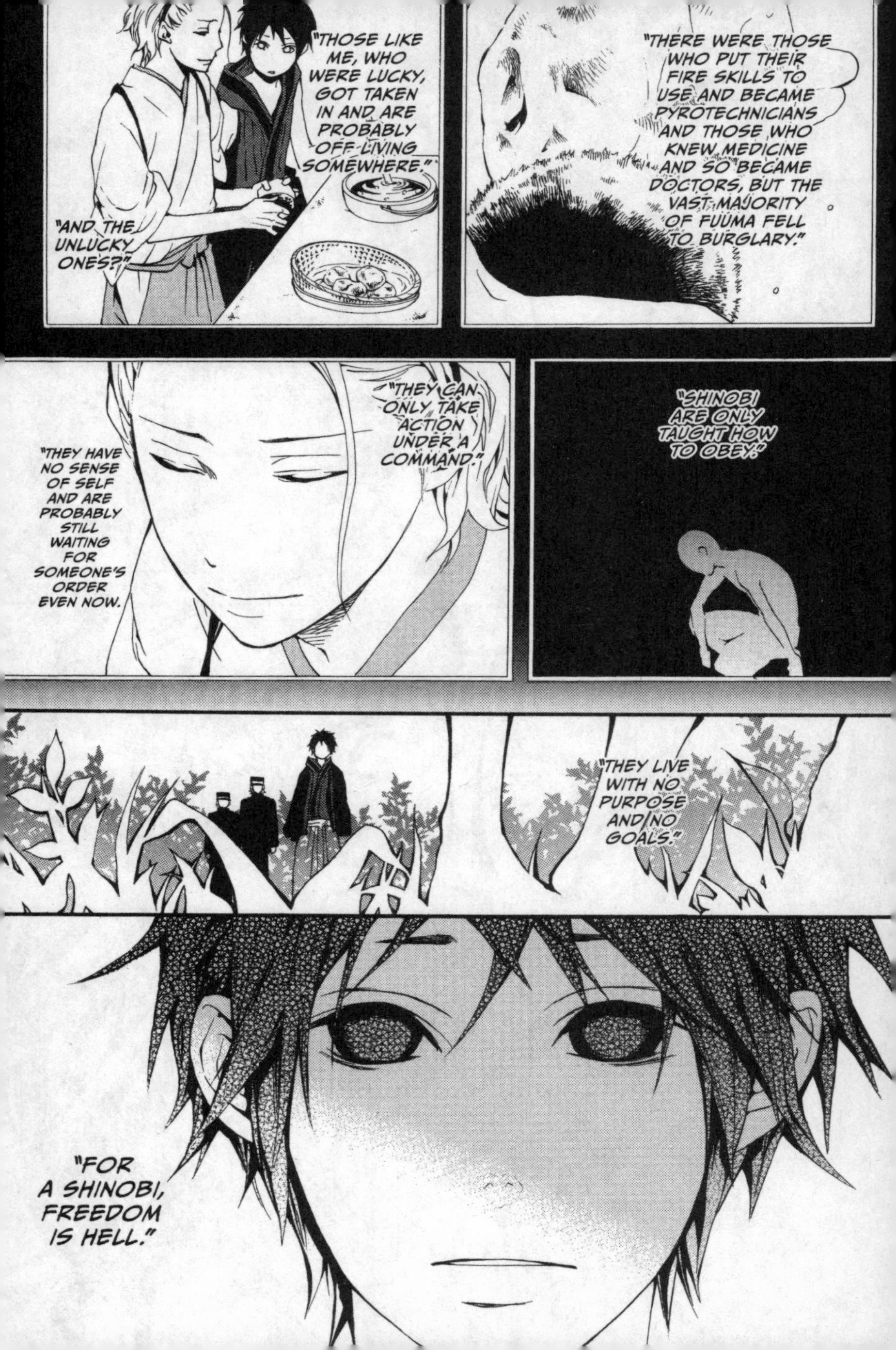
"THERE WERE THOSE WHO PUT THEIR FIRE SKILLS TO USE AND BECAME PYROTECHNICIANS AND THOSE WHO KNEW MEDICINE AND SO BECAME DOCTORS, BUT THE VAST MAJORITY OF FUUMA FELL TO BURGLARY."
"THOSE LIKE ME, WHO WERE LUCKY, GOT TAKEN IN AND ARE PROBABLY OFF LIVING SOMEWHERE."
"AND THE UNLUCKY ONES?"
"SHINOBI ARE ONLY TAUGHT HOW TO OBEY."
"THEY CAN ONLY TAKE ACTION UNDER A COMMAND."
"THEY HAVE NO SENSE OF SELF AND ARE PROBABLY STILL WAITING FOR SOMEONE'S ORDER EVEN NOW.
"THEY LIVE WITH NO PURPOSE AND NO GOALS."
"FOR A SHINOBI, FREEDOM IS HELL."

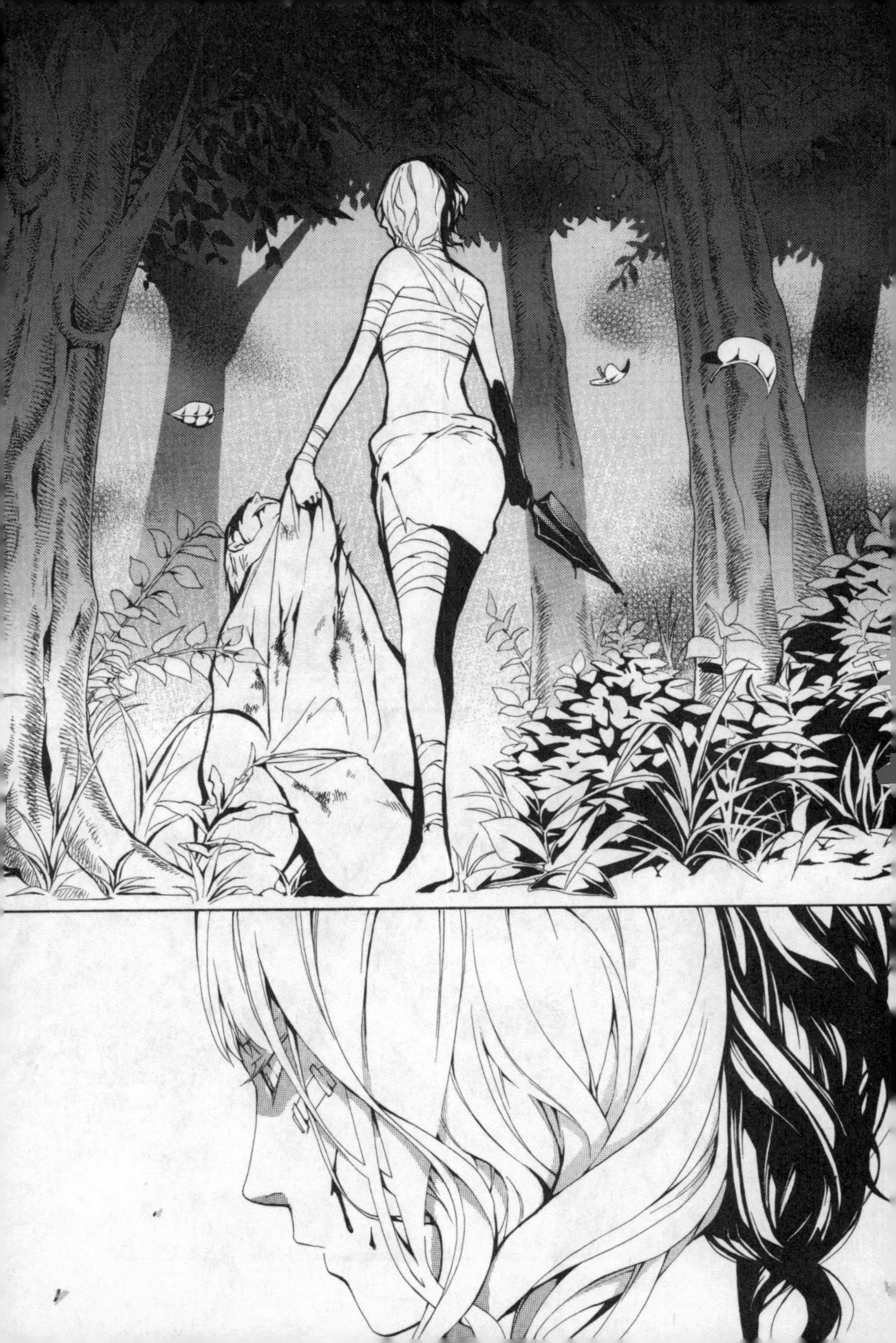

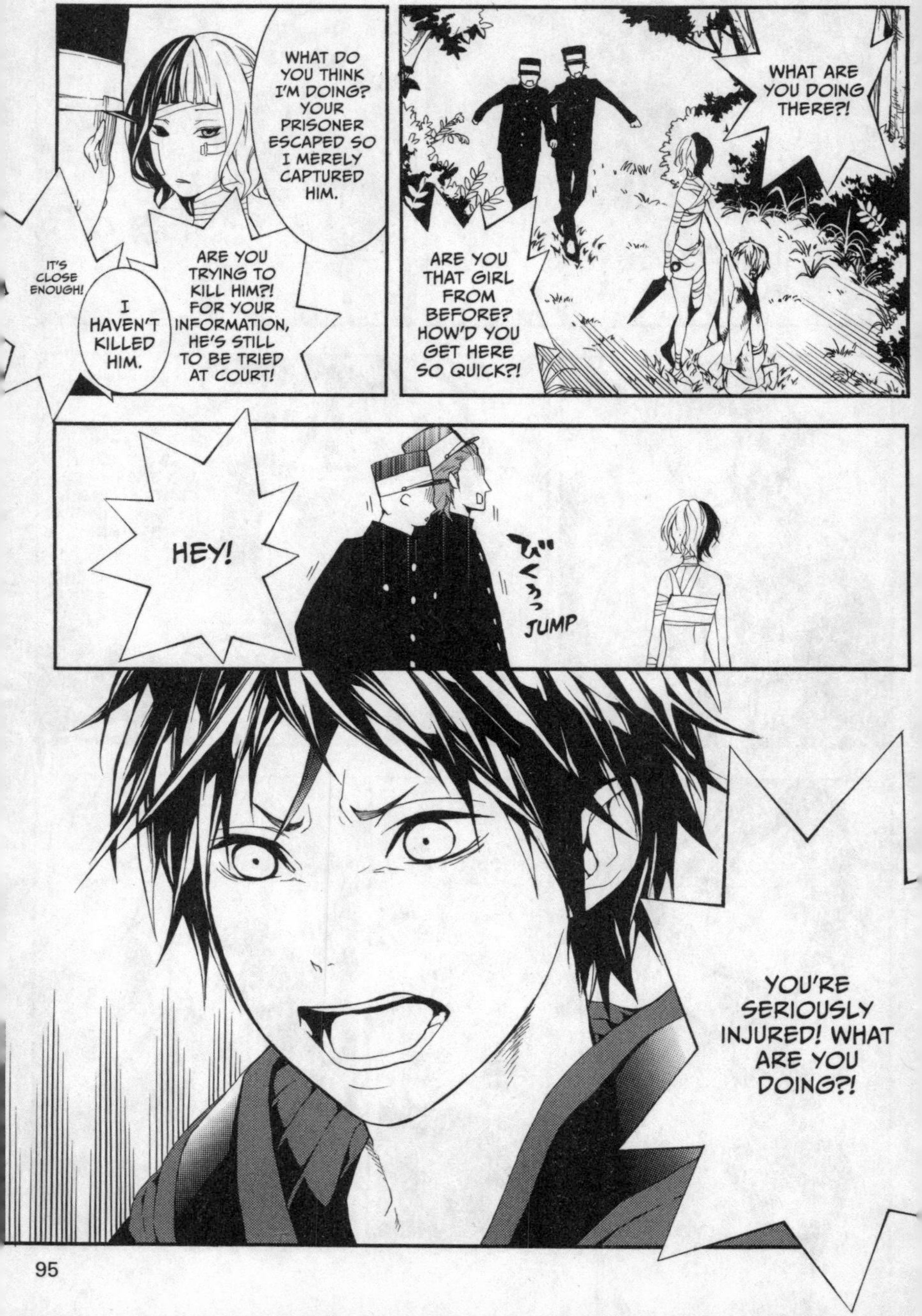
WHAT ARE YOU DOING THERE?!
ARE YOU THAT GIRL FROM BEFORE? HOW'D YOU GET HERE SO QUICK?!
WHAT DO YOU THINK I'M DOING? YOUR PRISONER ESCAPED SO I MERELY CAPTURED HIM.
ARE YOU TRYING TO KILL HIM?! FOR YOUR INFORMATION, HE'S STILL TO BE TRIED AT COURT!
I HAVEN'T KILLED HIM.
IT'S CLOSE ENOUGH!
びくっ
JUMP
HEY!
YOU'RE SERIOUSLY INJURED! WHAT ARE YOU DOING?!

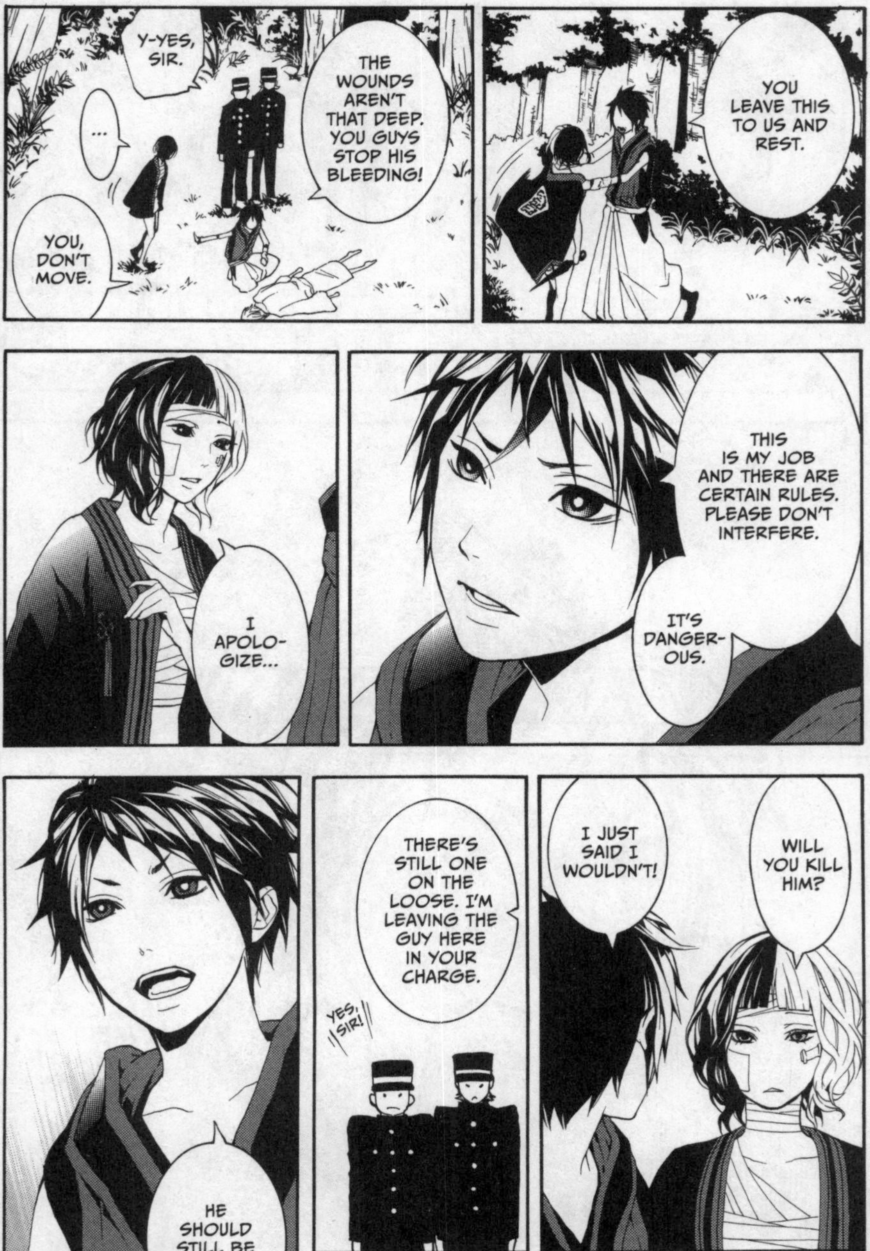
YOU LEAVE THIS TO US AND REST.
THE WOUNDS AREN'T THAT DEEP. YOU GUYS STOP HIS BLEEDING!
Y-YES, SIR.
...
YOU, DON'T MOVE.
THIS IS MY JOB AND THERE ARE CERTAIN RULES. PLEASE DON'T INTERFERE.
IT'S DANGER-OUS.
I APOLO-GIZE...
WILL YOU KILL HIM?
I JUST SAID I WOULDN'T!
THERE'S STILL ONE ON THE LOOSE. I'M LEAVING THE GUY HERE IN YOUR CHARGE.
YES, SIR!
HE SHOULD STILL BE NEARBY.

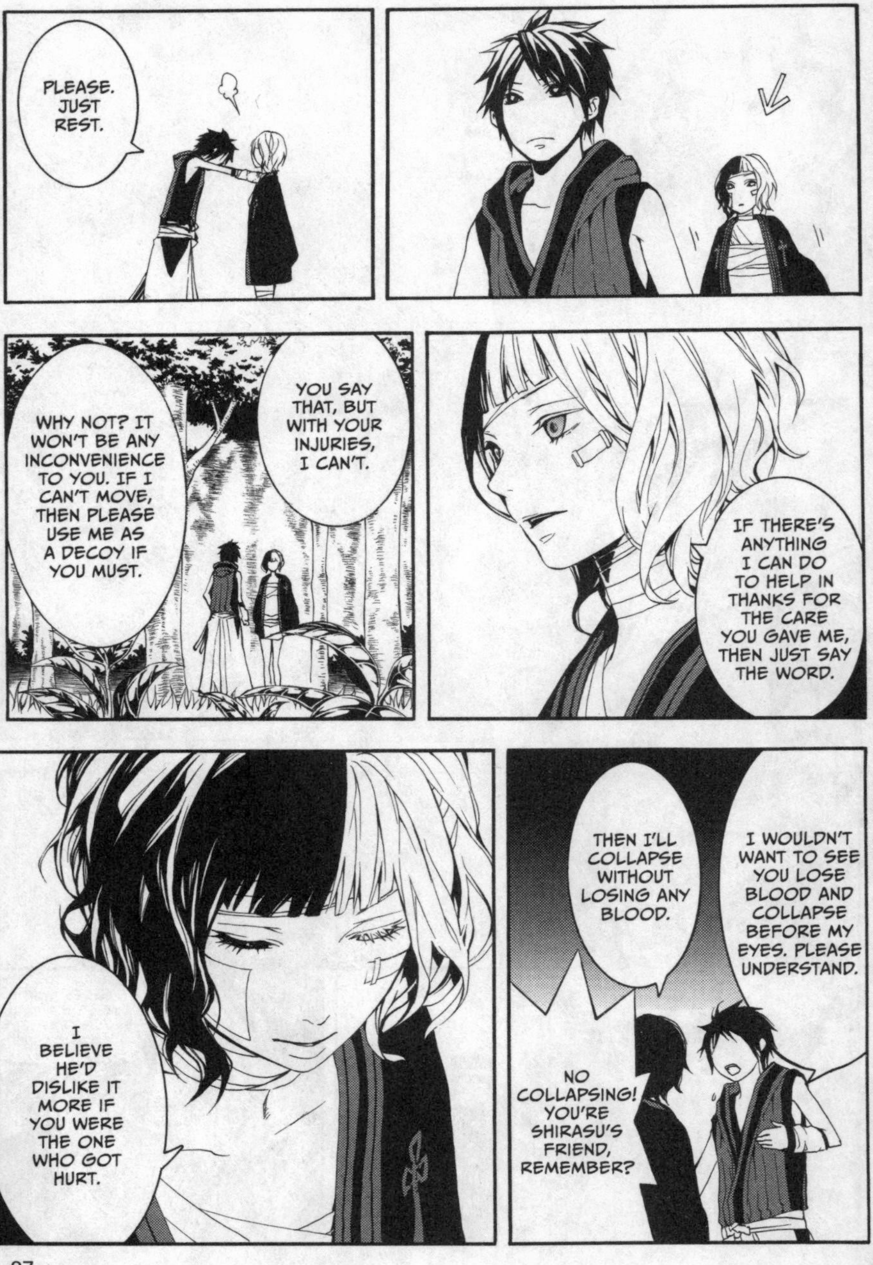
PLEASE. JUST REST.
IF THERE'S ANYTHING I CAN DO TO HELP IN THANKS FOR THE CARE YOU GAVE ME, THEN JUST SAY THE WORD.
YOU SAY THAT, BUT WITH YOUR INJURIES, I CAN'T.
WHY NOT? IT WON'T BE ANY INCONVENIENCE TO YOU. IF I CAN'T MOVE, THEN PLEASE USE ME AS A DECOY IF YOU MUST.
I WOULDN'T WANT TO SEE YOU LOSE BLOOD AND COLLAPSE BEFORE MY EYES. PLEASE UNDERSTAND.
THEN I'LL COLLAPSE WITHOUT LOSING ANY BLOOD.
NO COLLAPSING! YOU'RE SHIRASU'S FRIEND, REMEMBER?
I BELIEVE HE'D DISLIKE IT MORE IF YOU WERE THE ONE WHO GOT HURT.

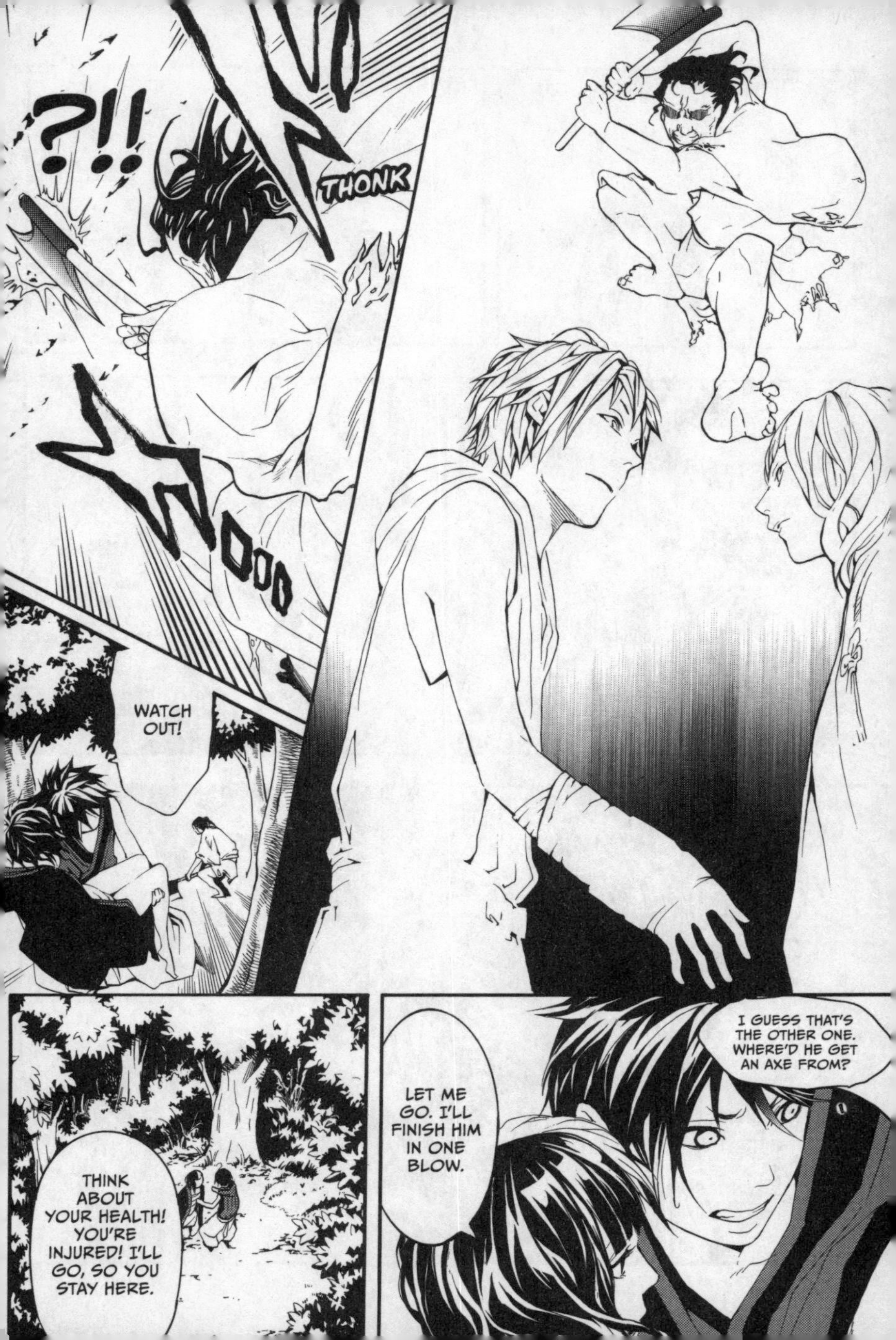
?!!
THONK
WOOO
WATCH OUT!
I GUESS THAT'S THE OTHER ONE. WHERE'D HE GET AN AXE FROM?
LET ME GO. I'LL FINISH HIM IN ONE BLOW.
THINK ABOUT YOUR HEALTH! YOU'RE INJURED! I'LL GO, SO YOU STAY HERE.

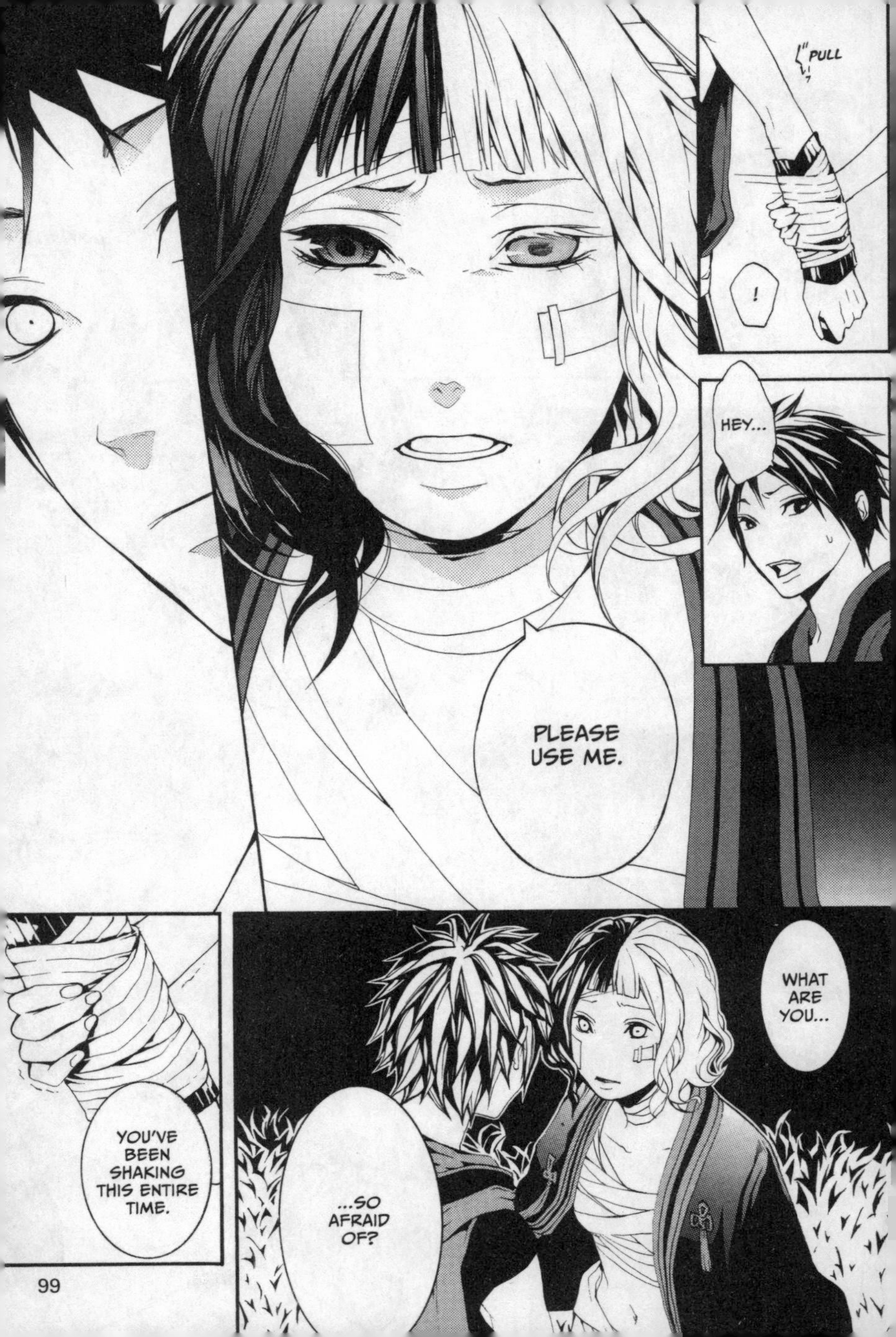
PULL
!
HEY...
PLEASE USE ME.
WHAT ARE YOU...
...SO AFRAID OF?
YOU'VE BEEN SHAKING THIS ENTIRE TIME.

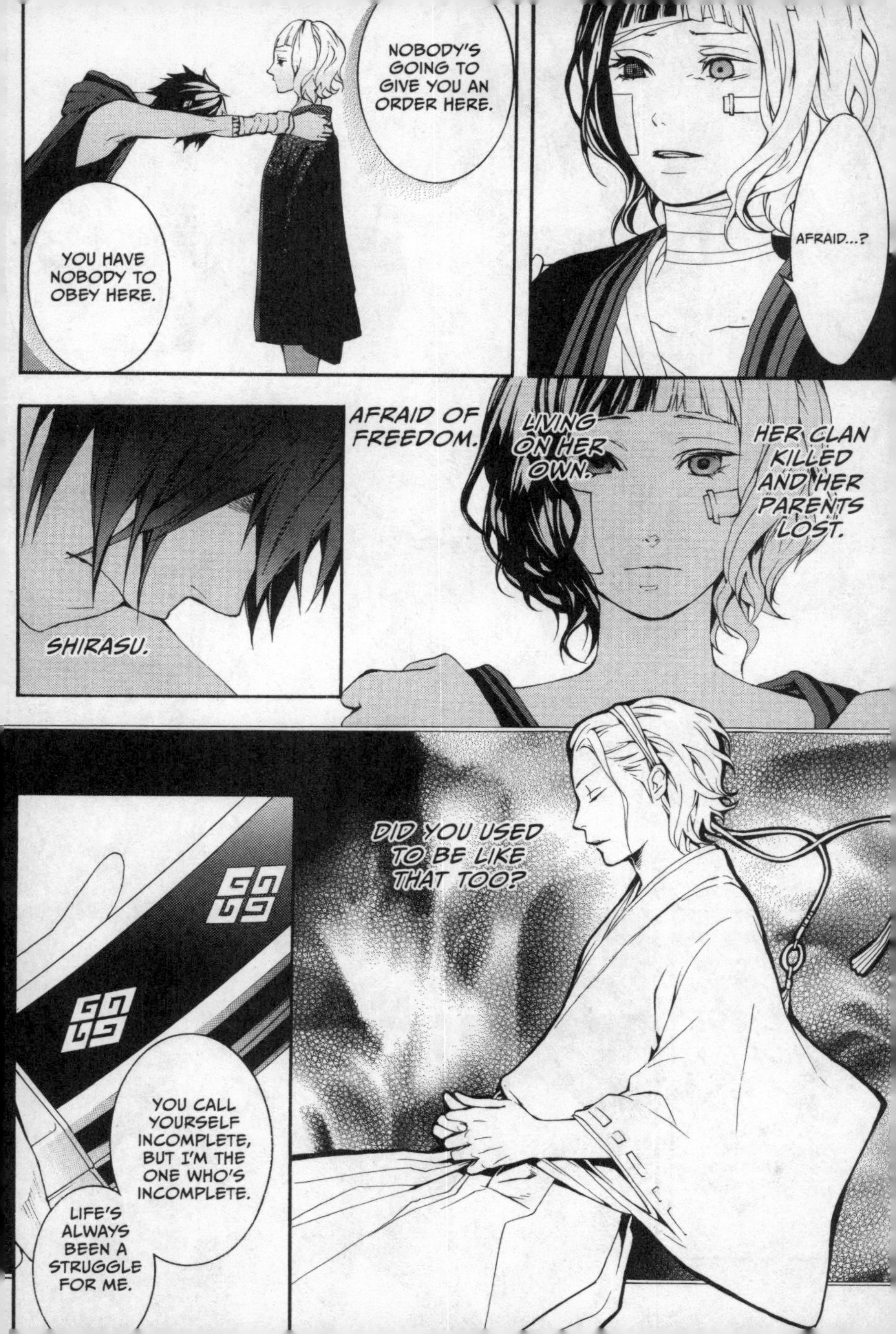
AFRAID...?
NOBODY'S GOING TO GIVE YOU AN ORDER HERE.
YOU HAVE NOBODY TO OBEY HERE.
HER CLAN KILLED AND HER PARENTS LOST.
LIVING ON HER OWN.
AFRAID OF FREEDOM.
SHIRASU.
DID YOU USED TO BE LIKE THAT TOO?
YOU CALL YOURSELF INCOMPLETE, BUT I'M THE ONE WHO'S INCOMPLETE.
LIFE'S ALWAYS BEEN A STRUGGLE FOR ME.

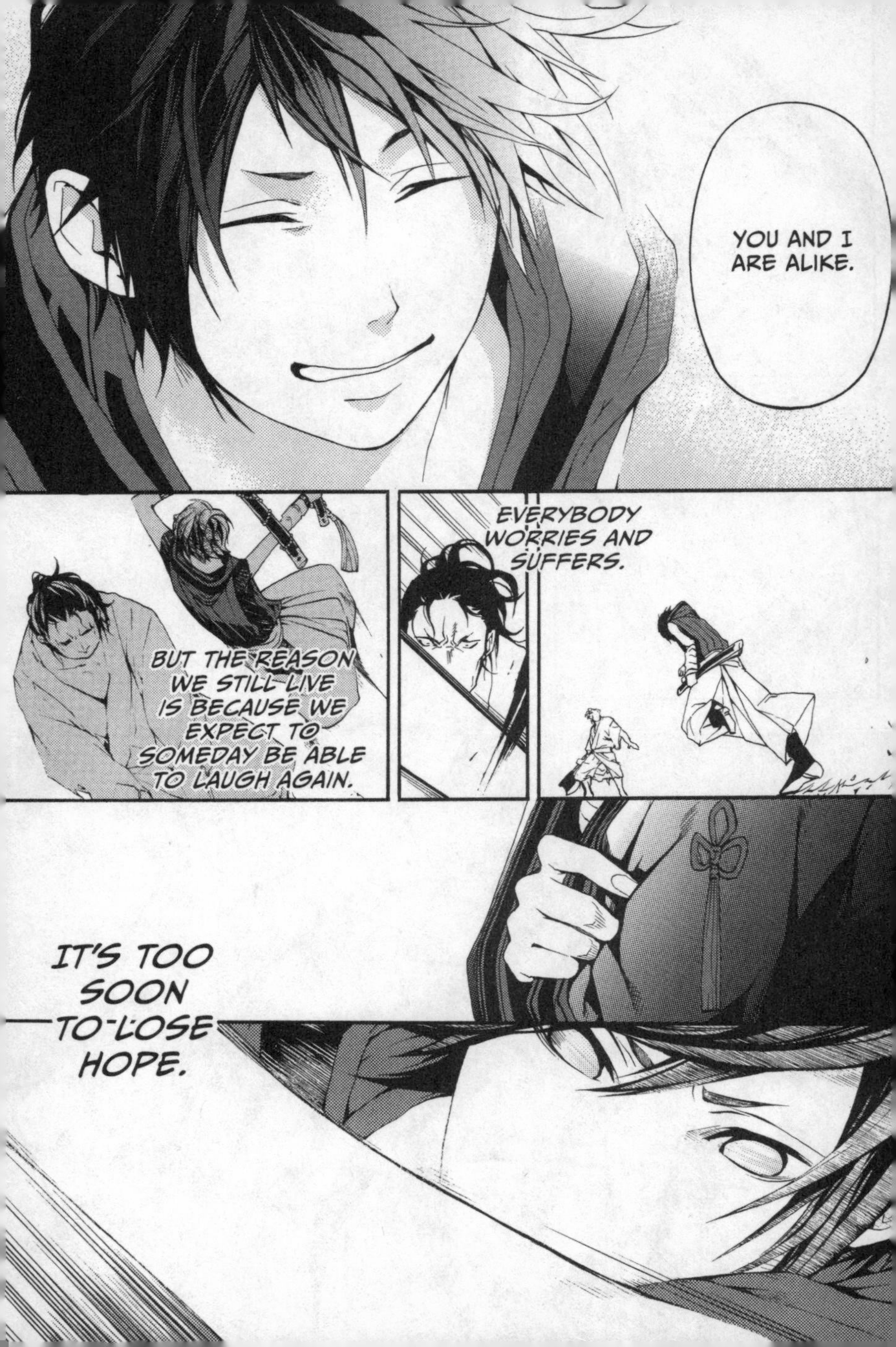
YOU AND I ARE ALIKE.
EVERYBODY WORRIES AND SUFFERS.
BUT THE REASON WE STILL LIVE IS BECAUSE WE EXPECT TO SOMEDAY BE ABLE TO LAUGH AGAIN.
IT'S TOO SOON TO LOSE HOPE.

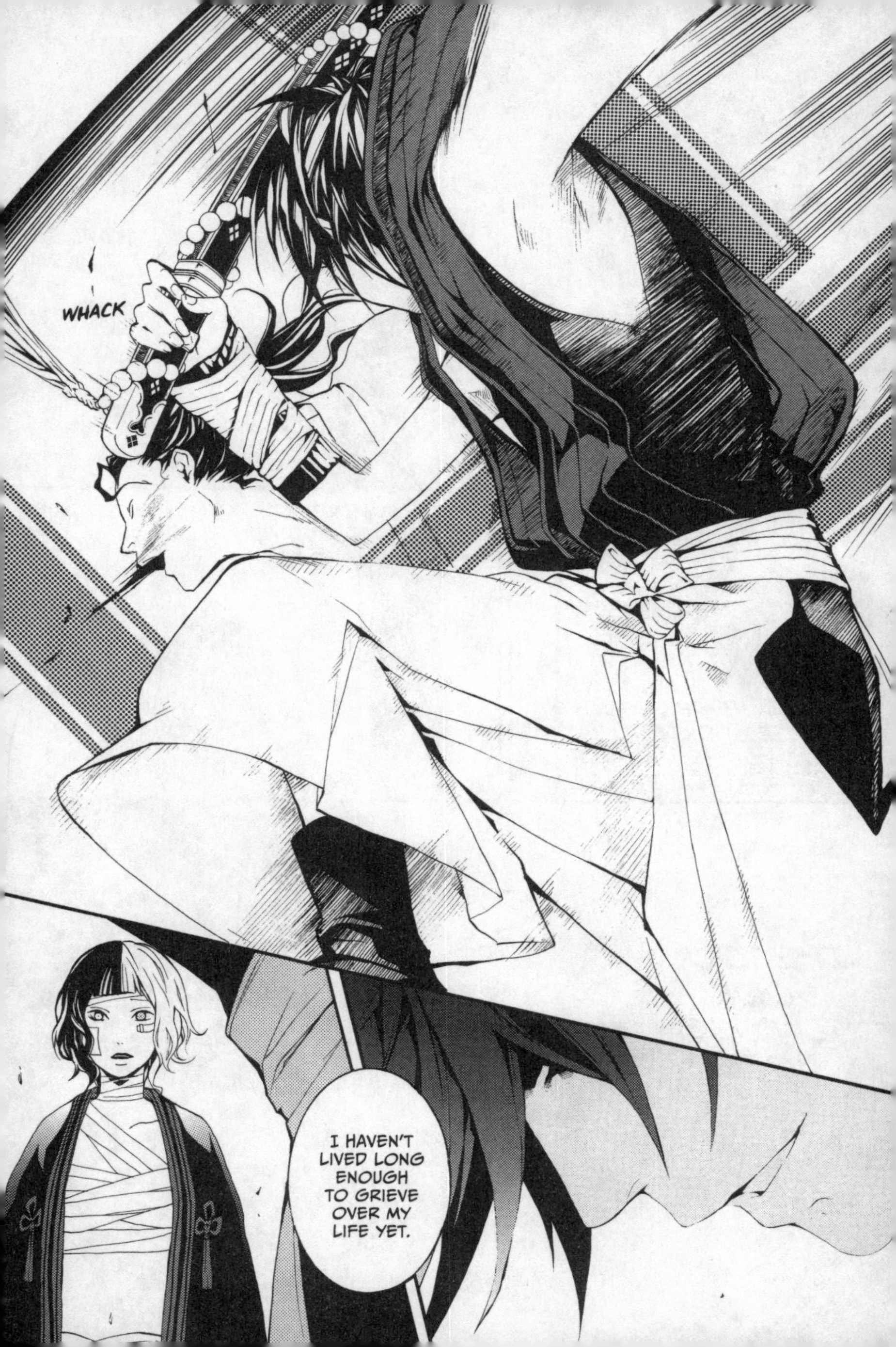
WHACK
I HAVEN'T LIVED LONG ENOUGH TO GRIEVE OVER MY LIFE YET.

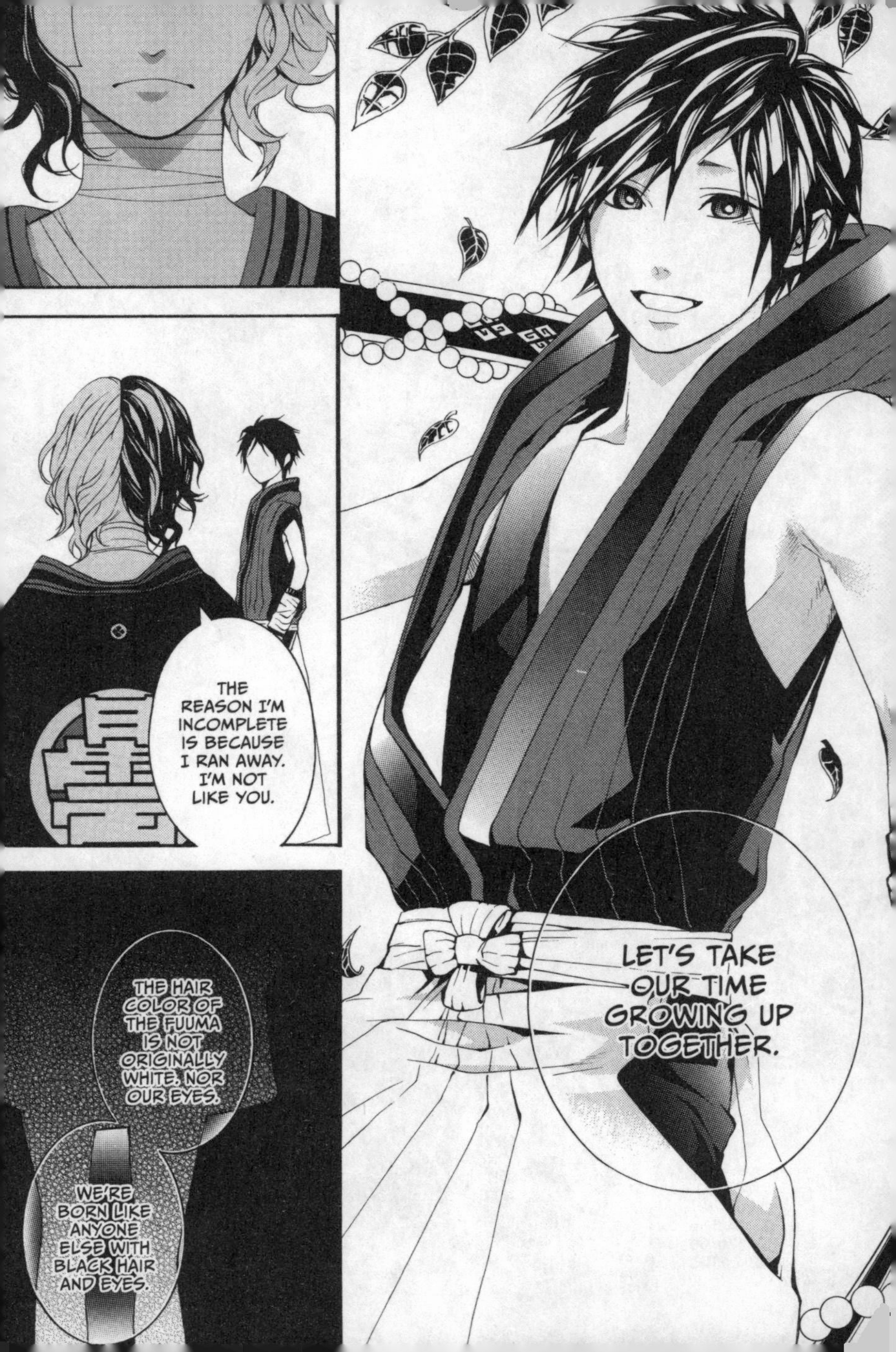
LET'S TAKE OUR TIME GROWING UP TOGETHER.
THE REASON I'M INCOMPLETE IS BECAUSE I RAN AWAY. I'M NOT LIKE YOU.
THE HAIR COLOR OF THE FUUMA IS NOT ORIGINALLY WHITE, NOR OUR EYES.
WE'RE BORN LIKE ANYONE ELSE WITH BLACK HAIR AND EYES.

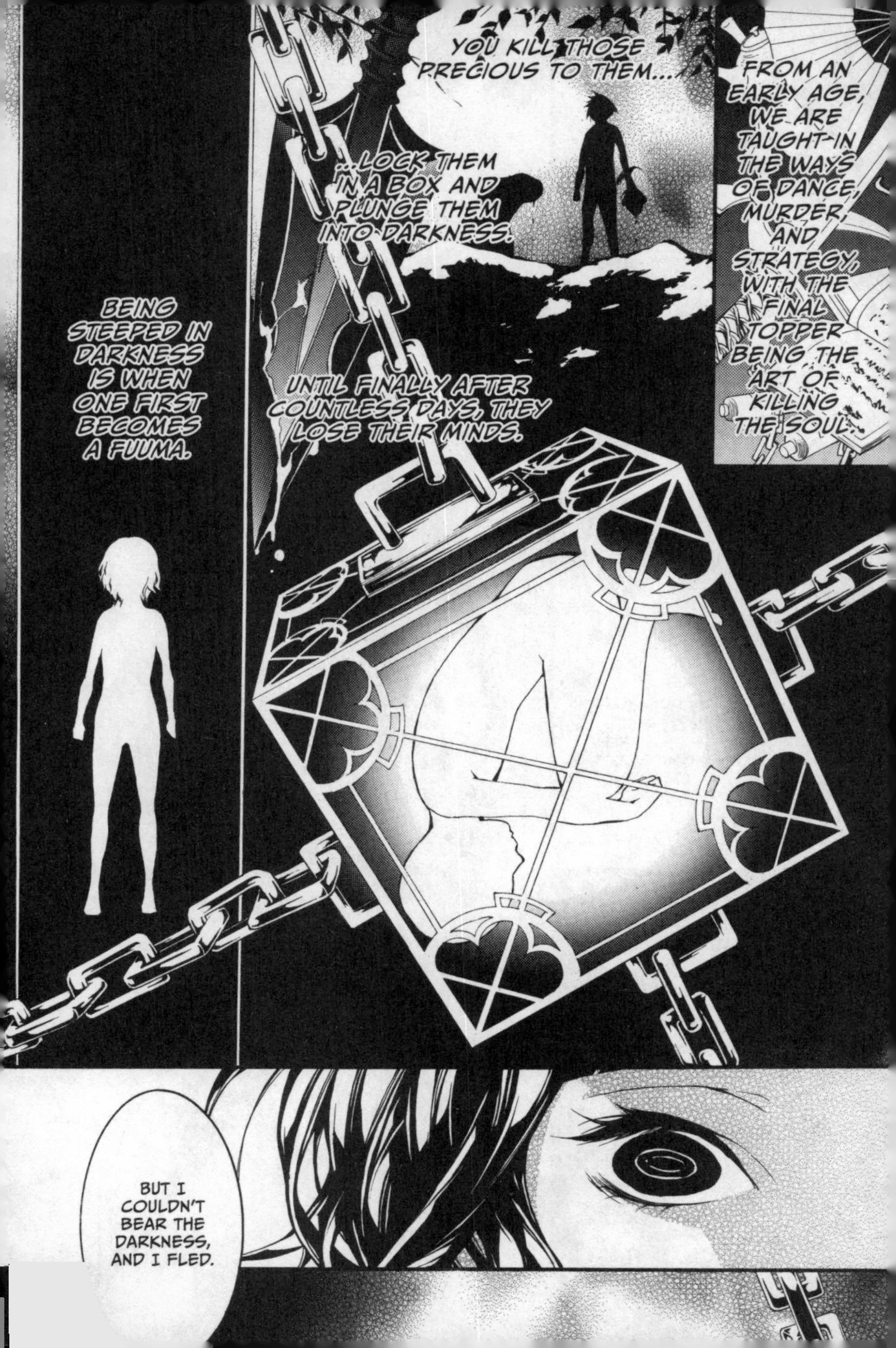
FROM AN EARLY AGE, WE ARE TAUGHT IN THE WAYS OF DANCE, MURDER, AND STRATEGY, WITH THE FINAL TOPPER BEING THE ART OF KILLING THE SOUL.
YOU KILL THOSE PRECIOUS TO THEM...
...LOCK THEM IN A BOX AND PLUNGE THEM INTO DARKNESS.
UNTIL FINALLY AFTER COUNTLESS DAYS, THEY LOSE THEIR MINDS.
BEING STEEPED IN DARKNESS IS WHEN ONE FIRST BECOMES A FUUMA.
BUT I COULDN'T BEAR THE DARKNESS, AND I FLED.

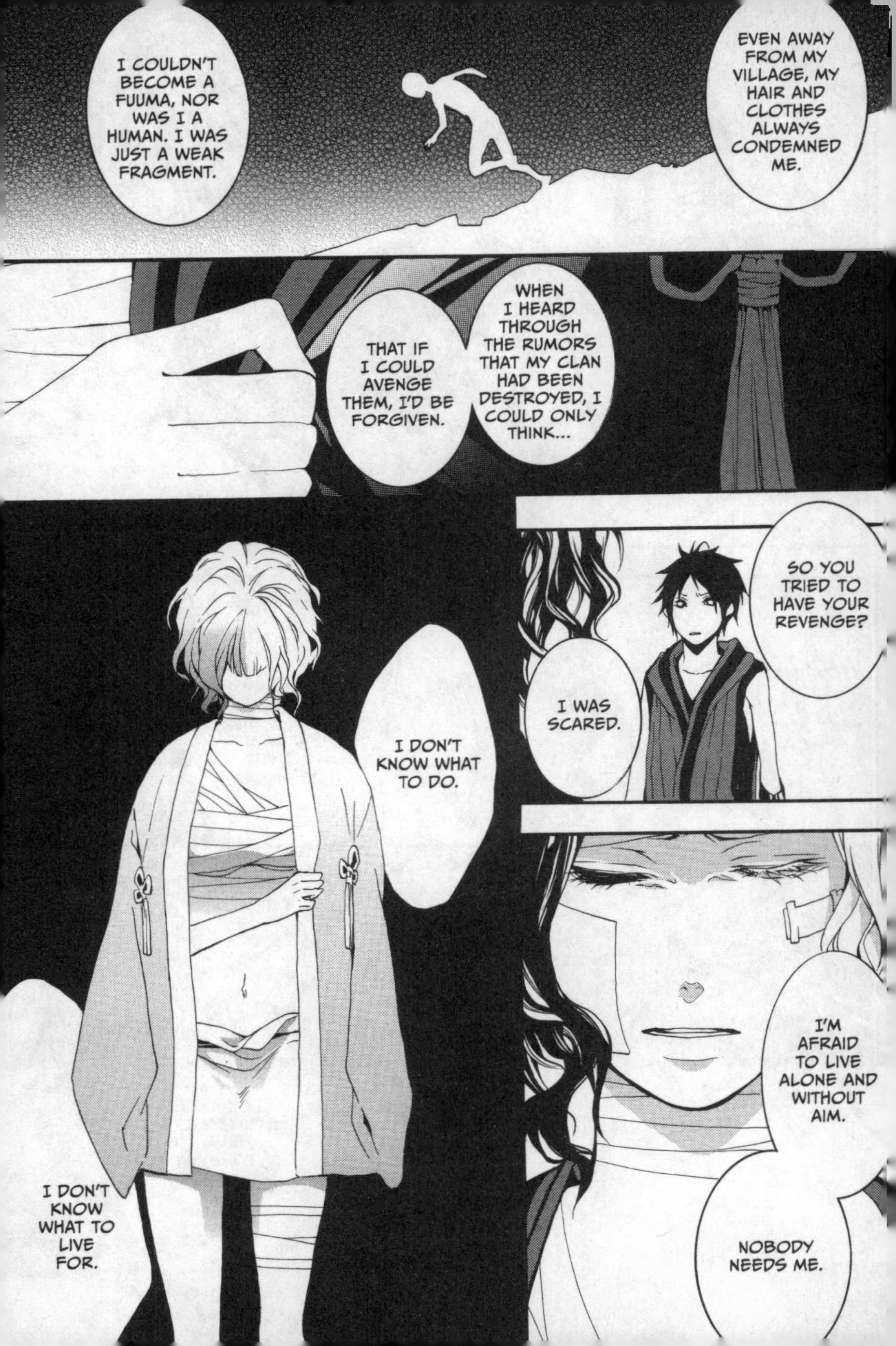
EVEN AWAY FROM MY VILLAGE, MY HAIR AND CLOTHES ALWAYS CONDEMNED ME.
I COULDN'T BECOME A FUUMA, NOR WAS I A HUMAN. I WAS JUST A WEAK FRAGMENT.
WHEN I HEARD THROUGH THE RUMORS THAT MY CLAN HAD BEEN DESTROYED, I COULD ONLY THINK...
THAT IF I COULD AVENGE THEM, I'D BE FORGIVEN.
SO YOU TRIED TO HAVE YOUR REVENGE?
I WAS SCARED.
I'M AFRAID TO LIVE ALONE AND WITHOUT AIM.
NOBODY NEEDS ME.
I DON'T KNOW WHAT TO DO.
I DON'T KNOW WHAT TO LIVE FOR.

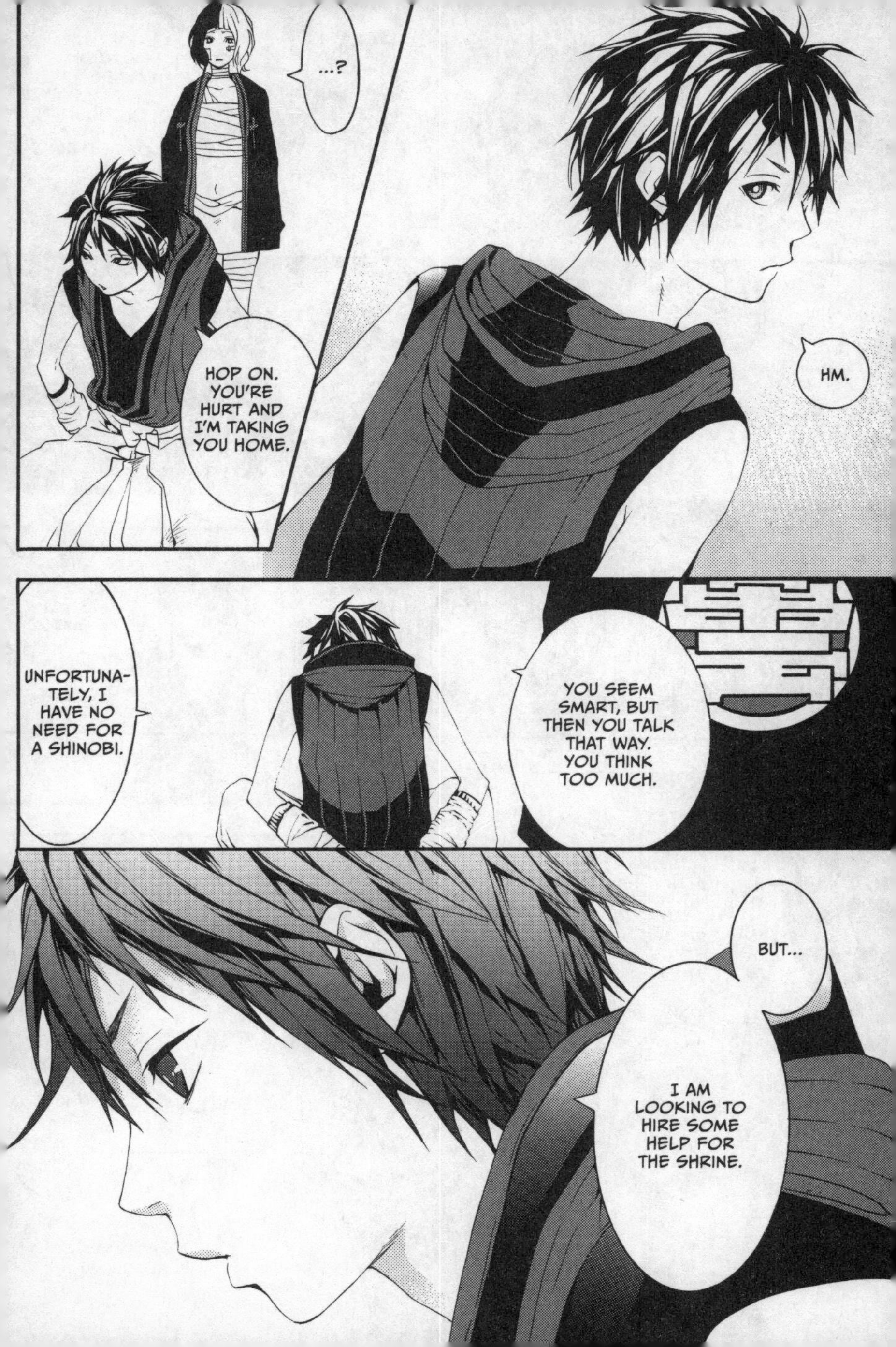

HM.
...?
HOP ON. YOU'RE HURT AND I'M TAKING YOU HOME.
YOU SEEM SMART, BUT THEN YOU TALK THAT WAY. YOU THINK TOO MUCH.
UNFORTUNA-TELY, I HAVE NO NEED FOR A SHINOBI.
BUT...
I AM LOOKING TO HIRE SOME HELP FOR THE SHRINE.

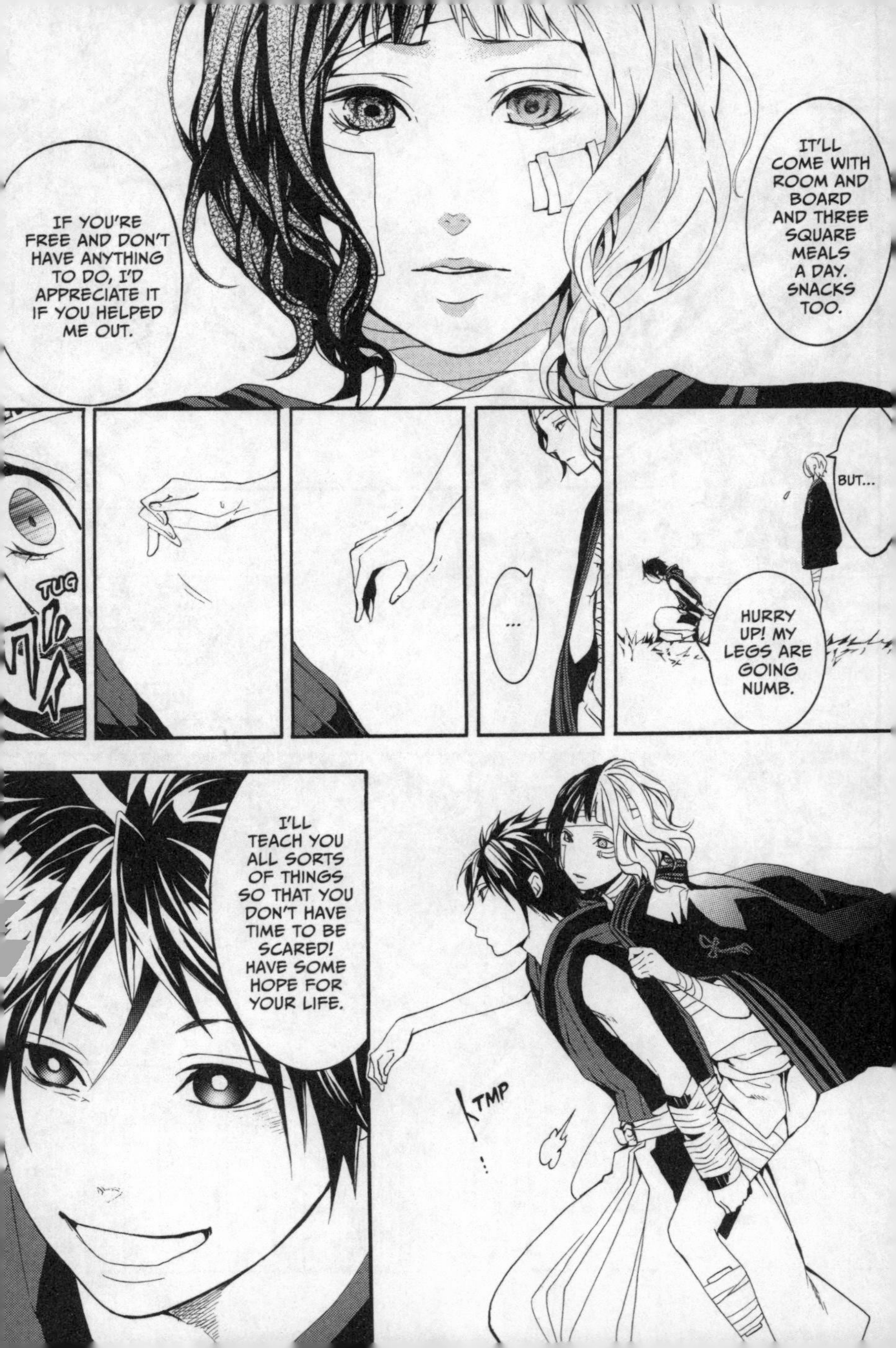

IT'LL COME WITH ROOM AND BOARD AND THREE SQUARE MEALS A DAY. SNACKS TOO.
IF YOU'RE FREE AND DON'T HAVE ANYTHING TO DO, I'D APPRECIATE IT IF YOU HELPED ME OUT.
BUT...
HURRY UP! MY LEGS ARE GOING NUMB.
...
TUG
I'LL TEACH YOU ALL SORTS OF THINGS SO THAT YOU DON'T HAVE TIME TO BE SCARED! HAVE SOME HOPE FOR YOUR LIFE.
TMP

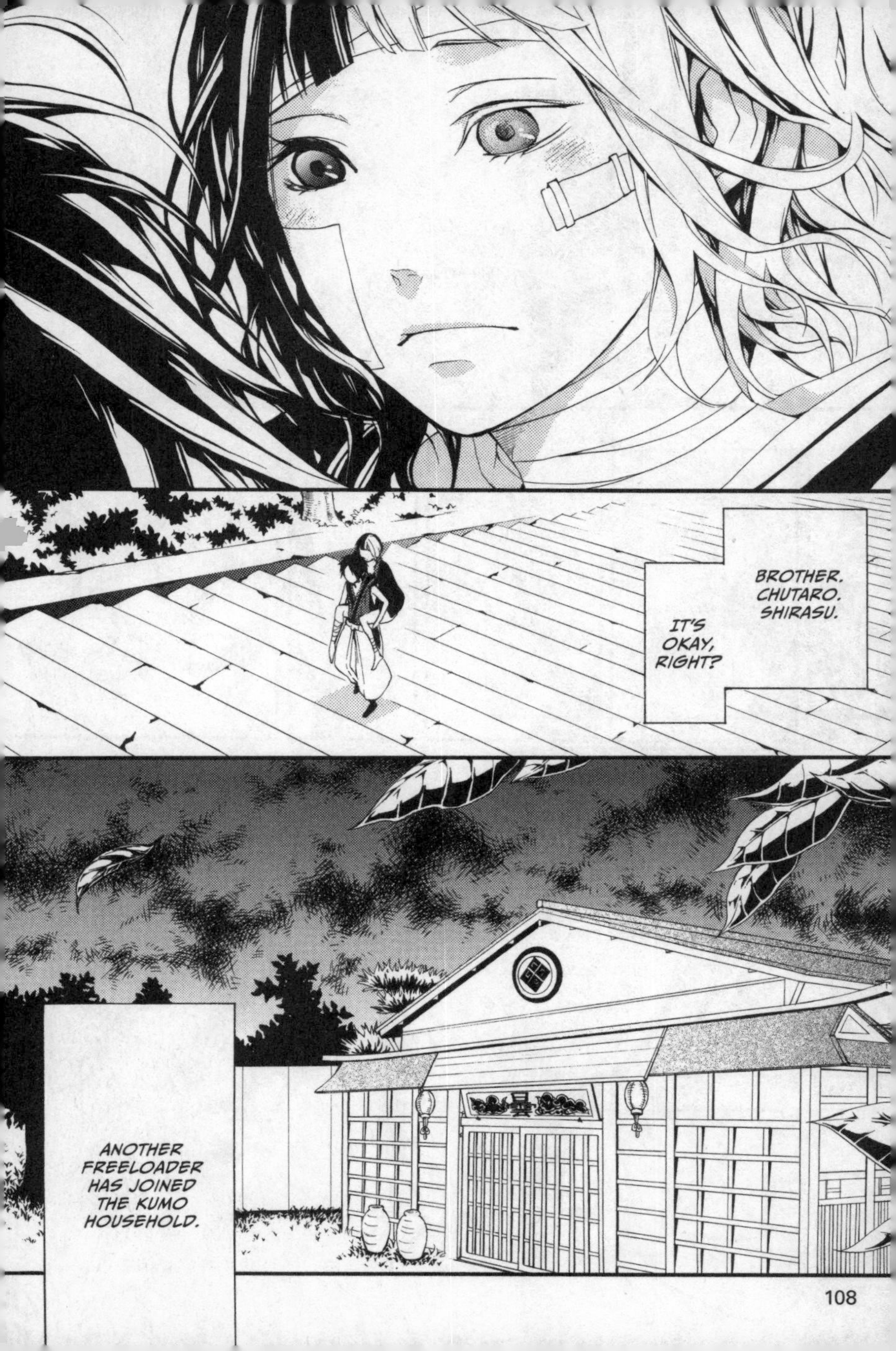
BROTHER. CHUTARO. SHIRASU.
IT'S OKAY, RIGHT?
ANOTHER FREELOADER HAS JOINED THE KUMO HOUSEHOLD.

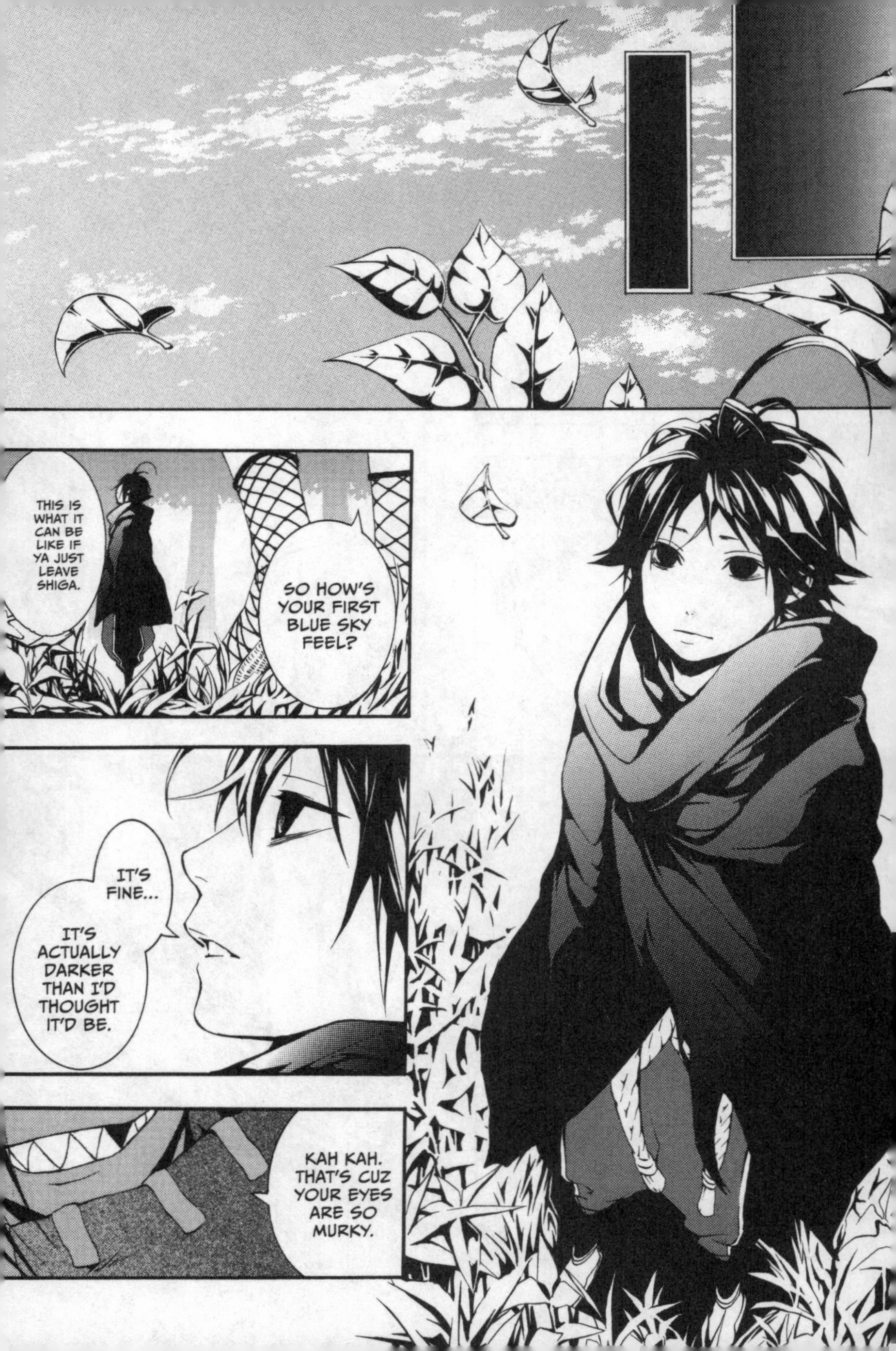
SO HOW'S YOUR FIRST BLUE SKY FEEL?
THIS IS WHAT IT CAN BE LIKE IF YA JUST LEAVE SHIGA.
IT'S FINE...
IT'S ACTUALLY DARKER THAN I'D THOUGHT IT'D BE.
KAH KAH. THAT'S CUZ YOUR EYES ARE SO MURKY.

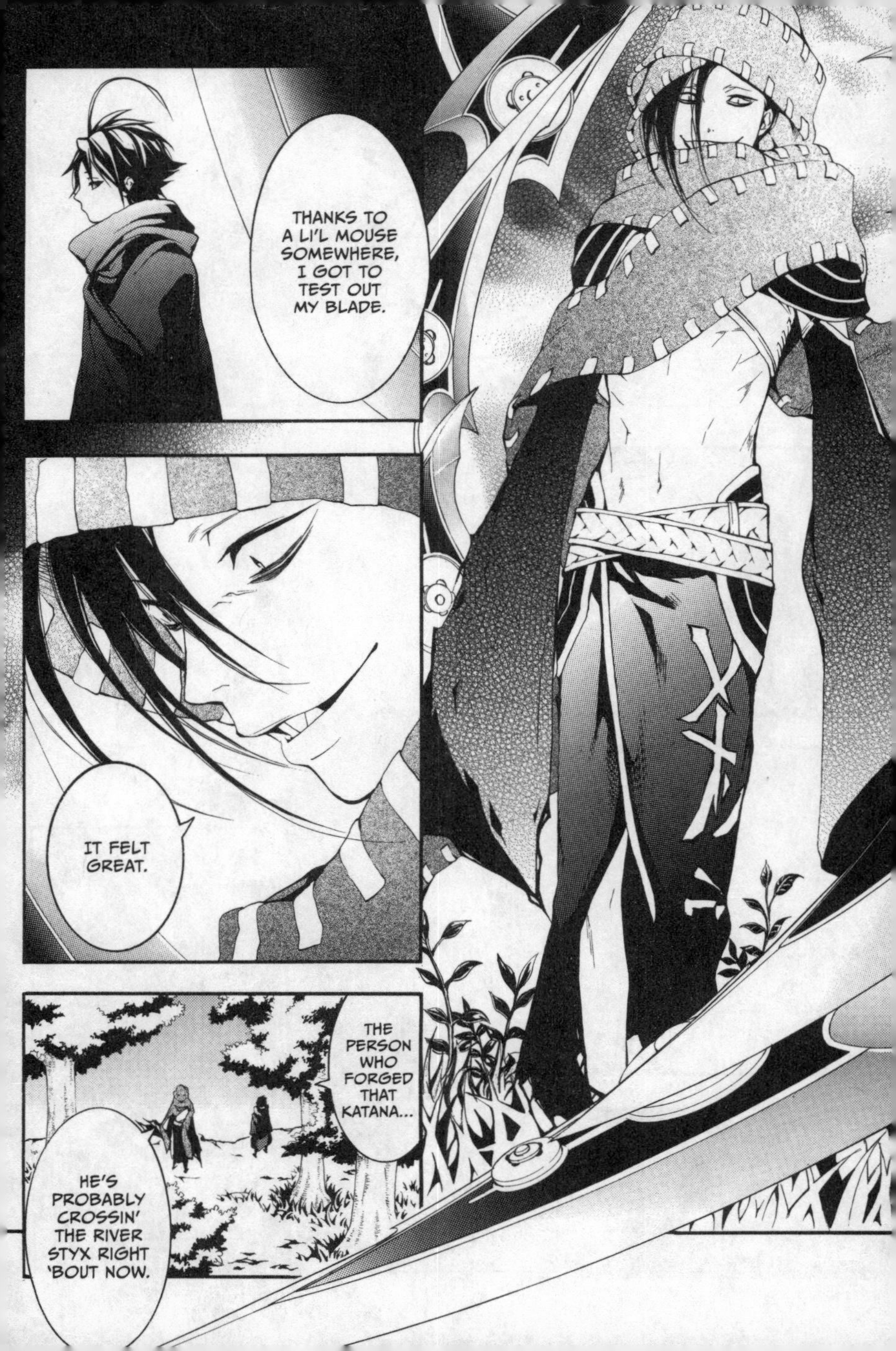
THANKS TO A LI'L MOUSE SOMEWHERE, I GOT TO TEST OUT MY BLADE.
IT FELT GREAT.
THE PERSON WHO FORGED THAT KATANA...
HE'S PROBABLY CROSSIN' THE RIVER STYX RIGHT 'BOUT NOW.

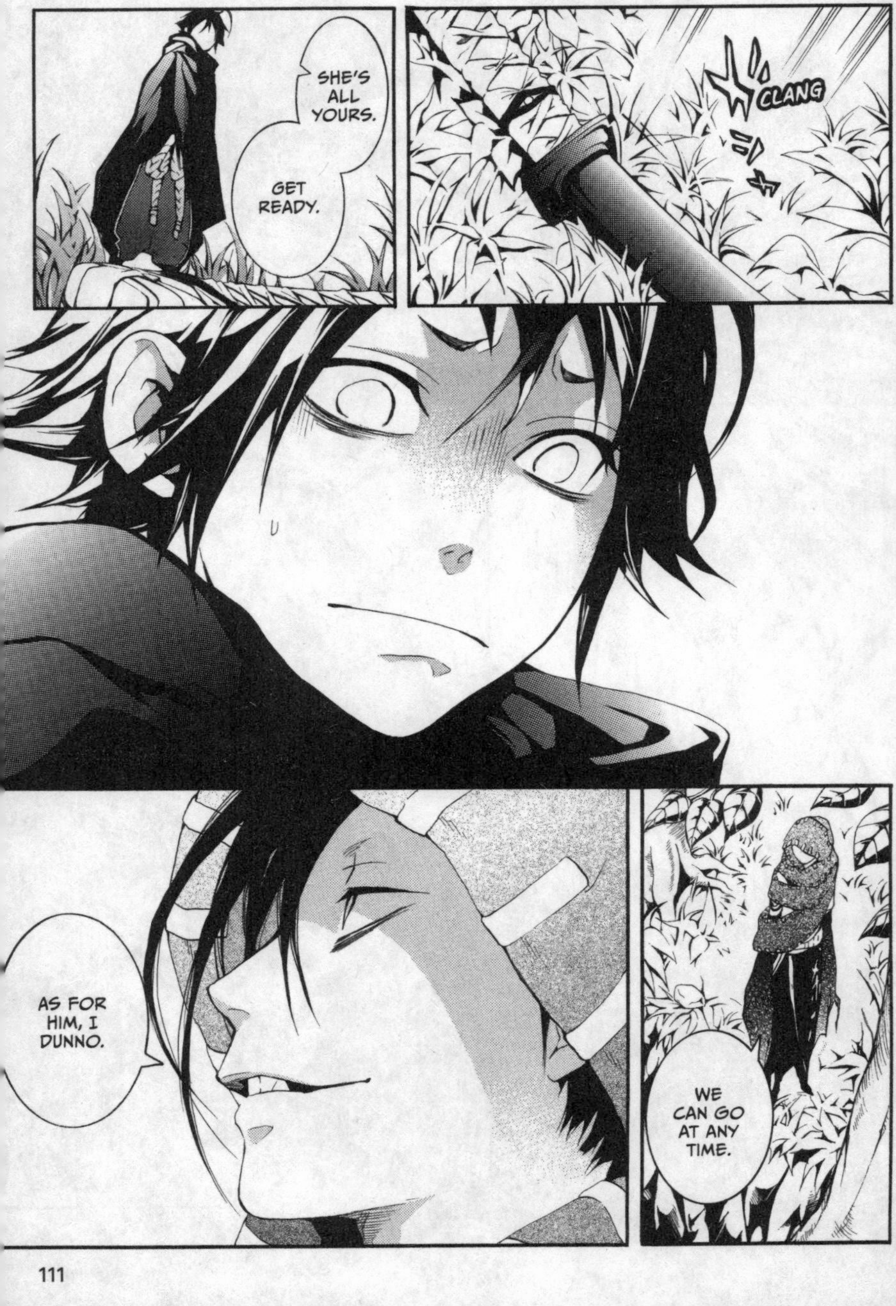
CLANG
SHE'S ALL YOURS.
GET READY.
WE CAN GO AT ANY TIME.
AS FOR HIM, I DUNNO.

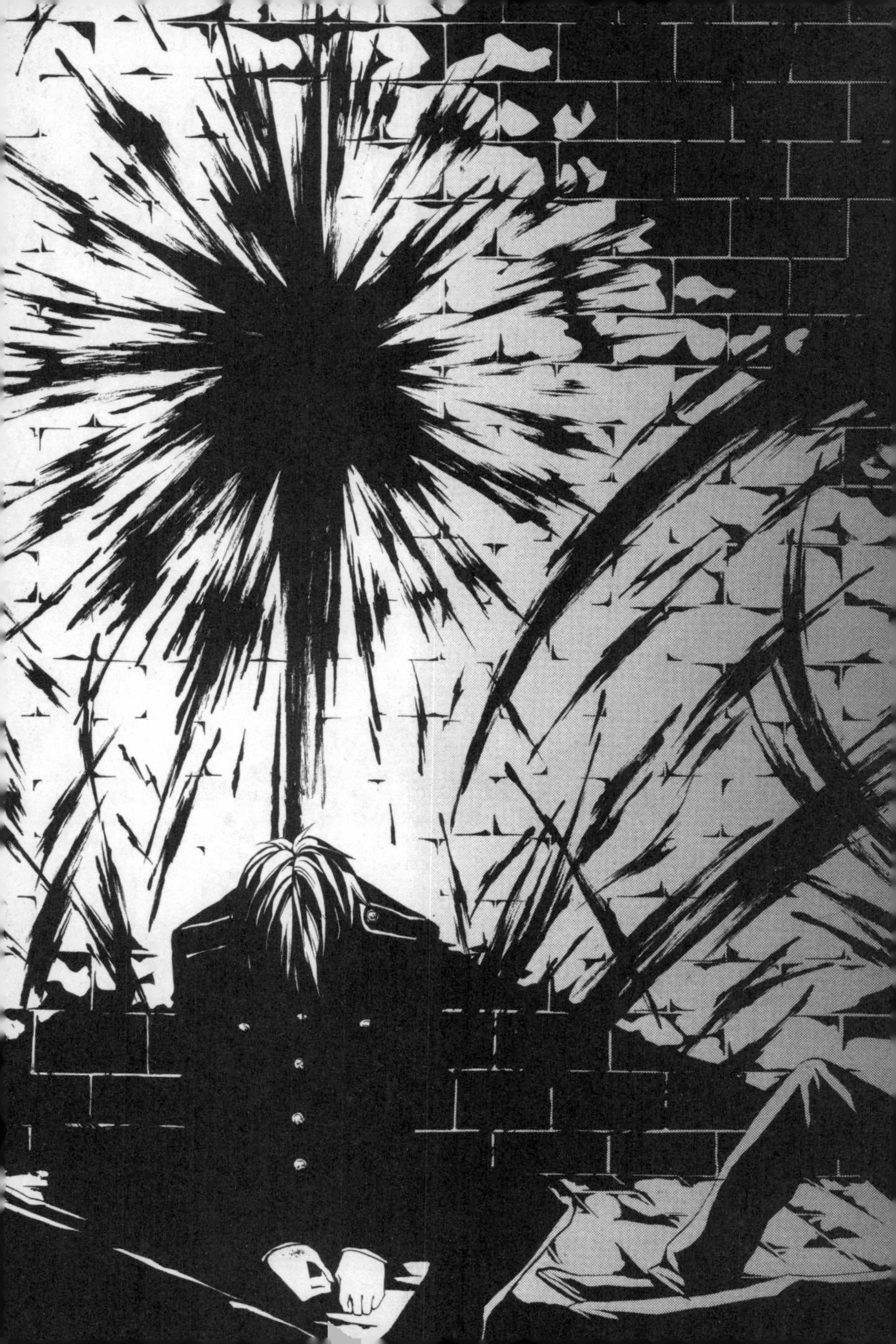

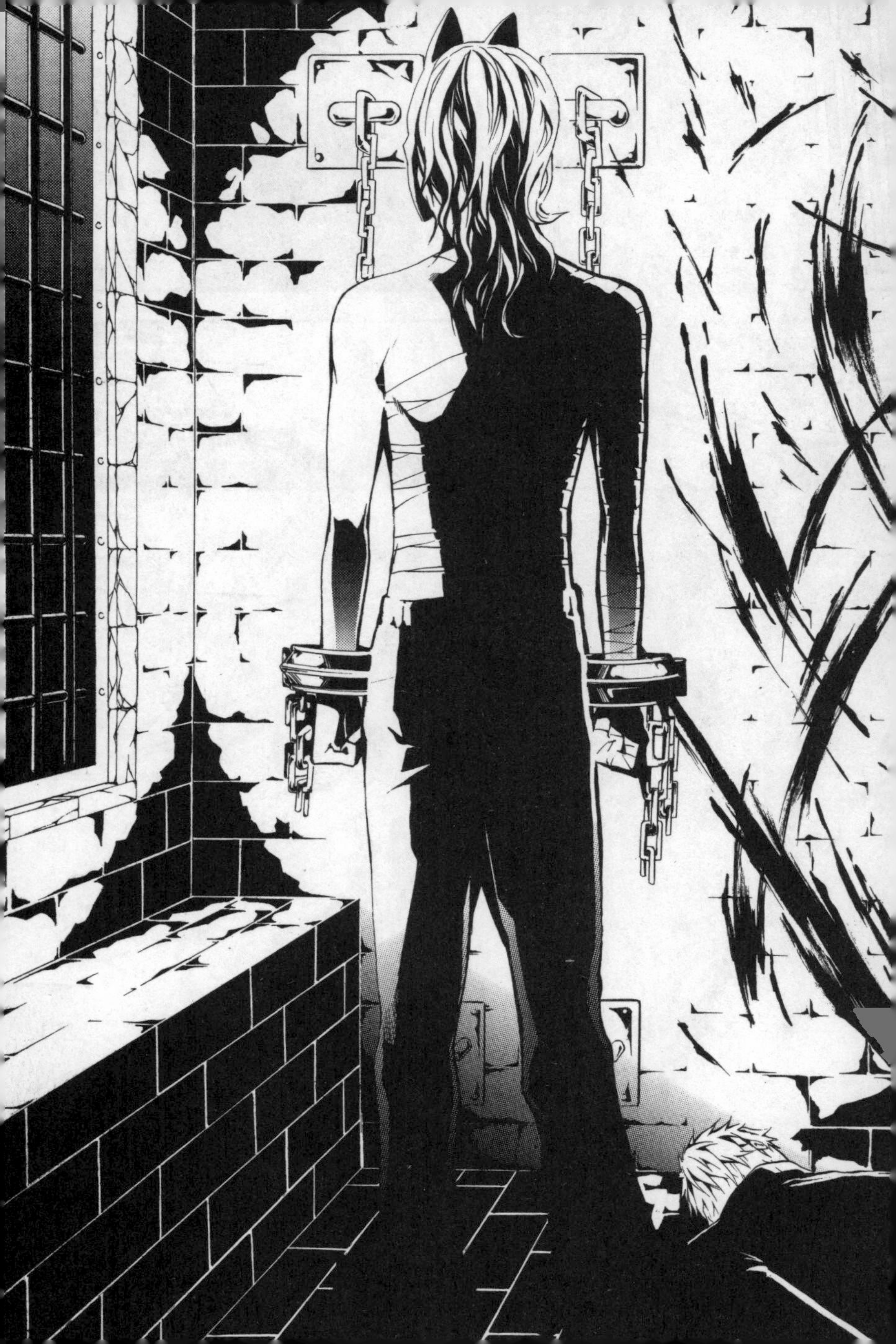

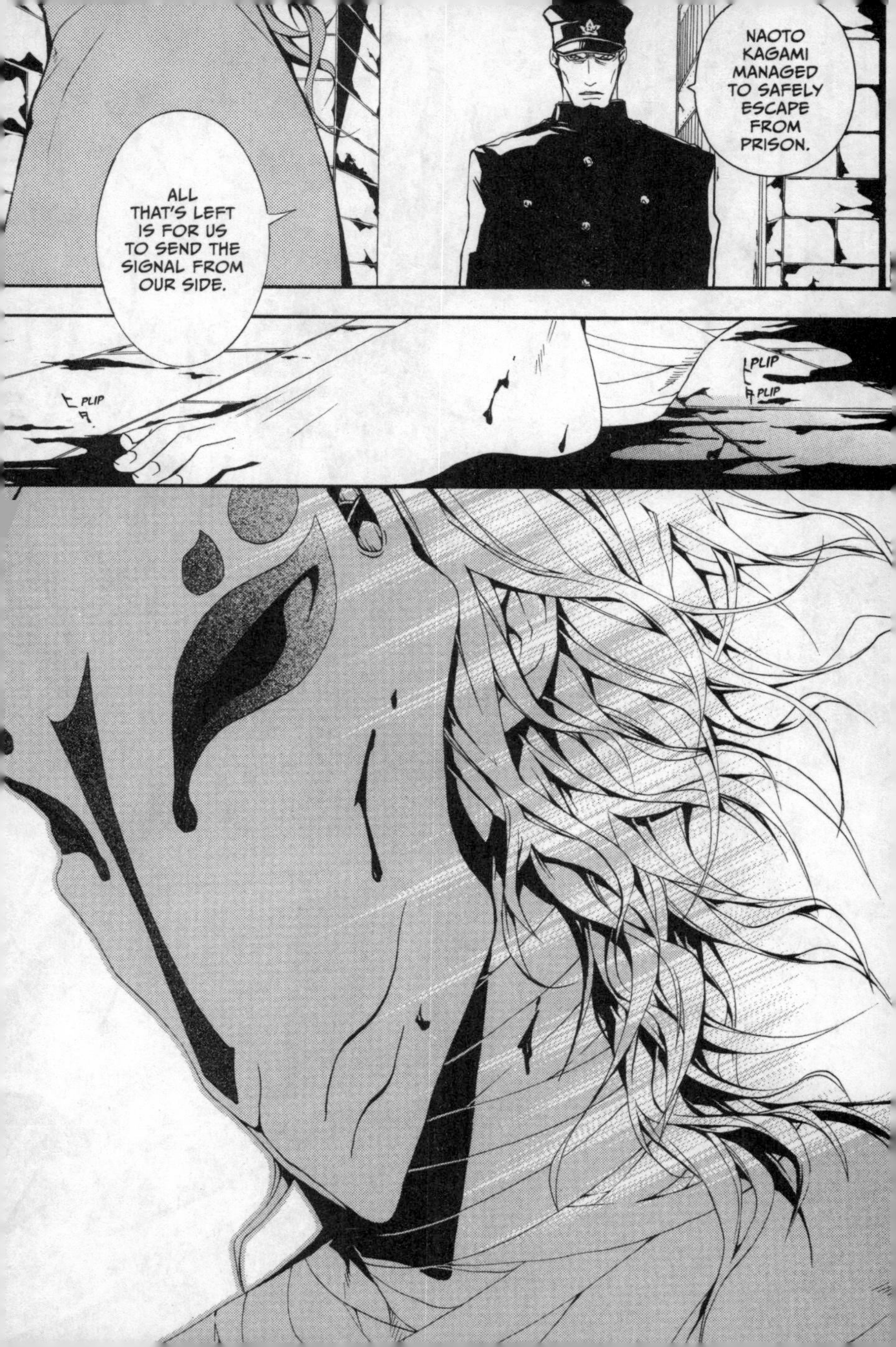
NAOTO KAGAMI MANAGED TO SAFELY ESCAPE FROM PRISON.
ALL THAT'S LEFT IS FOR US TO SEND THE SIGNAL FROM OUR SIDE.
PLIP
PLIP
PLIP

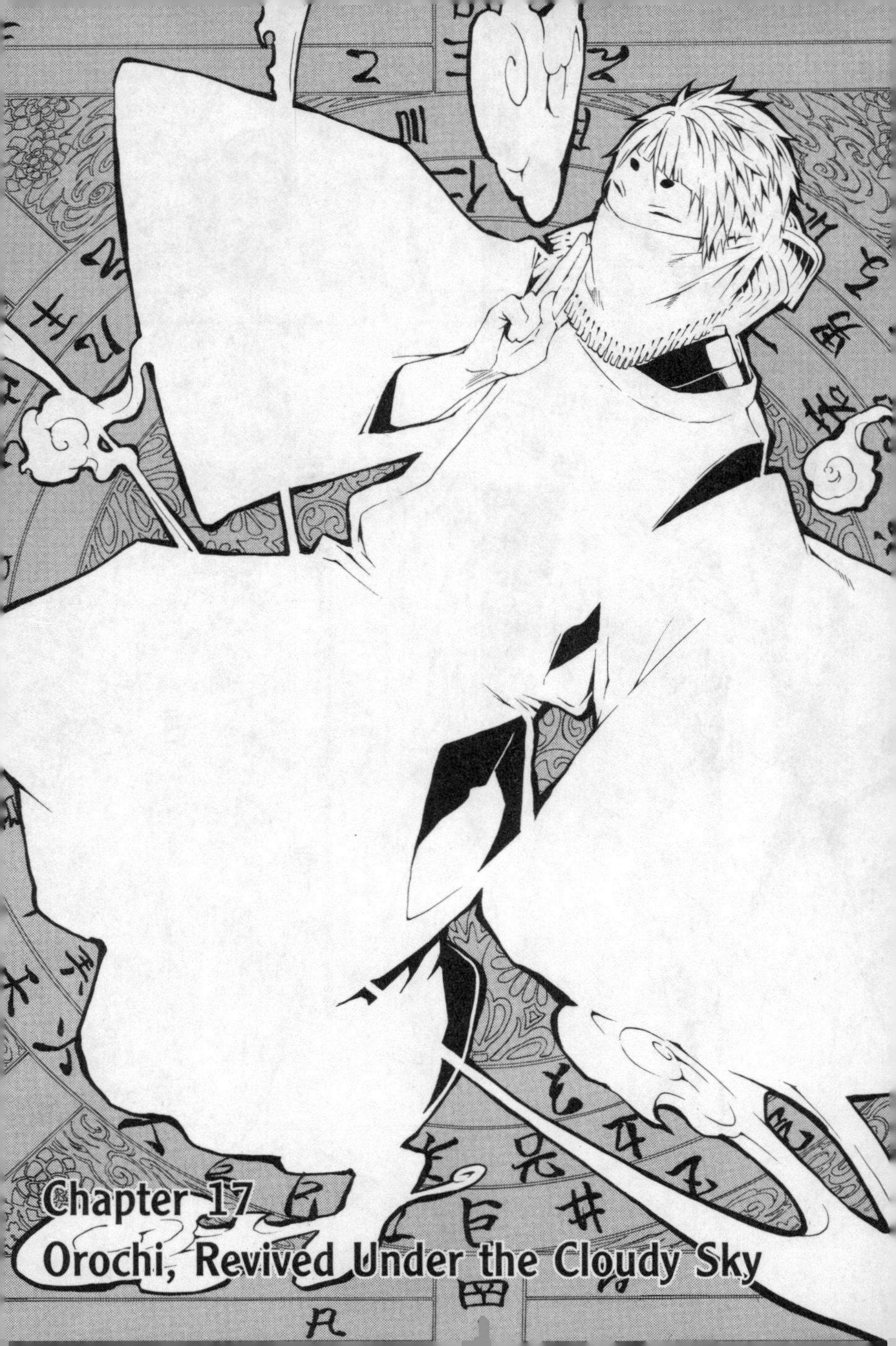

Chapter 17
Orochi, Revived Under the Cloudy Sky

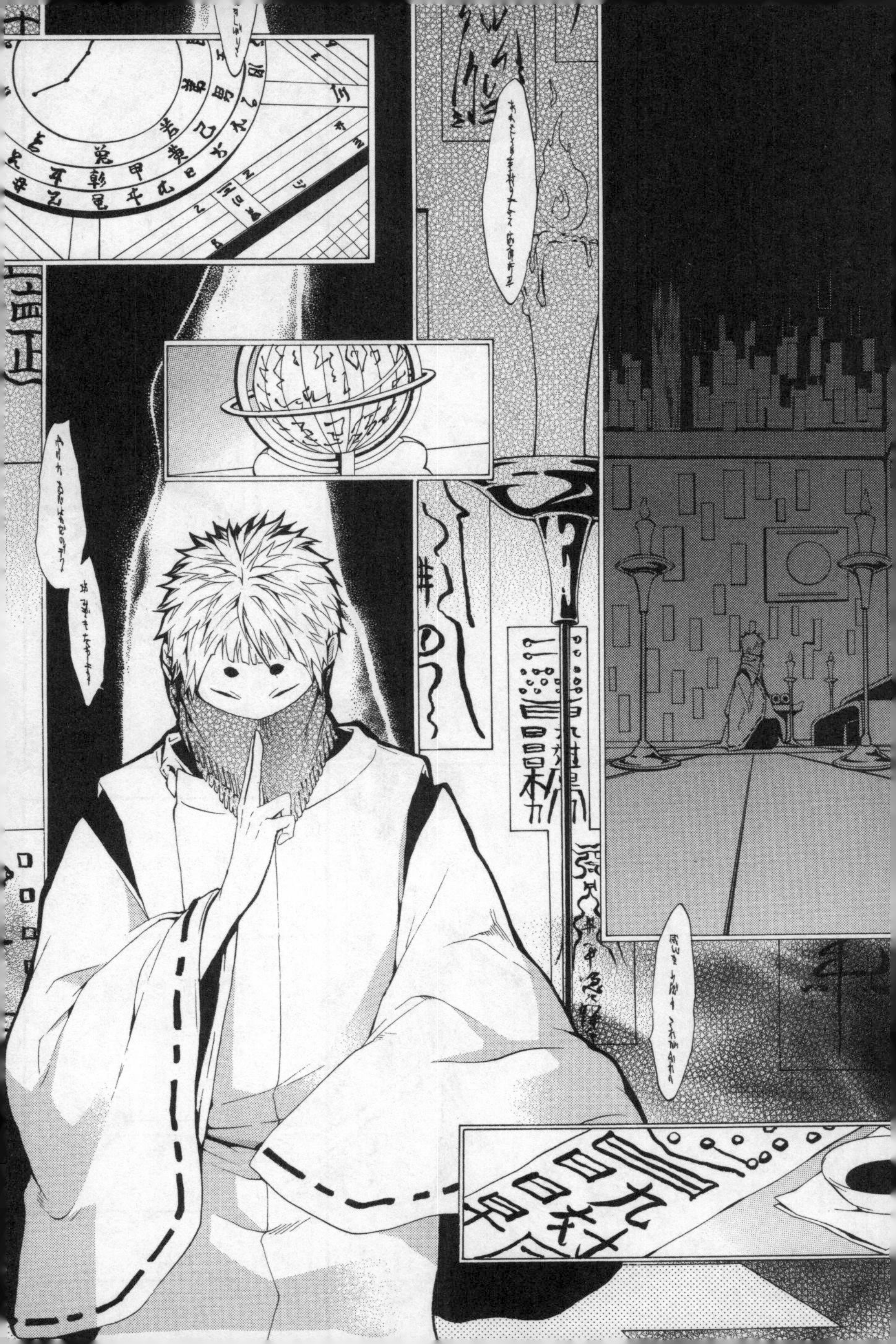

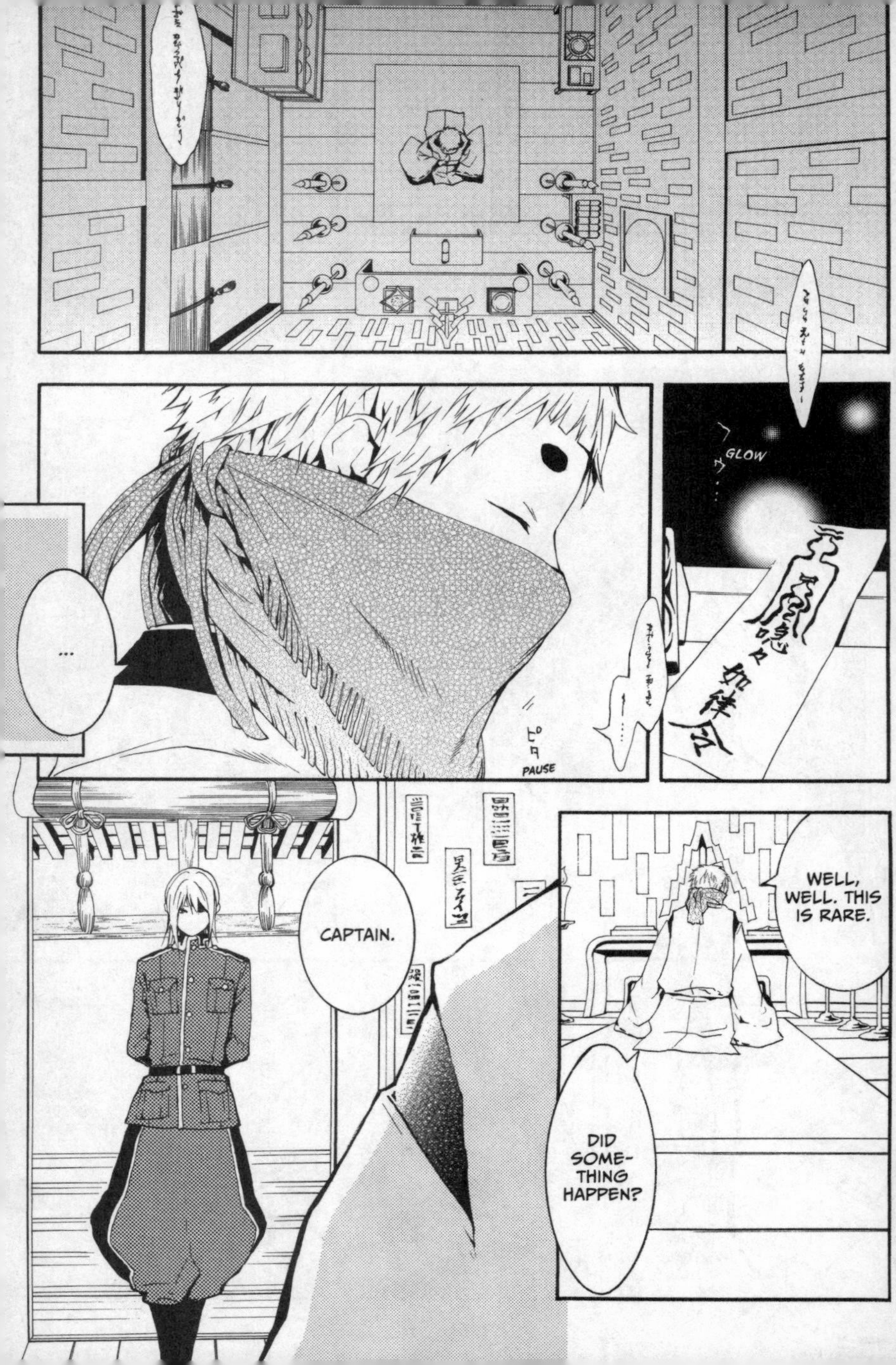
GLOW
...
PAUSE
WELL, WELL. THIS IS RARE.
DID SOME-THING HAPPEN?
CAPTAIN.

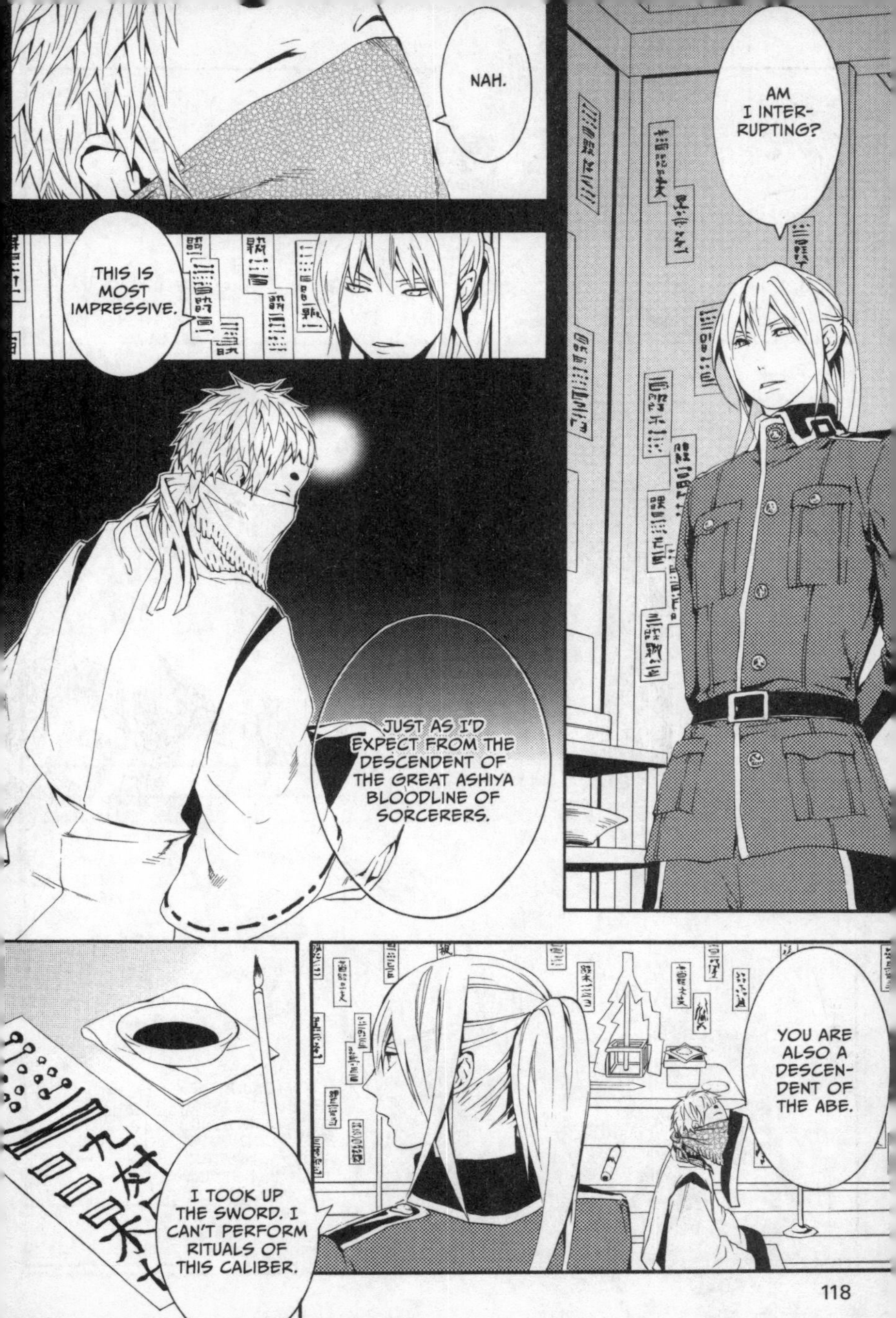
AM I INTER-RUPTING?
NAH.
THIS IS MOST IMPRESSIVE.
JUST AS I'D EXPECT FROM THE DESCENDENT OF THE GREAT ASHIYA BLOODLINE OF SORCERERS.
YOU ARE ALSO A DESCEN-DENT OF THE ABE.
I TOOK UP THE SWORD. I CAN'T PERFORM RITUALS OF THIS CALIBER.

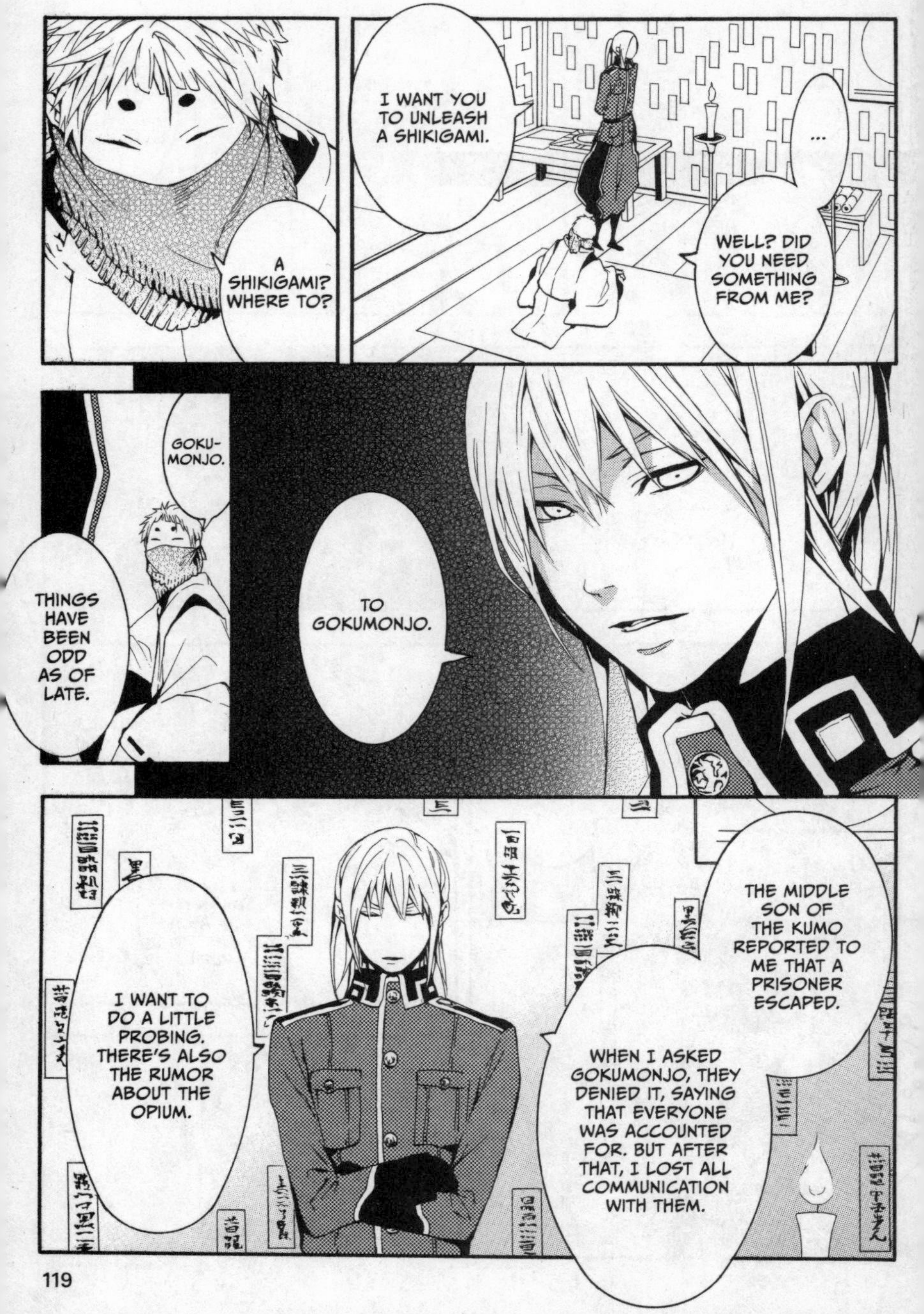
...
WELL? DID YOU NEED SOMETHING FROM ME?
I WANT YOU TO UNLEASH A SHIKIGAMI.
A SHIKIGAMI? WHERE TO?
TO GOKUMONJO.
GOKU-MONJO.
THINGS HAVE BEEN ODD AS OF LATE.
THE MIDDLE SON OF THE KUMO REPORTED TO ME THAT A PRISONER ESCAPED.
WHEN I ASKED GOKUMONJO, THEY DENIED IT, SAYING THAT EVERYONE WAS ACCOUNTED FOR. BUT AFTER THAT, I LOST ALL COMMUNICATION WITH THEM.
I WANT TO DO A LITTLE PROBING. THERE'S ALSO THE RUMOR ABOUT THE OPIUM.

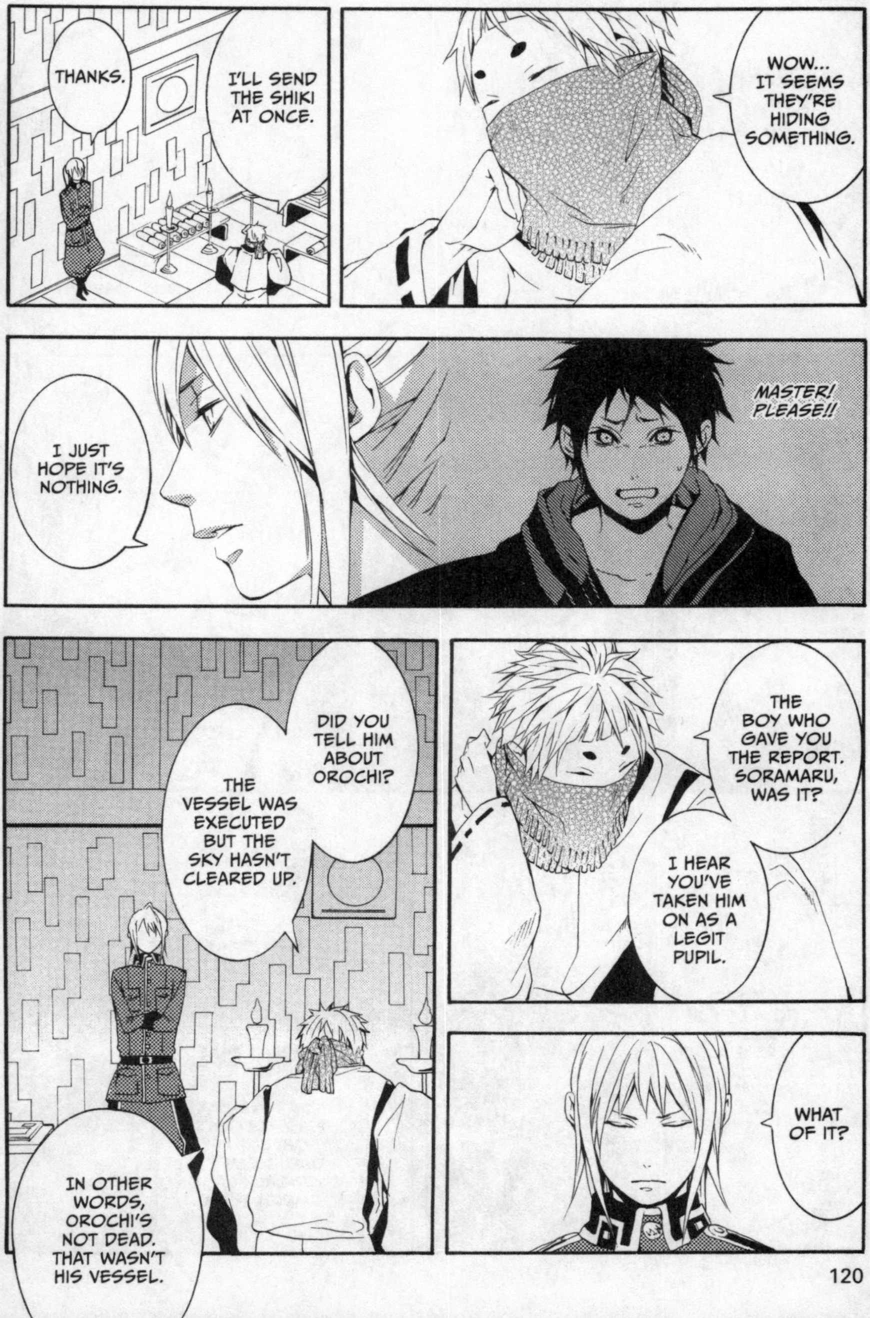
WOW... IT SEEMS THEY'RE HIDING SOMETHING.
I'LL SEND THE SHIKI AT ONCE.
THANKS.
MASTER! PLEASE!!
I JUST HOPE IT'S NOTHING.
THE BOY WHO GAVE YOU THE REPORT. SORAMARU, WAS IT?
I HEAR YOU'VE TAKEN HIM ON AS A LEGIT PUPIL.
WHAT OF IT?
DID YOU TELL HIM ABOUT OROCHI?
THE VESSEL WAS EXECUTED BUT THE SKY HASN'T CLEARED UP.
IN OTHER WORDS, OROCHI'S NOT DEAD. THAT WASN'T HIS VESSEL.

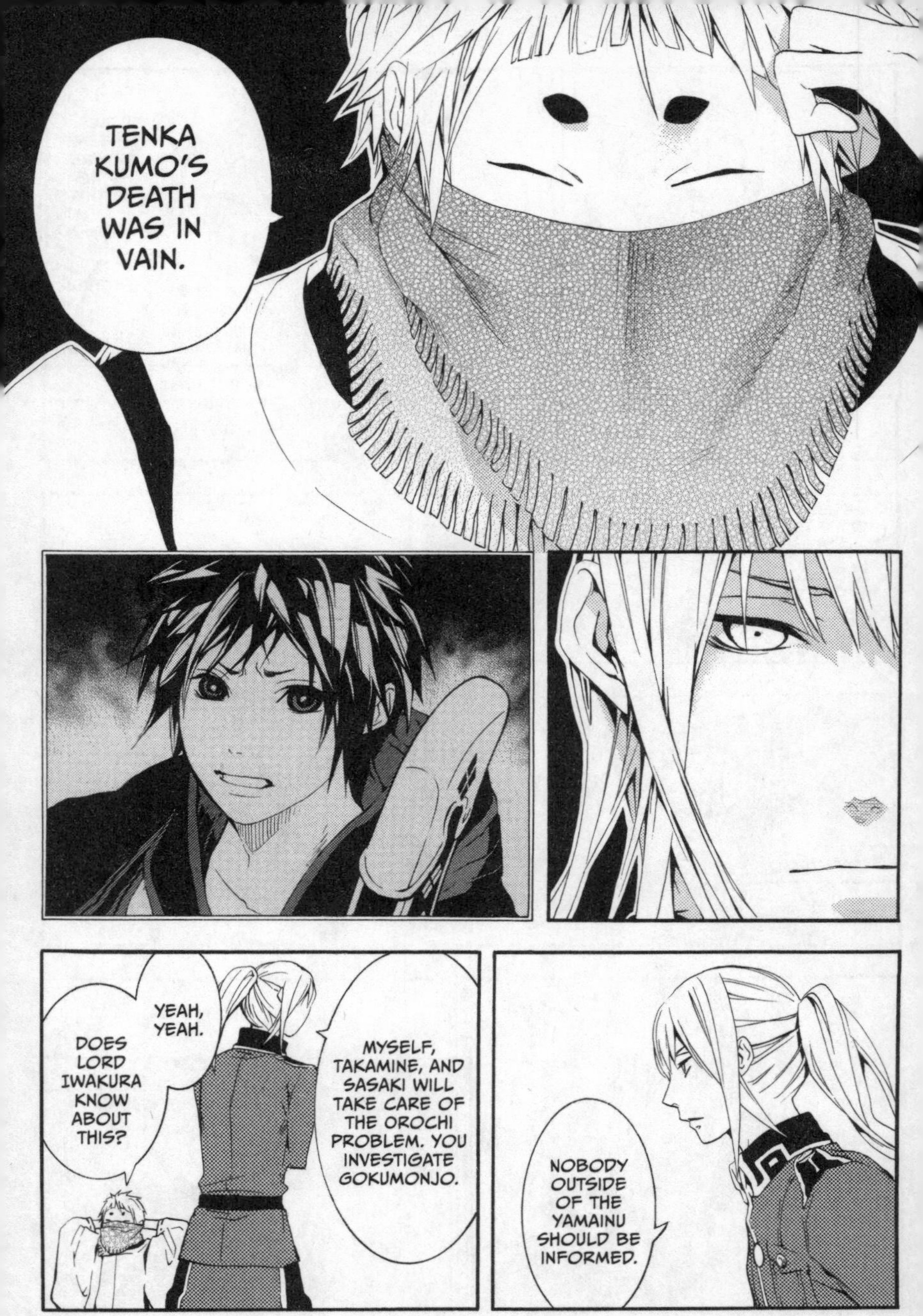
TENKA KUMO'S DEATH WAS IN VAIN.
NOBODY OUTSIDE OF THE YAMAINU SHOULD BE INFORMED.
MYSELF, TAKAMINE, AND SASAKI WILL TAKE CARE OF THE OROCHI PROBLEM. YOU INVESTIGATE GOKUMONJO.
YEAH, YEAH.
DOES LORD IWAKURA KNOW ABOUT THIS?

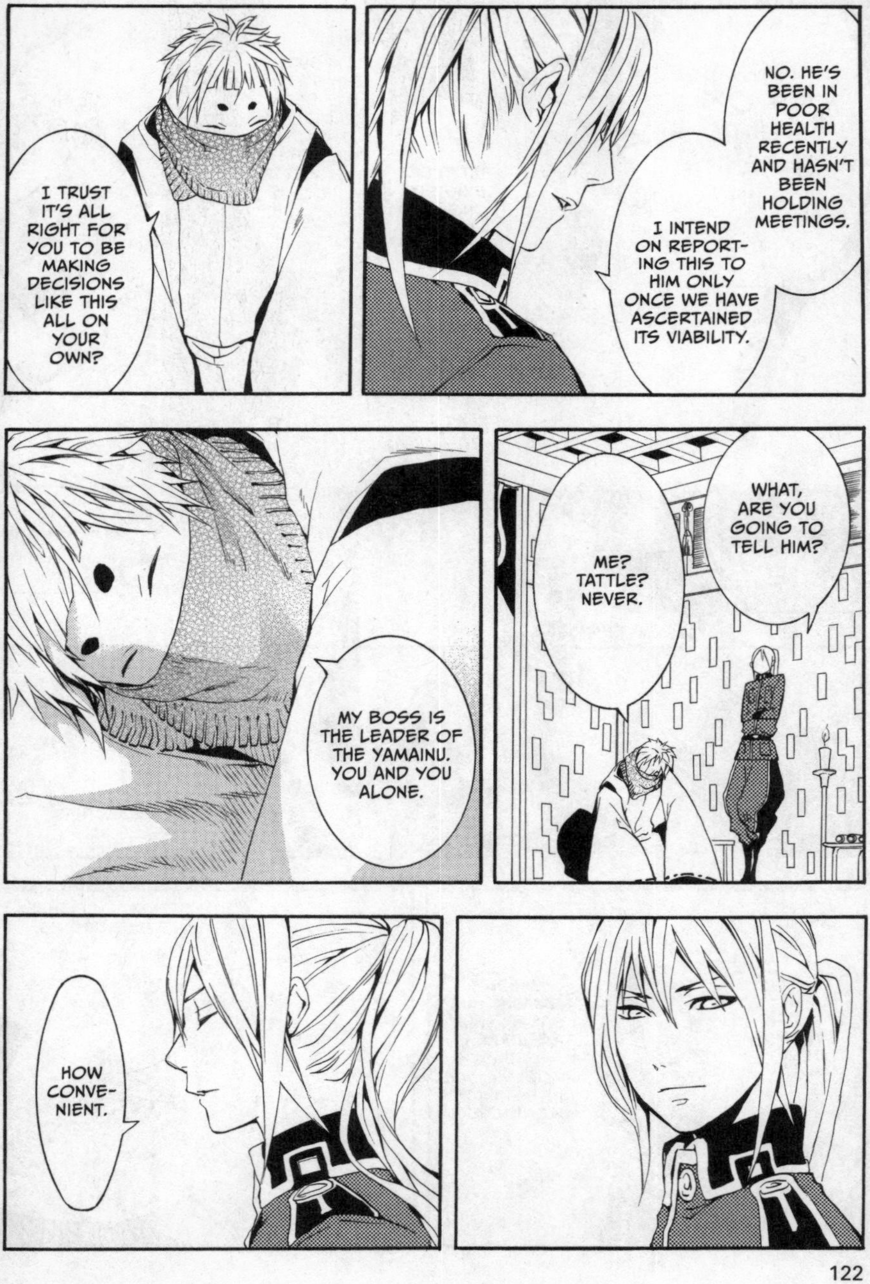
NO. HE'S BEEN IN POOR HEALTH RECENTLY AND HASN'T BEEN HOLDING MEETINGS.
I INTEND ON REPORTING THIS TO HIM ONLY ONCE WE HAVE ASCERTAINED ITS VIABILITY.
I TRUST IT'S ALL RIGHT FOR YOU TO BE MAKING DECISIONS LIKE THIS ALL ON YOUR OWN?
WHAT, ARE YOU GOING TO TELL HIM?
ME? TATTLE? NEVER.
MY BOSS IS THE LEADER OF THE YAMAINU. YOU AND YOU ALONE.
HOW CONVENIENT.

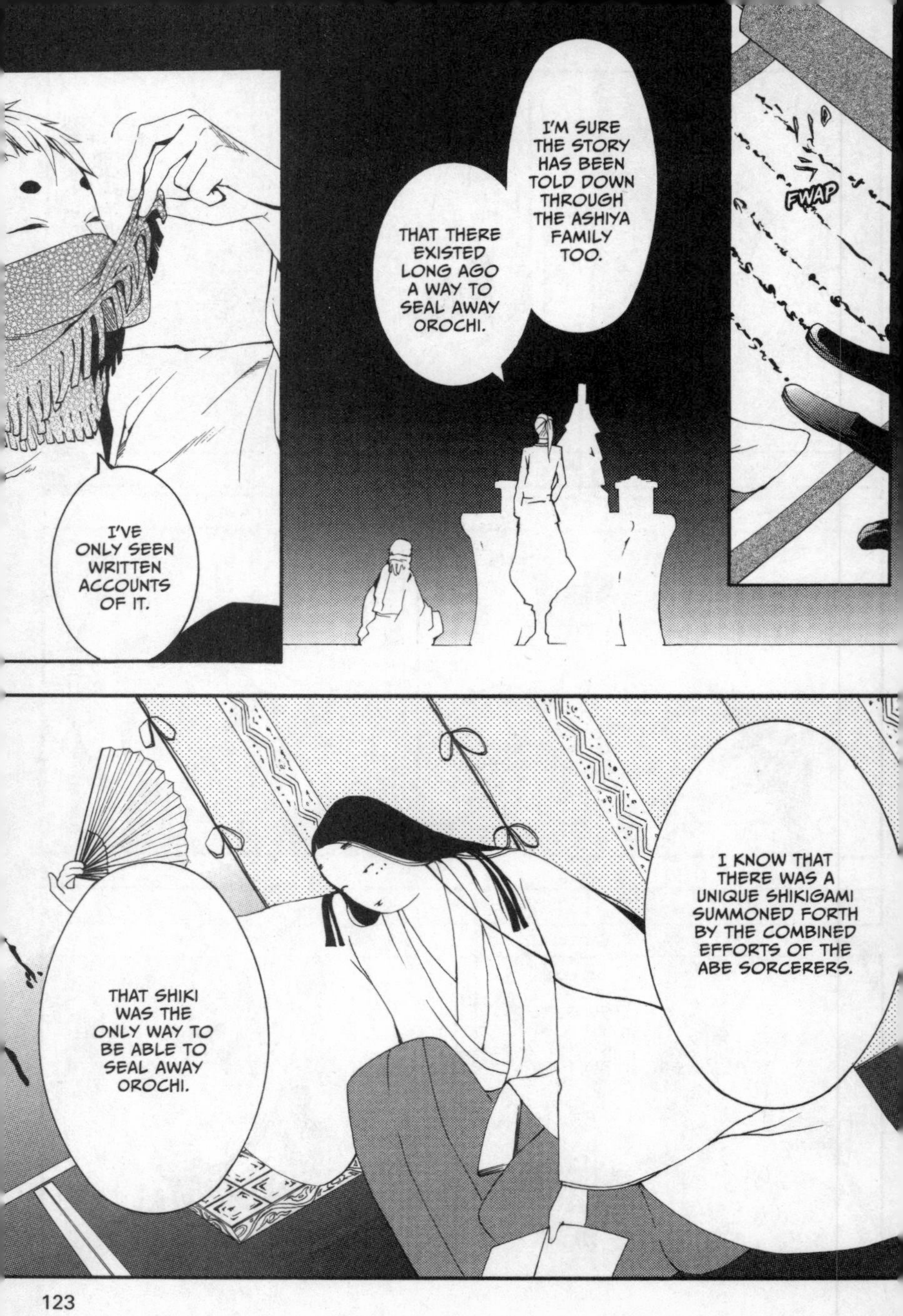

FWAP
I'M SURE THE STORY HAS BEEN TOLD DOWN THROUGH THE ASHIYA FAMILY TOO.
THAT THERE EXISTED LONG AGO A WAY TO SEAL AWAY OROCHI.
I'VE ONLY SEEN WRITTEN ACCOUNTS OF IT.
I KNOW THAT THERE WAS A UNIQUE SHIKIGAMI SUMMONED FORTH BY THE COMBINED EFFORTS OF THE ABE SORCERERS.
THAT SHIKI WAS THE ONLY WAY TO BE ABLE TO SEAL AWAY OROCHI.

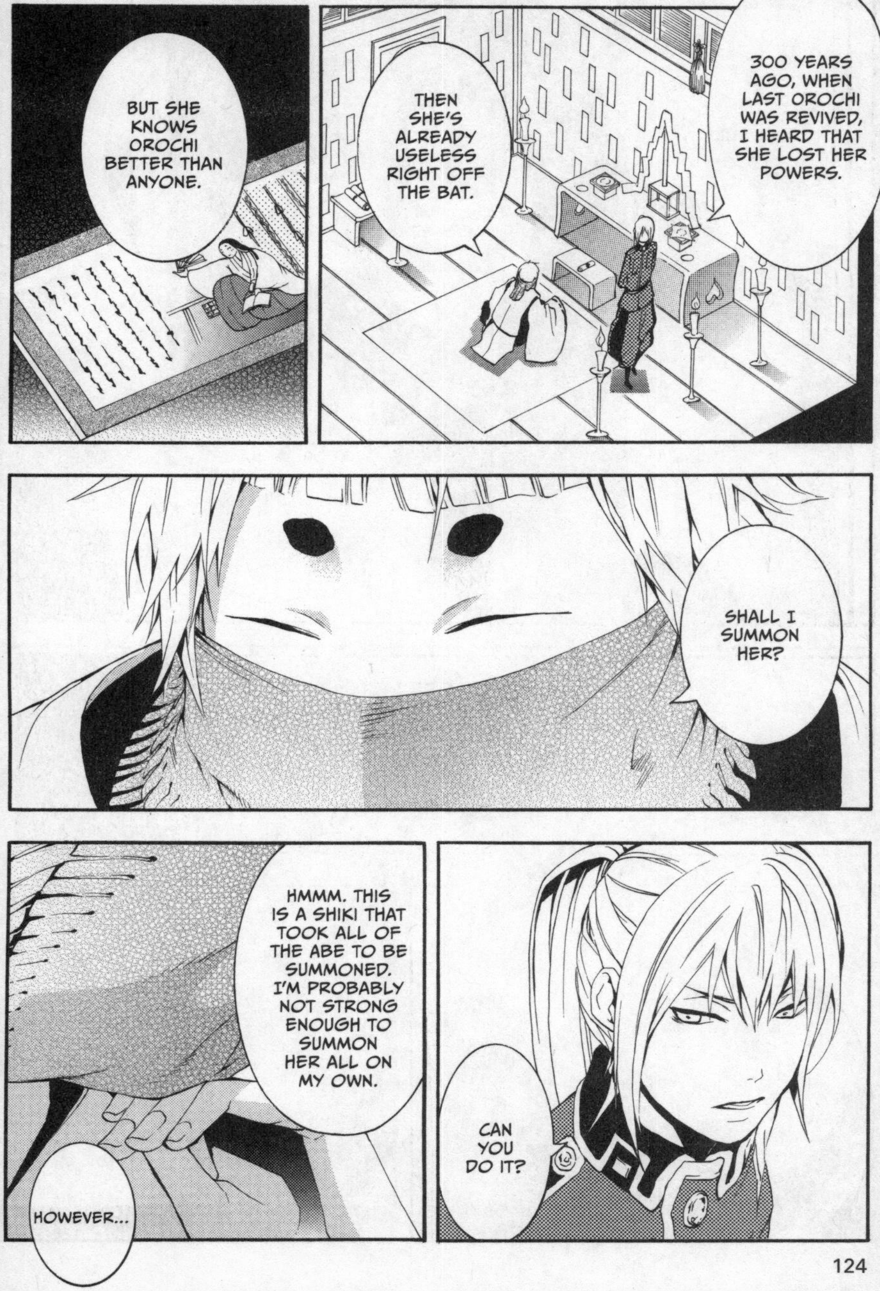
300 YEARS AGO, WHEN LAST OROCHI WAS REVIVED, I HEARD THAT SHE LOST HER POWERS.
THEN SHE'S ALREADY USELESS RIGHT OFF THE BAT.
BUT SHE KNOWS OROCHI BETTER THAN ANYONE.
SHALL I SUMMON HER?
CAN YOU DO IT?
HMMM. THIS IS A SHIKI THAT TOOK ALL OF THE ABE TO BE SUMMONED. I'M PROBABLY NOT STRONG ENOUGH TO SUMMON HER ALL ON MY OWN.
HOWEVER...

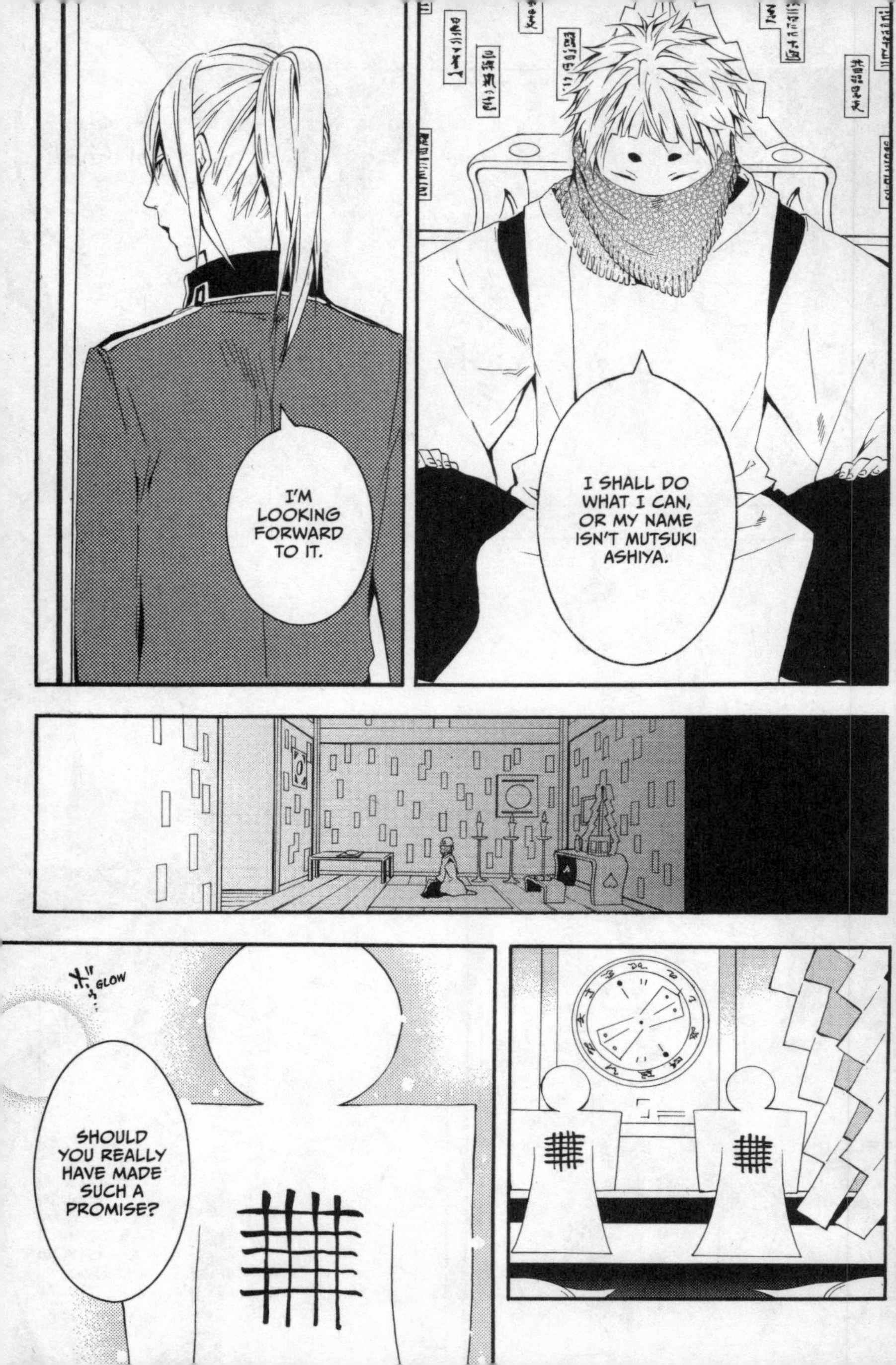
I SHALL DO WHAT I CAN, OR MY NAME ISN'T MUTSUKI ASHIYA.
I'M LOOKING FORWARD TO IT.
GLOW
SHOULD YOU REALLY HAVE MADE SUCH A PROMISE?

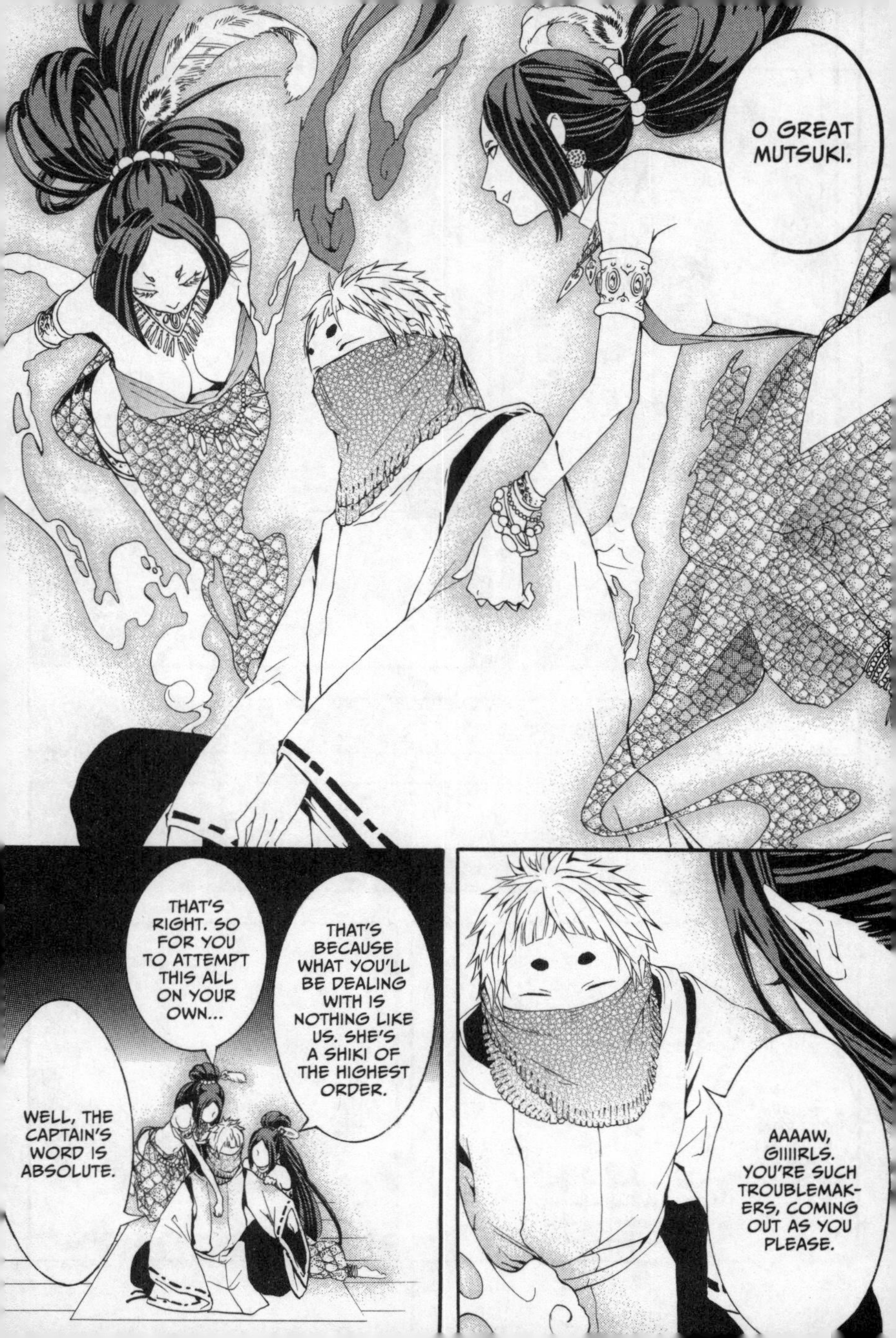
O GREAT MUTSUKI.
AAAAW, GIIIIRLS. YOU'RE SUCH TROUBLEMAKERS, COMING OUT AS YOU PLEASE.
THAT'S BECAUSE WHAT YOU'LL BE DEALING WITH IS NOTHING LIKE US. SHE'S A SHIKI OF THE HIGHEST ORDER.
THAT'S RIGHT. SO FOR YOU TO ATTEMPT THIS ALL ON YOUR OWN...
WELL, THE CAPTAIN'S WORD IS ABSOLUTE.

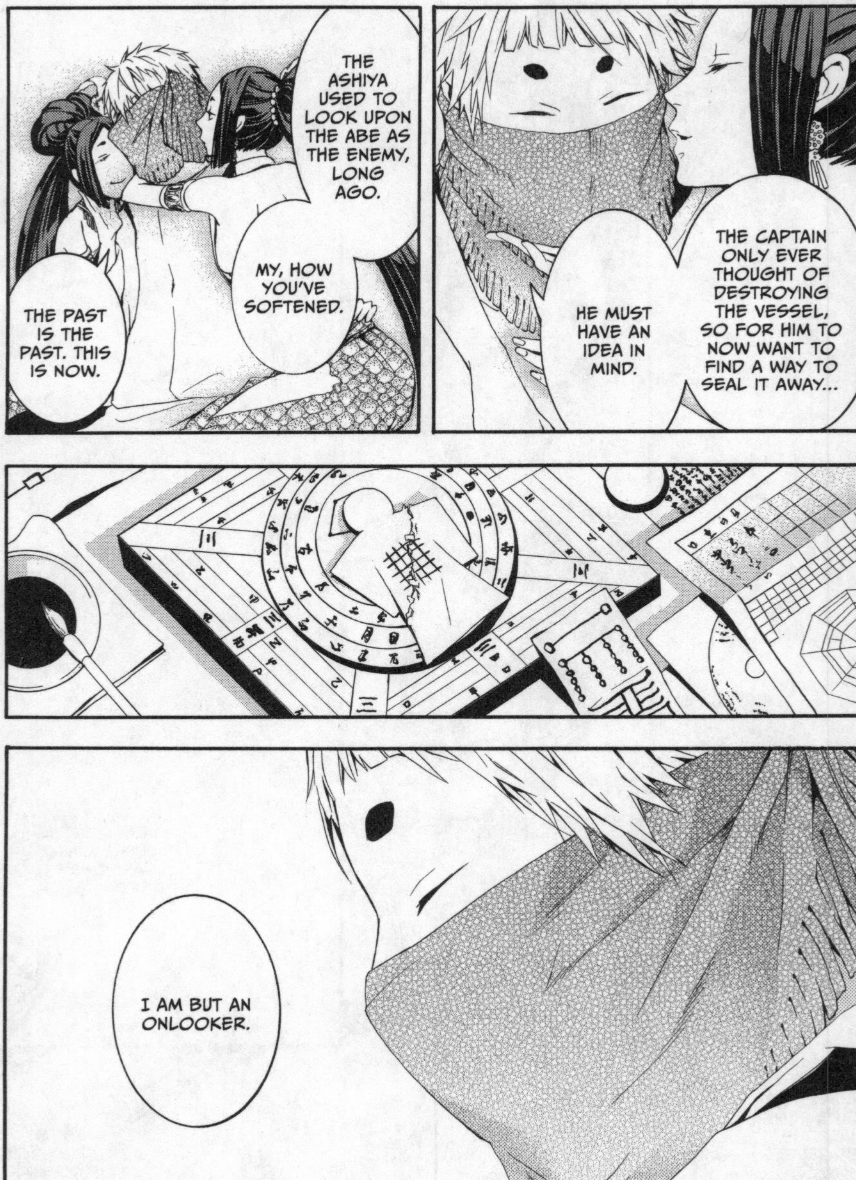
THE CAPTAIN ONLY EVER THOUGHT OF DESTROYING THE VESSEL, SO FOR HIM TO NOW WANT TO FIND A WAY TO SEAL IT AWAY...
HE MUST HAVE AN IDEA IN MIND.
THE ASHIYA USED TO LOOK UPON THE ABE AS THE ENEMY, LONG AGO.
MY, HOW YOU'VE SOFTENED.
THE PAST IS THE PAST. THIS IS NOW.
I AM BUT AN ONLOOKER.

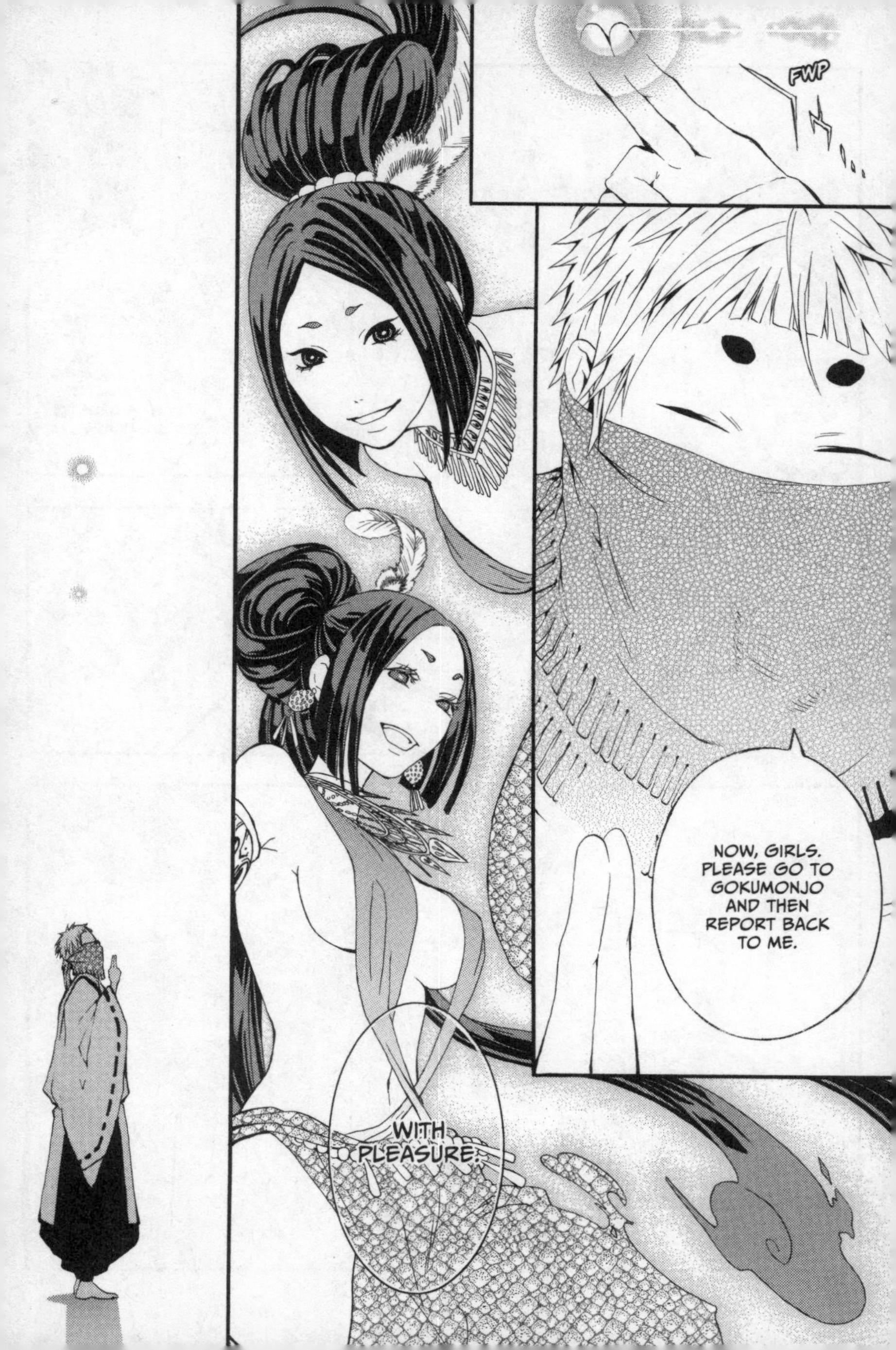
FWP
NOW, GIRLS. PLEASE GO TO GOKUMONJO AND THEN REPORT BACK TO ME.
WITH PLEASURE.

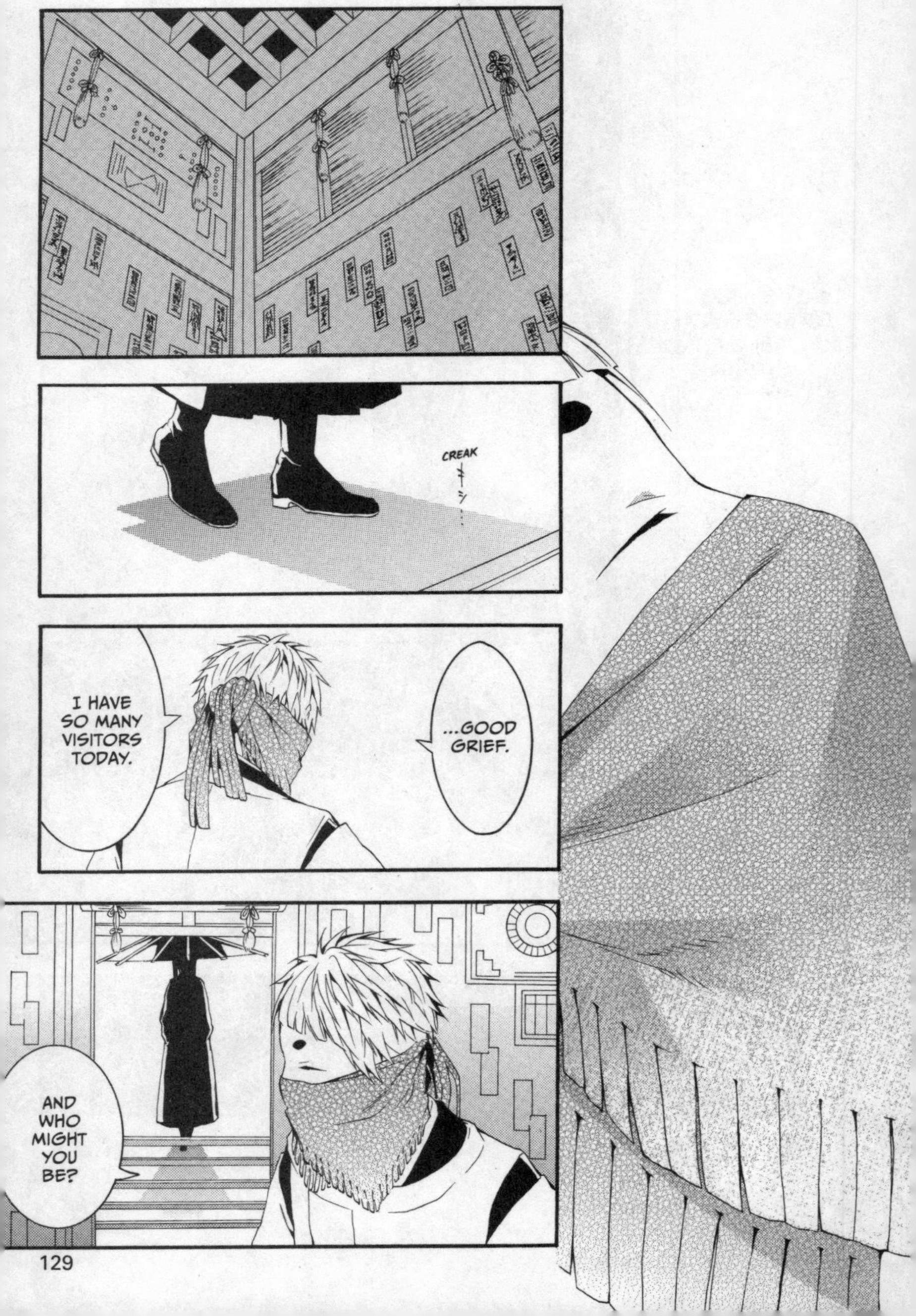
CREAK
...GOOD GRIEF.
I HAVE SO MANY VISITORS TODAY.
AND WHO MIGHT YOU BE?

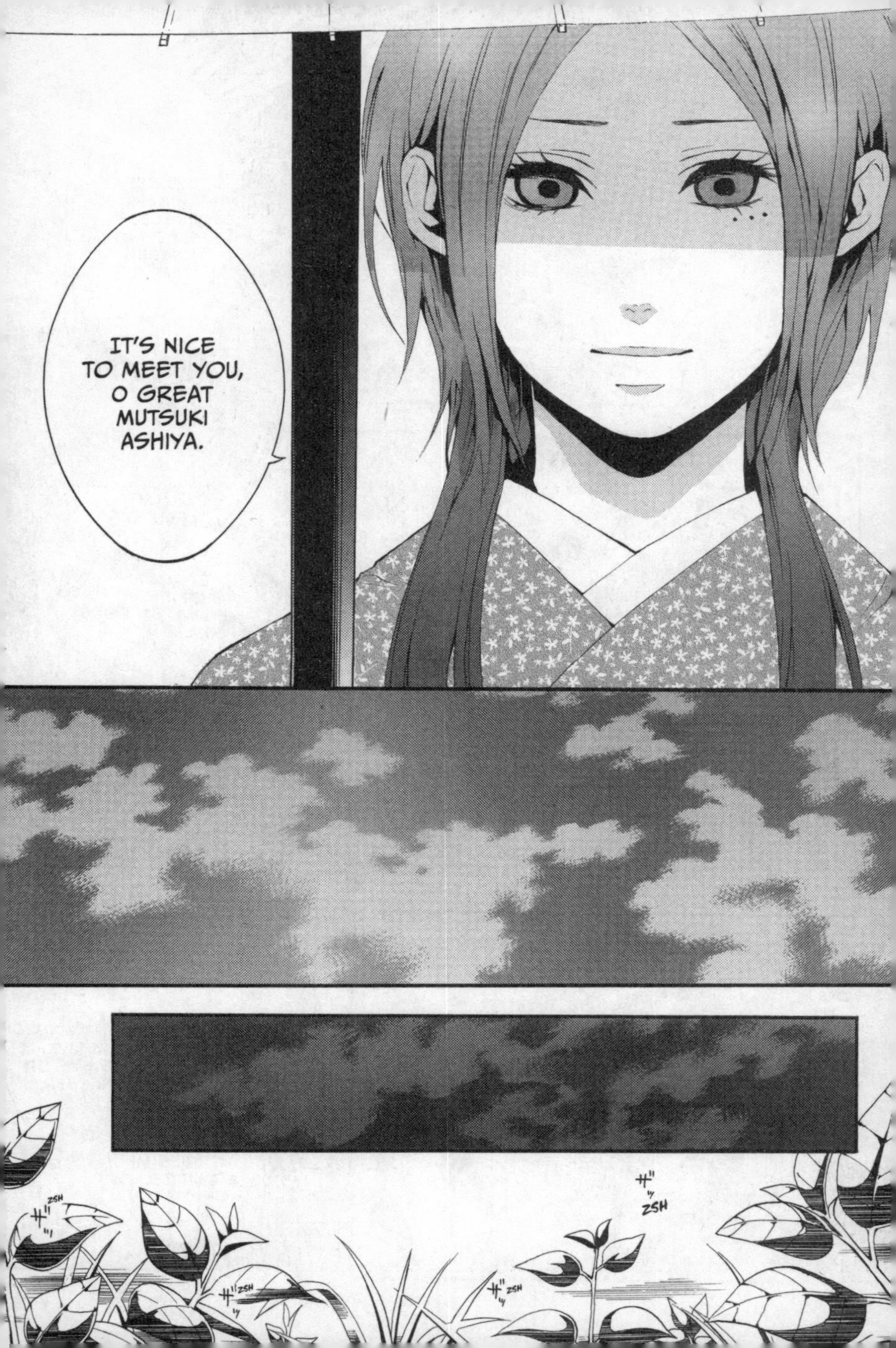
IT'S NICE TO MEET YOU, O GREAT MUTSUKI ASHIYA.
ZSH
ZSH
ZSH
ZSH

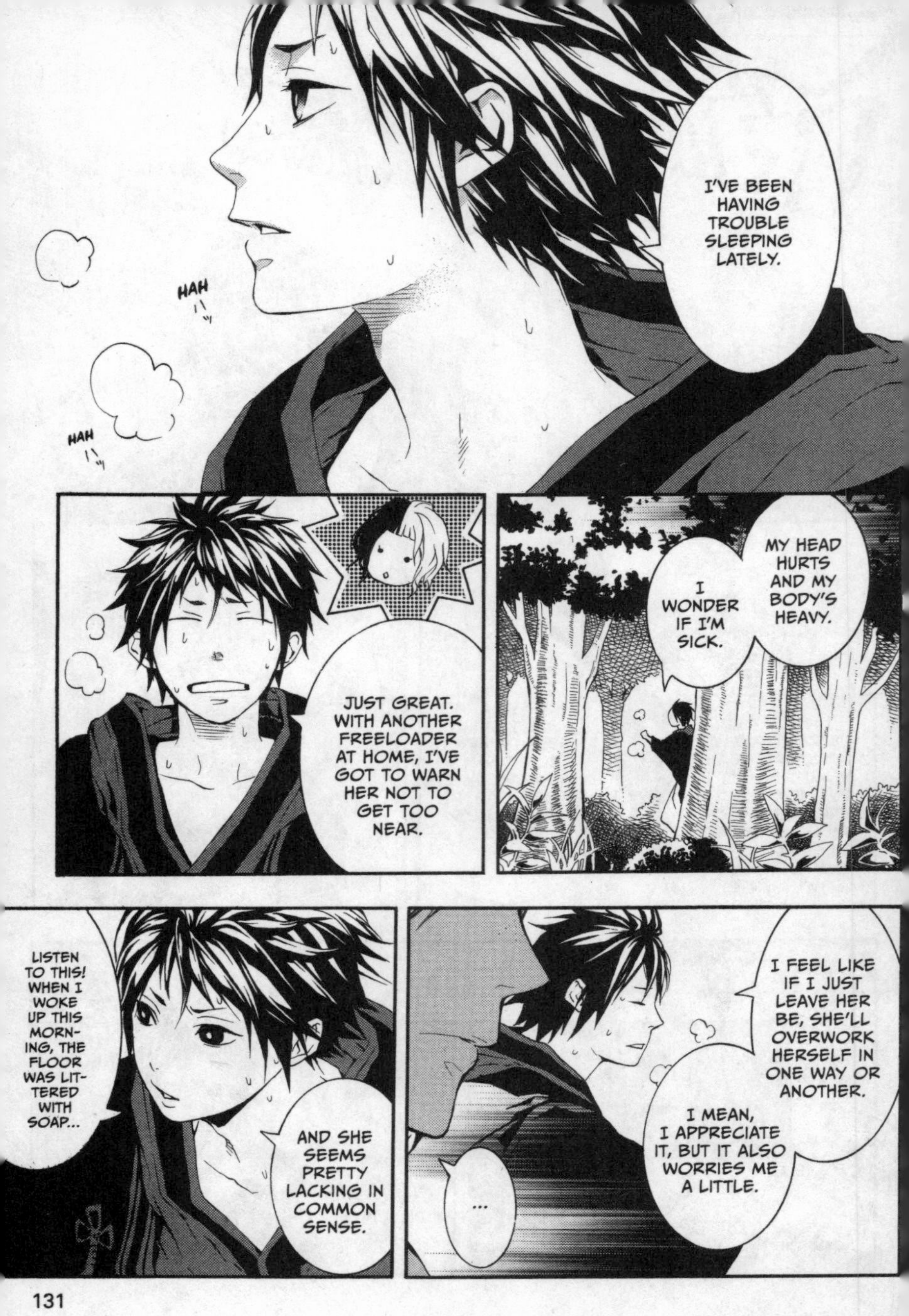
I'VE BEEN HAVING TROUBLE SLEEPING LATELY.
HAH
HAH
MY HEAD HURTS AND MY BODY'S HEAVY.
I WONDER IF I'M SICK.
JUST GREAT. WITH ANOTHER FREELOADER AT HOME, I'VE GOT TO WARN HER NOT TO GET TOO NEAR.
I FEEL LIKE IF I JUST LEAVE HER BE, SHE'LL OVERWORK HERSELF IN ONE WAY OR ANOTHER.
I MEAN, I APPRECIATE IT, BUT IT ALSO WORRIES ME A LITTLE.
...
LISTEN TO THIS! WHEN I WOKE UP THIS MORNING, THE FLOOR WAS LITTERED WITH SOAP...
AND SHE SEEMS PRETTY LACKING IN COMMON SENSE.

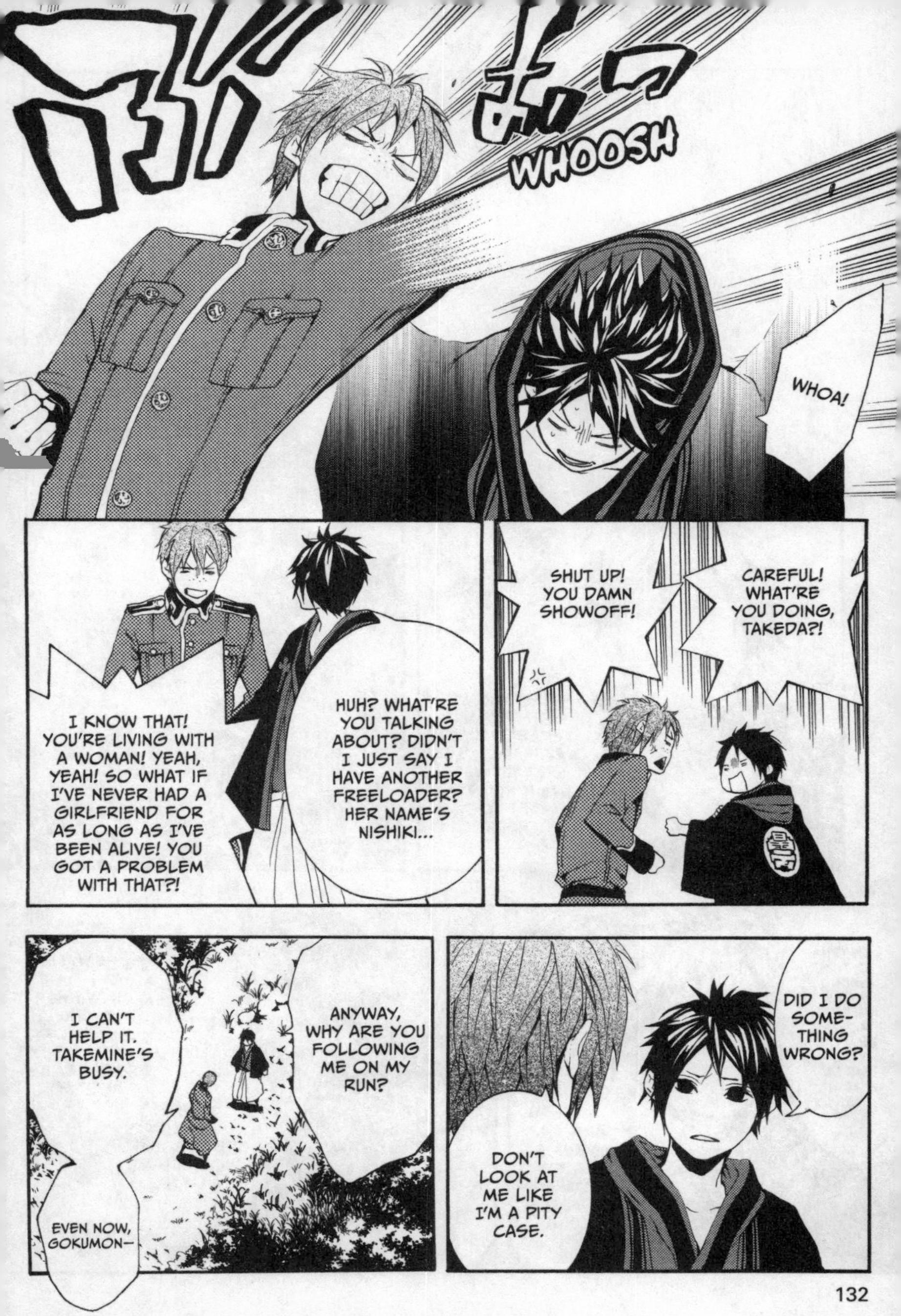
WHOOSH
WHOA!
CAREFUL! WHAT'RE YOU DOING, TAKEDA?!
SHUT UP! YOU DAMN SHOWOFF!
HUH? WHAT'RE YOU TALKING ABOUT? DIDN'T I JUST SAY I HAVE ANOTHER FREELOADER? HER NAME'S NISHIKI...
I KNOW THAT! YOU'RE LIVING WITH A WOMAN! YEAH, YEAH! SO WHAT IF I'VE NEVER HAD A GIRLFRIEND FOR AS LONG AS I'VE BEEN ALIVE! YOU GOT A PROBLEM WITH THAT?!
DID I DO SOME-THING WRONG?
DON'T LOOK AT ME LIKE I'M A PITY CASE.
ANYWAY, WHY ARE YOU FOLLOWING ME ON MY RUN?
I CAN'T HELP IT. TAKEMINE'S BUSY.
EVEN NOW, GOKUMON—

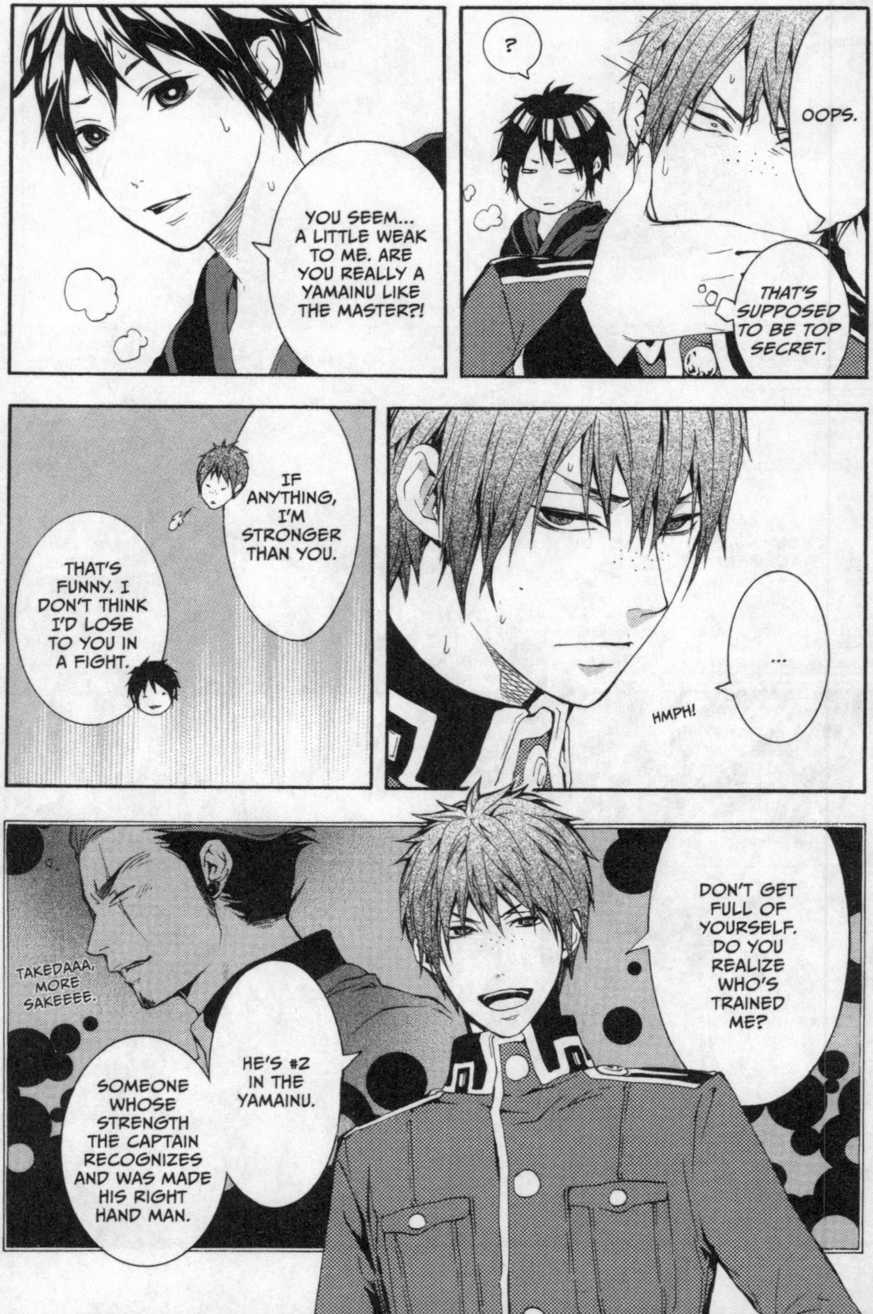
OOPS.
?
THAT'S SUPPOSED TO BE TOP SECRET.
YOU SEEM... A LITTLE WEAK TO ME. ARE YOU REALLY A YAMAINU LIKE THE MASTER?!
...
HMPH!
IF ANYTHING, I'M STRONGER THAN YOU.
THAT'S FUNNY. I DON'T THINK I'D LOSE TO YOU IN A FIGHT.
DON'T GET FULL OF YOURSELF. DO YOU REALIZE WHO'S TRAINED ME?
HE'S #2 IN THE YAMAINU.
SOMEONE WHOSE STRENGTH THE CAPTAIN RECOGNIZES AND WAS MADE HIS RIGHT HAND MAN.
TAKEDAAA, MORE SAKEEEE.

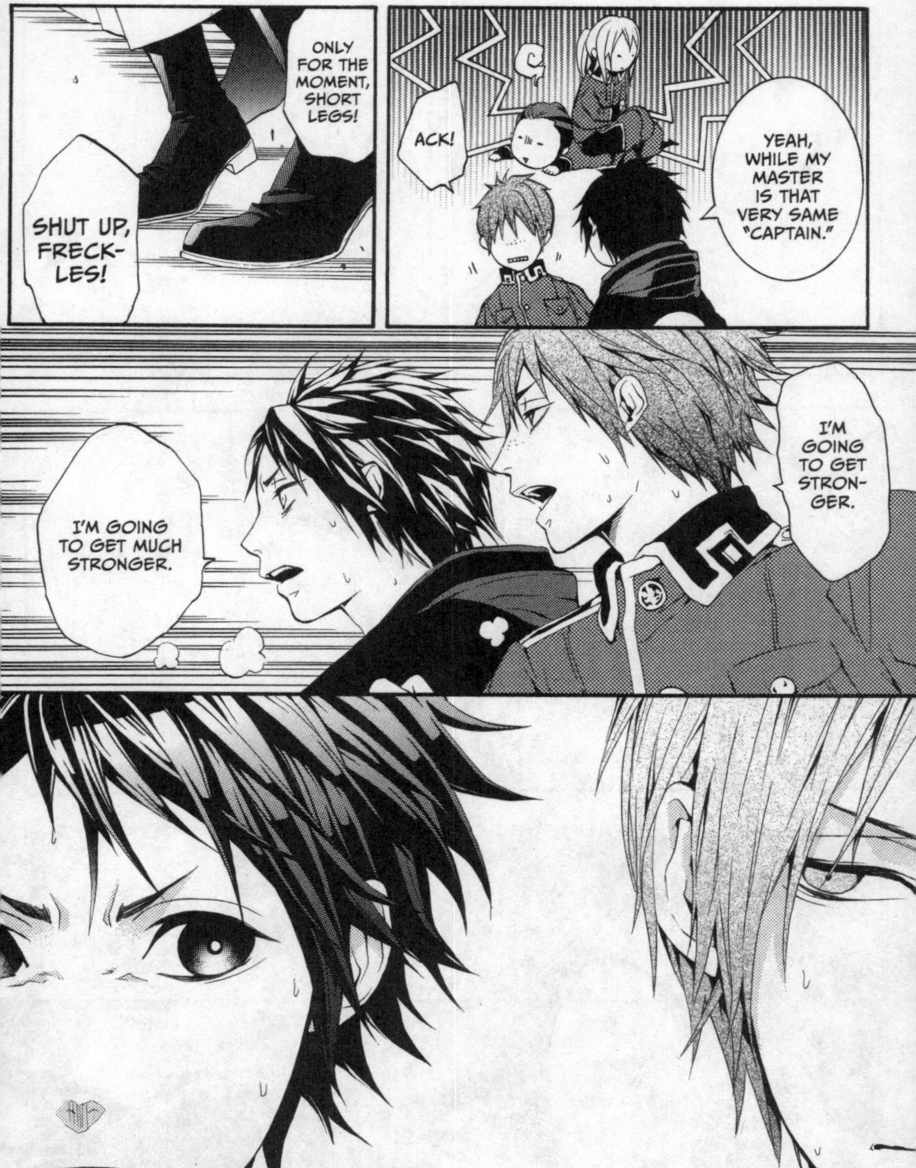
YEAH, WHILE MY MASTER IS THAT VERY SAME "CAPTAIN."
ACK!
ONLY FOR THE MOMENT, SHORT LEGS!
SHUT UP, FRECK-LES!
I'M GOING TO GET STRON-GER.
I'M GOING TO GET MUCH STRONGER.

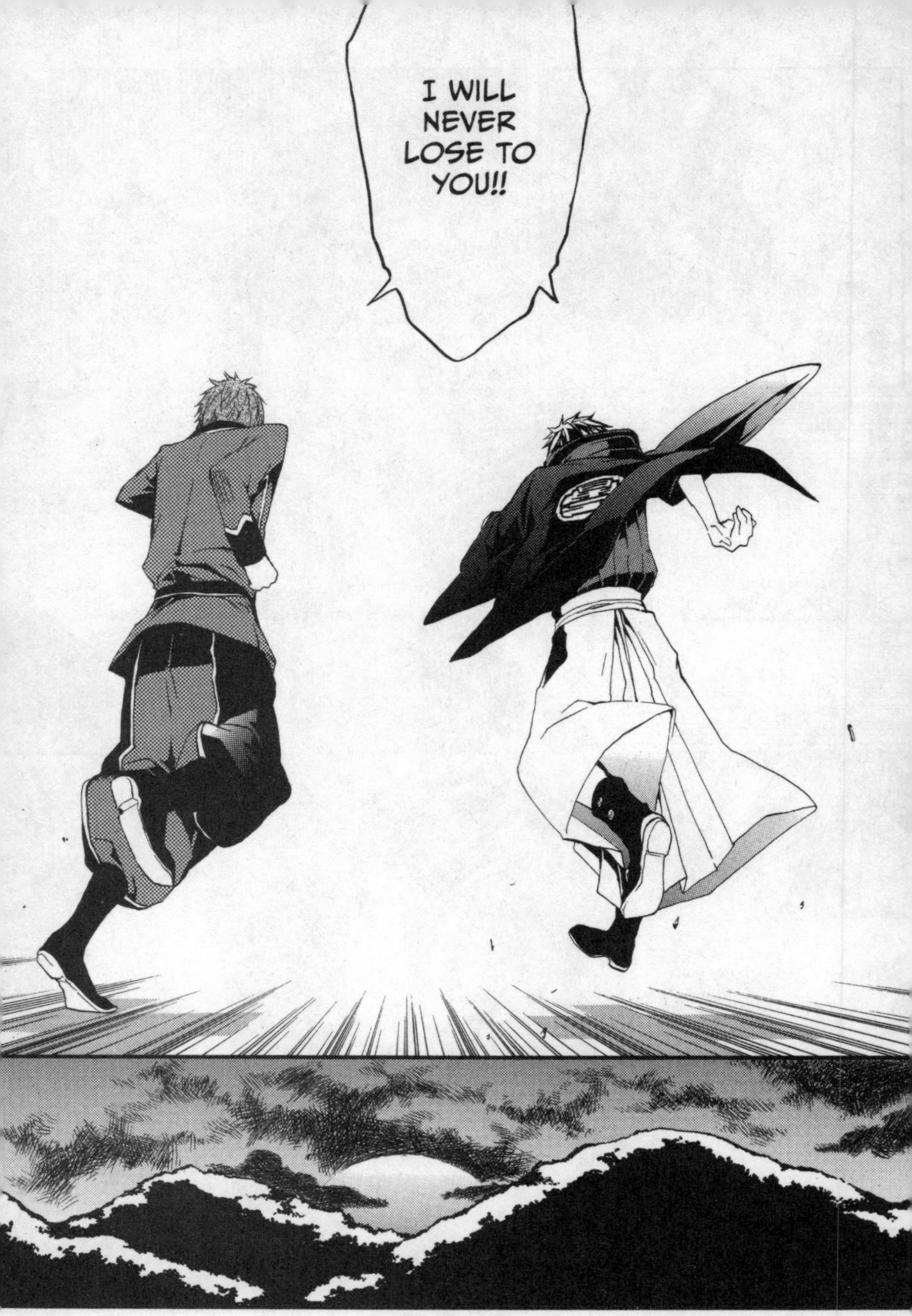
I WILL NEVER LOSE TO YOU!!

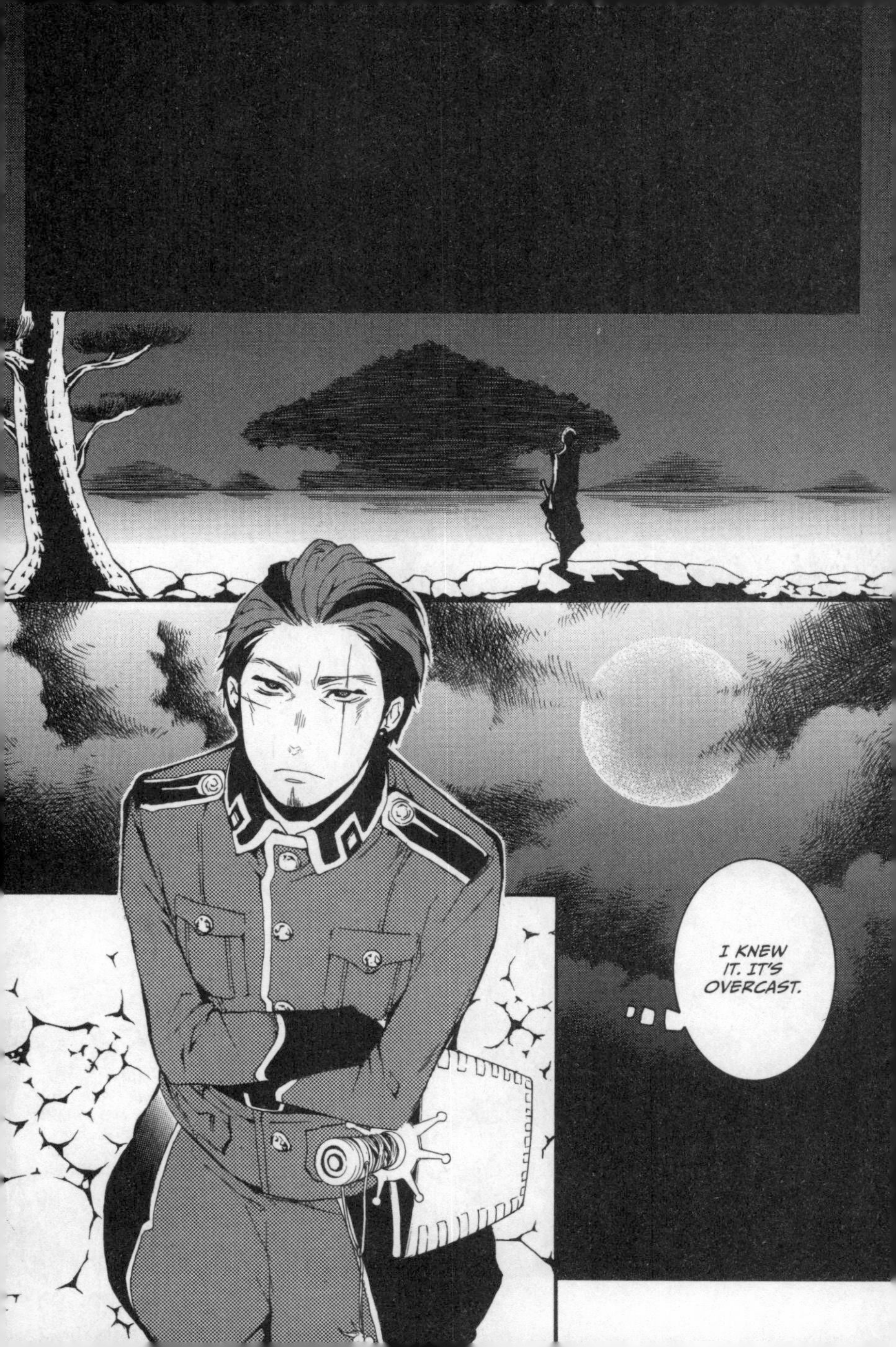
I KNEW
IT. IT'S
OVERCAST.

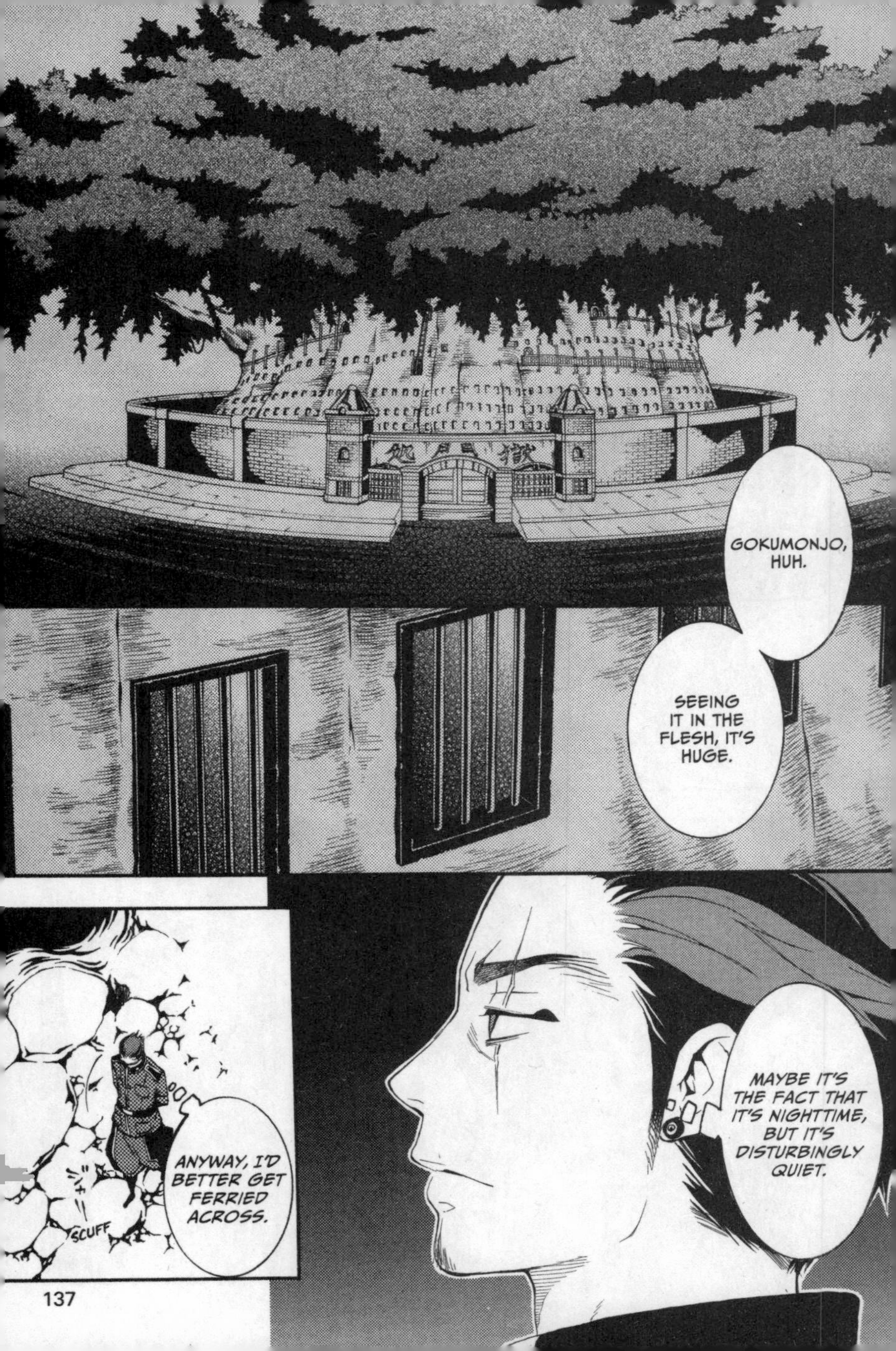
GOKUMONJO, HUH.
SEEING IT IN THE FLESH, IT'S HUGE.
MAYBE IT'S THE FACT THAT IT'S NIGHTTIME, BUT IT'S DISTURBINGLY QUIET.
ANYWAY, I'D BETTER GET FERRIED ACROSS.
SCUFF

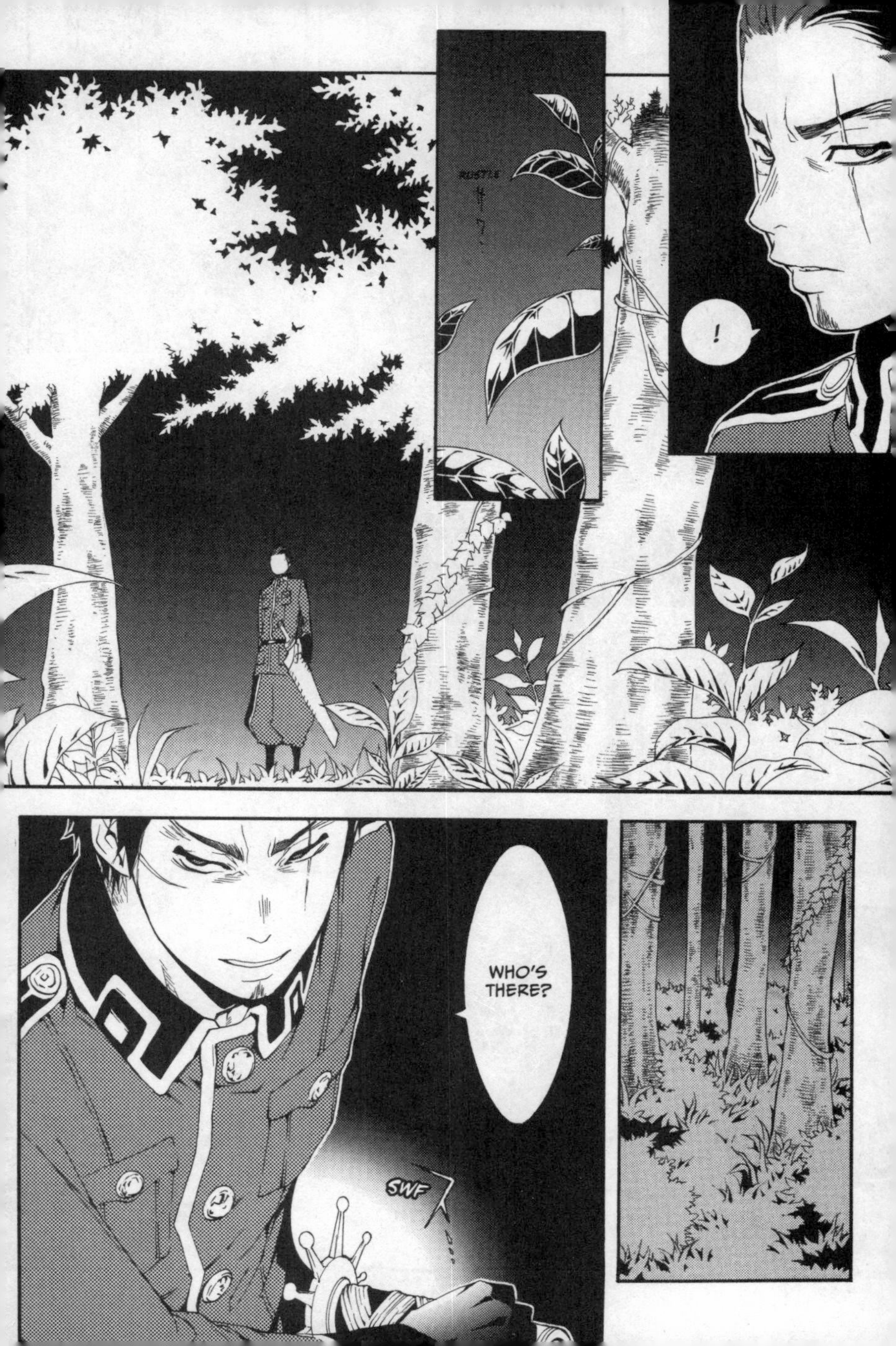
!
RUSTLE
WHO'S THERE?
SWF

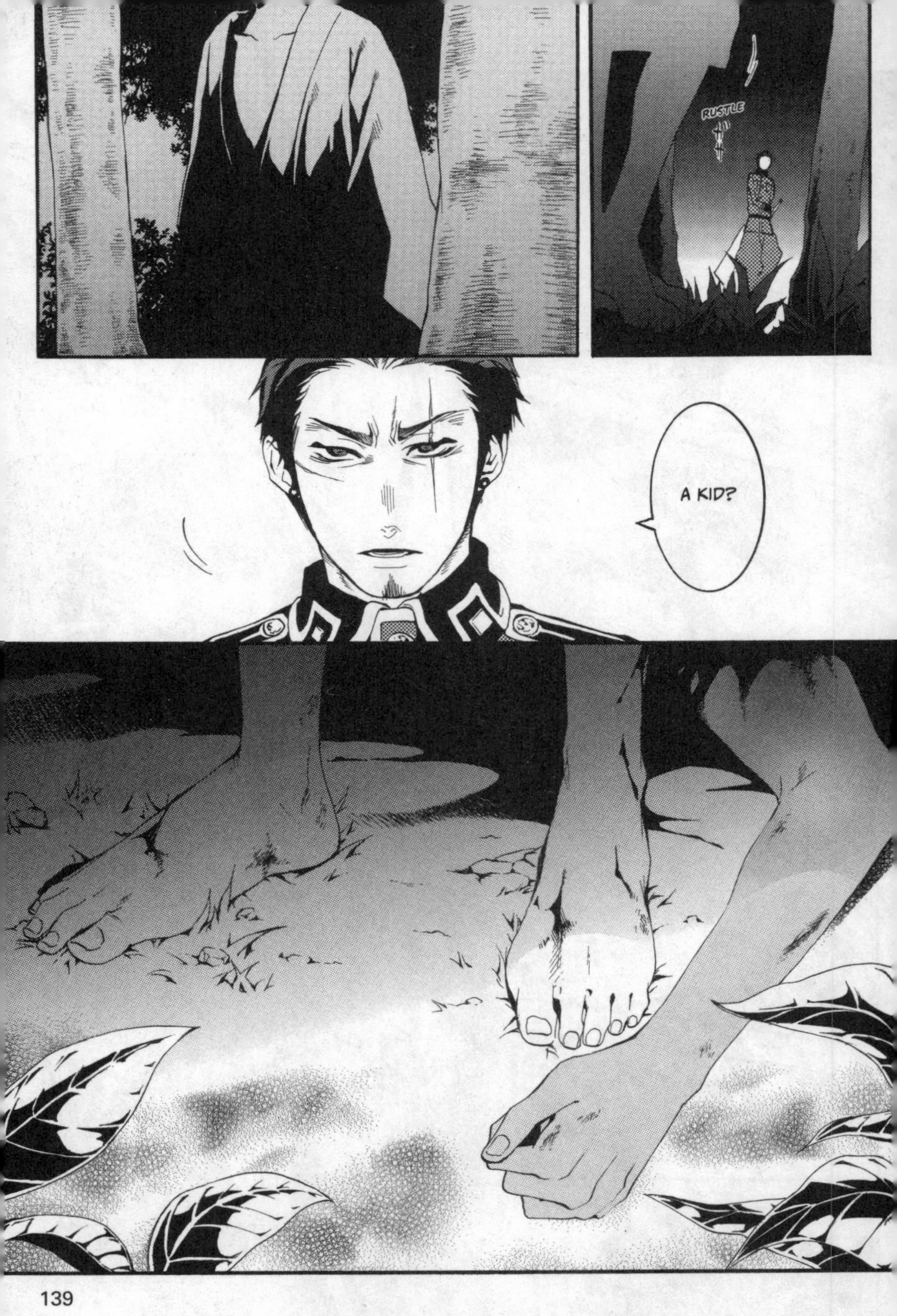
RUSTLE
A KID?

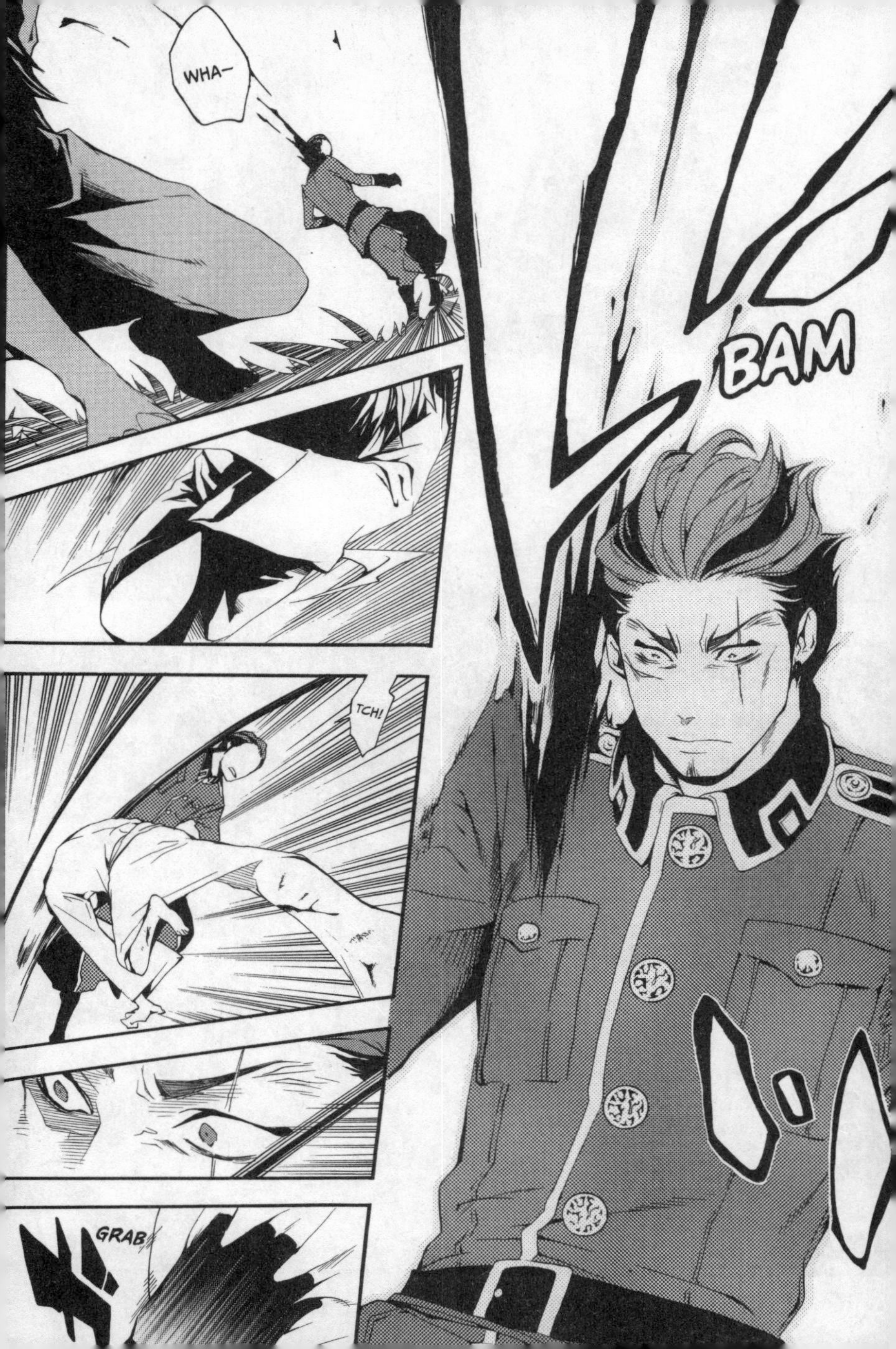
BAM
WHA–
TCH!
GRAB

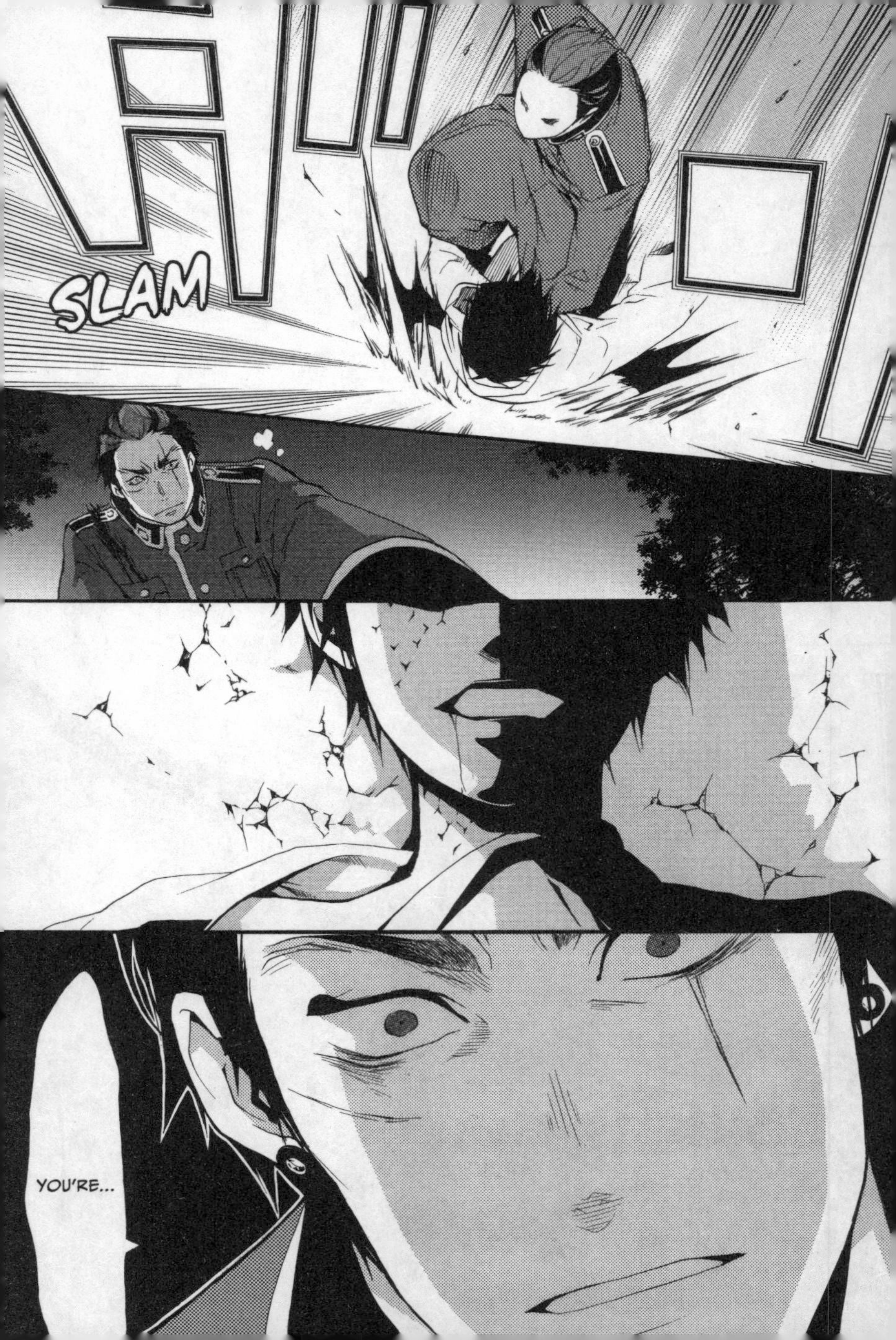
SLAM
YOU'RE...

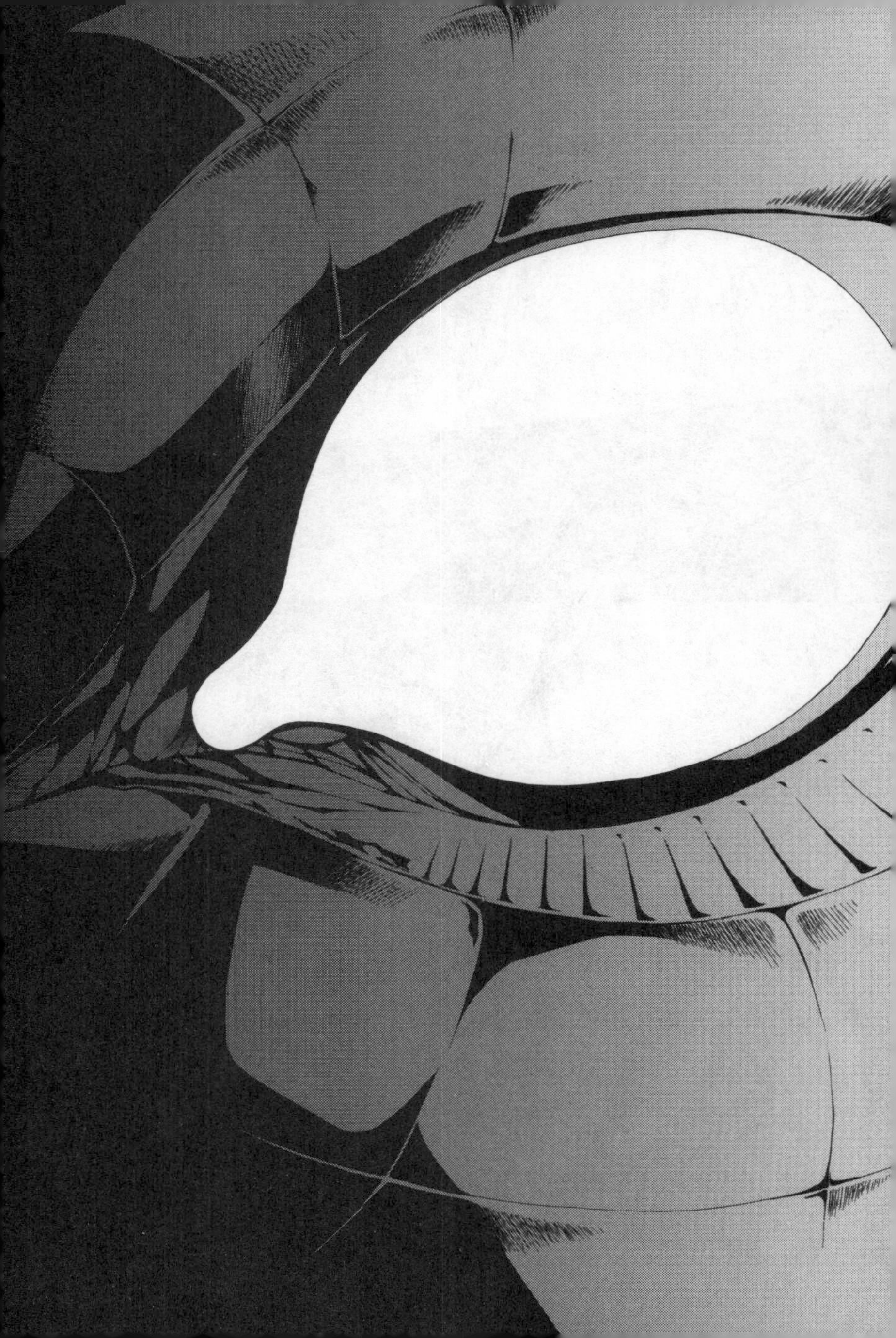

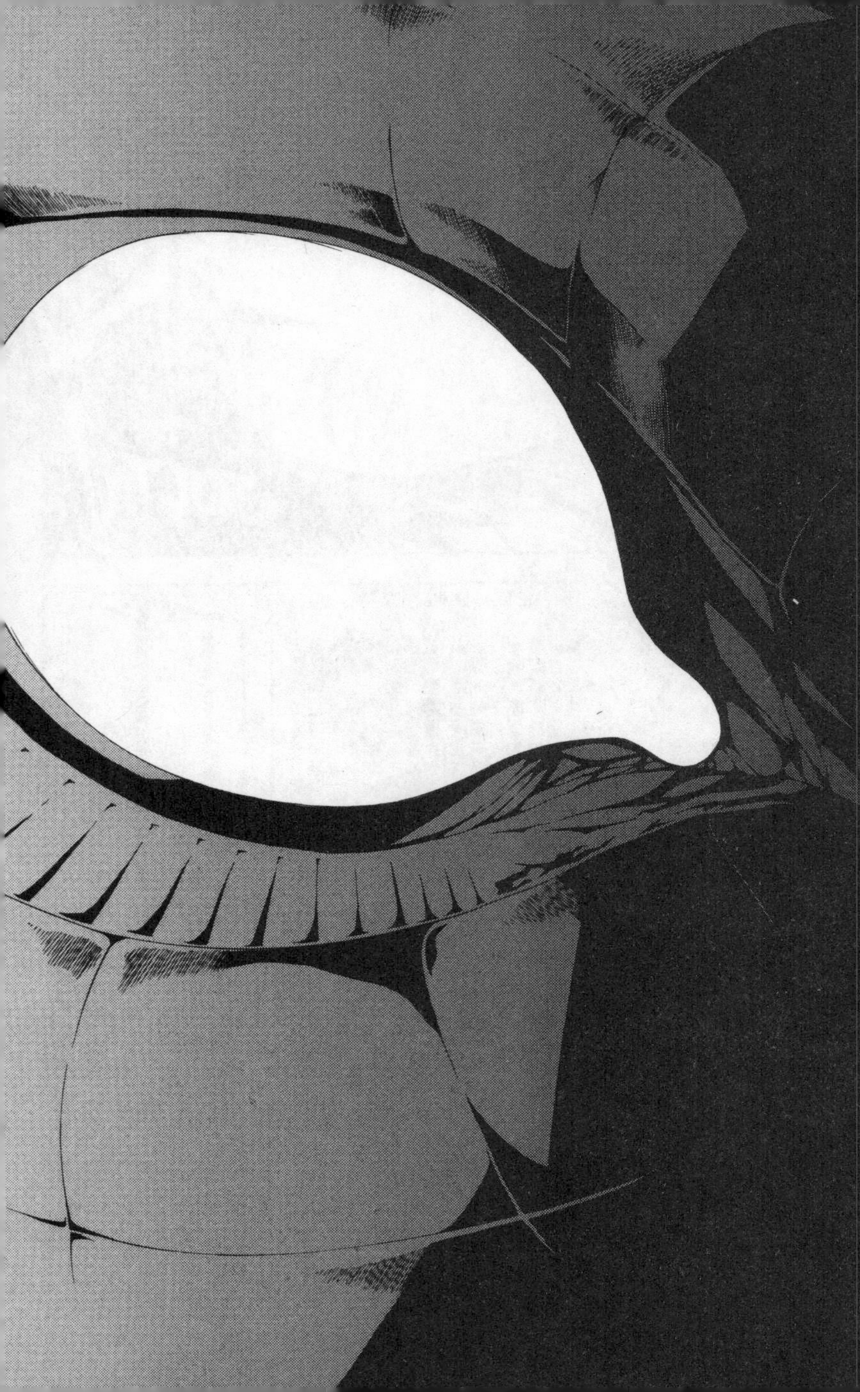

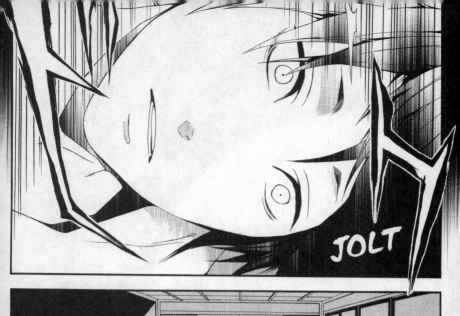

JOLT

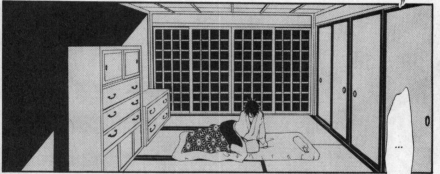

...

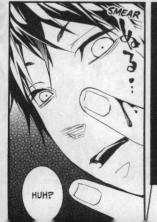

SMEAR

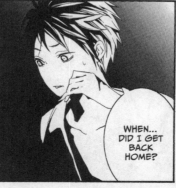

WHEN...
DID I GET
BACK
HOME?

HUH?

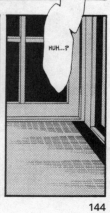

HUH...?

144

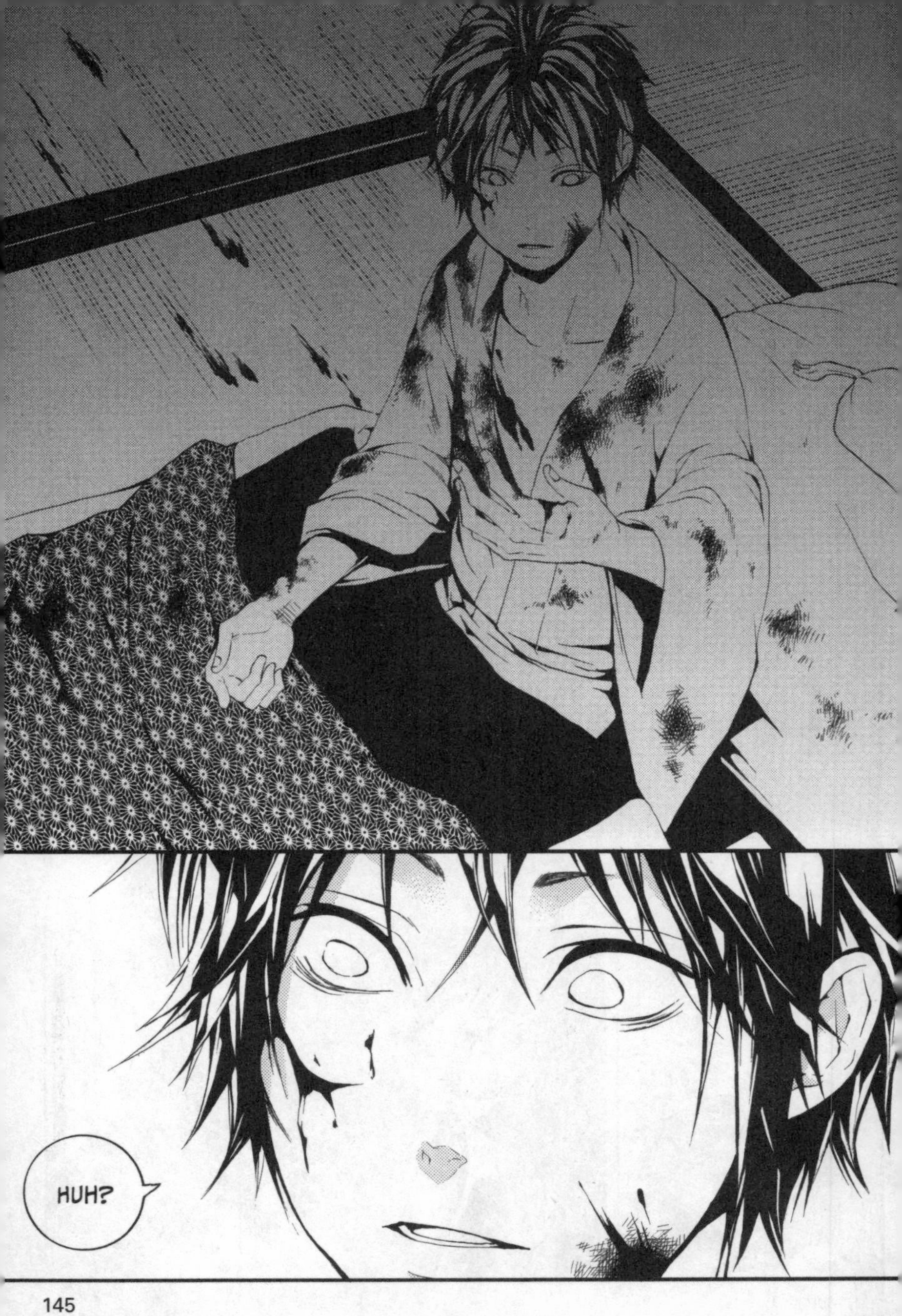
HUH?

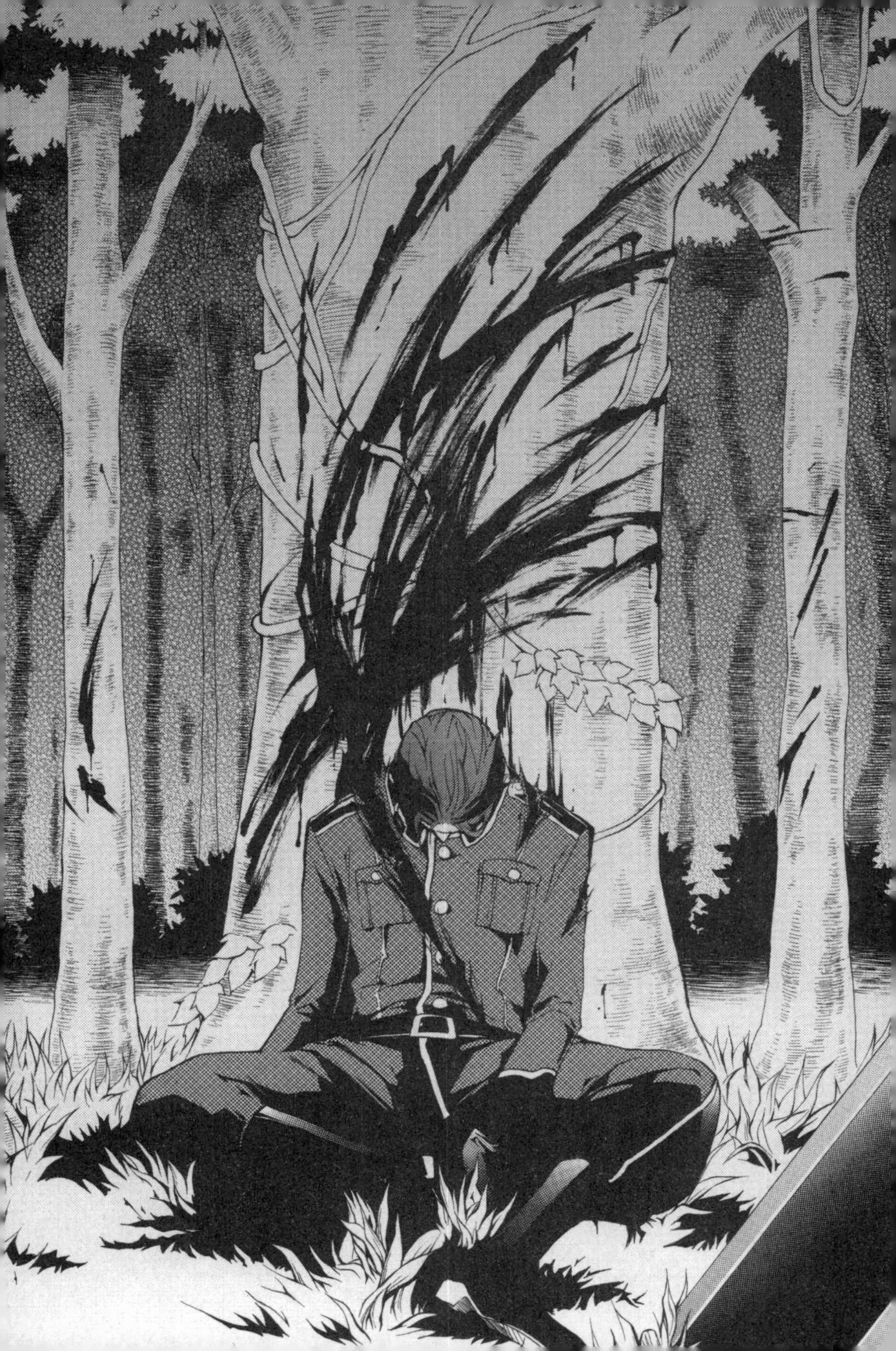

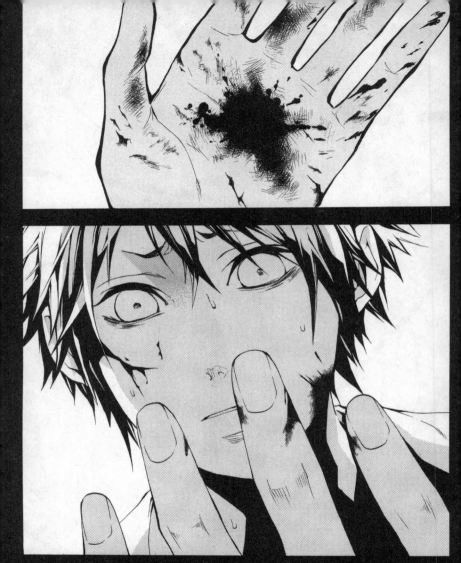

I CAN'T REMEMBER.

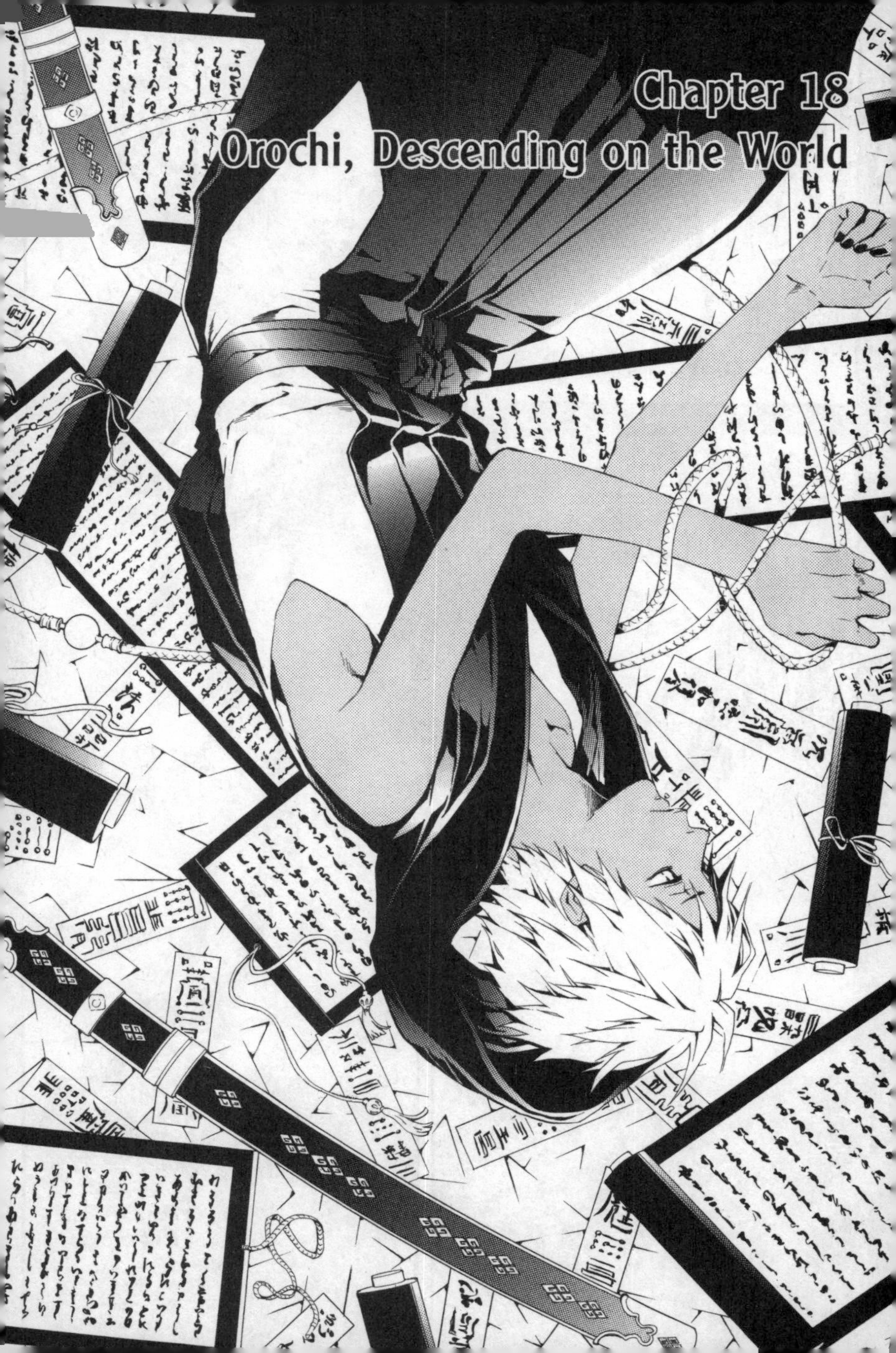
Chapter 18
Orochi, Descending on the World

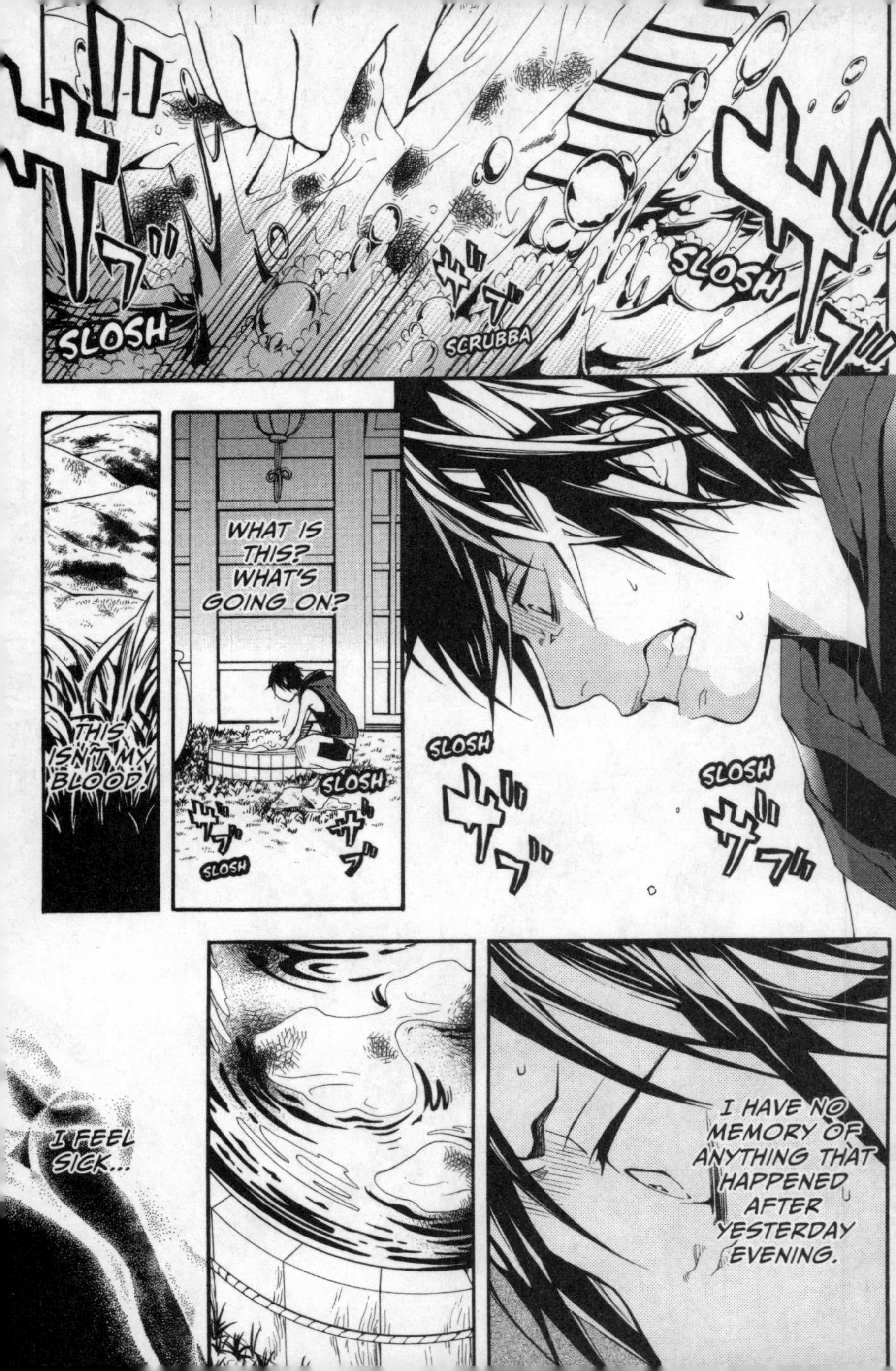
SLOSH
SCRUBBA
SLOSH
SLOSH
SLOSH
WHAT IS THIS? WHAT'S GOING ON?
SLOSH
SLOSH
THIS ISN'T MY BLOOD.
I HAVE NO MEMORY OF ANYTHING THAT HAPPENED AFTER YESTERDAY EVENING.
I FEEL SICK...

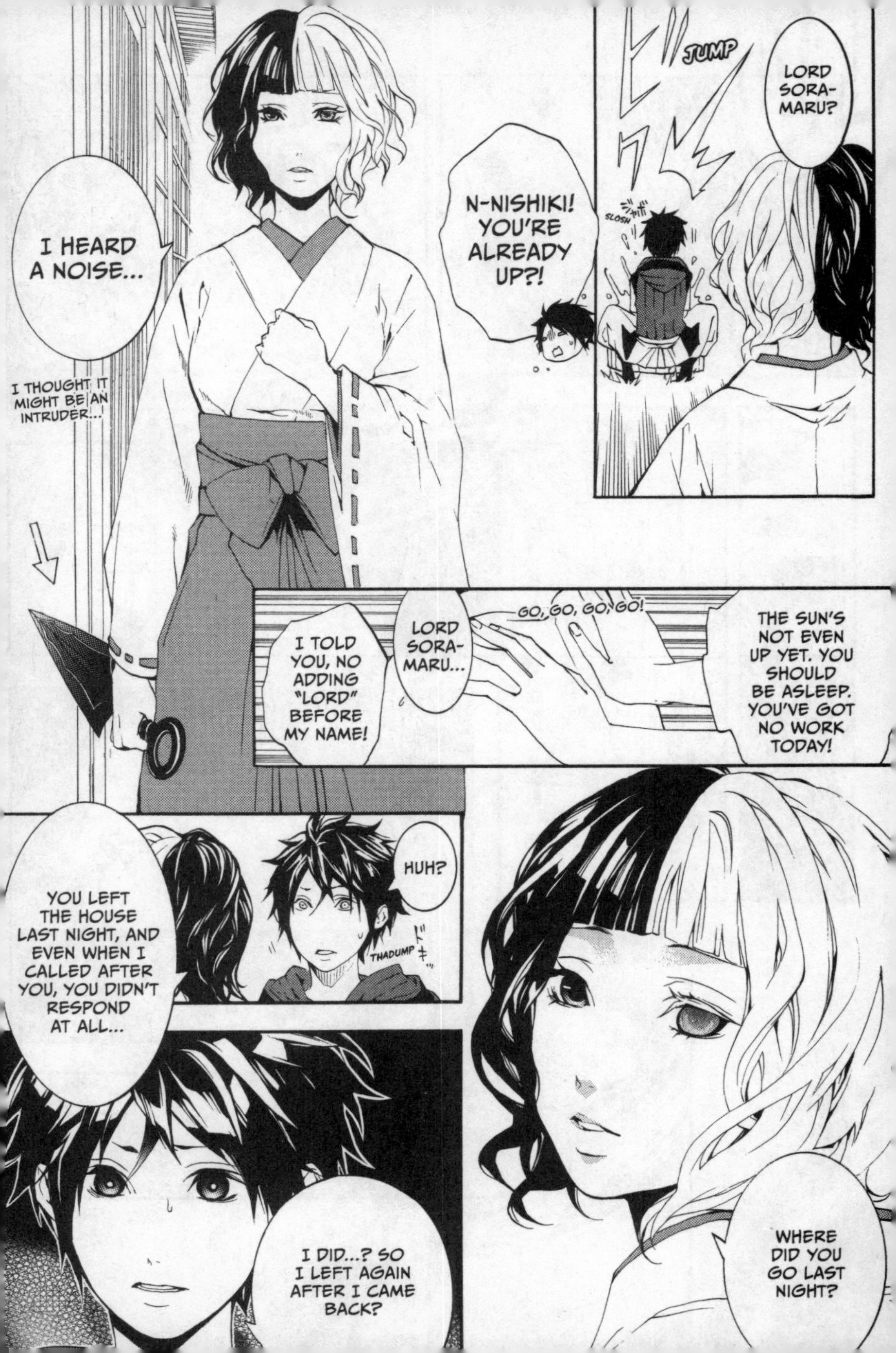
LORD SORA-MARU?
JUMP
SLOSH
N-NISHIKI! YOU'RE ALREADY UP?!
I HEARD A NOISE...
I THOUGHT IT MIGHT BE AN INTRUDER...!
THE SUN'S NOT EVEN UP YET. YOU SHOULD BE ASLEEP. YOU'VE GOT NO WORK TODAY!
GO, GO, GO, GO!
LORD SORA-MARU...
I TOLD YOU, NO ADDING "LORD" BEFORE MY NAME!
WHERE DID YOU GO LAST NIGHT?
YOU LEFT THE HOUSE LAST NIGHT, AND EVEN WHEN I CALLED AFTER YOU, YOU DIDN'T RESPOND AT ALL...
HUH?
THADUMP
I DID...? SO I LEFT AGAIN AFTER I CAME BACK?

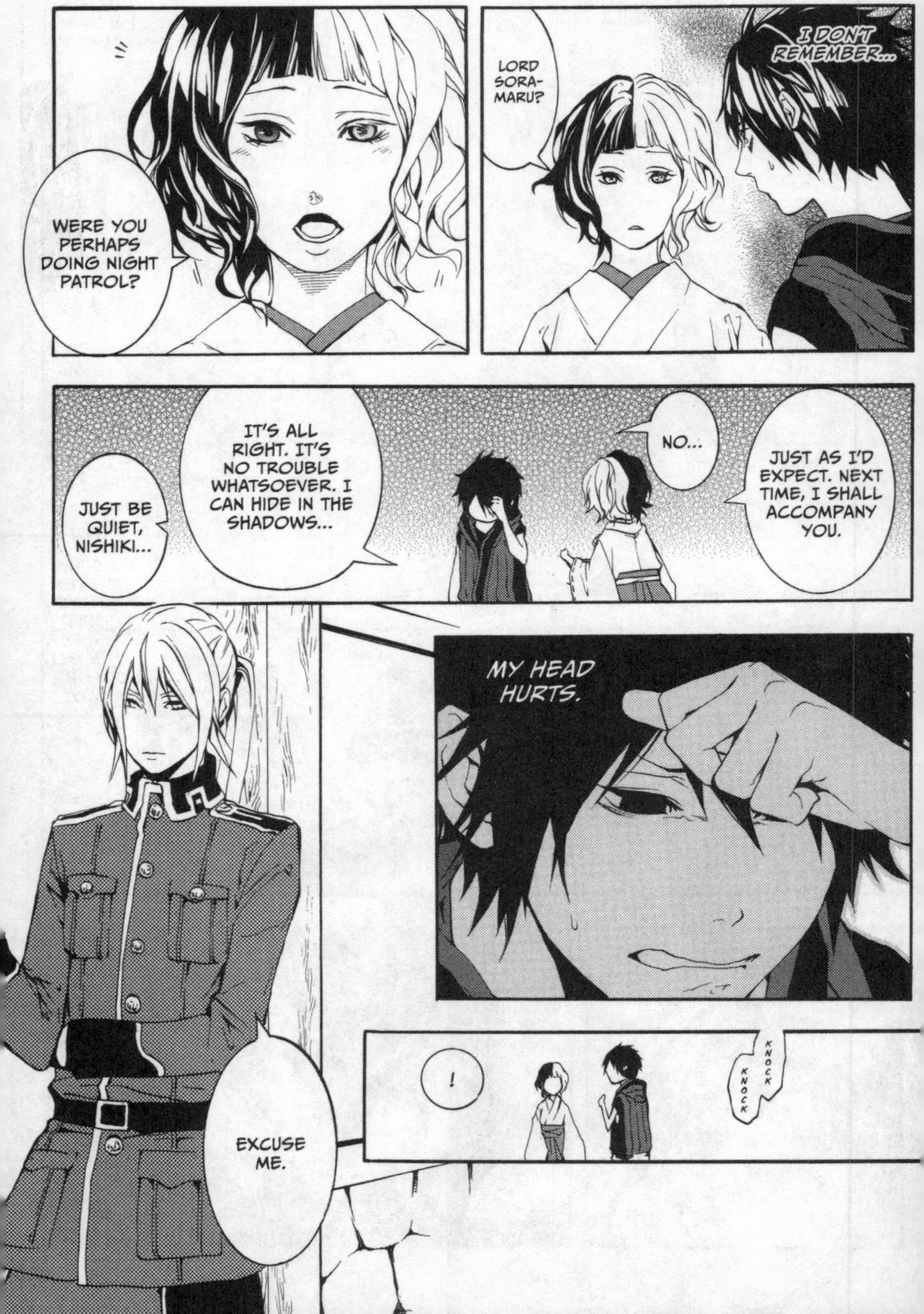
I DON'T REMEMBER...
LORD SORA-MARU?
WERE YOU PERHAPS DOING NIGHT PATROL?
JUST AS I'D EXPECT. NEXT TIME, I SHALL ACCOMPANY YOU.
NO...
IT'S ALL RIGHT. IT'S NO TROUBLE WHATSOEVER. I CAN HIDE IN THE SHADOWS...
JUST BE QUIET, NISHIKI...
MY HEAD HURTS.
KNOCK KNOCK
!
EXCUSE ME.

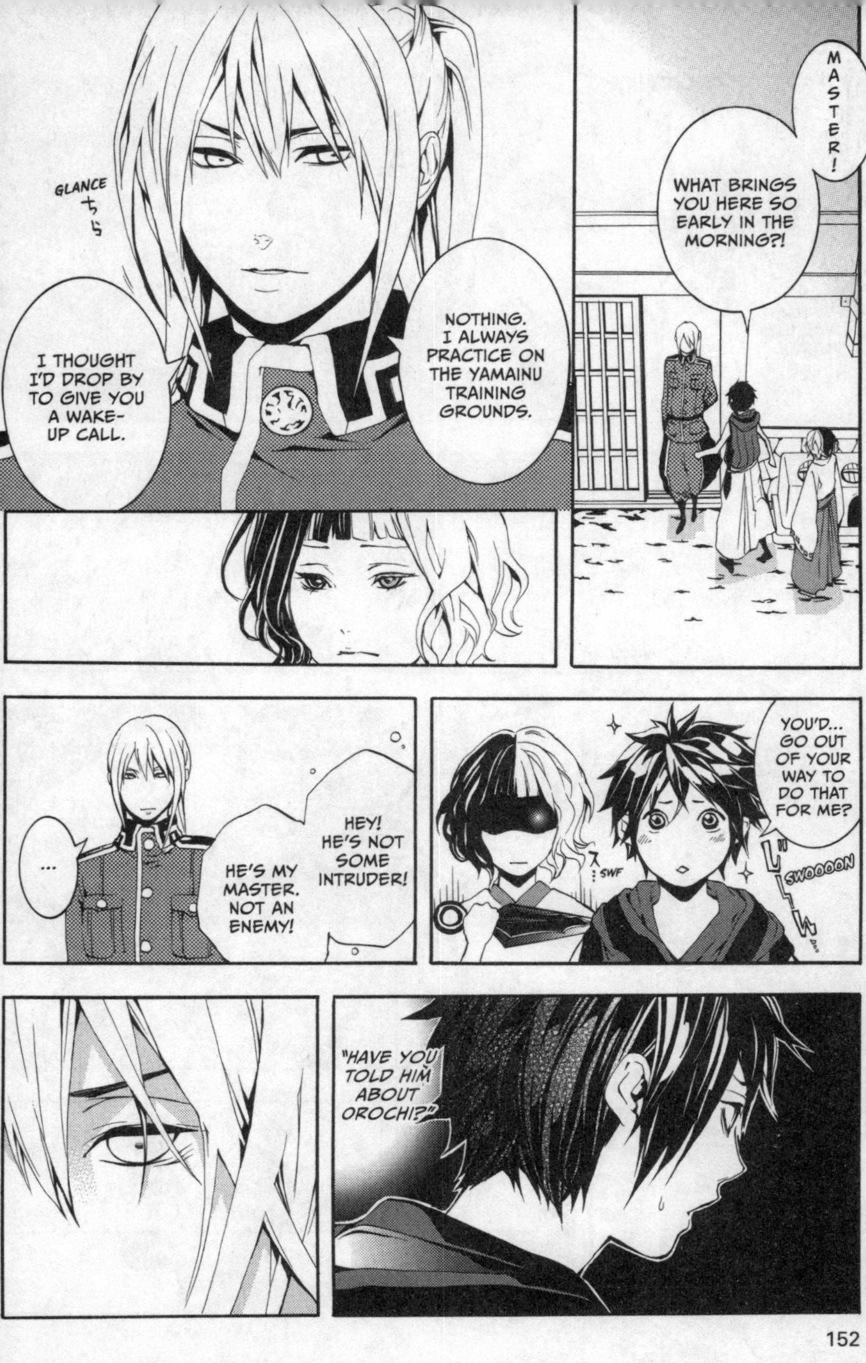
MASTER!
WHAT BRINGS YOU HERE SO EARLY IN THE MORNING?!
NOTHING. I ALWAYS PRACTICE ON THE YAMAINU TRAINING GROUNDS.
GLANCE
I THOUGHT I'D DROP BY TO GIVE YOU A WAKE-UP CALL.
YOU'D... GO OUT OF YOUR WAY TO DO THAT FOR ME?
SWOOOON
SWF
HEY! HE'S NOT SOME INTRUDER!
HE'S MY MASTER. NOT AN ENEMY!
...
"HAVE YOU TOLD HIM ABOUT OROCHI?"

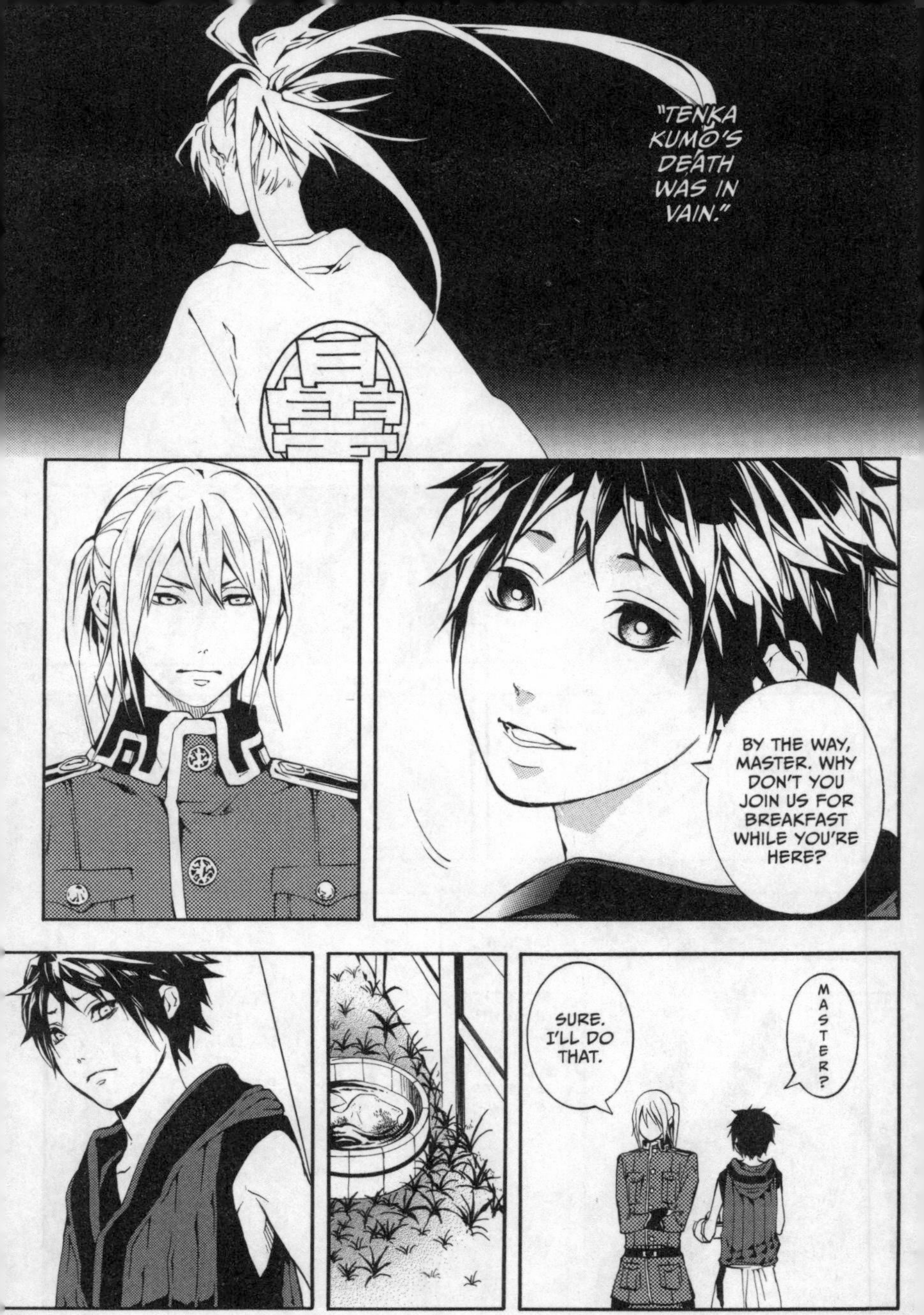
"TENKA KUMO'S DEATH WAS IN VAIN."
BY THE WAY, MASTER. WHY DON'T YOU JOIN US FOR BREAKFAST WHILE YOU'RE HERE?
MASTER?
SURE. I'LL DO THAT.

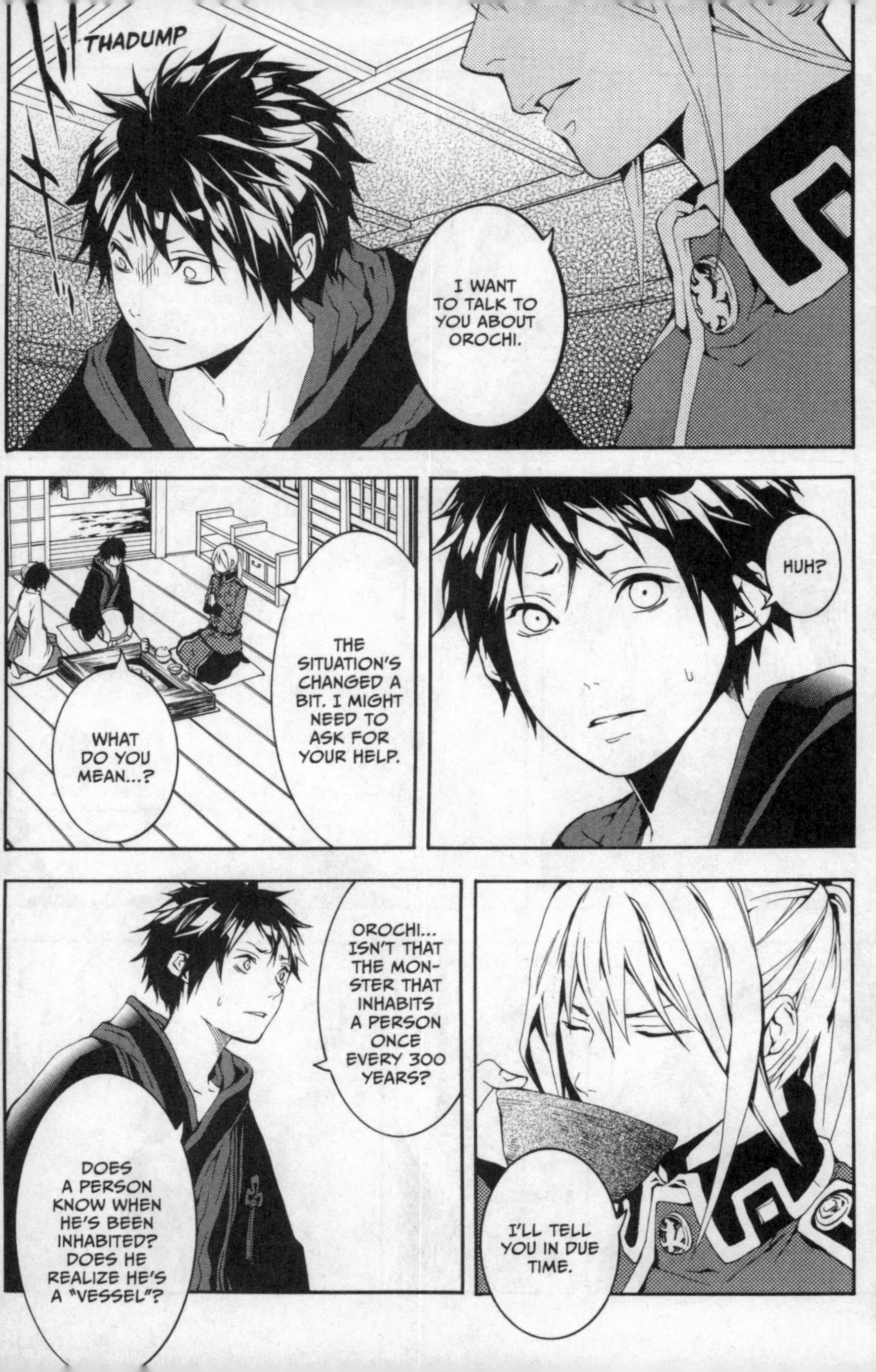
I WANT TO TALK TO YOU ABOUT OROCHI.
THADUMP
HUH?
THE SITUATION'S CHANGED A BIT. I MIGHT NEED TO ASK FOR YOUR HELP.
WHAT DO YOU MEAN...?
I'LL TELL YOU IN DUE TIME.
OROCHI... ISN'T THAT THE MON-STER THAT INHABITS A PERSON ONCE EVERY 300 YEARS?
DOES A PERSON KNOW WHEN HE'S BEEN INHABITED? DOES HE REALIZE HE'S A "VESSEL"?

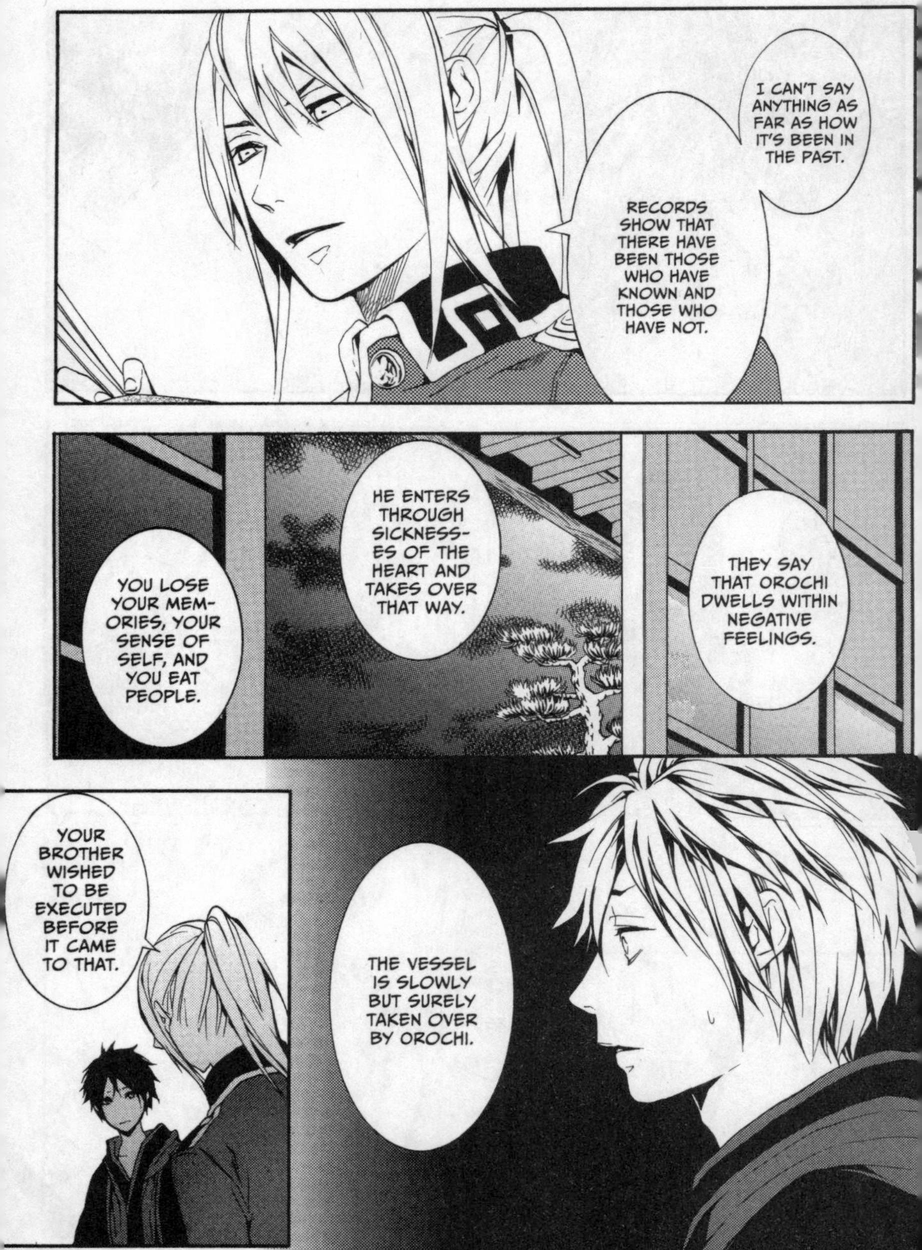
I CAN'T SAY ANYTHING AS FAR AS HOW IT'S BEEN IN THE PAST.
RECORDS SHOW THAT THERE HAVE BEEN THOSE WHO HAVE KNOWN AND THOSE WHO HAVE NOT.
THEY SAY THAT OROCHI DWELLS WITHIN NEGATIVE FEELINGS.
HE ENTERS THROUGH SICKNESS-ES OF THE HEART AND TAKES OVER THAT WAY.
YOU LOSE YOUR MEM-ORIES, YOUR SENSE OF SELF, AND YOU EAT PEOPLE.
THE VESSEL IS SLOWLY BUT SURELY TAKEN OVER BY OROCHI.
YOUR BROTHER WISHED TO BE EXECUTED BEFORE IT CAME TO THAT.

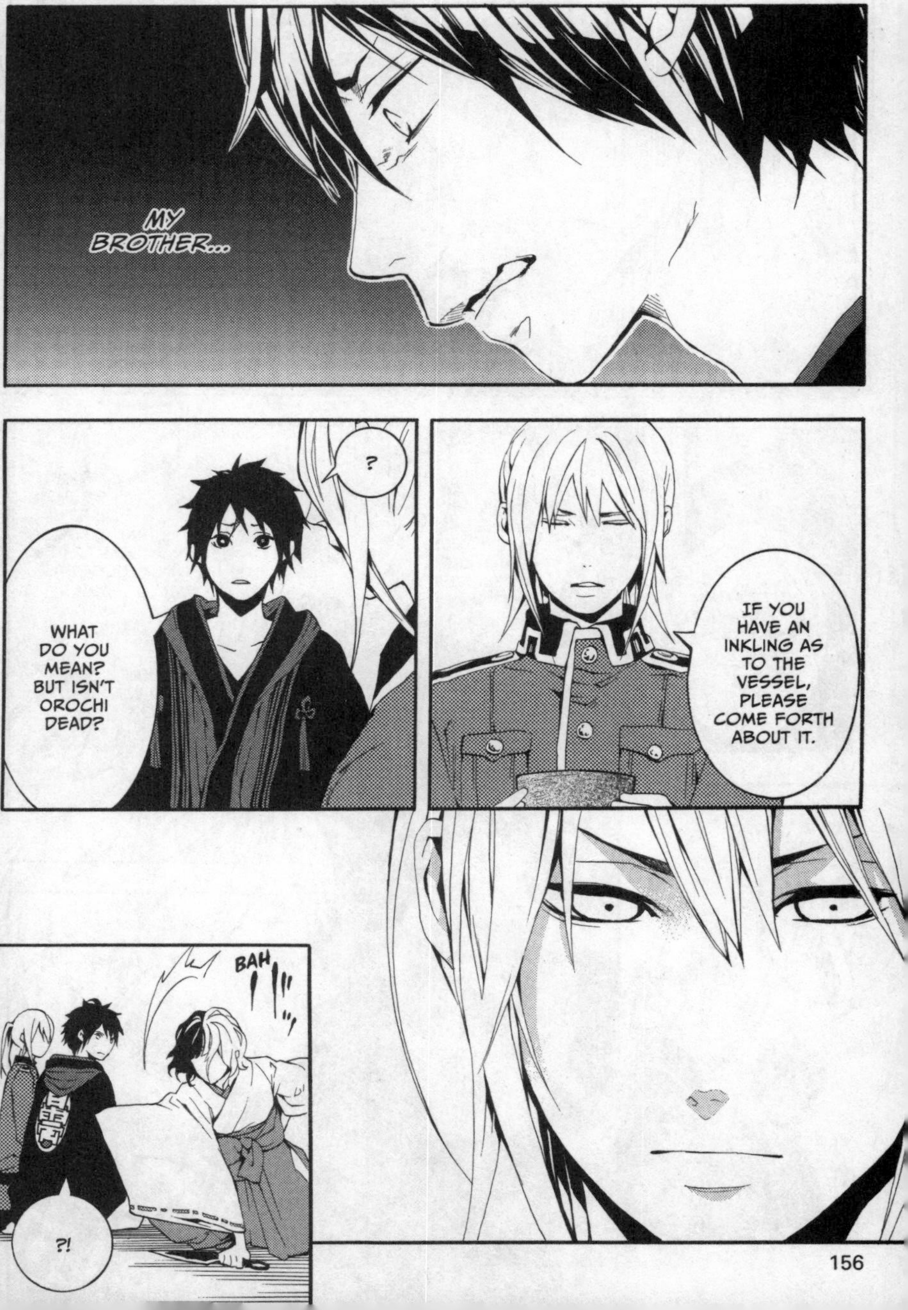
MY BROTHER...
IF YOU HAVE AN INKLING AS TO THE VESSEL, PLEASE COME FORTH ABOUT IT.
?
WHAT DO YOU MEAN? BUT ISN'T OROCHI DEAD?
BAH
?!

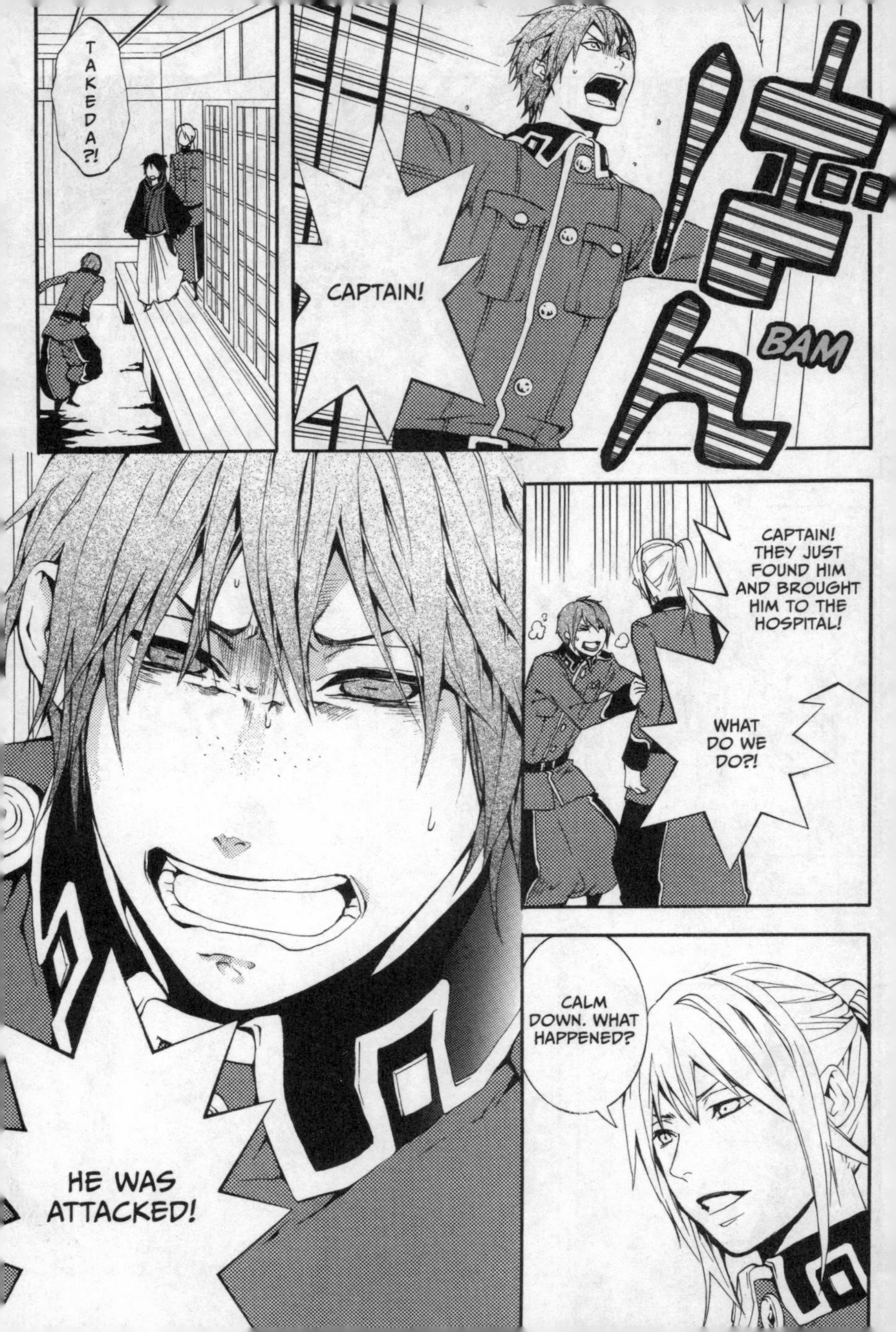
BAM
CAPTAIN!
TAKEDA?!
CAPTAIN! THEY JUST FOUND HIM AND BROUGHT HIM TO THE HOSPITAL!
WHAT DO WE DO?!
CALM DOWN. WHAT HAPPENED?
HE WAS ATTACKED!

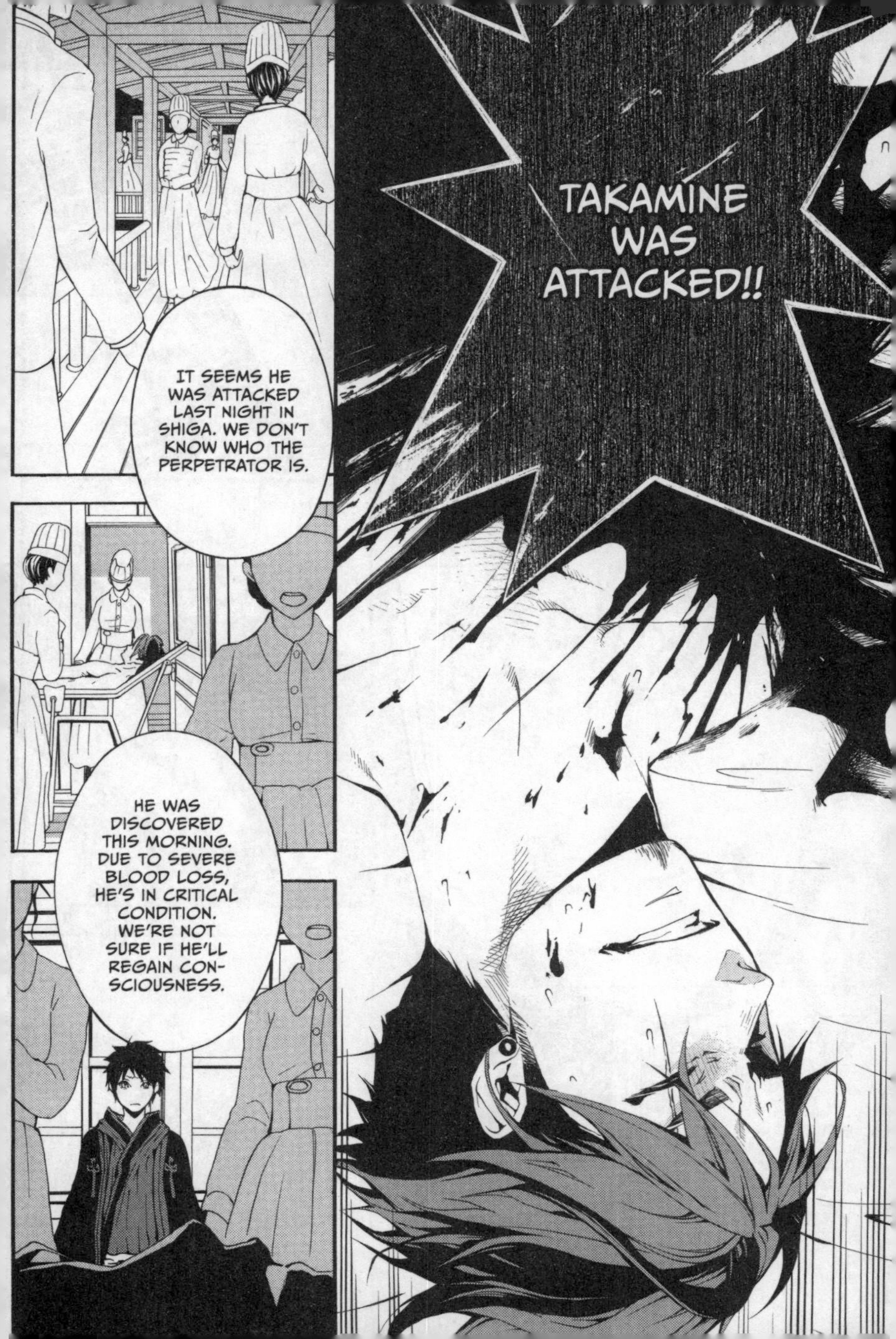
TAKAMINE WAS ATTACKED!!
IT SEEMS HE WAS ATTACKED LAST NIGHT IN SHIGA. WE DON'T KNOW WHO THE PERPETRATOR IS.
HE WAS DISCOVERED THIS MORNING. DUE TO SEVERE BLOOD LOSS, HE'S IN CRITICAL CONDITION. WE'RE NOT SURE IF HE'LL REGAIN CONSCIOUSNESS.

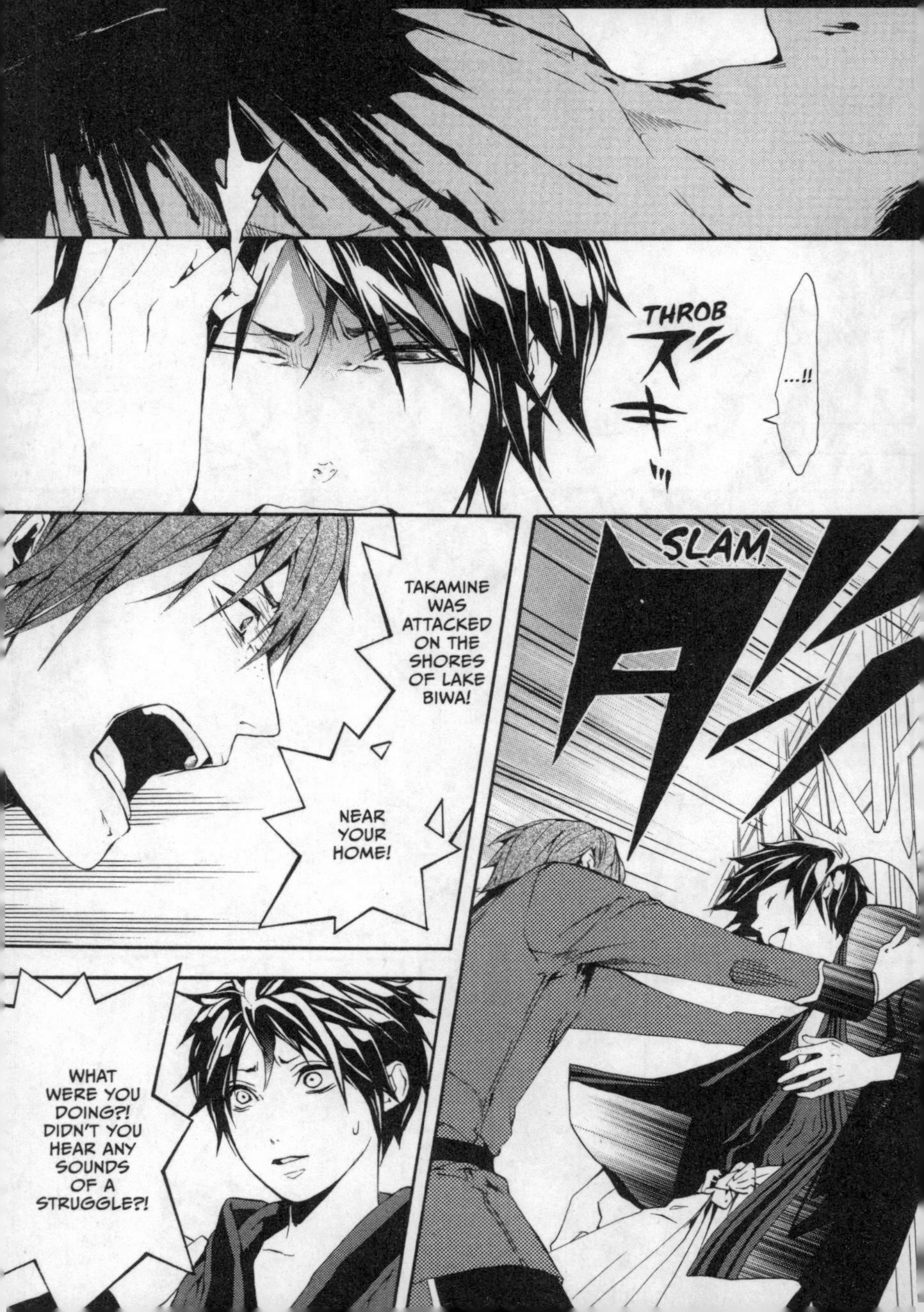
THROB
...!!
TAKAMINE WAS ATTACKED ON THE SHORES OF LAKE BIWA!
NEAR YOUR HOME!
SLAM
WHAT WERE YOU DOING?! DIDN'T YOU HEAR ANY SOUNDS OF A STRUGGLE?!

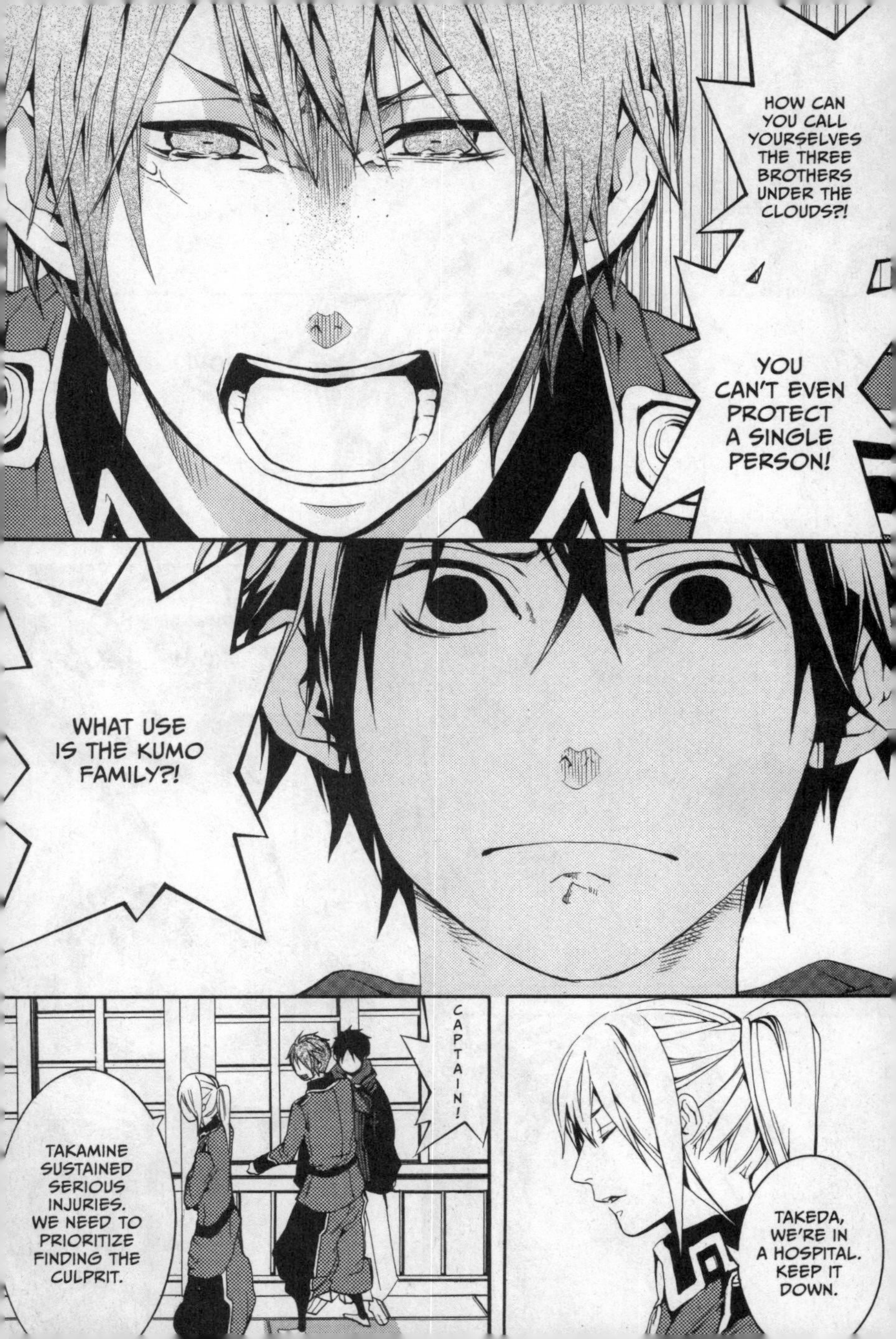
HOW CAN YOU CALL YOURSELVES THE THREE BROTHERS UNDER THE CLOUDS?!
YOU CAN'T EVEN PROTECT A SINGLE PERSON!
WHAT USE IS THE KUMO FAMILY?!
TAKEDA, WE'RE IN A HOSPITAL. KEEP IT DOWN.
CAPTAIN!
TAKAMINE SUSTAINED SERIOUS INJURIES. WE NEED TO PRIORITIZE FINDING THE CULPRIT.

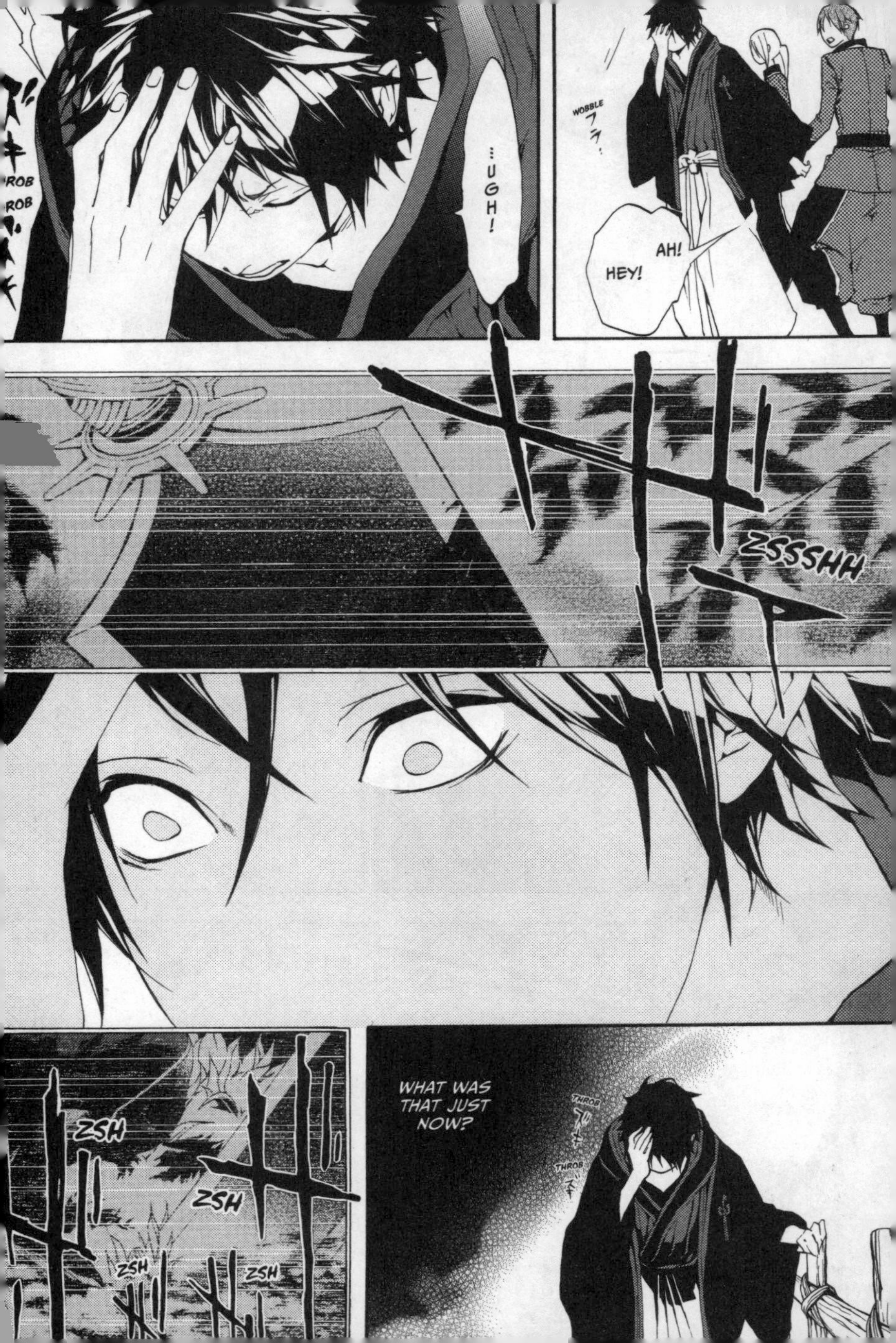
WOBBLE
フラ…
AH!
HEY!
ROB ROB
...UGH!
ZSSSHH
WHAT WAS THAT JUST NOW?
THROB
THROB
ZSH
ZSH
ZSH
ZSH

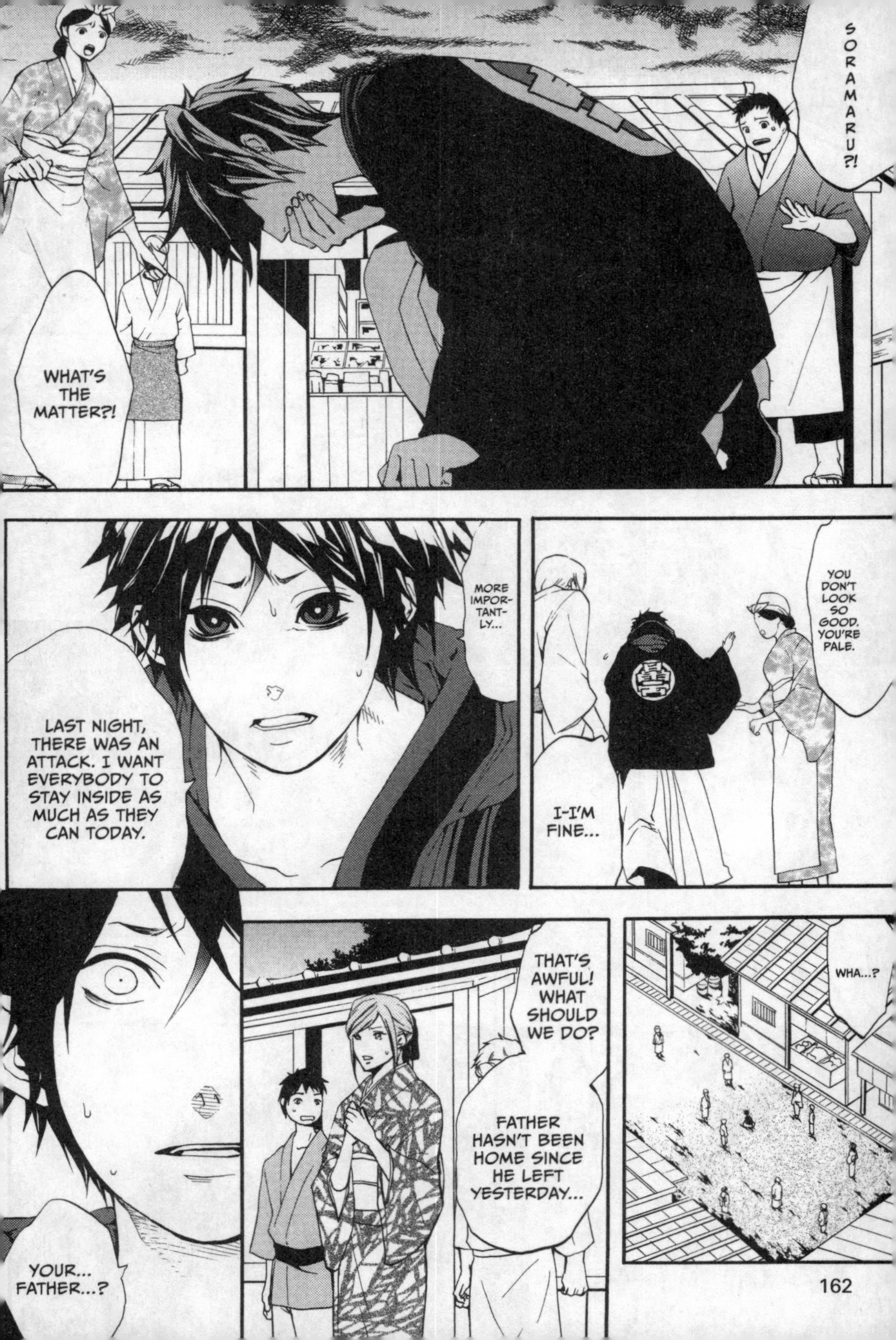
SORAMARU?!
WHAT'S THE MATTER?!
YOU DON'T LOOK SO GOOD. YOU'RE PALE.
I-I'M FINE...
MORE IMPORTANTLY...
LAST NIGHT, THERE WAS AN ATTACK. I WANT EVERYBODY TO STAY INSIDE AS MUCH AS THEY CAN TODAY.
WHA...?
THAT'S AWFUL! WHAT SHOULD WE DO?
FATHER HASN'T BEEN HOME SINCE HE LEFT YESTERDAY...
YOUR... FATHER...?

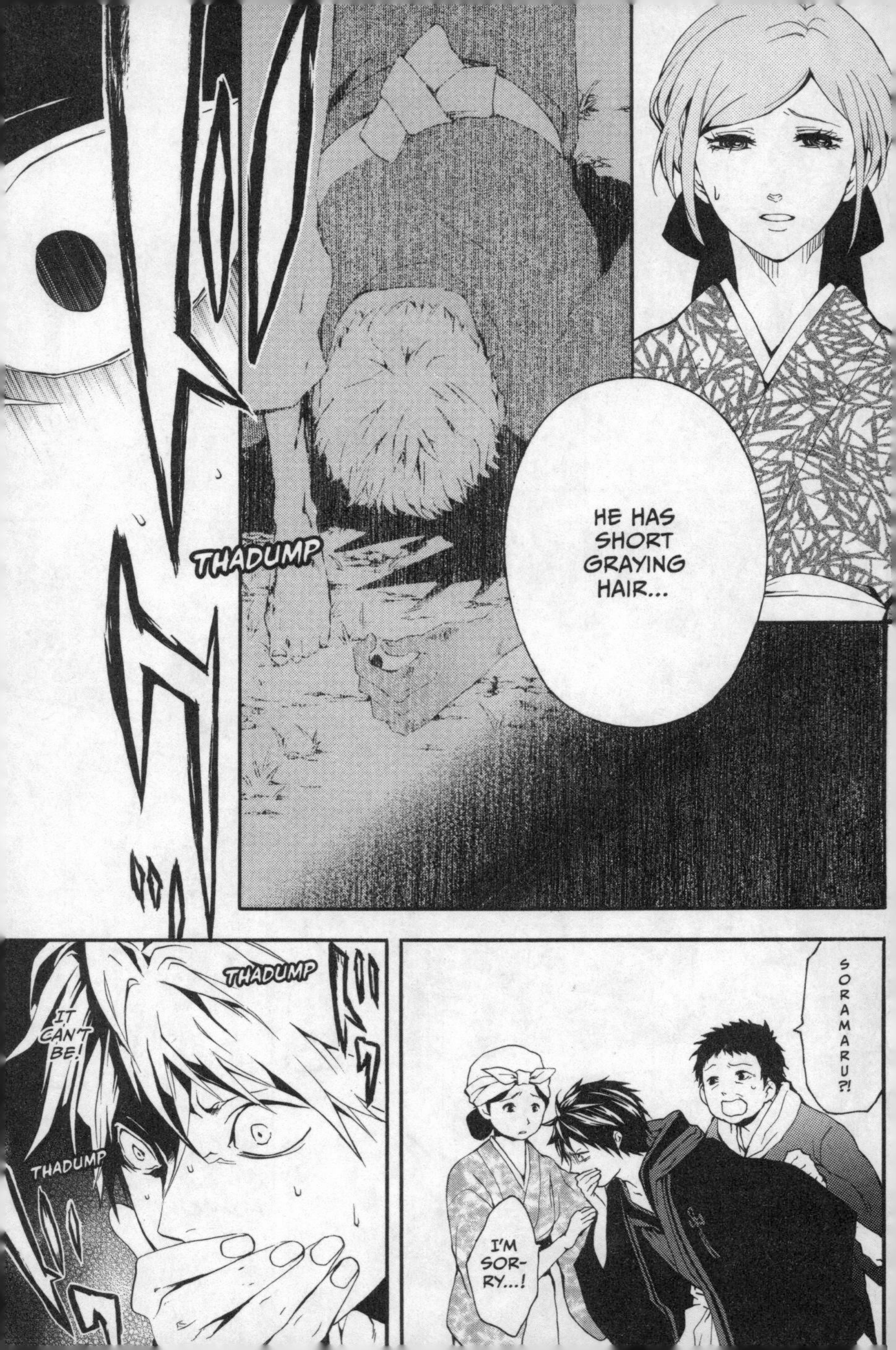
HE HAS SHORT GRAYING HAIR...
THADUMP
SORAMARU?!
I'M SORRY...!
THADUMP
IT CAN'T BE!
THADUMP

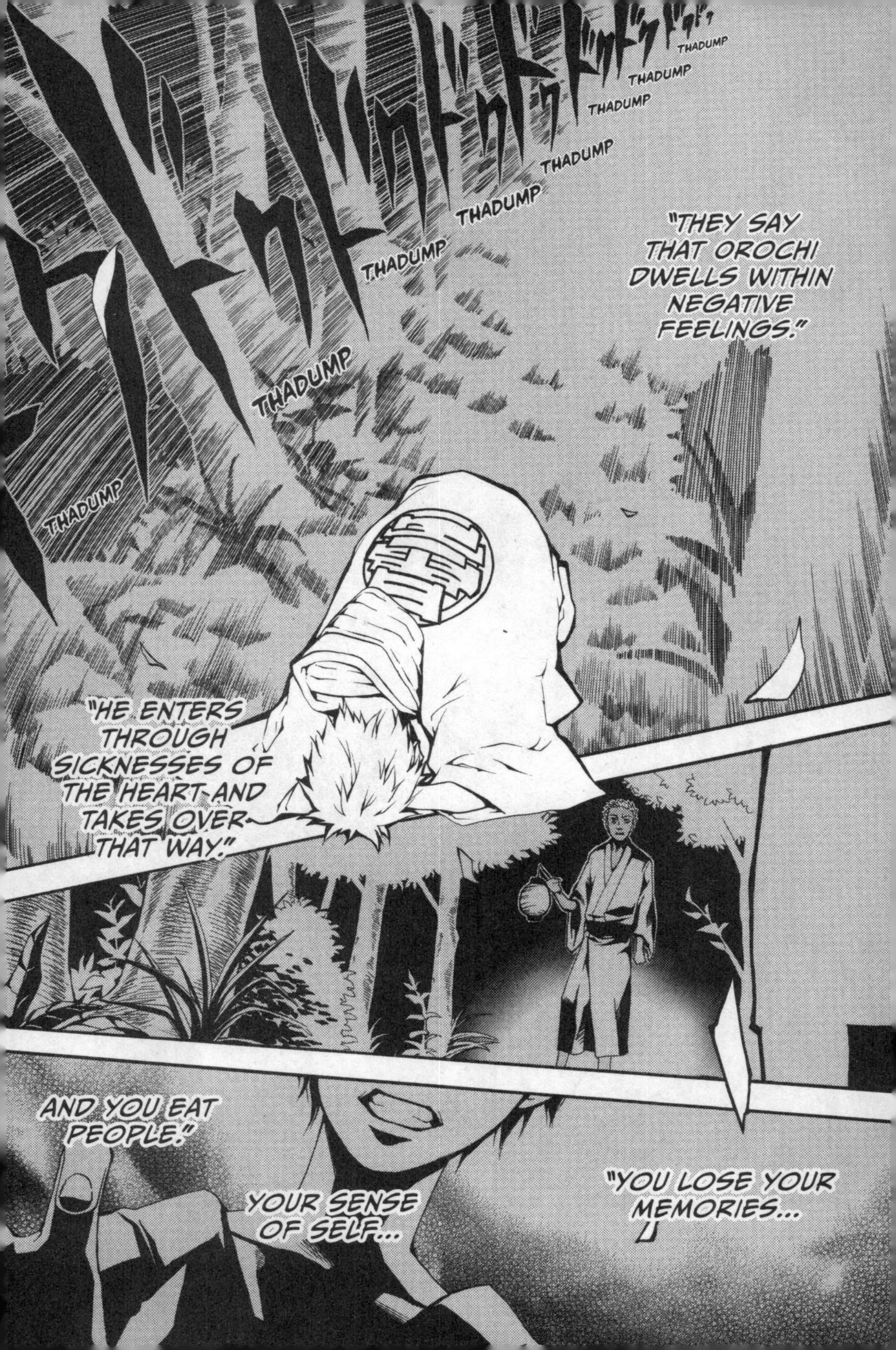
"THEY SAY THAT OROCHI DWELLS WITHIN NEGATIVE FEELINGS."
THADUMP
THADUMP
THADUMP
THADUMP
THADUMP
THADUMP
THADUMP
THADUMP
"HE ENTERS THROUGH SICKNESSES OF THE HEART AND TAKES OVER THAT WAY."
"YOU LOSE YOUR MEMORIES...
YOUR SENSE OF SELF...
AND YOU EAT PEOPLE."

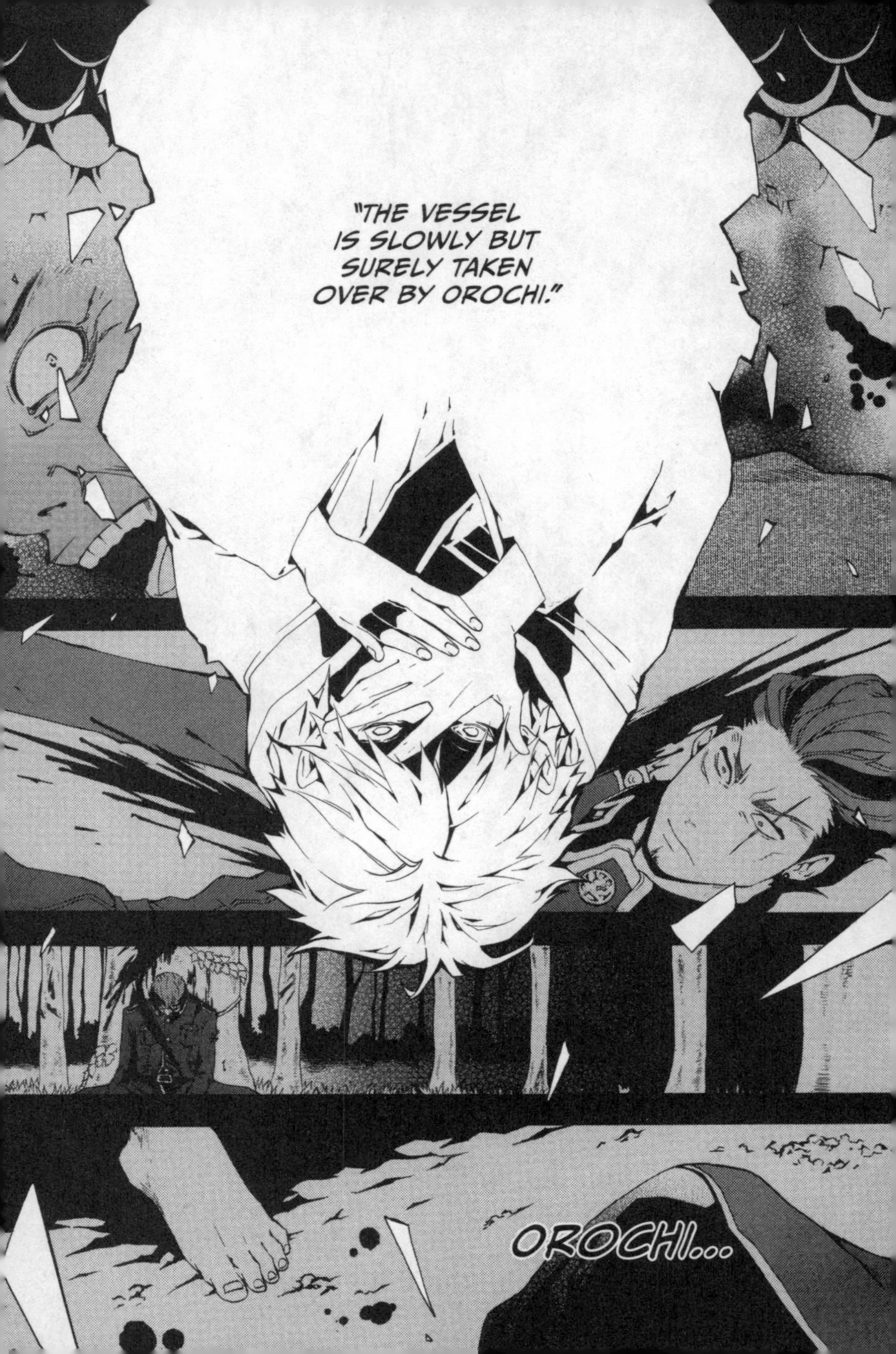
"THE VESSEL IS SLOWLY BUT SURELY TAKEN OVER BY OROCHI."
OROCHI...

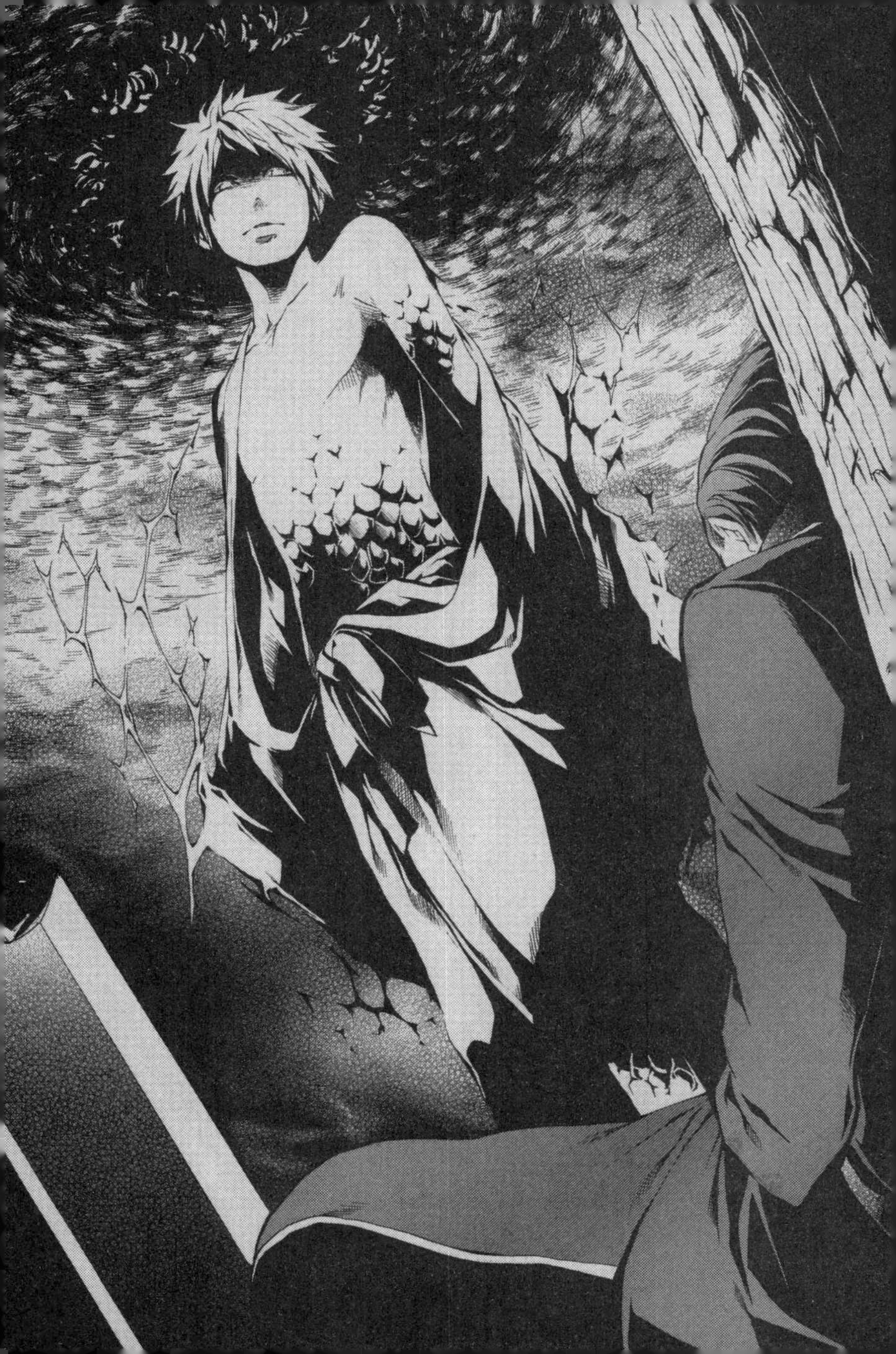

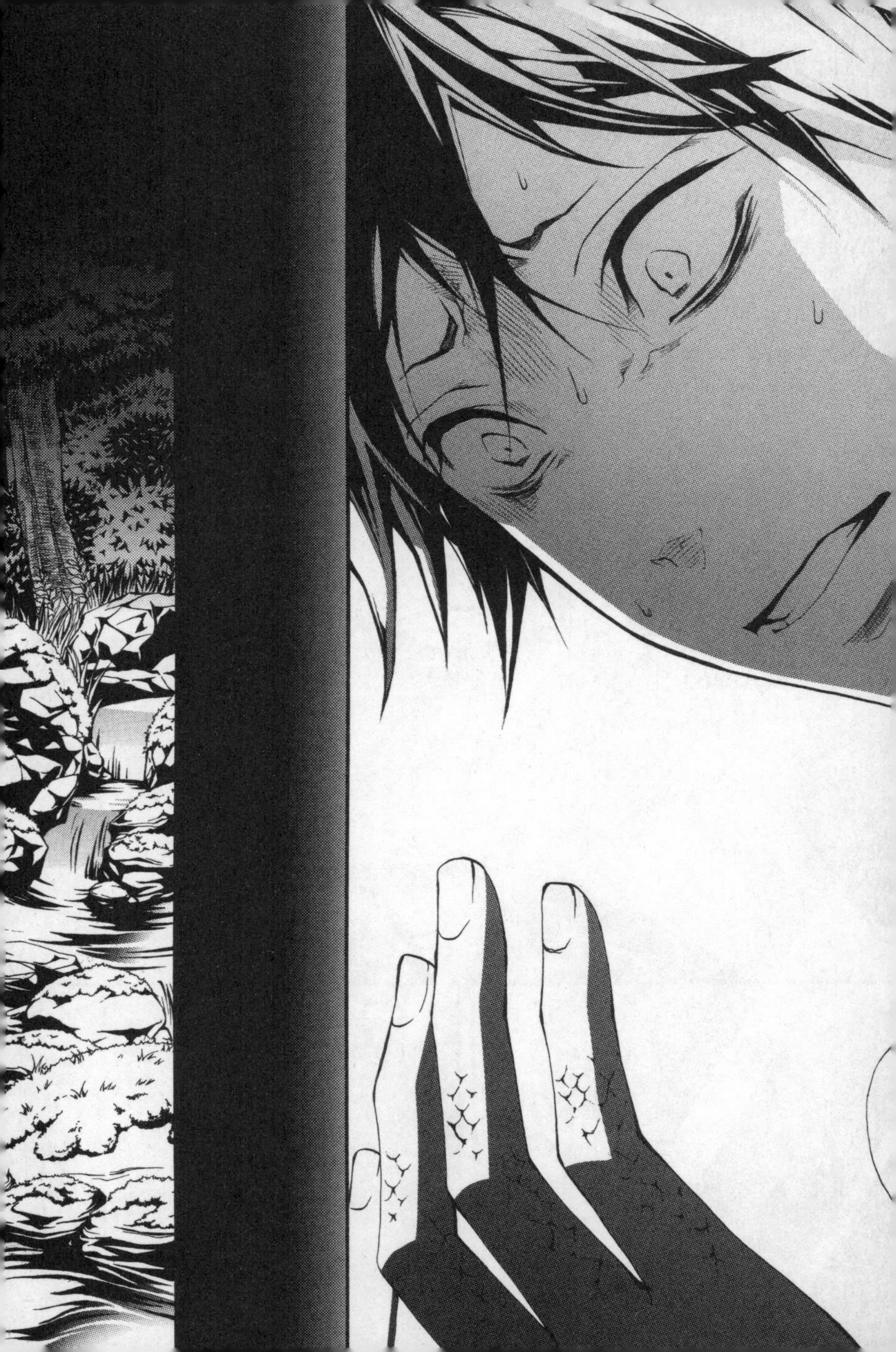

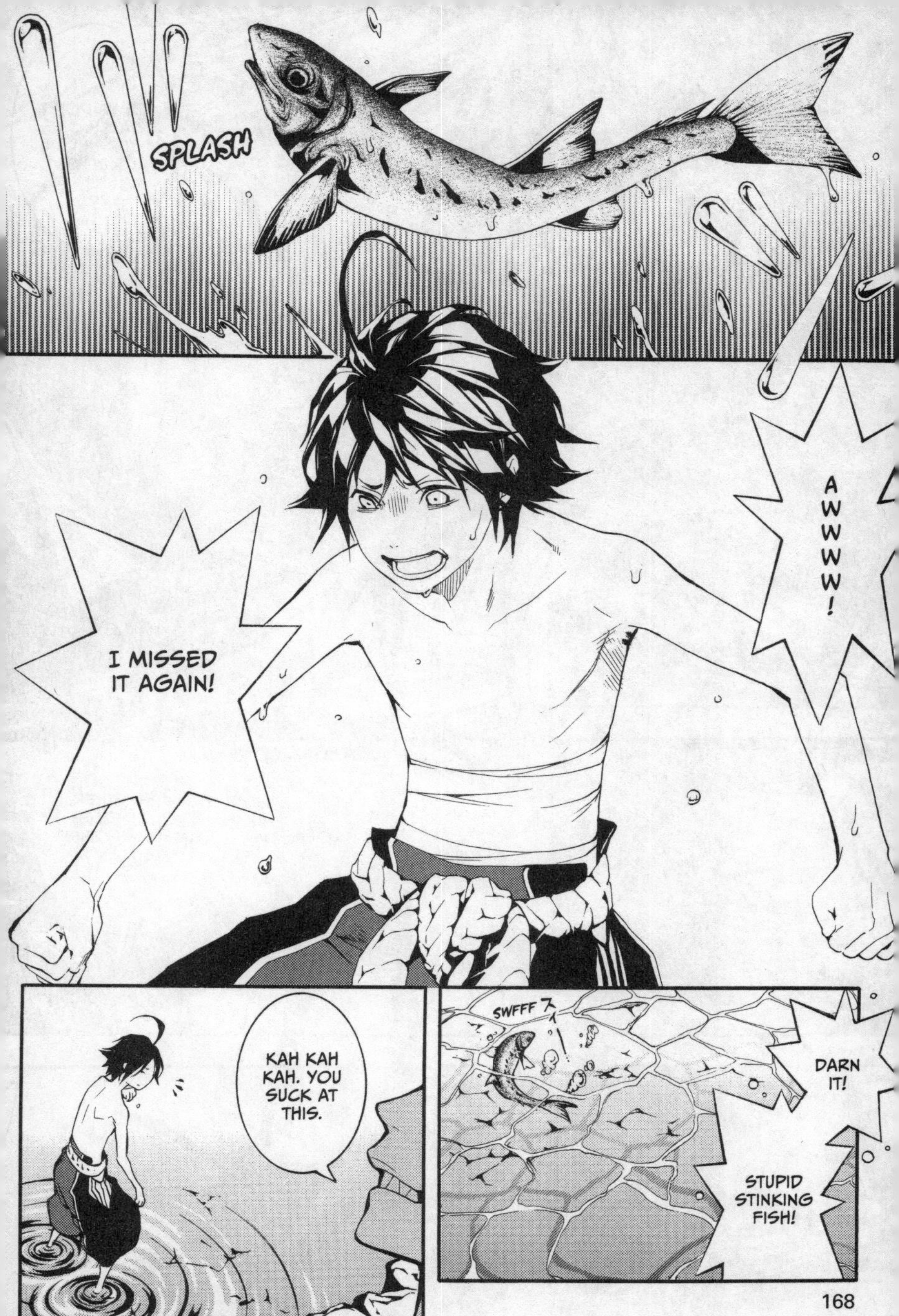
SPLASH
AWWWWW!
I MISSED IT AGAIN!
SWFFF スイ
DARN IT!
STUPID STINKING FISH!
KAH KAH KAH. YOU SUCK AT THIS.

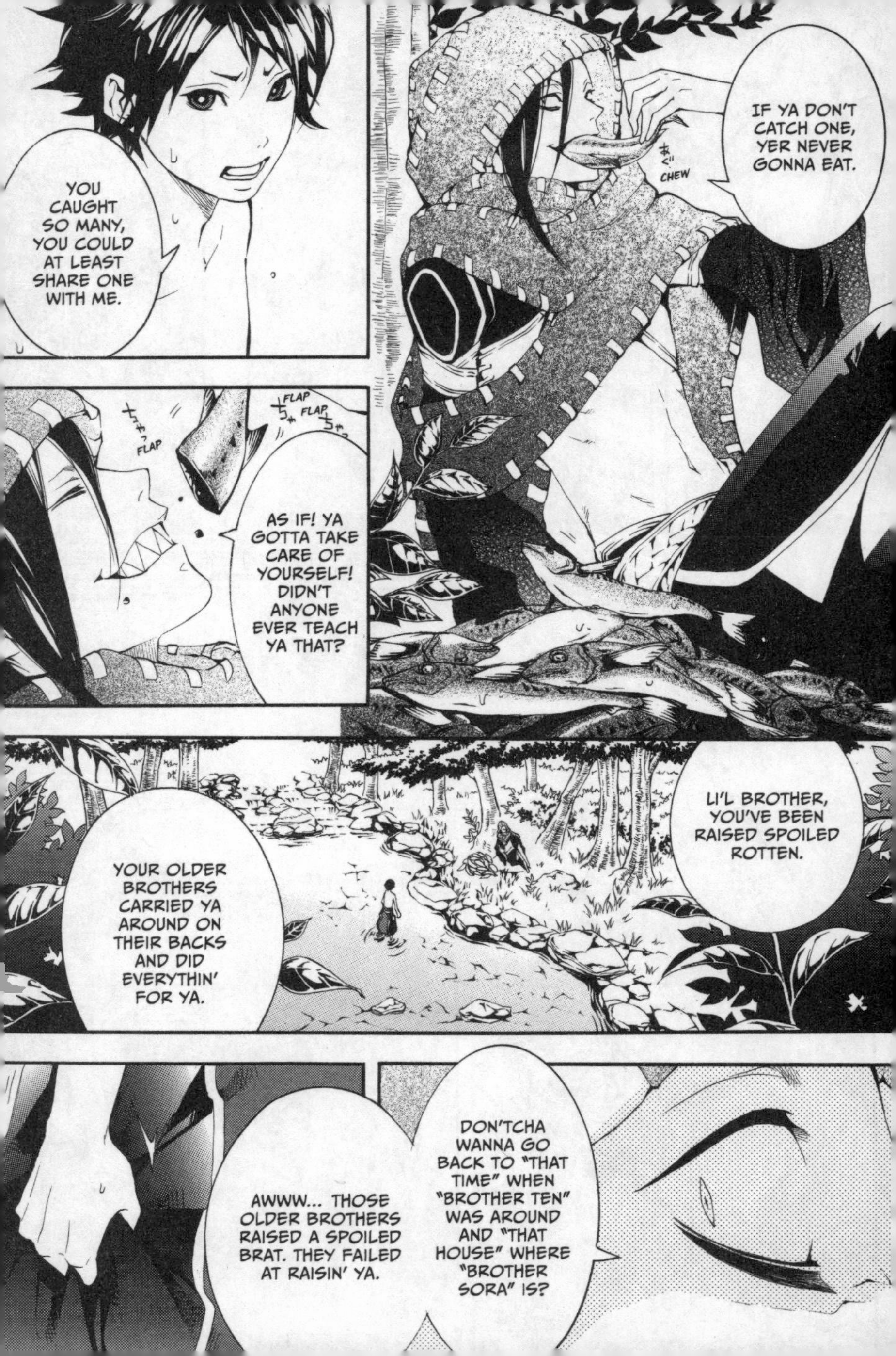

CHEW
IF YA DON'T CATCH ONE, YER NEVER GONNA EAT.
YOU CAUGHT SO MANY, YOU COULD AT LEAST SHARE ONE WITH ME.
FLAP FLAP FLAP
AS IF! YA GOTTA TAKE CARE OF YOURSELF! DIDN'T ANYONE EVER TEACH YA THAT?
LI'L BROTHER, YOU'VE BEEN RAISED SPOILED ROTTEN.
YOUR OLDER BROTHERS CARRIED YA AROUND ON THEIR BACKS AND DID EVERYTHIN' FOR YA.
DON'TCHA WANNA GO BACK TO "THAT TIME" WHEN "BROTHER TEN" WAS AROUND AND "THAT HOUSE" WHERE "BROTHER SORA" IS?
AWWW... THOSE OLDER BROTHERS RAISED A SPOILED BRAT. THEY FAILED AT RAISIN' YA.

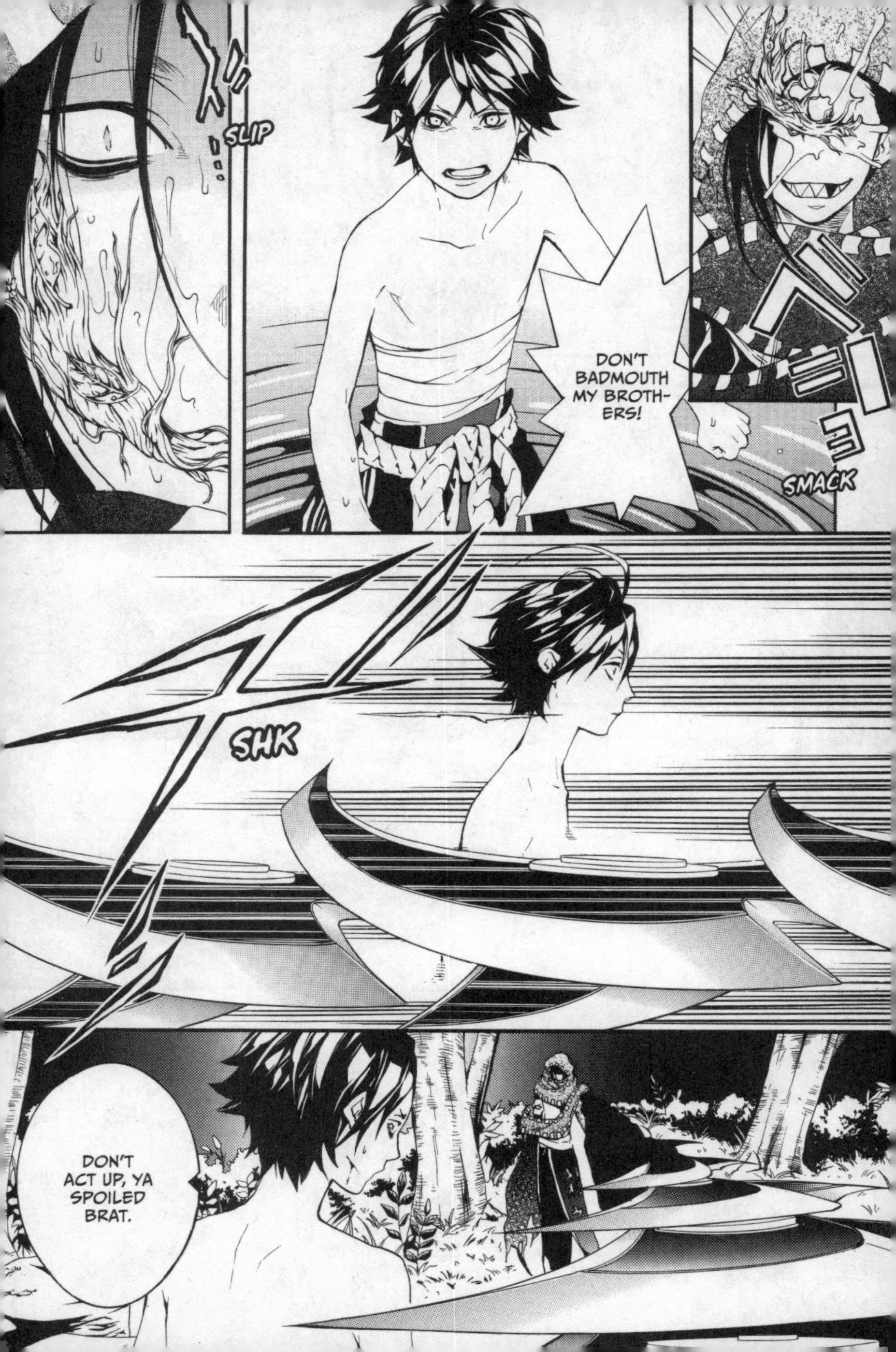
SMACK
DON'T BADMOUTH MY BROTHERS!
SLIP
SHK
DON'T ACT UP, YA SPOILED BRAT.

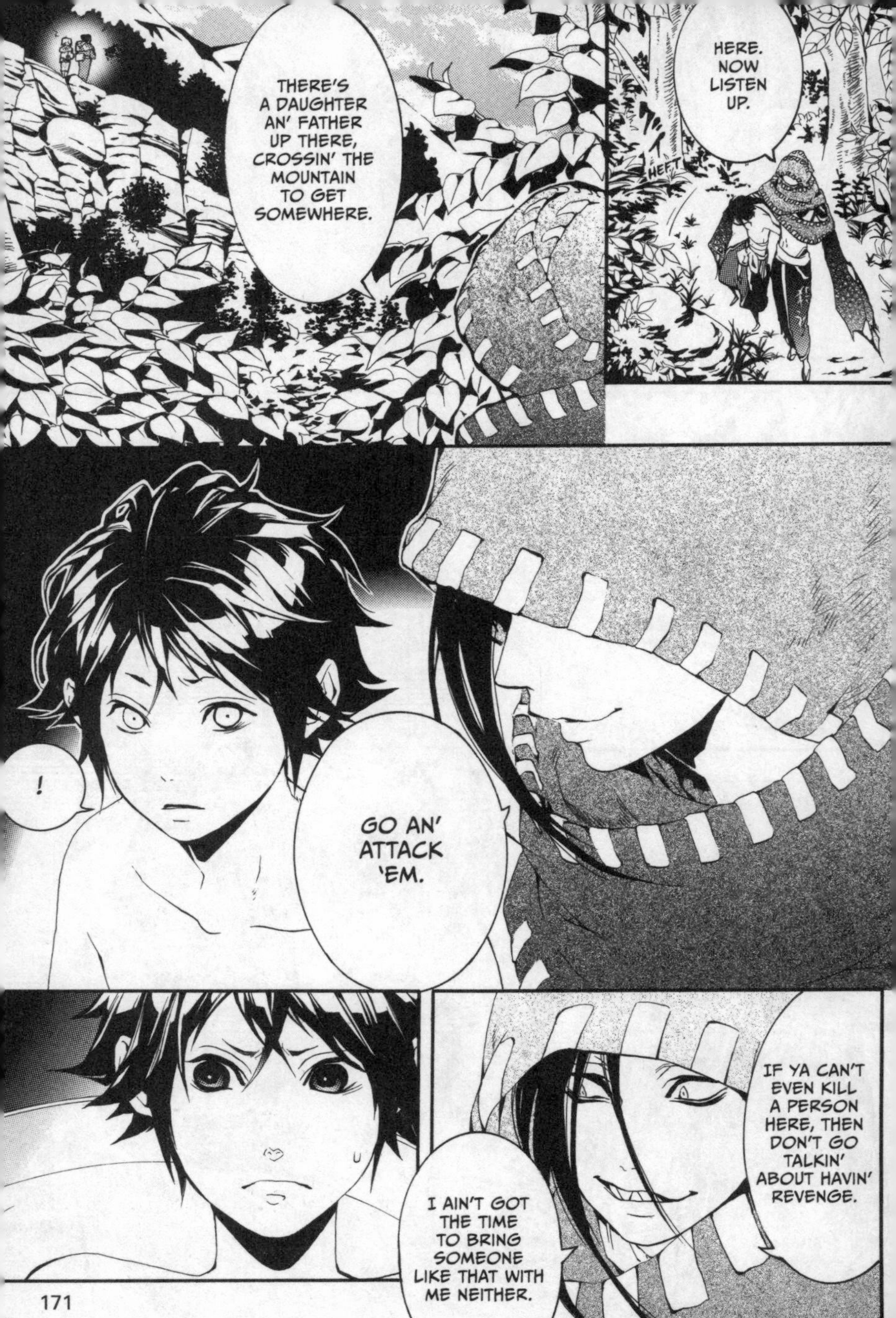
HERE. NOW LISTEN UP.
HEFT
THERE'S A DAUGHTER AN' FATHER UP THERE, CROSSIN' THE MOUNTAIN TO GET SOMEWHERE.
GO AN' ATTACK 'EM.
!
IF YA CAN'T EVEN KILL A PERSON HERE, THEN DON'T GO TALKIN' ABOUT HAVIN' REVENGE.
I AIN'T GOT THE TIME TO BRING SOMEONE LIKE THAT WITH ME NEITHER.

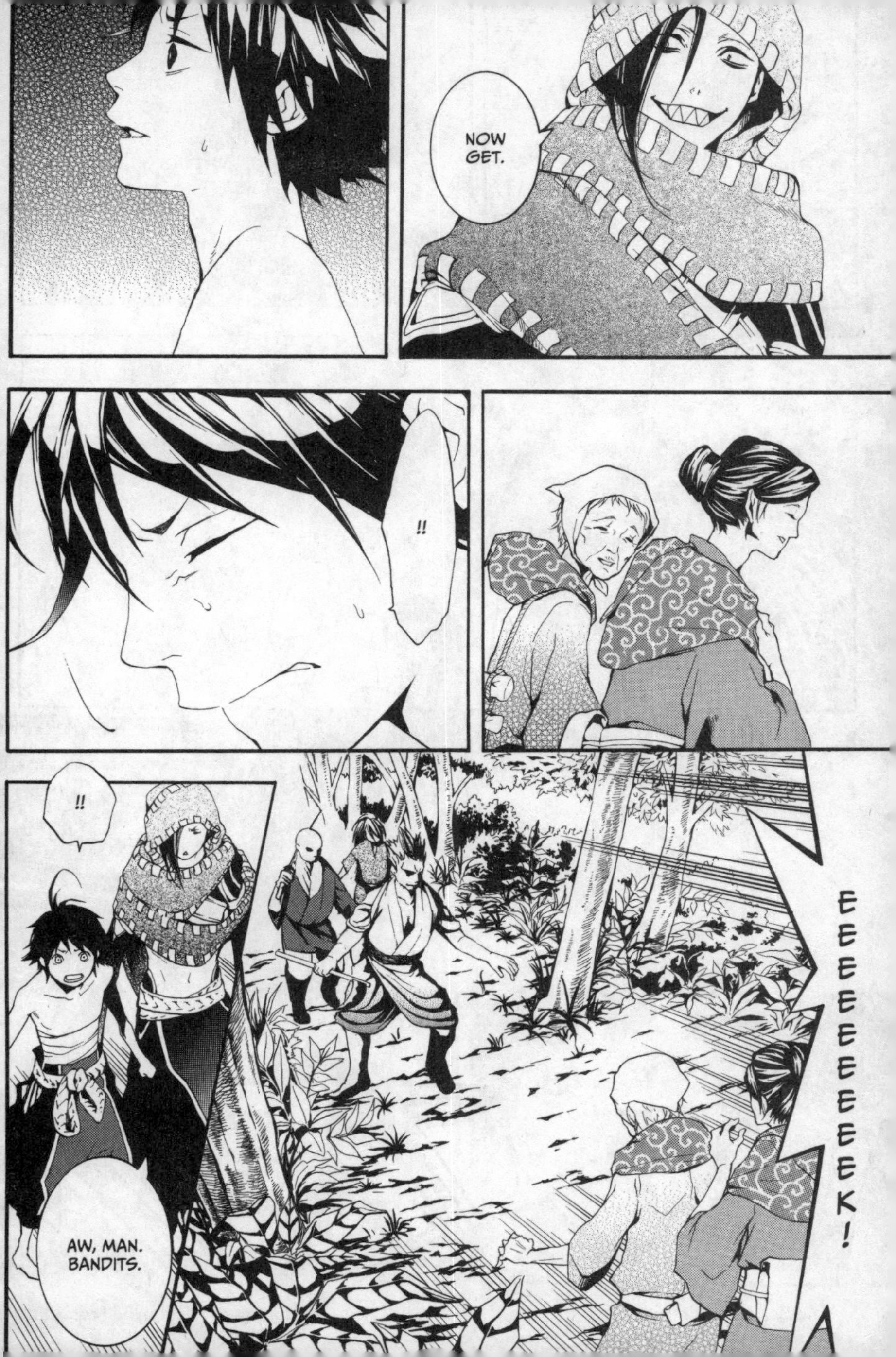
NOW GET.
!!
EEEEEEEEEEEK!
!!
AW, MAN. BANDITS.

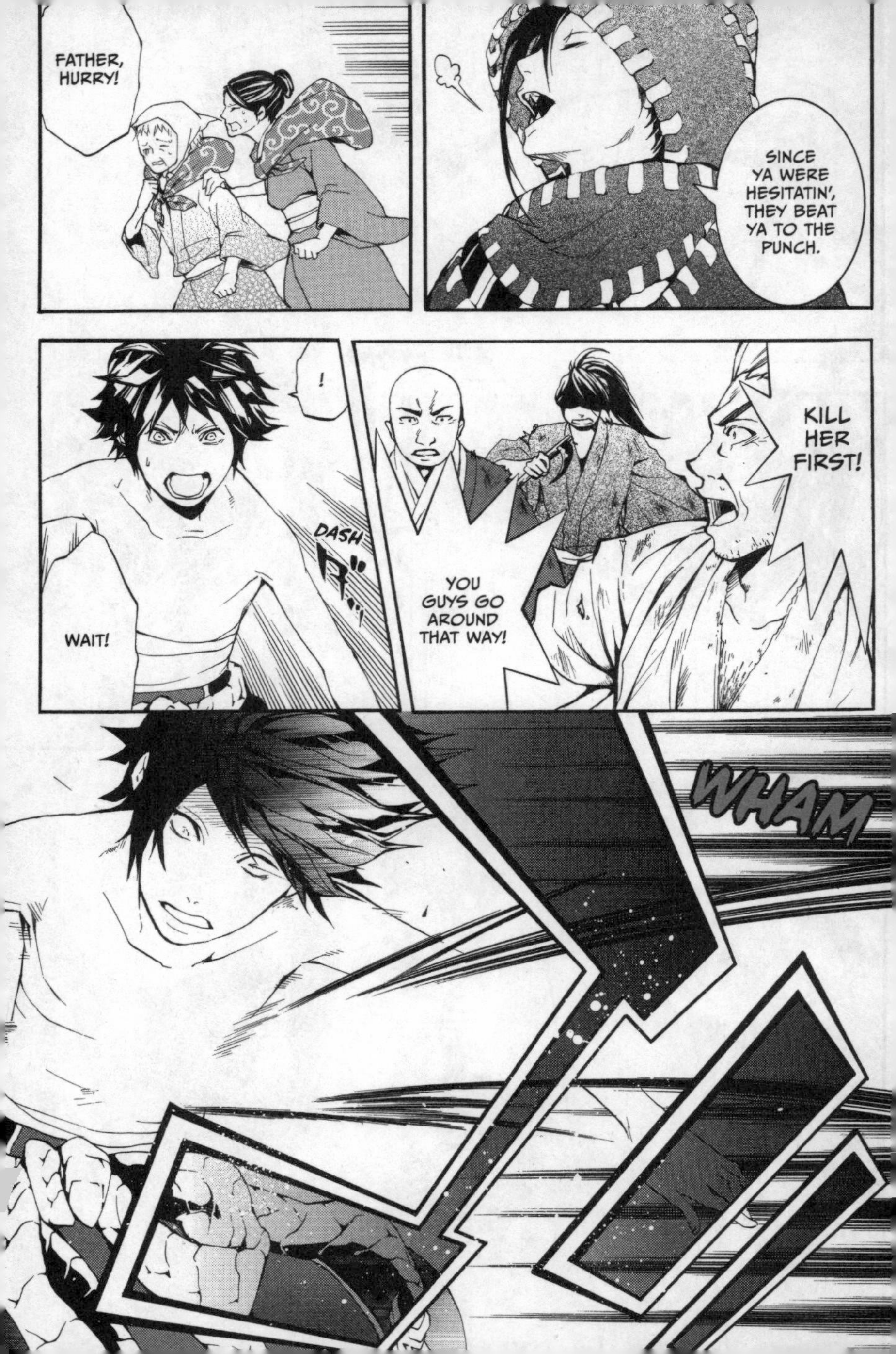
SINCE YA WERE HESITATIN', THEY BEAT YA TO THE PUNCH.
FATHER, HURRY!
KILL HER FIRST!
YOU GUYS GO AROUND THAT WAY!
!
DASH
WAIT!
WHAM

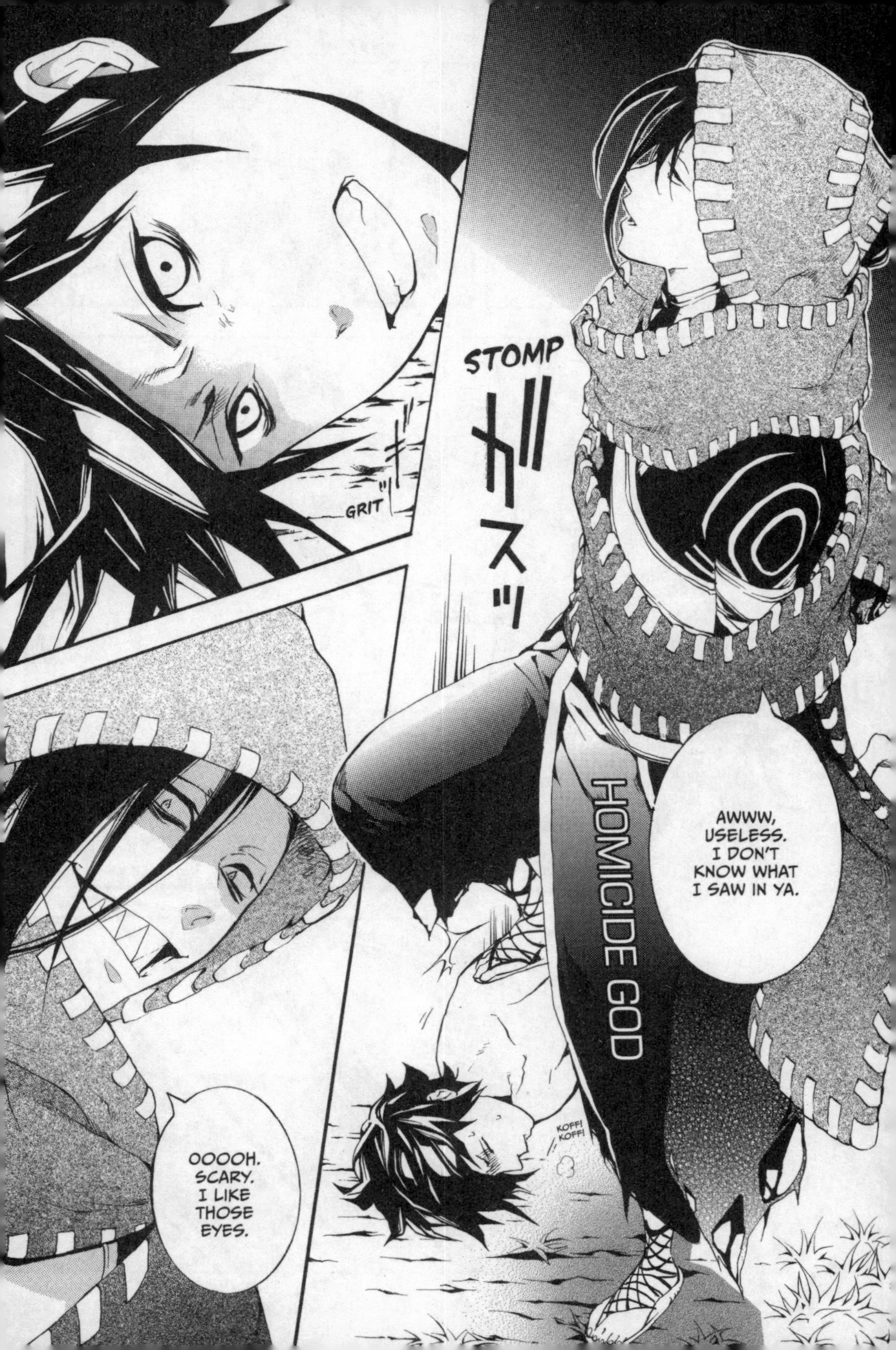
STOMP
ガスッ
AWWW, USELESS. I DON'T KNOW WHAT I SAW IN YA.
HOMICIDE GOD
KOFF! KOFF!
GRIT
OOOOH. SCARY. I LIKE THOSE EYES.

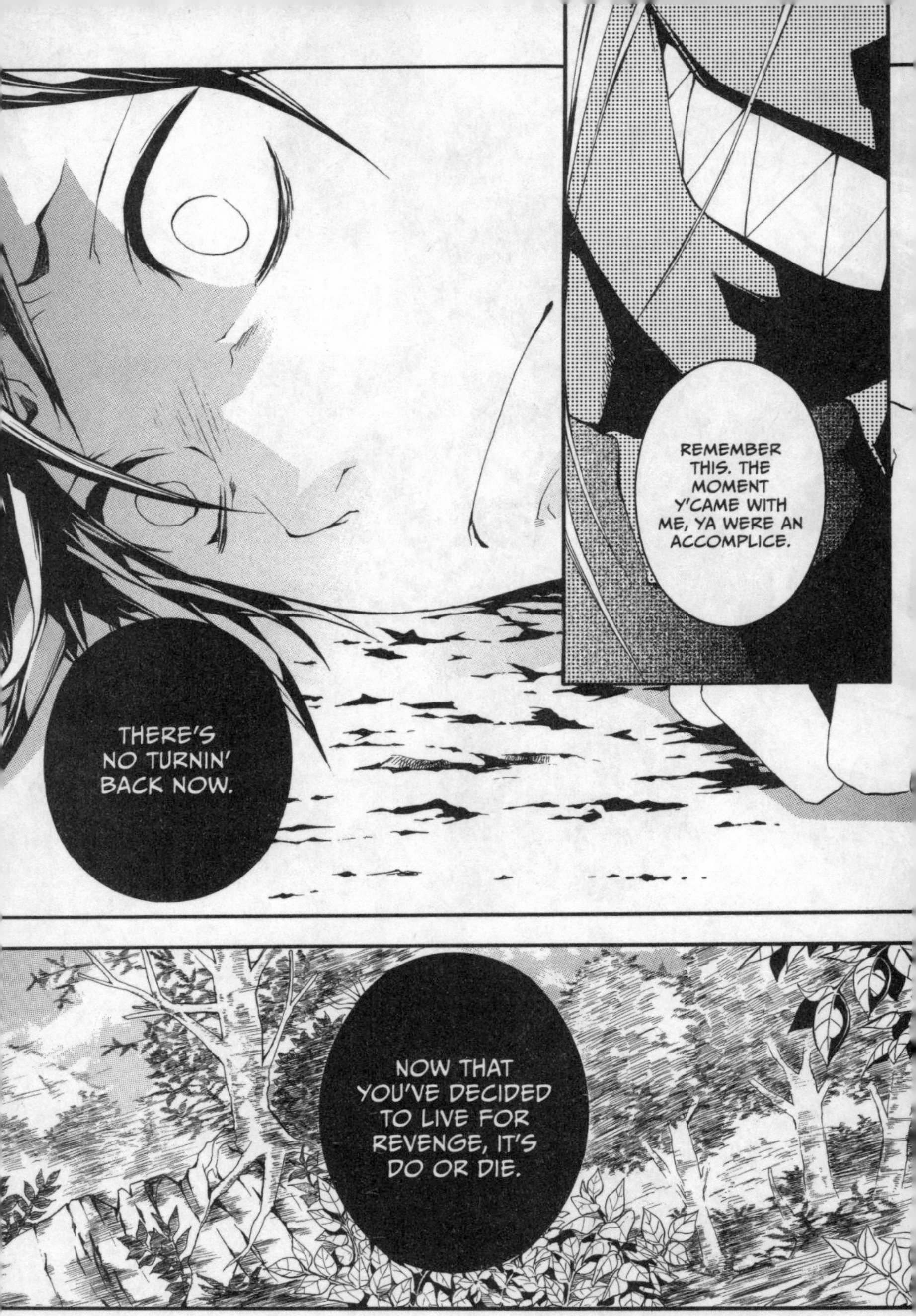
REMEMBER THIS. THE MOMENT Y'CAME WITH ME, YA WERE AN ACCOMPLICE.
THERE'S NO TURNIN' BACK NOW.
NOW THAT YOU'VE DECIDED TO LIVE FOR REVENGE, IT'S DO OR DIE.

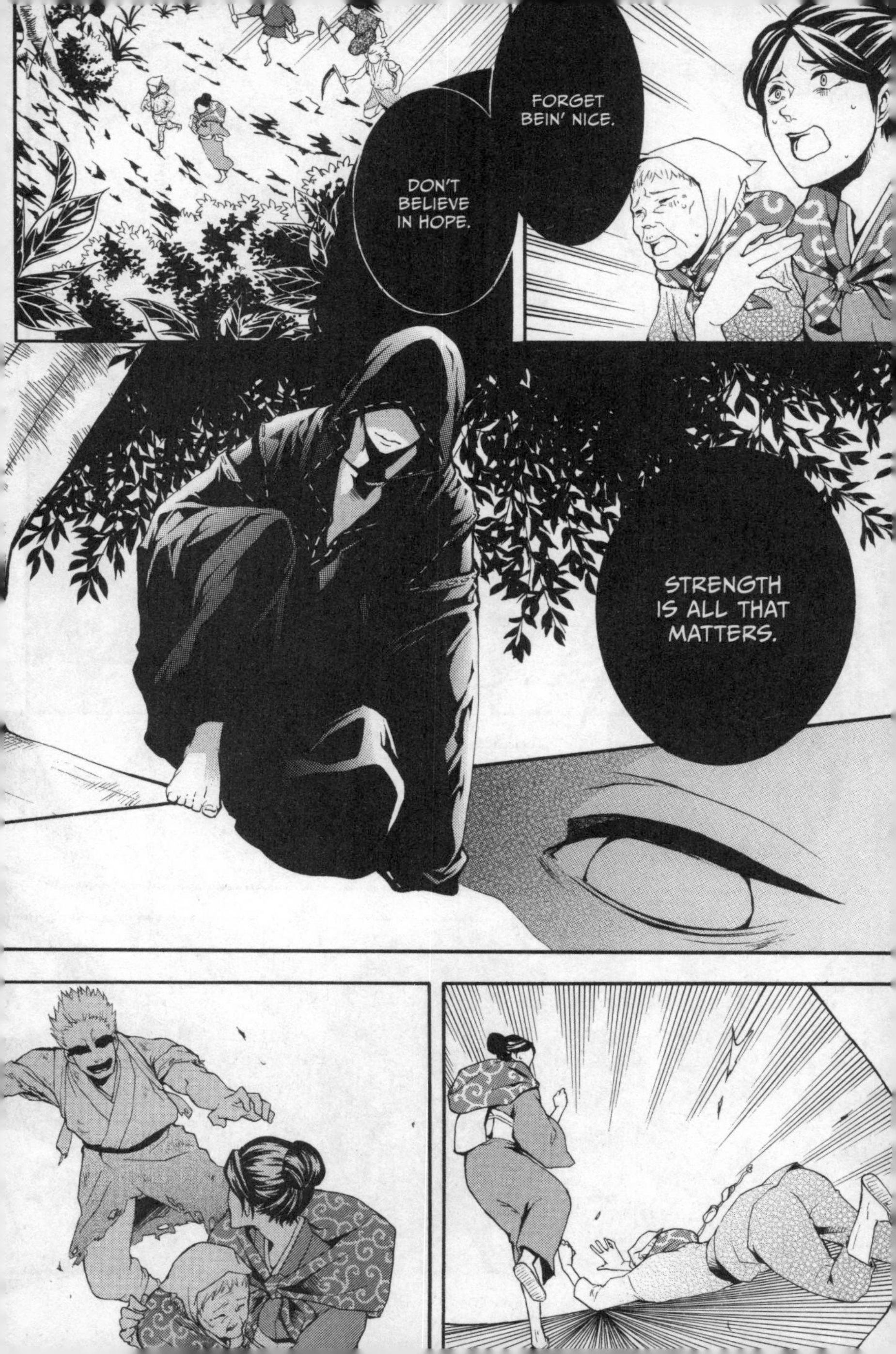
FORGET BEIN' NICE.
DON'T BELIEVE IN HOPE.
STRENGTH IS ALL THAT MATTERS.

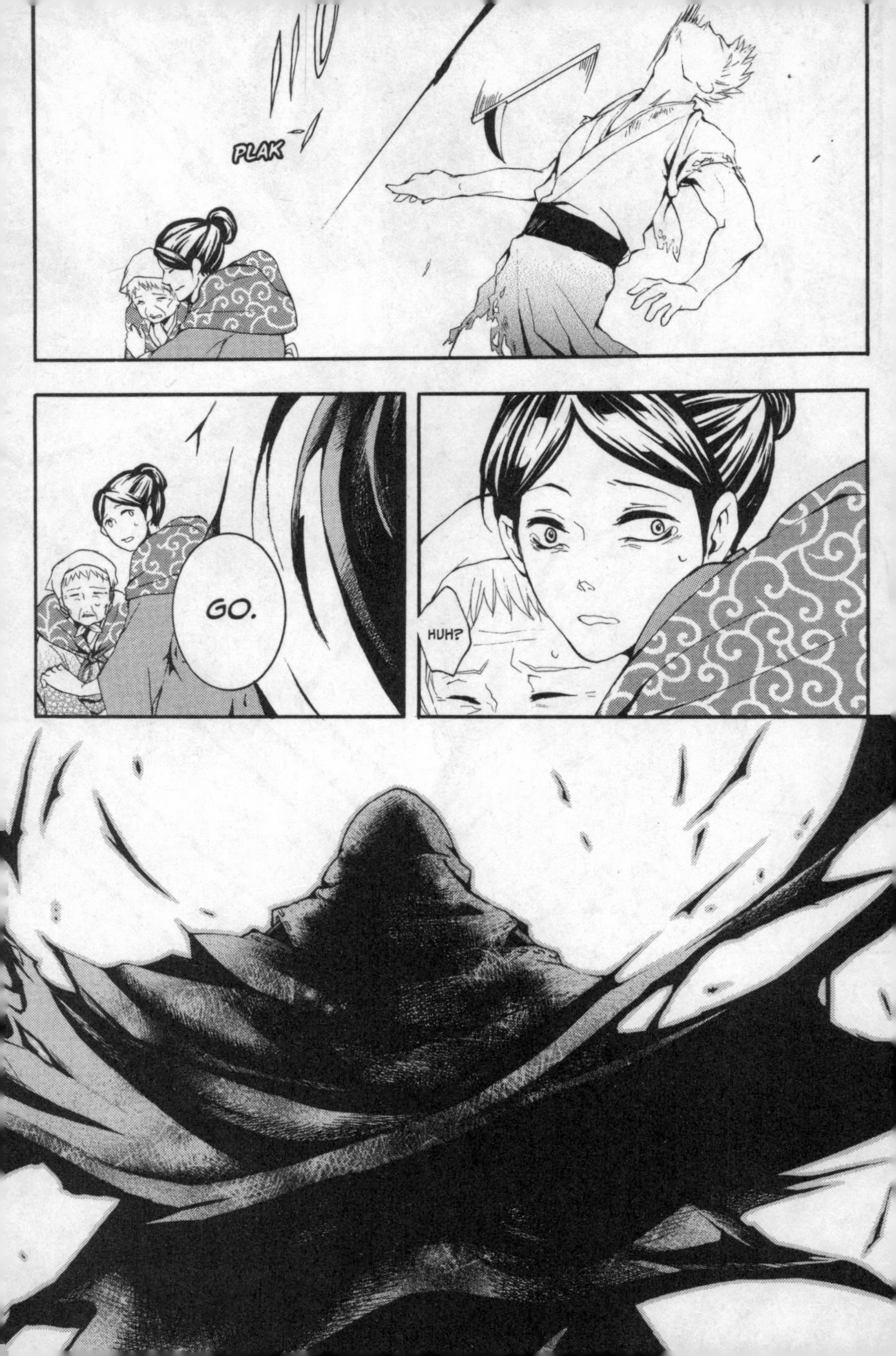
PLAK
HUH?
GO.

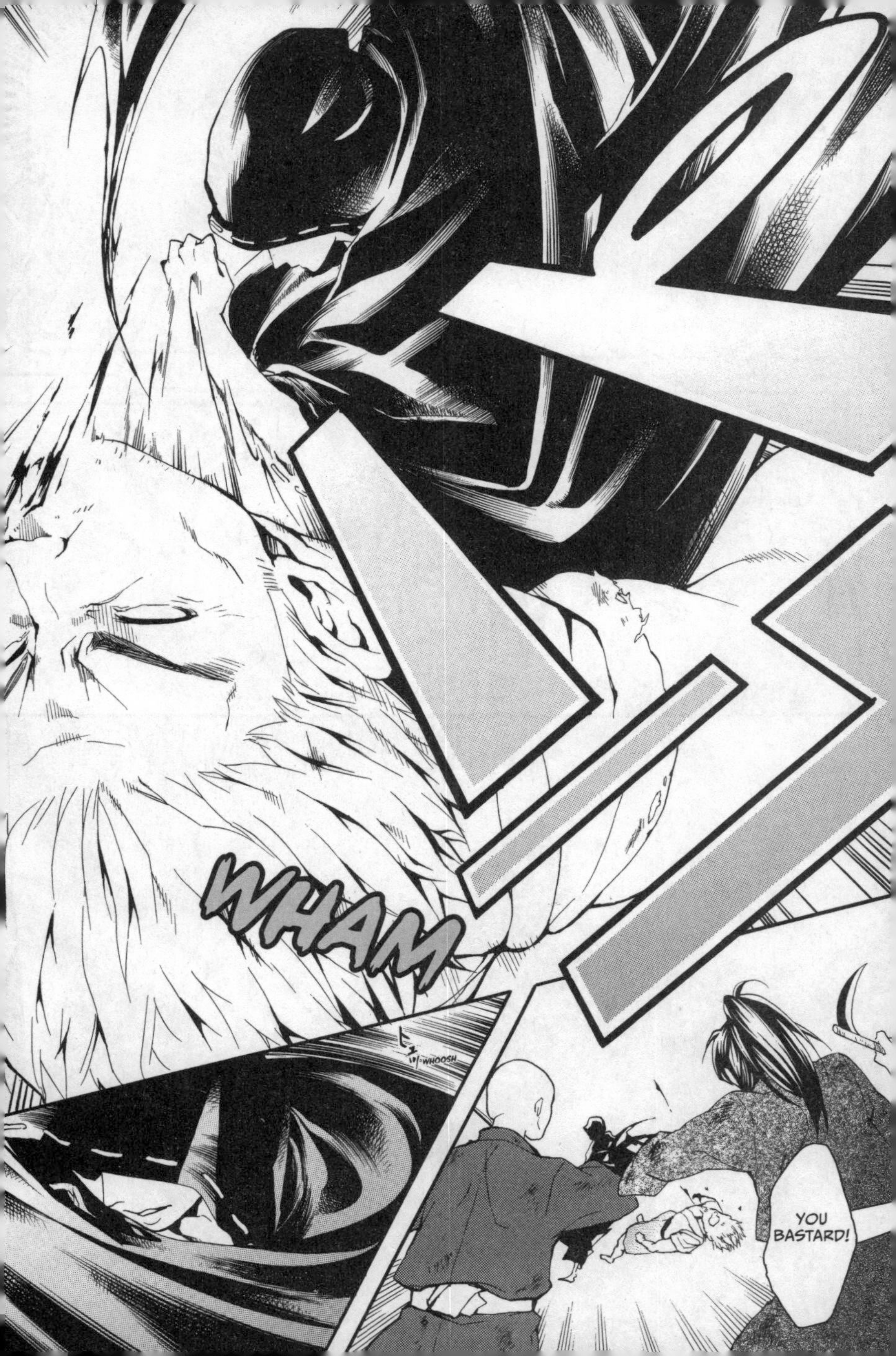
WHAM
YOU BASTARD!
WHOOSH

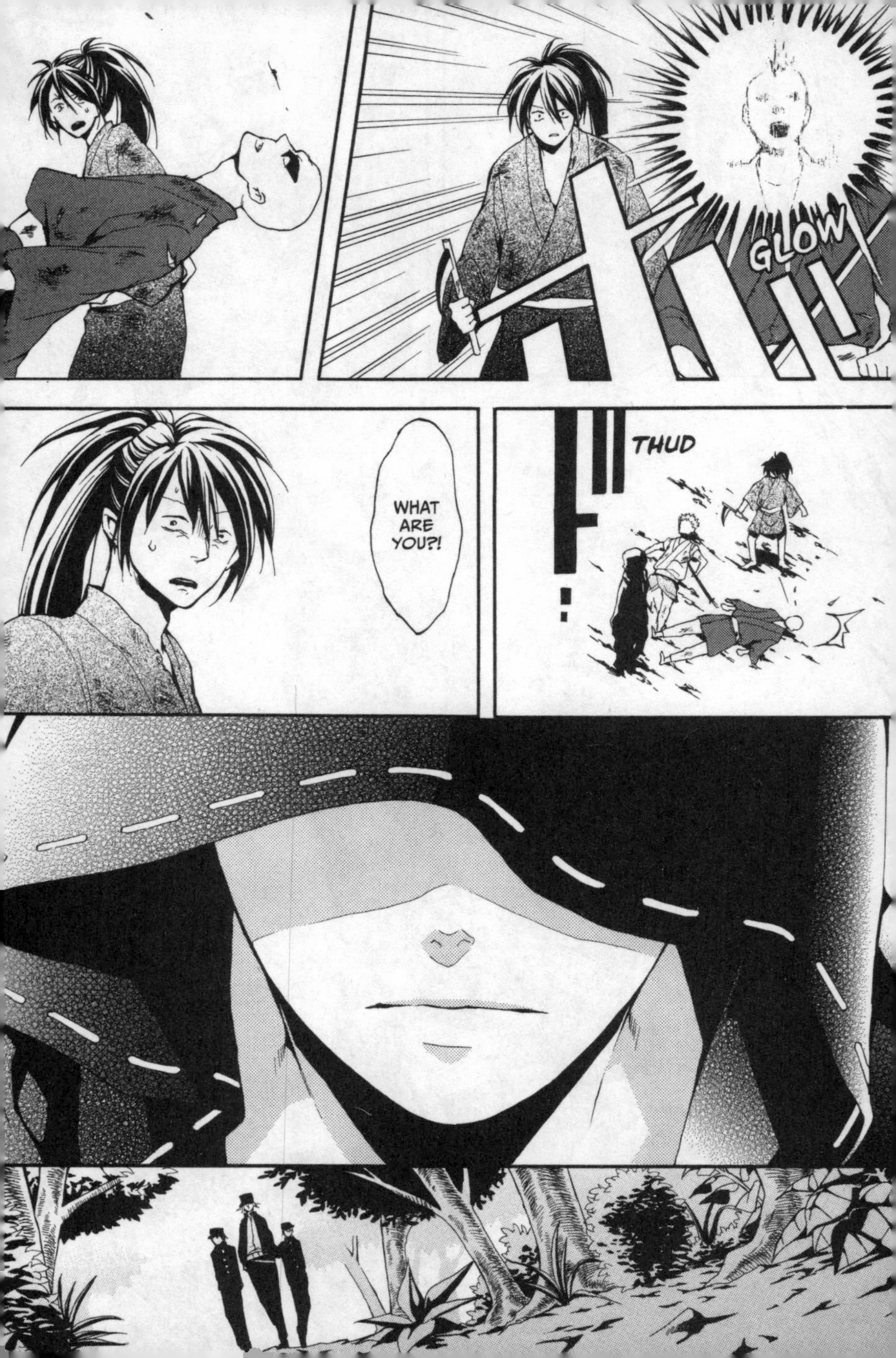
GLOW
THUD
WHAT ARE YOU?!

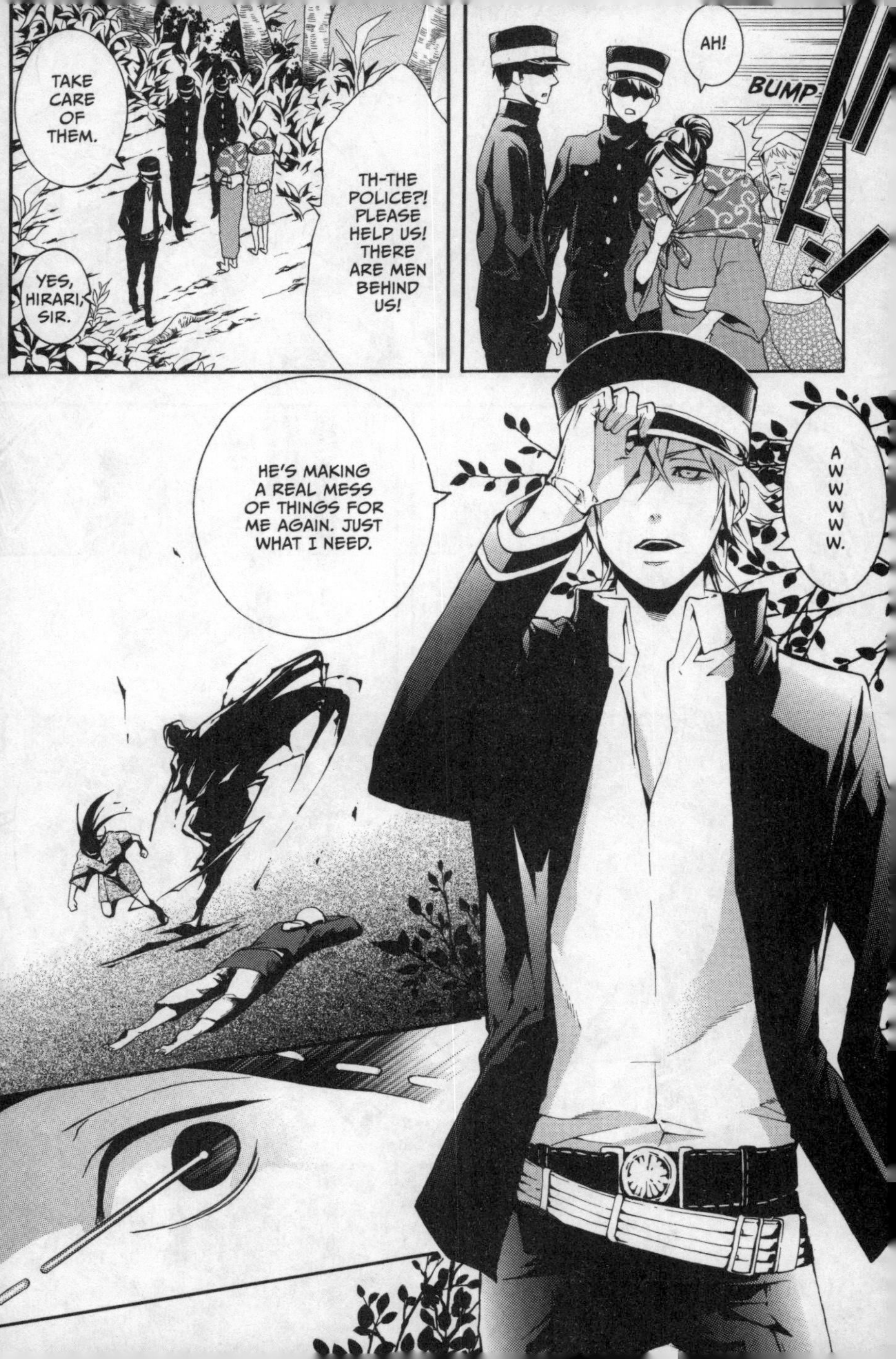
AH!
BUMP
TH-THE POLICE?! PLEASE HELP US! THERE ARE MEN BEHIND US!
TAKE CARE OF THEM.
YES, HIRARI, SIR.
AWWWWW.
HE'S MAKING A REAL MESS OF THINGS FOR ME AGAIN. JUST WHAT I NEED.

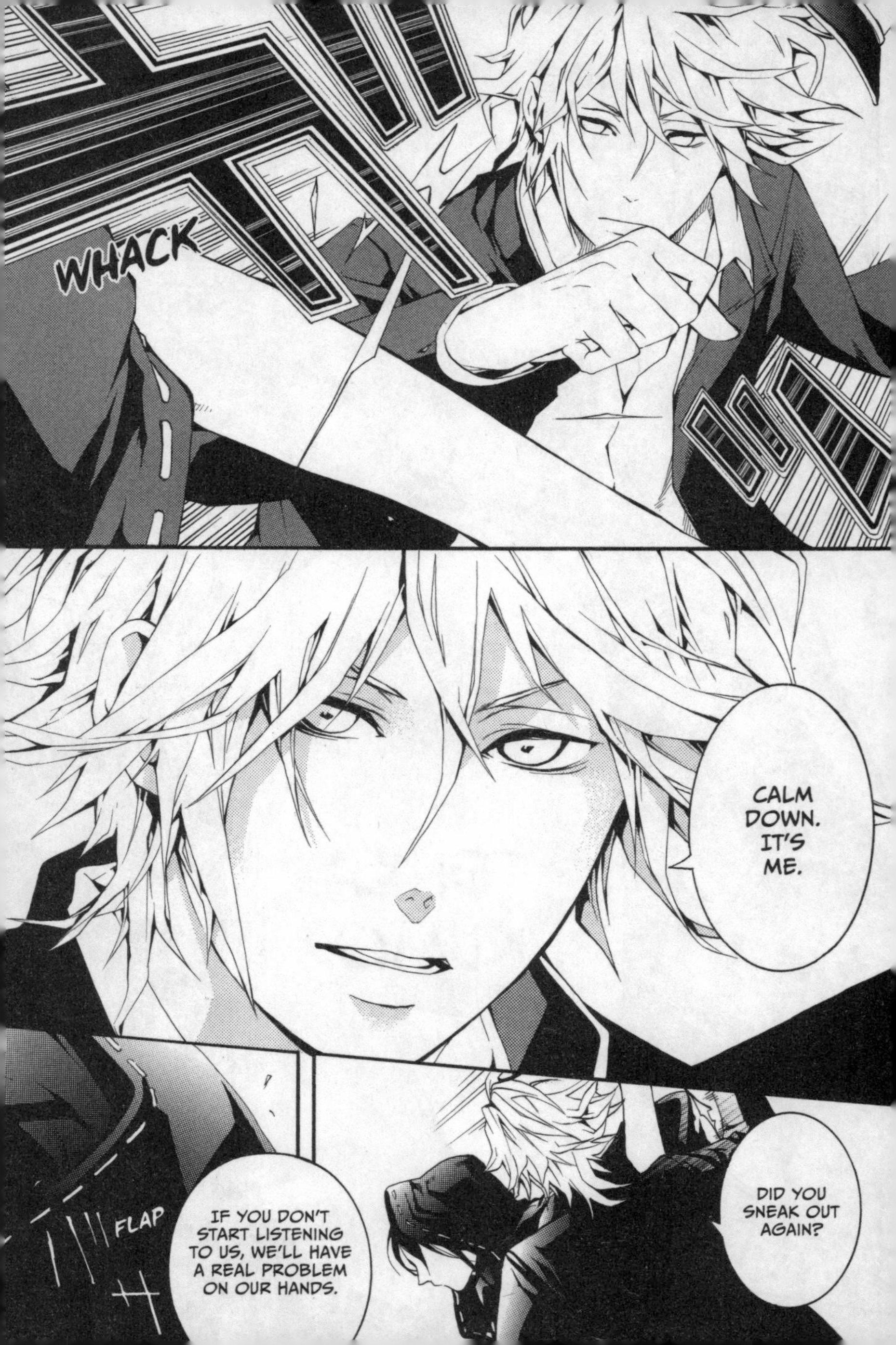
WHACK
CALM DOWN. IT'S ME.
DID YOU SNEAK OUT AGAIN?
IF YOU DON'T START LISTENING TO US, WE'LL HAVE A REAL PROBLEM ON OUR HANDS.
FLAP

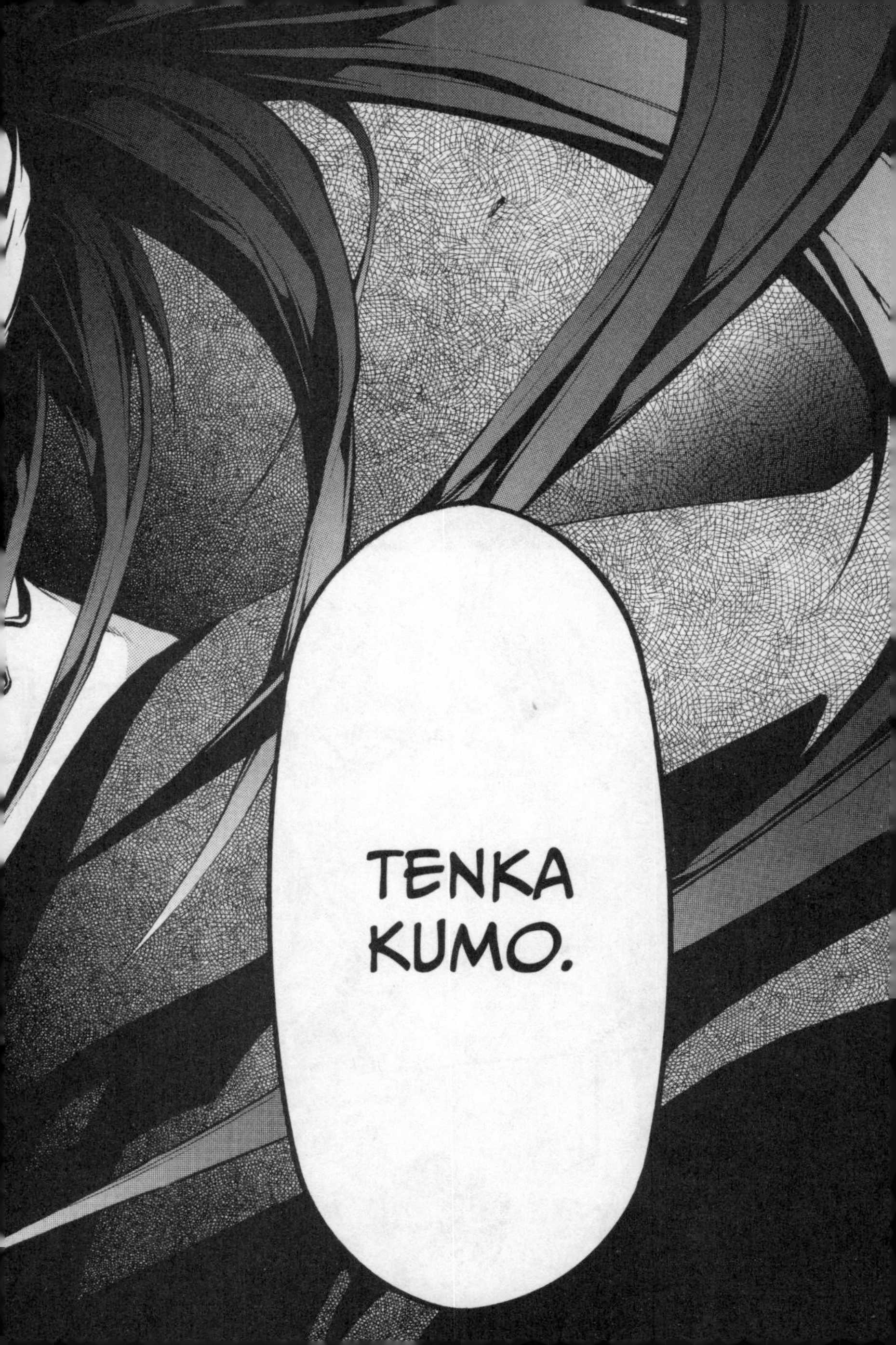
TENKA KUMO.

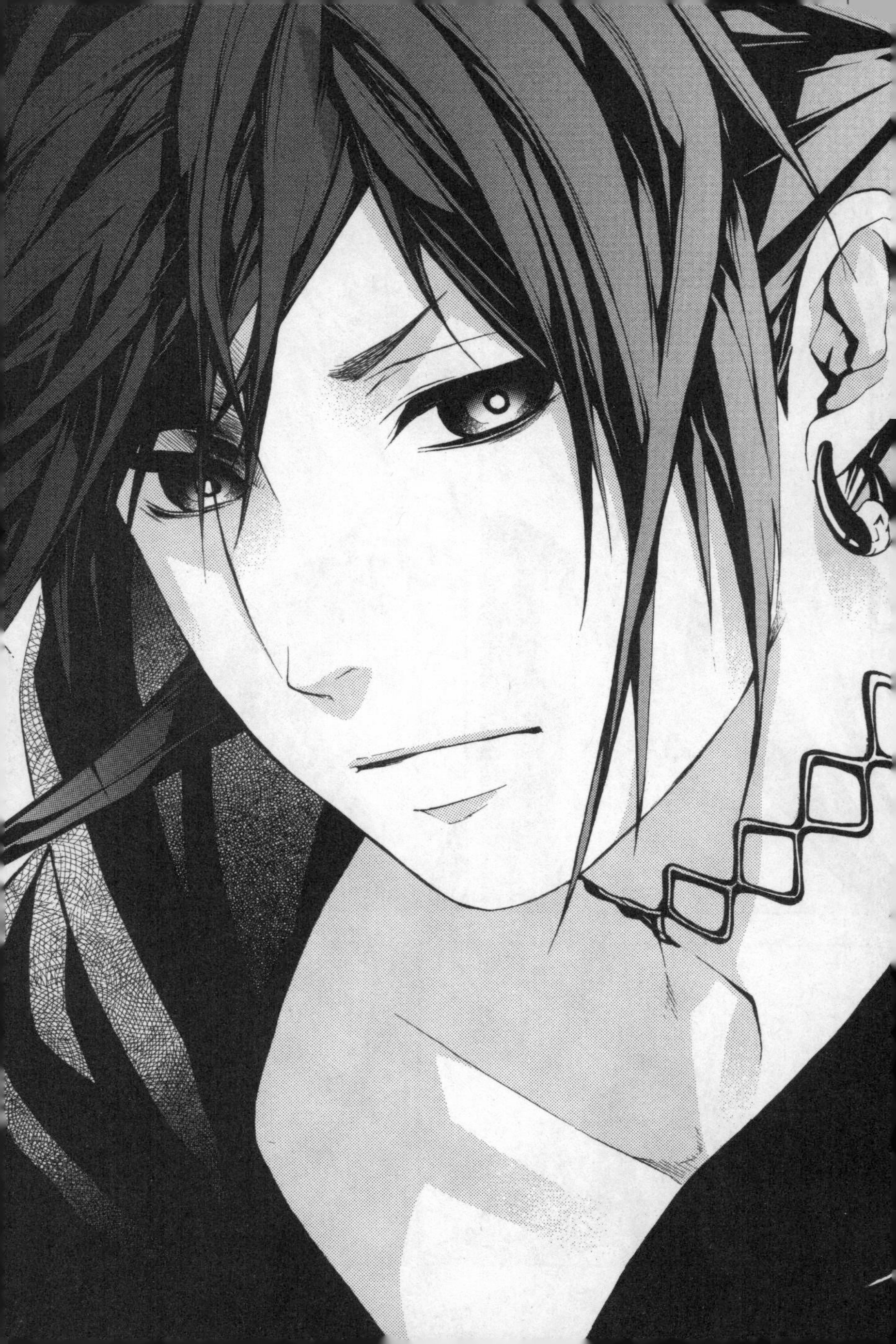

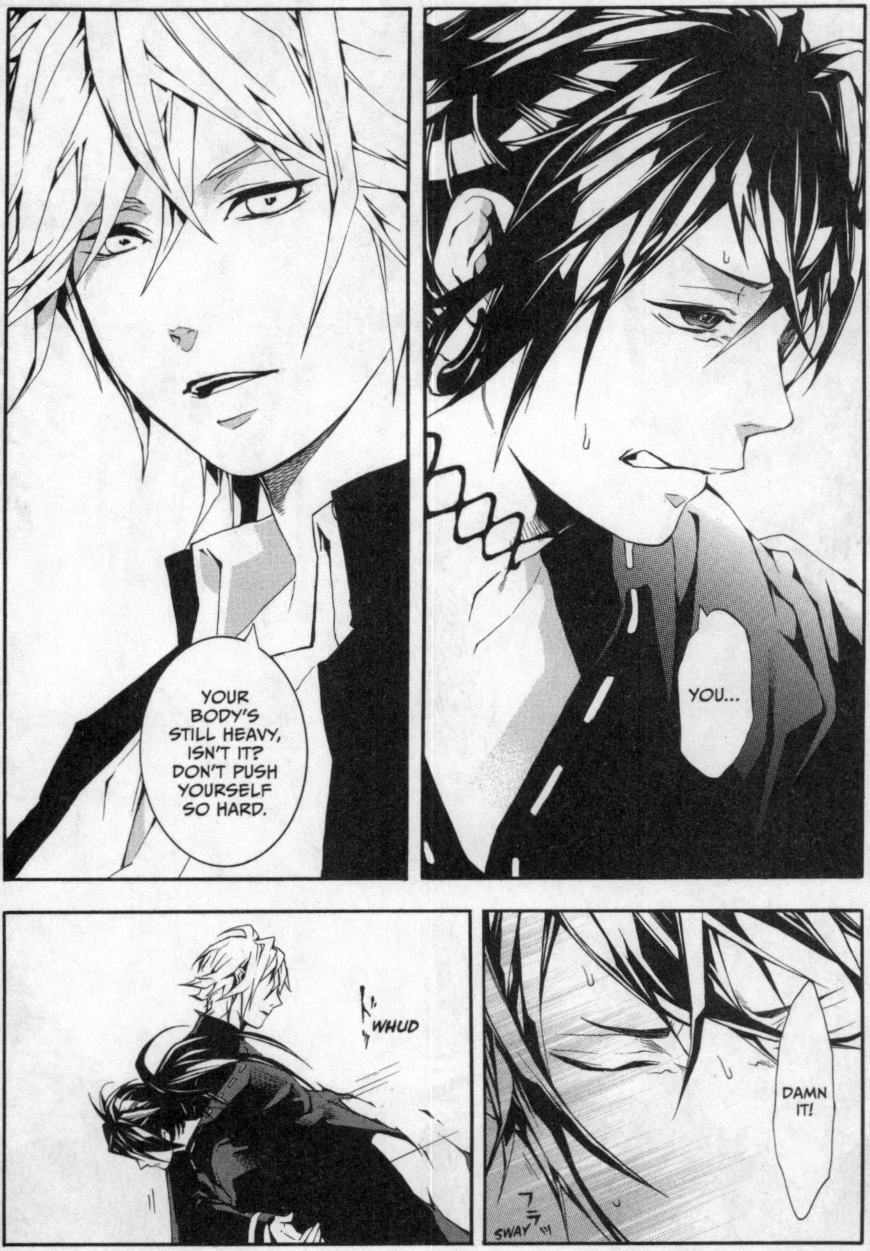

YOU...
YOUR BODY'S STILL HEAVY, ISN'T IT? DON'T PUSH YOURSELF SO HARD.
DAMN IT!
SWAY
WHUD

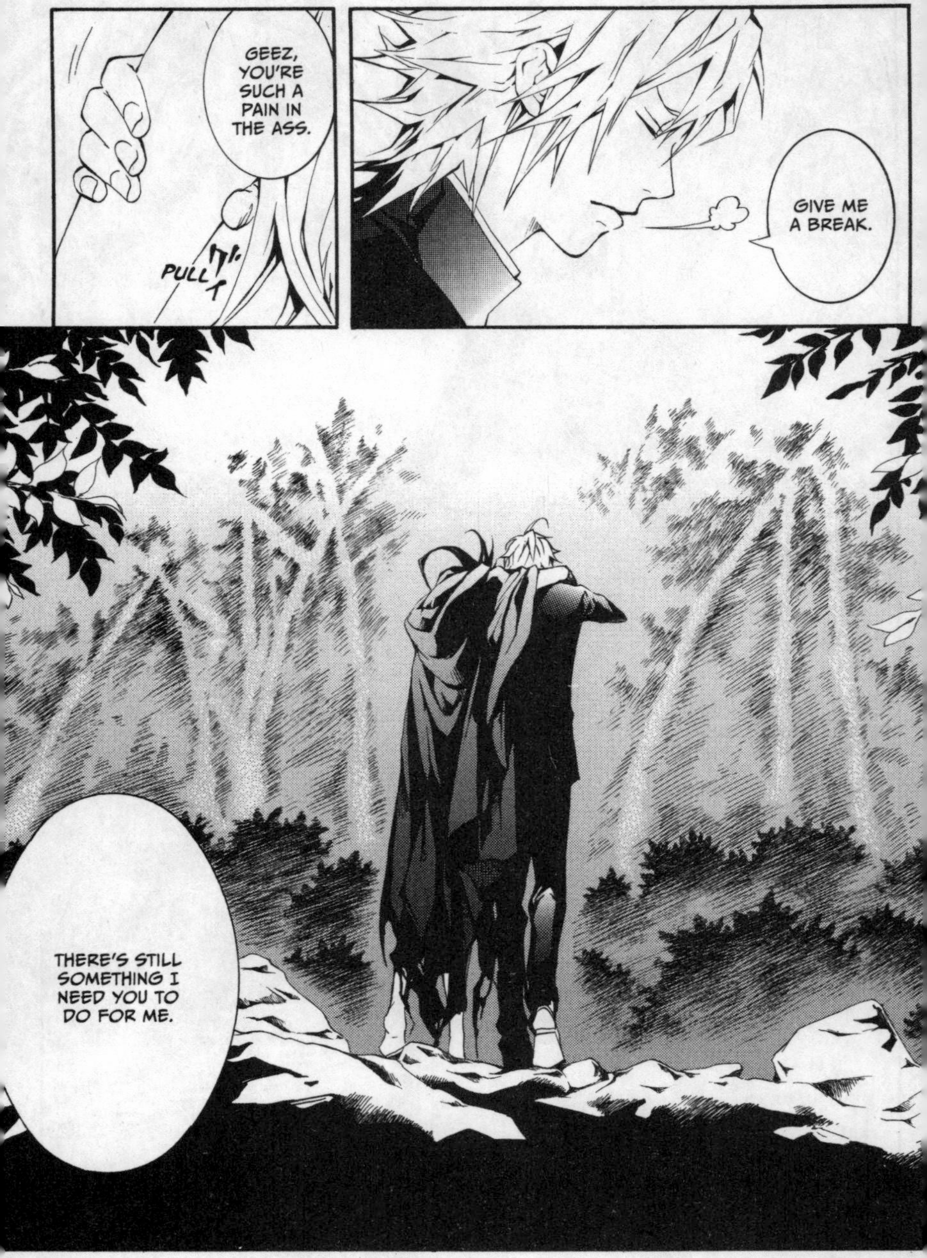
GIVE ME A BREAK.
GEEZ, YOU'RE SUCH A PAIN IN THE ASS.
PULL
THERE'S STILL SOMETHING I NEED YOU TO DO FOR ME.

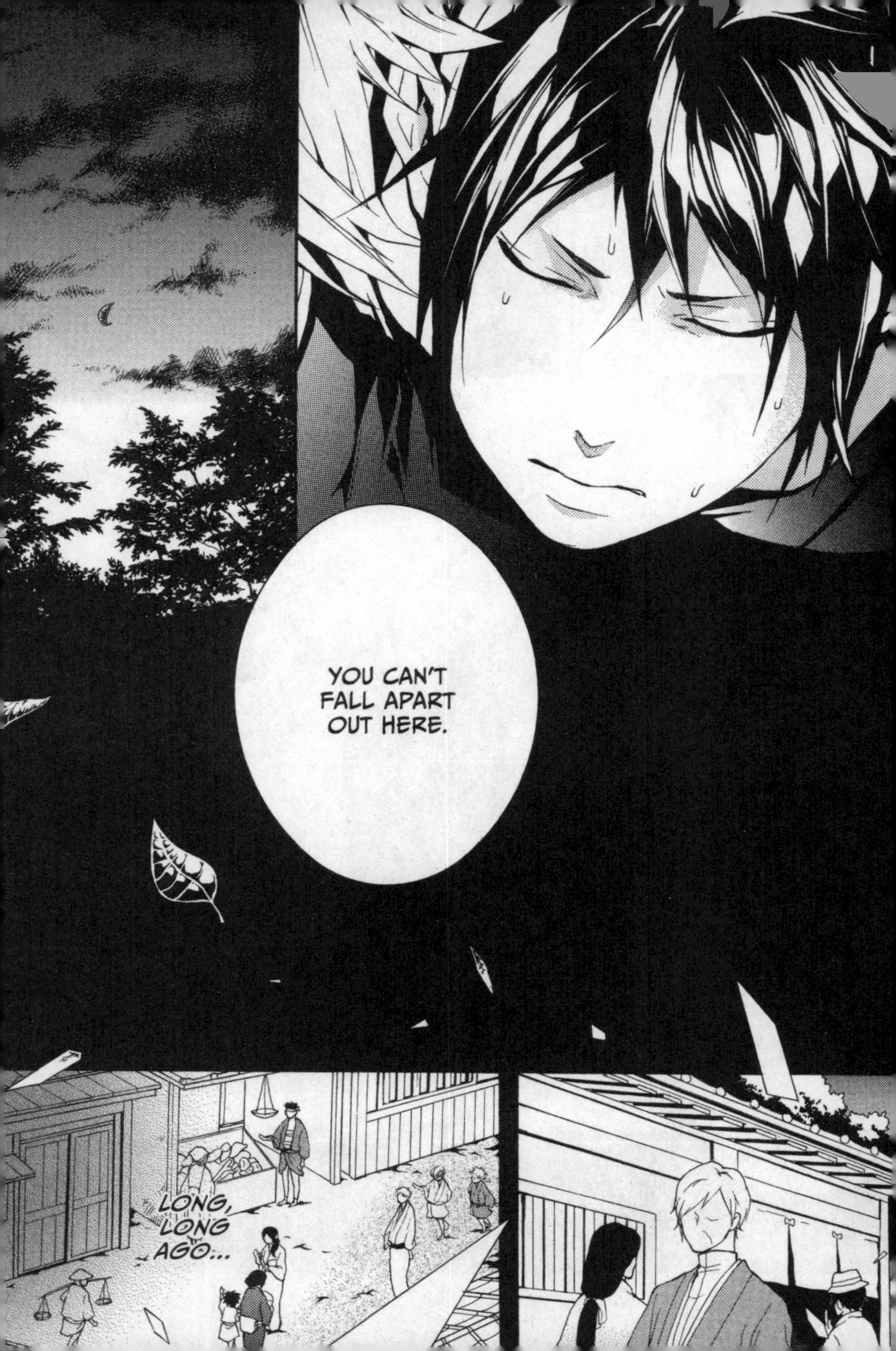
YOU CAN'T FALL APART OUT HERE.
LONG, LONG AGO...

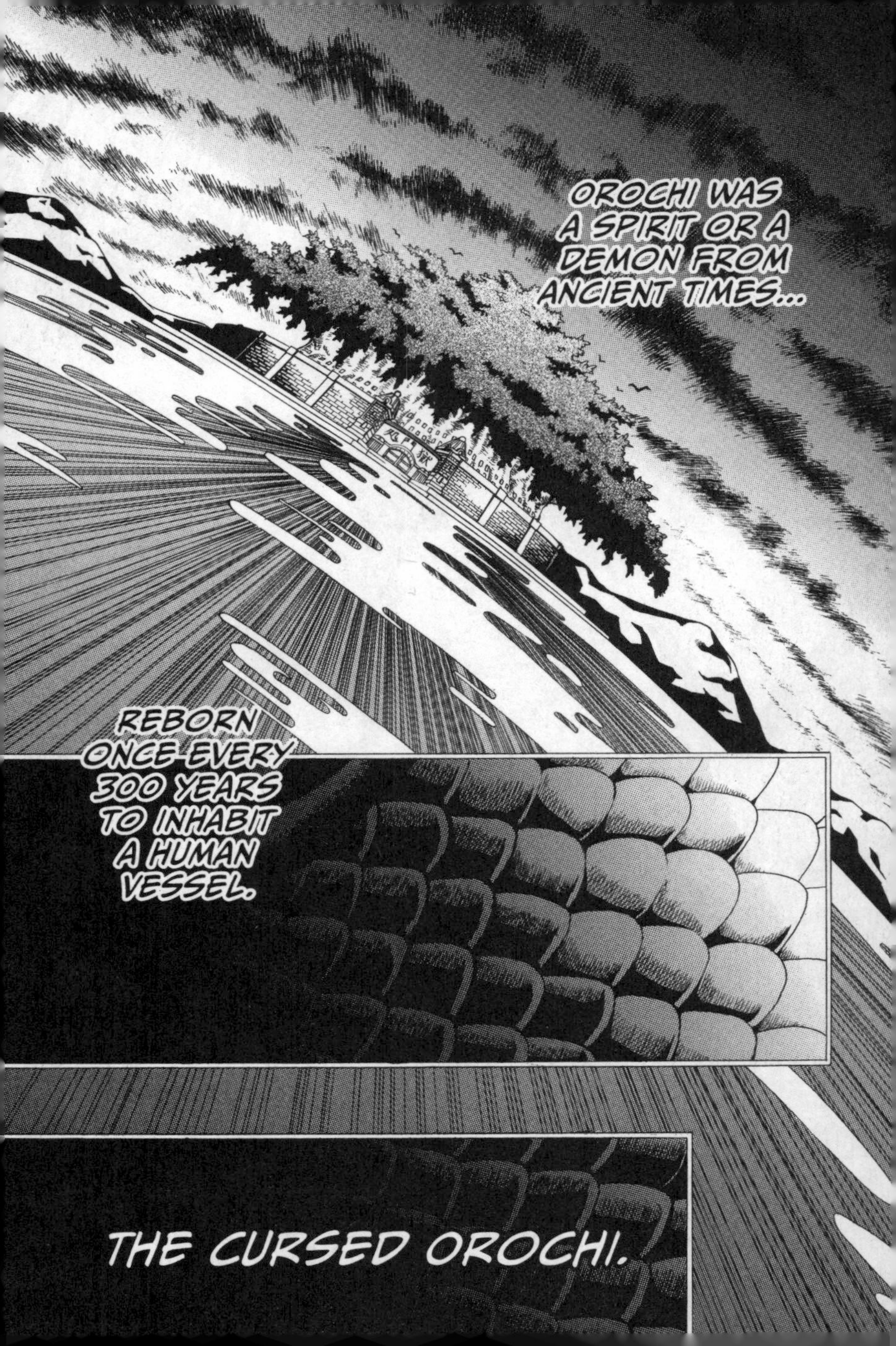
OROCHI WAS A SPIRIT OR A DEMON FROM ANCIENT TIMES...
REBORN ONCE EVERY 300 YEARS TO INHABIT A HUMAN VESSEL.
THE CURSED OROCHI.

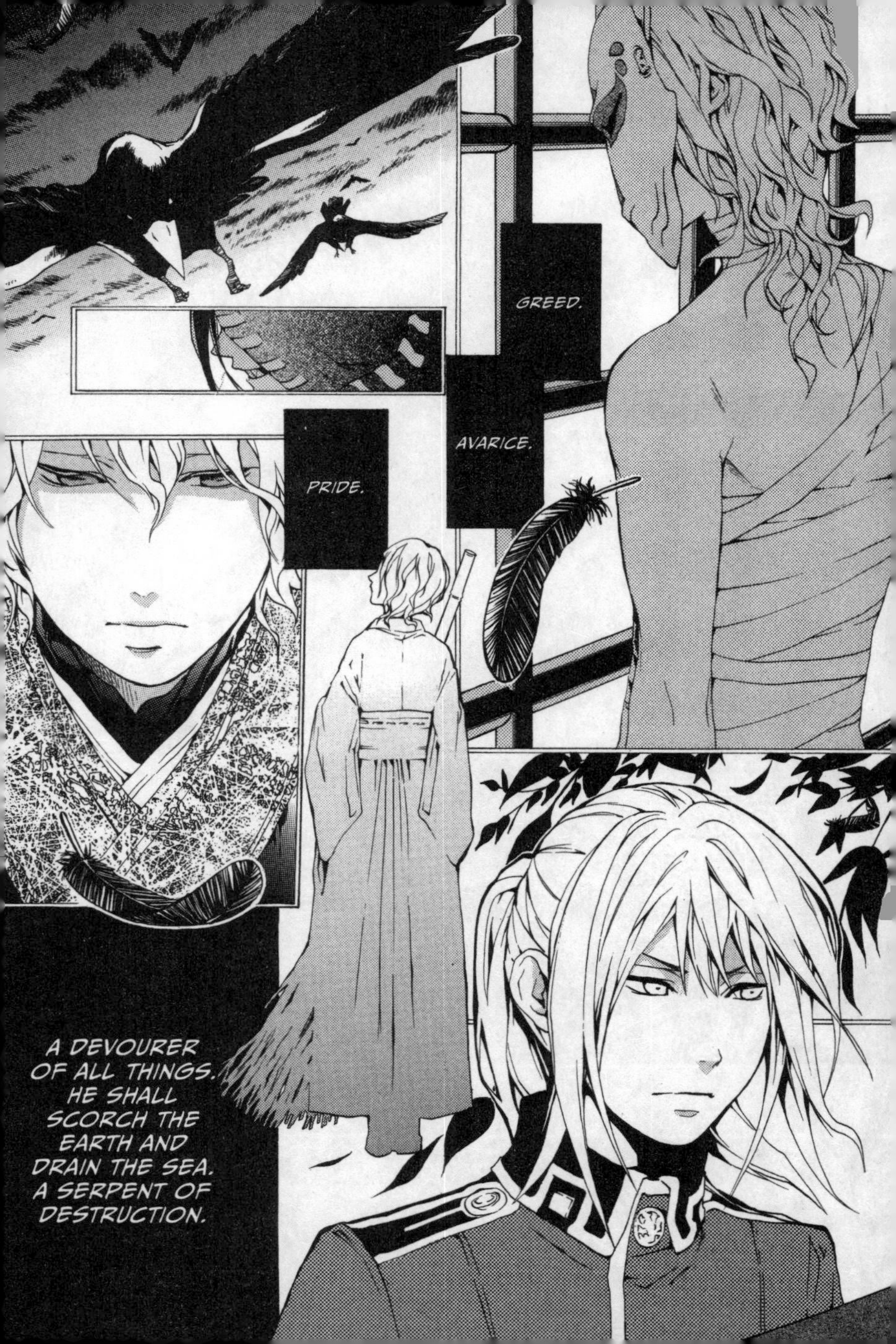
GREED.
AVARICE.
PRIDE.
A DEVOURER OF ALL THINGS. HE SHALL SCORCH THE EARTH AND DRAIN THE SEA. A SERPENT OF DESTRUCTION.

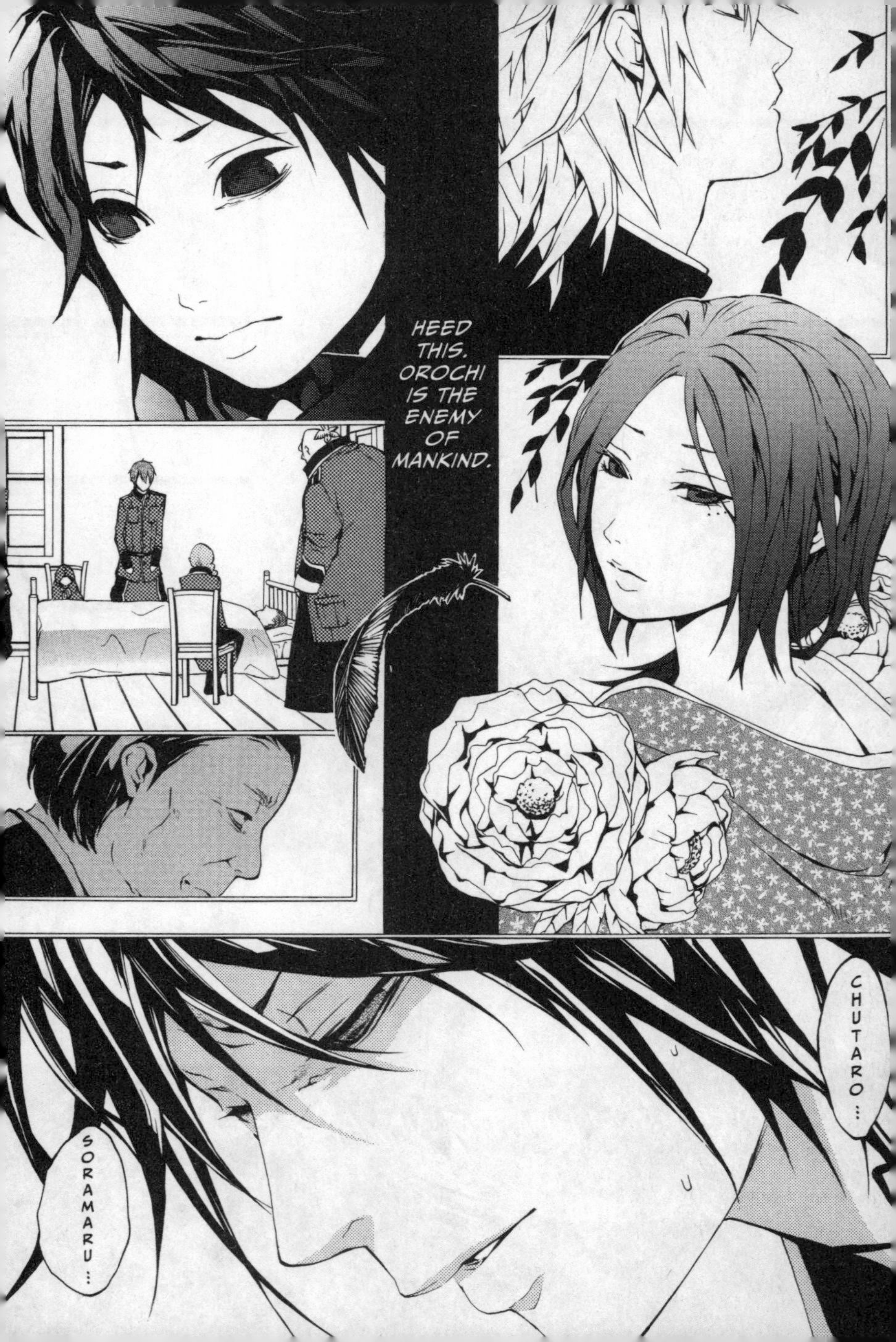
HEED THIS. OROCHI IS THE ENEMY OF MANKIND.
CHUTARO...
SORAMARU...

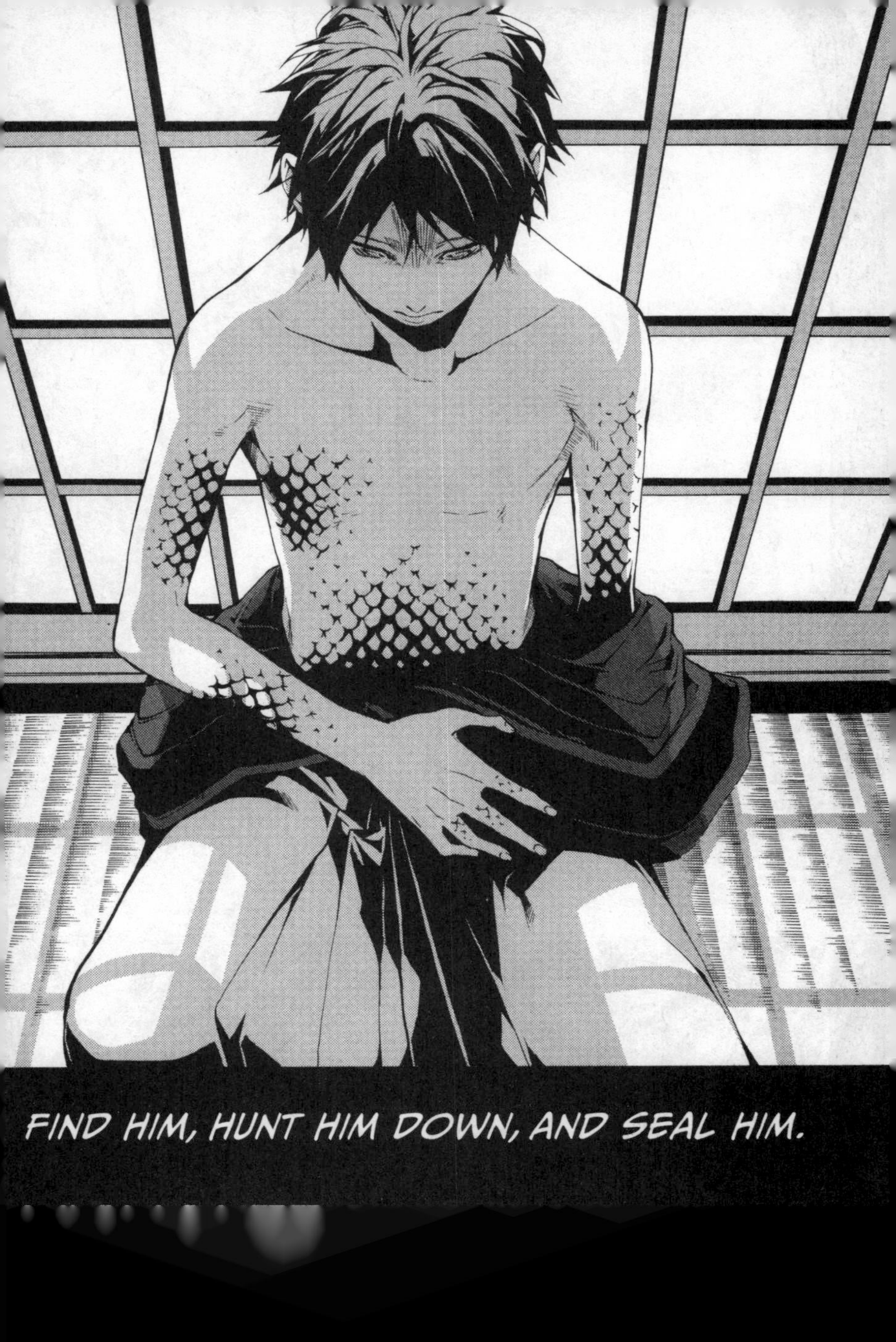
FIND HIM, HUNT HIM DOWN, AND SEAL HIM.

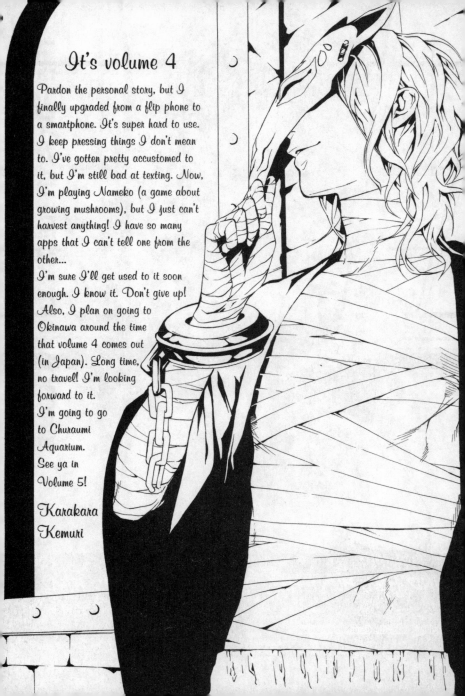

It's volume 4

Pardon the personal story, but I finally upgraded from a flip phone to a smartphone. It's super hard to use. I keep pressing things I don't mean to. I've gotten pretty accustomed to it, but I'm still bad at texting. Now, I'm playing Nameko (a game about growing mushrooms), but I just can't harvest anything! I have so many apps that I can't tell one from the other...
I'm sure I'll get used to it soon enough. I know it. Don't give up!
Also, I plan on going to Okinawa around the time that volume 4 comes out (in Japan). Long time, no travel! I'm looking forward to it.
I'm going to go to Churaumi Aquarium.
See ya in Volume 5!

Karakara Kemuri

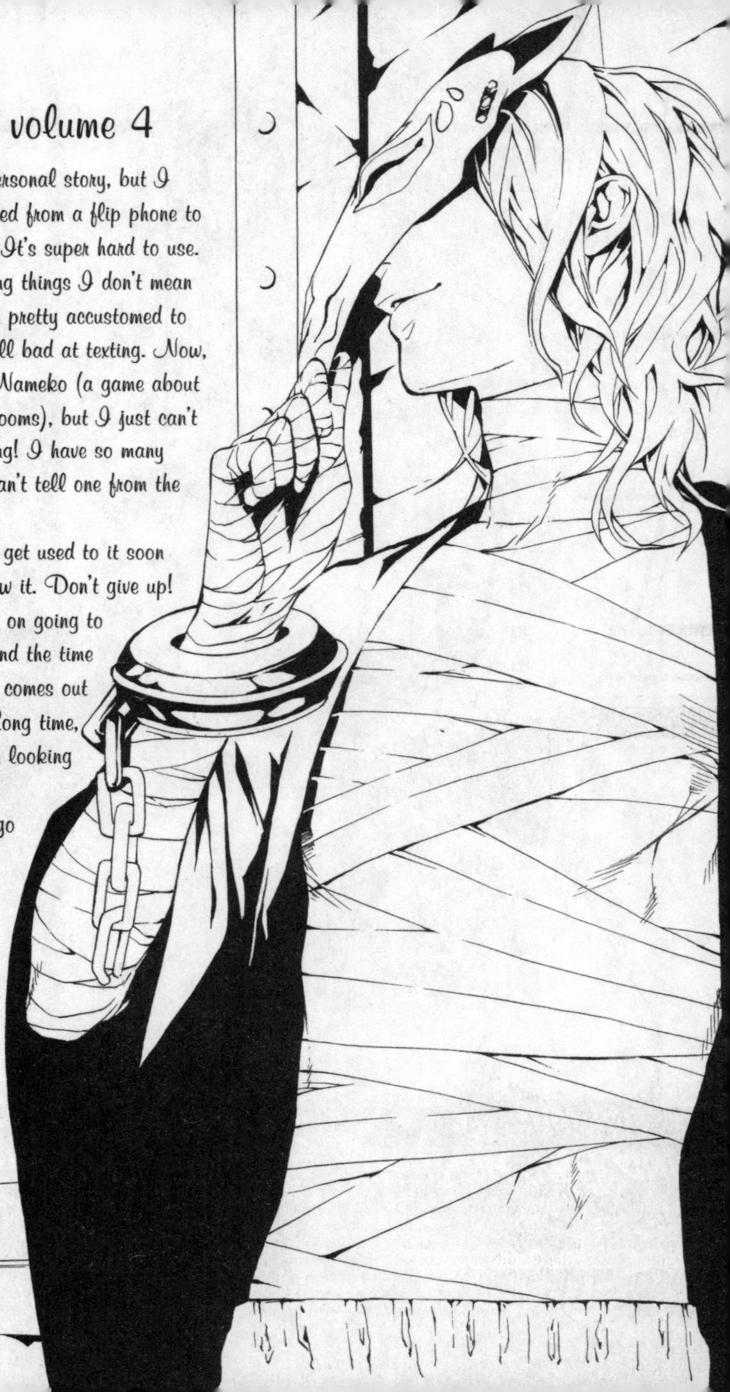

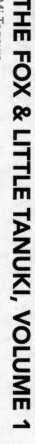

THE FOX & LITTLE TANUKI, VOLUME 1

Mi Tagawa

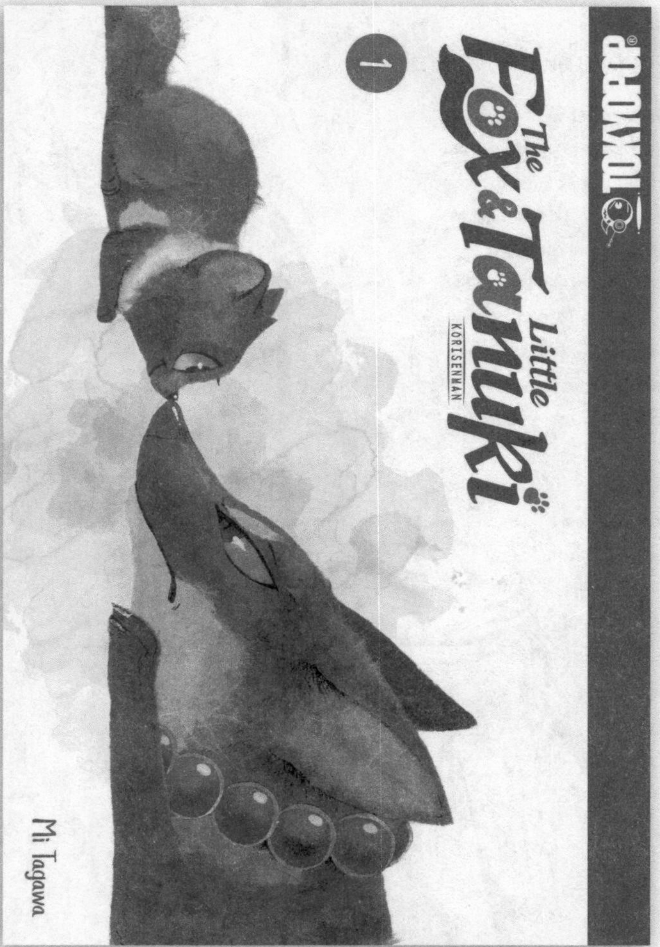
TOKYOPOP
The Fox & Little Tanuki
KORISENMAN
1
Mi Tagawa

FANTASY

It is said that there are some special animals occasionally born with great powers. Senzou the black fox is one of those... but instead of using his powers for good, he abused his strength until the Sun Goddess imprisoned him for his bad behavior. Three hundred years later, he's finally been released, but only on one condition — he can't have any of his abilities back until he successfully helps a tanuki cub named Manpachi become an assistant to the gods. Unfortunately for Senzou, there's no cheating when it comes to completing his task! The magic beads around his neck make sure he can't wander too far from his charge or ignore his duties, and so... Senzou the once-great Fox Spirit must figure out how to be an actually-great babysitter to an innocent little tanuki or risk being stuck without his powers forever!

TOKYOPOP

THE FOX & LITTLE TANUKI, VOLUME 2

Mi Tagawa

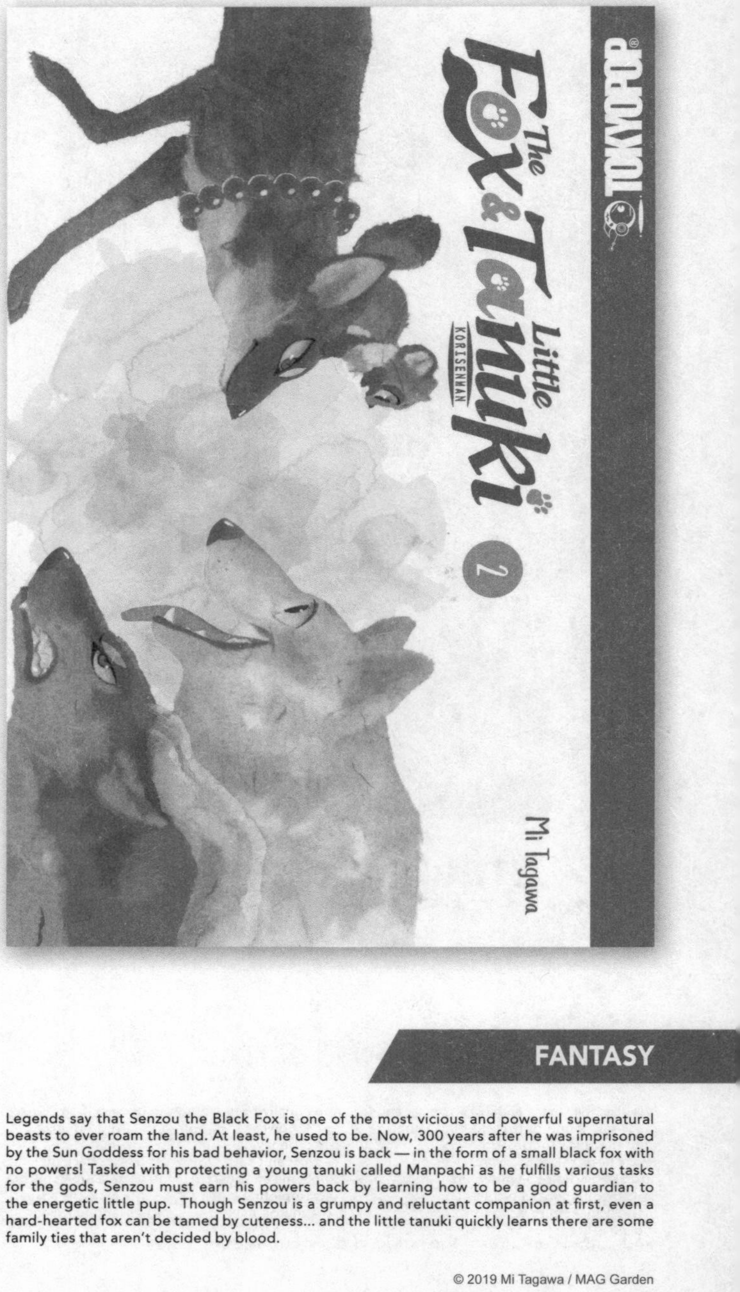
TOKYOPOP
The Fox & Little Tanuki
KORISENMAN
2
Mi Tagawa

FANTASY

Legends say that Senzou the Black Fox is one of the most vicious and powerful supernatural beasts to ever roam the land. At least, he used to be. Now, 300 years after he was imprisoned by the Sun Goddess for his bad behavior, Senzou is back — in the form of a small black fox with no powers! Tasked with protecting a young tanuki called Manpachi as he fulfills various tasks for the gods, Senzou must earn his powers back by learning how to be a good guardian to the energetic little pup. Though Senzou is a grumpy and reluctant companion at first, even a hard-hearted fox can be tamed by cuteness... and the little tanuki quickly learns there are some family ties that aren't decided by blood.

TOKYOPOP

DISNEY STITCH AND THE SAMURAI, VOLUME 1

Hiroto Wada

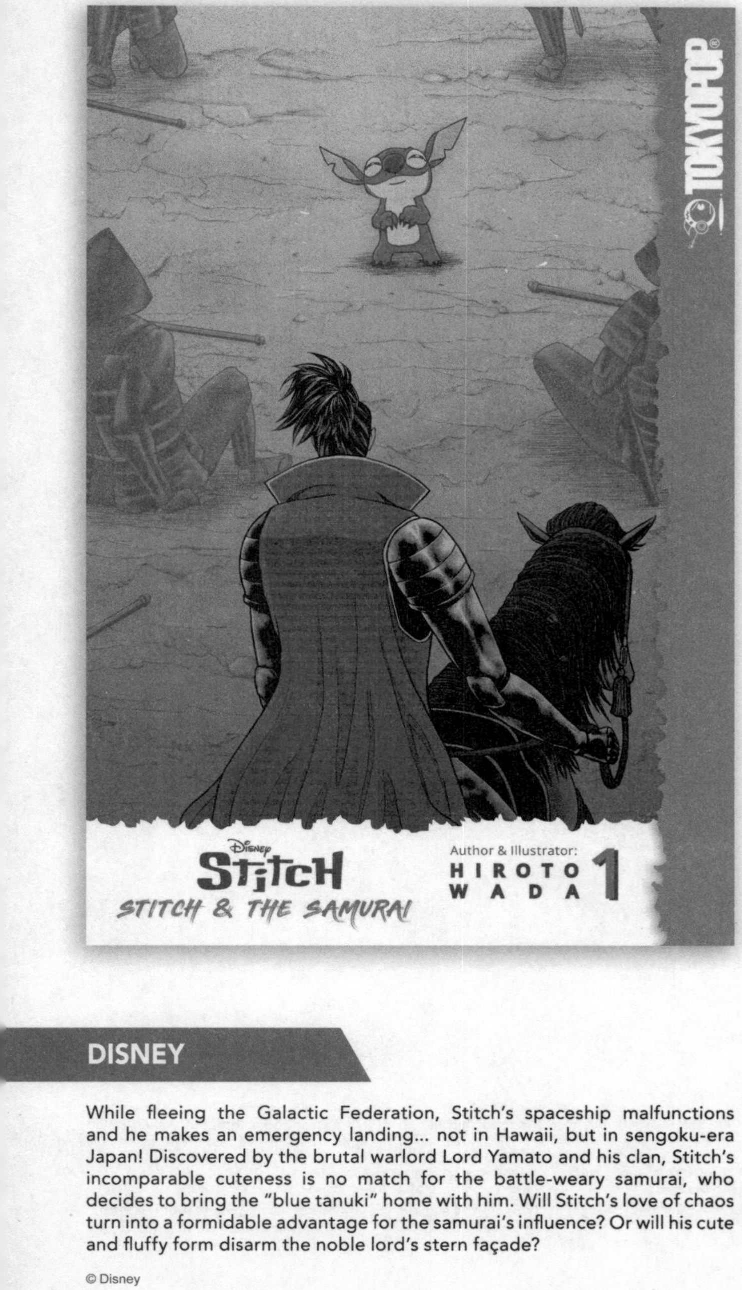
TOKYOPOP
Disney
Stitch
STITCH & THE SAMURAI
Author & Illustrator:
HIROTO WADA
1

DISNEY

While fleeing the Galactic Federation, Stitch's spaceship malfunctions and he makes an emergency landing... not in Hawaii, but in sengoku-era Japan! Discovered by the brutal warlord Lord Yamato and his clan, Stitch's incomparable cuteness is no match for the battle-weary samurai, who decides to bring the "blue tanuki" home with him. Will Stitch's love of chaos turn into a formidable advantage for the samurai's influence? Or will his cute and fluffy form disarm the noble lord's stern façade?

TOKYOPOP

DISNEY STITCH AND THE SAMURAI, VOLUME 2

Hiroto Wada

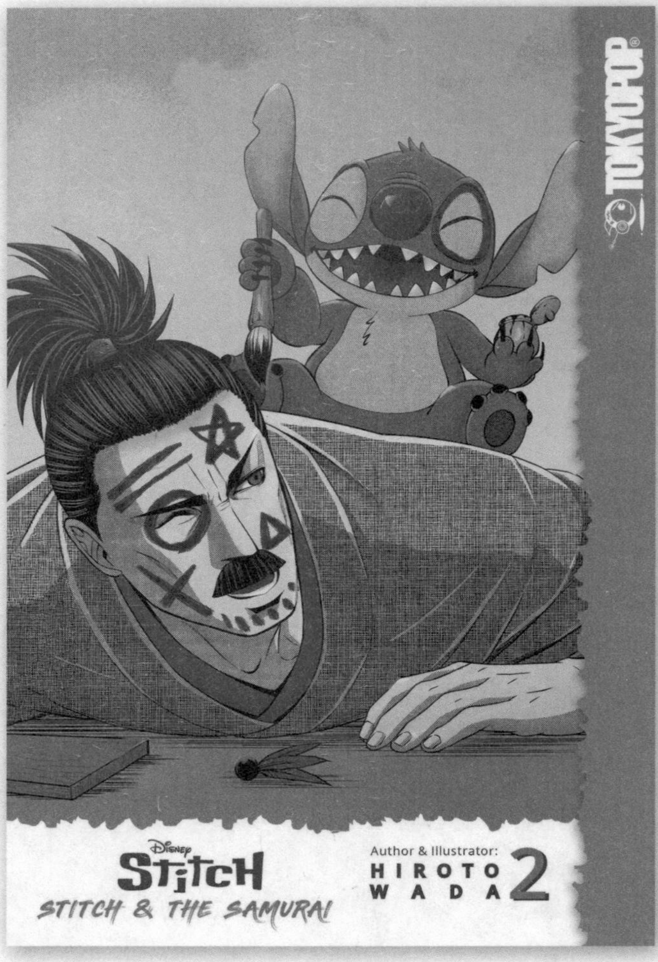
TOKYOPOP
Disney
Stitch
STITCH & THE SAMURAI
Author & Illustrator:
HIROTO WADA
2

DISNEY

After a chance encounter with what he thought was a falling star, Lord Meison Yamato was startled to discover a crashed spaceship along with its passenger: a wild, fluffy alien called Stitch. Believing him to be a blue tanuki, Yamato took him back to his castle and eventually befriended the "energetic" creature. But now the Galactic Federation has come searching for Stitch, sending Jumba and Pleakley to Earth to recapture the escaped experiment.

Can Stitch and the warlord deal with the alien invaders without alerting the rest of the locals? Will Stitch ruin Yamato's plans for political power? And what about the mysterious ghost that has taken up residence in the castle? Stitch's adventures in feudal Japan continue!

TOKYOPOP

THE TREASURE OF THE KING AND THE CAT

You Kajika

TOKYOPOP
YOU
KAJIKA
The Treasure of the KING and the Cat

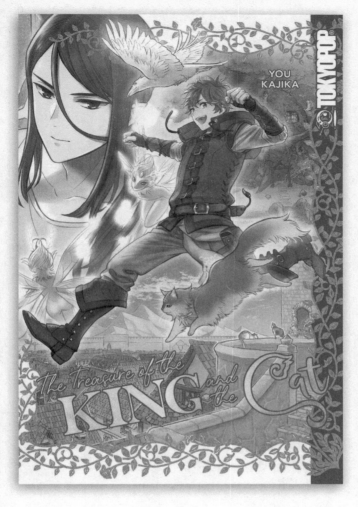

LOVE-x-LOVE

One day, a large number of people suddenly disappeared in the royal capital. When young King Castio goes out to investigate this occurrence, he comes across the culprit... but the criminal puts a spell on him! To help him out, the king calls the wizard O'Feuille to his castle, along with Prince Volks and his loyal retainer Nios. Together, they're determined to solve this strange, fluffy mystery full of cats, swords and magic!

TOKYOPOP

THE GOD AND THE FLIGHTLESS MESSENGER

Hagi

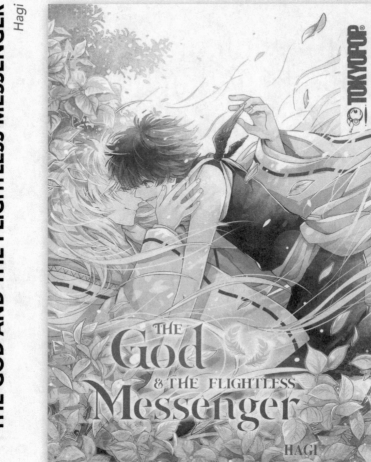

THE
God
& THE FLIGHTLESS
Messenger

HAGI

♂LOVE·x·LOVE♂

A messenger's duty is to care for and protect the god they've been assigned to. In order to complete these tasks, such messengers require wings. Shin, however, can't fly. His tiny, useless wings make him the target of ridicule and scorn among the other messengers and have kept him from being able to serve a god... until now. Determined to prove himself as a capable messenger despite his flightlessness, Shin accepts his assignment to a mysterious being on one of the nearby mountains. At first, it seems an easy task to keep his charge safe and happy — especially when the deity in question is just a cute, fluffy ball of fur. But things aren't always what they seem. Recently, messengers flying over the strange god's mountain have been disappearing. Even as suspicion mounts against his deity, Shin just can't bring himself to think that such a gentle god could have a dark side. It's strange, but for some reason... the mysterious, fluffy being feels so familiar to him.

NO VAMPIRE, NO HAPPY ENDING, VOLUME 1

Shinya Shinya

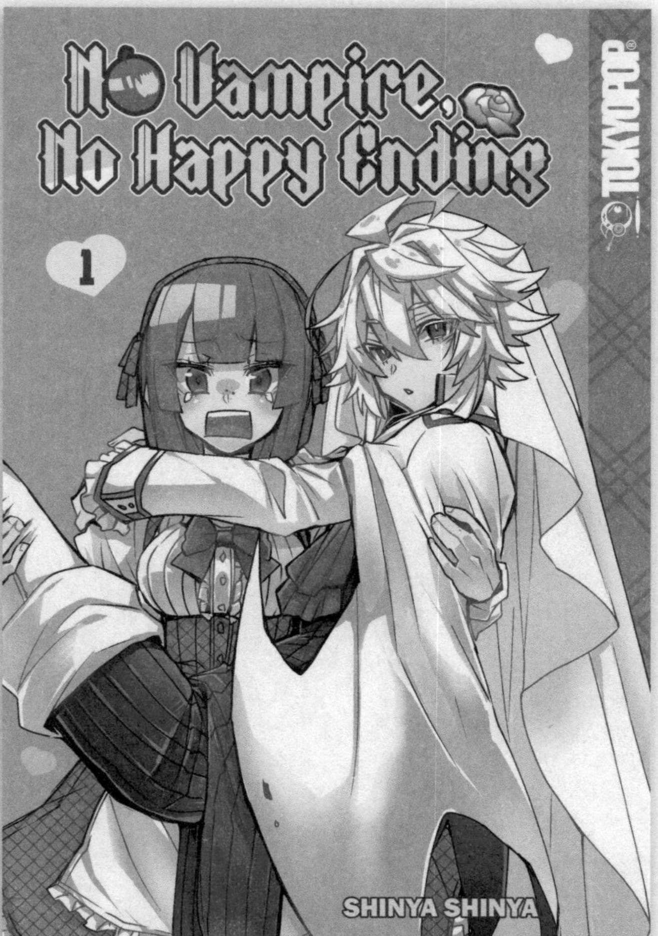
No Vampire, No Happy Ending
1
TOKYOPOP
SHINYA SHINYA

LOVE-x-LOVE

Arika is what you could charitably call a vampire "enthusiast." When she stumbles across the beautiful and mysterious vampire Divo however, her excitement quickly turns to disappointment as she discovers he's not exactly like the seductive, manipulative villains in her stories. His looks win first place, but his head's a space case. Armed with her extensive knowledge of vampire lore, Arika downgrades Divo to a beta vampire and begins their long, long... long journey to educate him in the ways of the undead.

TOKYOPOP

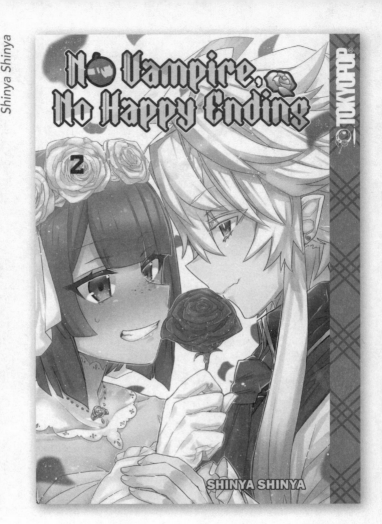

NO VAMPIRE, NO HAPPY ENDING, VOLUME 2

Shinya Shinya

No Vampire, No Happy Ending
2
SHINYA SHINYA
TOKYOPOP

LOVE-x-LOVE

TOKYOPOP

When die-hard vampire enthusiast Arika comes across a mysterious young man named Divo, it seems she struck the jackpot-- she's found a drop-dead gorgeous vampire of her own! Unfortunately, she quickly finds out the disappointing truth: Divo is all beauty, no brains, and no vampire instincts whatsoever. What's a vampire-loving girl to do? Teach him, of course! The grand finale of the laugh-out-loud supernatural love comedy featuring a vampire in beta and the vampire fangirl determined to make him worth her time!

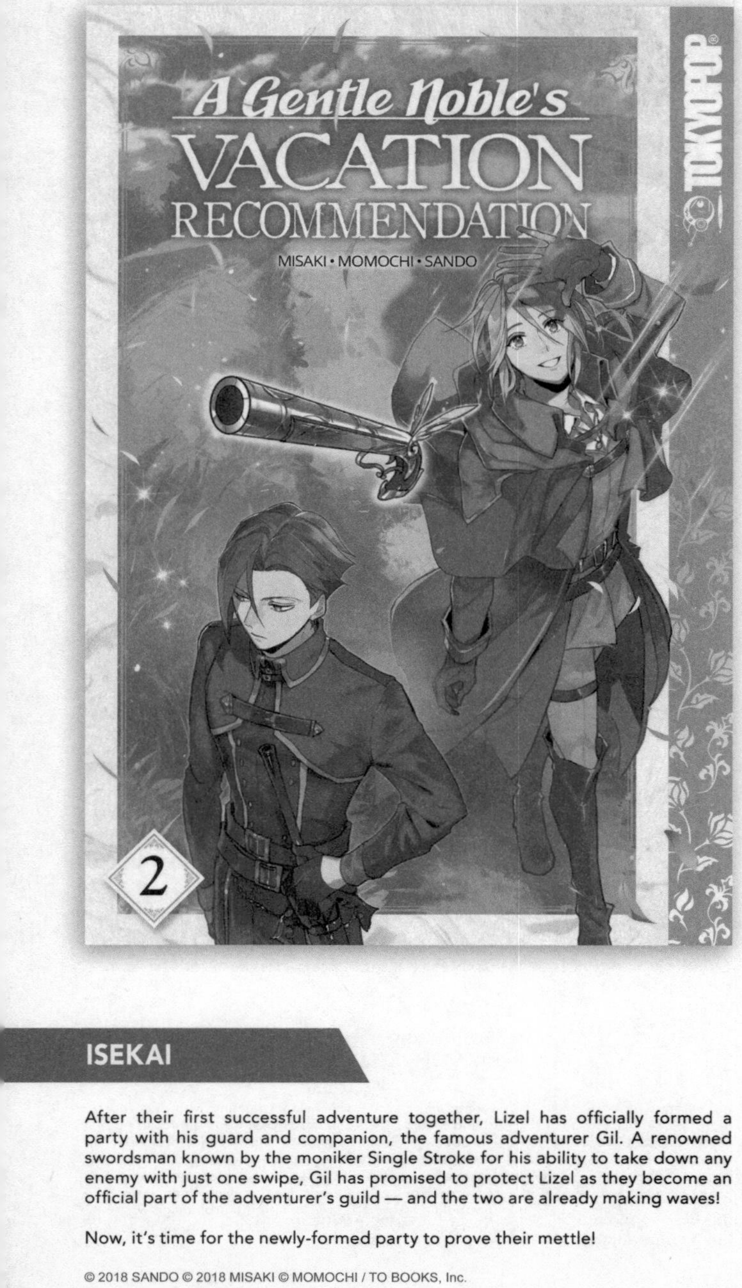
TOKYOPOP
A Gentle Noble's
VACATION
RECOMMENDATION
MISAKI • MOMOCHI • SANDO
2

A GENTLE NOBLE'S VACATION RECOMMENDATION, VOLUME 2

Misaki, Momochi & Sando

ISEKAI

After their first successful adventure together, Lizel has officially formed a party with his guard and companion, the famous adventurer Gil. A renowned swordsman known by the moniker Single Stroke for his ability to take down any enemy with just one swipe, Gil has promised to protect Lizel as they become an official part of the adventurer's guild — and the two are already making waves!

Now, it's time for the newly-formed party to prove their mettle!

TOKYOPOP

PARHAM ITAN: TALES FROM BEYOND, VOLUME 2

Kaili Sorano

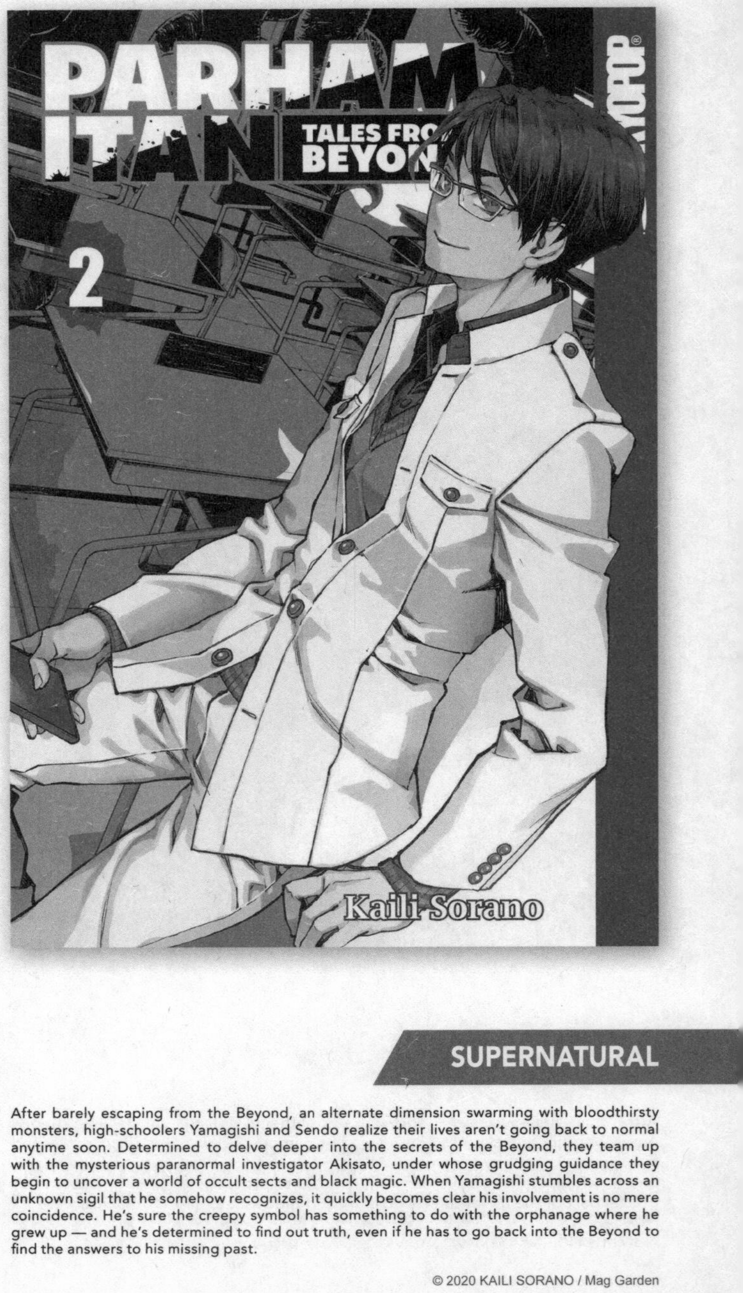
PARHAM
ITAN
TALES FRO
BEYON
TOKYOPOP
2
Kaili Sorano

SUPERNATURAL

After barely escaping from the Beyond, an alternate dimension swarming with bloodthirsty monsters, high-schoolers Yamagishi and Sendo realize their lives aren't going back to normal anytime soon. Determined to delve deeper into the secrets of the Beyond, they team up with the mysterious paranormal investigator Akisato, under whose grudging guidance they begin to uncover a world of occult sects and black magic. When Yamagishi stumbles across an unknown sigil that he somehow recognizes, it quickly becomes clear his involvement is no mere coincidence. He's sure the creepy symbol has something to do with the orphanage where he grew up — and he's determined to find out truth, even if he has to go back into the Beyond to find the answers to his missing past.

TOKYOPOP

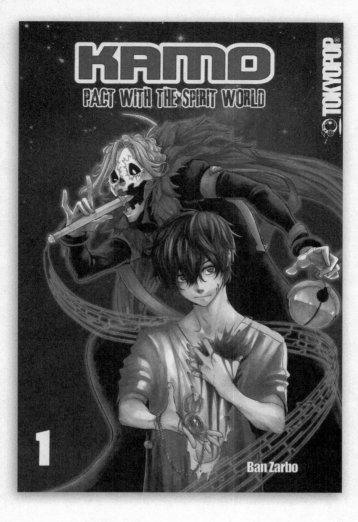

KAMO
PACT WITH THE SPIRIT WORLD

1

Ban Zarbo

INTERNATIONAL
WOMEN of MANGA

Born with a failing heart, Kamo has fought death his whole life, but to no avail. As his body weakens and he readies to draw his final breath, he's visited by a powerful spirit named Crimson who offers him a deal: defeat and capture the souls of twelve spirits in exchange for a new heart. It seems too good to be true... and maybe it is. A pact with the spirit world; what could possibly go wrong?

KAMO: PACT WITH THE SPIRIT WORLD, VOLUME 2

Ban Zarbo

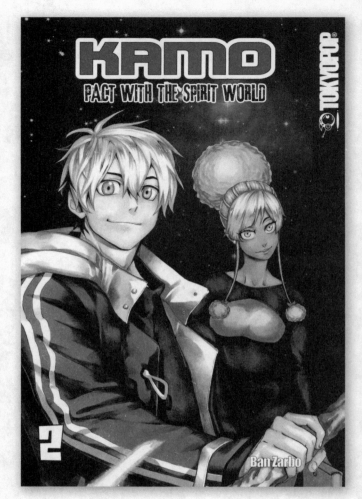

INTERNATIONAL
WOMEN of MANGA

After making a pact with the spirit Crimson to heal his deadly heart condition, Kamo must defeat and capture twelve spirits in order to complete his side of the bargain. That's no small task, and lately spirits have been hard to come by, disappearing before Kamo can capture them. Thankfully, Shokola has just the spell in mind to curse Kamo as an Obscuro Magnético — a magnet for all things phantasmal — making him the center of attention for otherworldly creatures and bringing them straight to him. Surely nothing can go wrong with this plan...

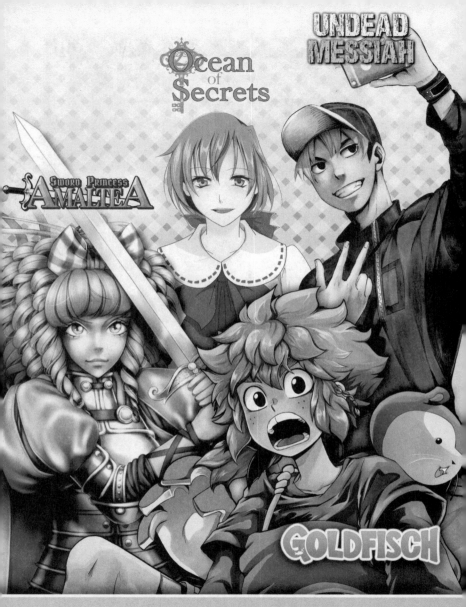

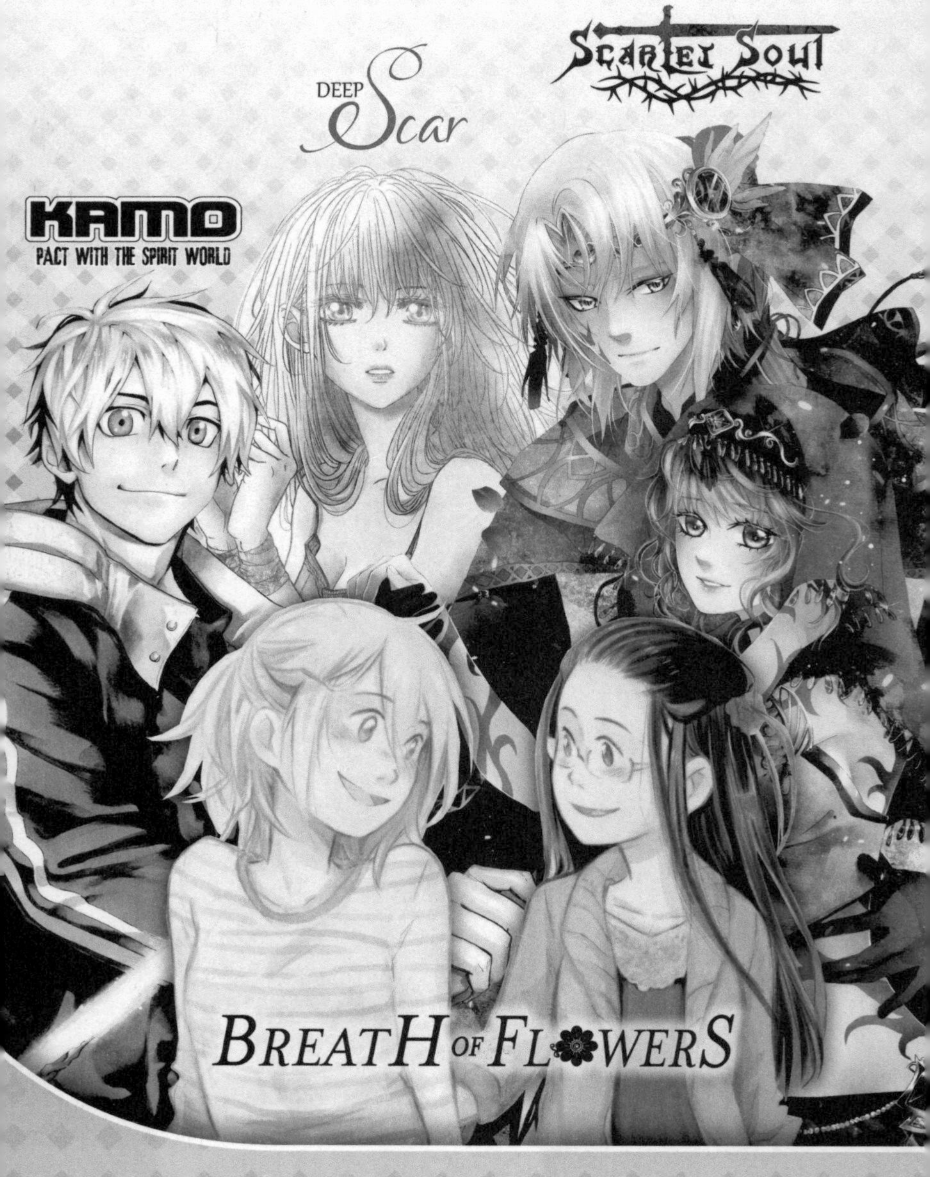
Scarlet Soul
DEEP Scar
KAMO
PACT WITH THE SPIRIT WORLD
BREATH OF FLOWERS

INTERNATIONAL WOMEN of MANGA